Drinking Cultures

DATE DUE

MAR 2 1 2011	
DEC 0 5 2011	

Drinking Cultures

Alcohol and Identity

Edited by
Thomas M. Wilson

Oxford • New York

First published in 2005 by
Berg
Editorial offices:
1st Floor, Angel Court, 81 St Clements Street, Oxford OX4 1AW, UK
175 Fifth Avenue, New York, NY 10010, USA

Paperback reprinted 2006

Berg is the imprint of Oxford International Publishers Ltd.

Library of Congress Cataloging-in-Publication Data
Drinking cultures : alcohol and identity / edited by Thomas M. Wilson.
    p. cm.
  Includes bibliographical references and index.
  ISBN 1-85973-873-7 (pbk.) — ISBN 1-85973-868-0 (cloth)
 1. Drinking of alcoholic beverages. 2. Drinking customs. 3.
Alcoholic beverages—Social aspects. I. Wilson, Thomas M., 1951–
  GT2884.D75 2005
    394.1′2—dc22
                                                    2005003348

British Library Cataloguing-in-Publication Data
A catalogue record for this book is available from the British Library.

ISBN-13 978 185973 868 9 (Cloth)
        978 1 85973 873 3 (Paper)

ISBN-10 1 85973 868 0 (Cloth)
        1 85973 873 7 (Paper)

Typeset by JS Typesetting Ltd, Porthcawl, Mid Glamorgan.
Printed in the United Kingdom by Biddles Ltd, King's Lynn.

www.bergpublishers.com

To Edward C. Hansen

Contents

Contents

List of Tables

Acknowledgements

My interest in the themes of this book began during my doctoral field research, when the boundaries of my American ethnic identity were clarified in the land of my ancestors, when even those things I had come to believe were second nature to 'the Irish' were revealed as contestable sites and disputable practices. The performances of local, class, ethnic, gender and national identity which I observed and in which I participated in the Irish midlands and in Dublin a quarter of a century ago were the start of my research interest in the politics of culture, and a fascination with the intersections of identity, culture and power in drinking arenas and through drinking practices. I am grateful to the Western Europe Program of the Social Science Research Council, the National Science Foundation, and the Wenner Gren Foundation for Anthropological Research for their financial support of my original research in Ireland, and to Wenner Gren, the National Endowment for the Humanities, the Leverhulme Trust and the British Academy for their support of my later research in Northern Ireland; both research projects have informed my contribution to this volume and allowed me to develop the perspectives on national identity which originally led me to conceive the idea of this book. I would also like to thank the following people for their various forms of aid and efforts on my behalf, recently and over the years, all of which facilitated the production of this book: William Cosgrave, Andrew Dawson, Eddie Farrell, Jim FitzSimons, Paddy FitzSimons, Colm Geraghty, Jonathan Hill, Sharryn Kasmir, Mac Marshall, A. Lynn Martin, Anahid Ordjanian, Vincent and Kate O'Reilly, Barney Reilly, David Sutton and Damian Usher.

Special thanks are due to Teodora Corina Hasegan for her editorial support in proofreading, formatting and copyediting, and overall good cheer as we balanced the preparation of this manuscript with other editorial duties, and to Kathryn Earle, Anne Hobbs, Jennifer Howell and Hannah Shakespeare at Berg Publishers for their help at every stage of a process which turned out to be much longer than anticipated. Kathryn's enthusiastic and critical reception of the themes of this book was the primary stimulus to its initiation, and her continuing patience and understanding over the course of its production are much appreciated. I am grateful for the graciousness of the contributors to this book, who allowed me to put the project on hold for some time while my family and I uprooted ourselves from Northern Ireland to move to a new job and home in the Southern Tier of New York State. Finally, I wish to dedicate this book to my friend and mentor, Edward C. Hansen, whose efforts at one point in my graduate education kept my eyes on the goal of a Ph.D., and whose critical approaches to politics, power, culture and drinking first made me aware of the issues which the contributors to this book address. While the follies of youth have begun to recede, and Ed and I no longer pass the time over a drink, the memories of learning anthropology with him will always prove intoxicating.

Contributors

Gary Armstrong lectures in the Department of Sport Sciences at Brunel University. He has written *Football Hooligans: Knowing the Score* (1998), and has co-edited (with Richard Giulianotti) *Entering the Field: New Perspectives on World Football* (1997), *Football Cultures and Identities* (1999), and *Fear and Loathing in World Football* (2001) – all published by Berg.

Steffan Igor Ayora-Diaz received his Ph.D. in 1993 at McGill University and has conducted research among Sardinian pastoralists, Chiapas healers and currently, in Yucatan, Mexico, conducts research on cuisine and regional identity. His book *Globalización, conocimiento y poder: Médicos locales y sus luchas por el Reconocimiento en Chiapas*, was published in 2002 by Plaza y Valdés and the Universidad Autónoma de Yucatán. He is Professor of Anthropology at the Facultad de Ciencias Antropológicas of the Universidad Autónoma de Yucatán.

Marion Demossier is Senior Lecturer in French and European Studies at the University of Bath. She is the author of various works on wine producers and wine consumers in France and has published on culture and identity in France and Europe. Her teaching is mainly in French and European Politics and Society. Her first monograph, *Hommes et vins: Une anthropologie du vignoble bourguignon* (1999, Editions universitaires de Dijon) won the prix Lucien Perriaux. She is the treasurer for ICAF Europe (International Commission for the Anthropology of Food) and is currently writing a book entitled *The Wandering Drinker: An Anthropology of Wine Culture and Consumption in France*.

Pauline Garvey is a lecturer in the Department of Anthropology in the National University of Ireland, Maynooth. Among her other publications are 'Drinking, Driving and Daring in Norway', in D. Miller, ed. *Car Cultures* (2001, Berg), and 'How to Have a "Good Home": The Practical Aesthetic and Normativity in Norway', *Journal of Design History* (2003).

Timothy M. Hall completed his Ph.D. at the University of California – San Diego with a specialization in psychiatric anthropology in 2003, and will receive an MD from the same university in 2005.

Geoffrey P. Hunt is a social anthropologist, who has done extensive ethnographic research in West Africa, England and most recently in the United States. He received his Ph.D. in Social Anthropology at the University of Kent. Currently he is the Principal Investigator on two National Institutes of Health-funded research projects: one on street gangs, motherhood and violence and the second on the social context of club drugs. From research data gleaned from research on street gangs, Dr Hunt and his research team have published over thirty articles focusing on gangs, gang members and violent behaviour.

Karen Joe-Laidler received her Ph.D. in sociology at the University of California at Davis. She is currently Associate Professor in the Department of Sociology at the University of Hong Kong. For the past ten years, her research and writing have focused on ethnic youth gangs and violence, and drug use and problems concentrating specifically on issues associated with young women. She is currently the Co-Principal Investigator with Geoffrey Hunt on two ongoing National Institute of Health studies on youth gangs and on the social context of club drugs use.

Sharryn Kasmir is the author of *The Myth of Mondragón: Cooperatives, Politics, and Working-Class Life in a Basque Town* (1996, SUNY Press), as well as articles and essays on the intersections of working-class and nationalist politics in the Basque region of Spain. Currently, she is writing about issues of working-class identity and activism in a US automobile factory. She is Associate Professor of Anthropology at Hofstra University.

Kathleen MacKenzie received her MA in anthropology at San Jose State University. Currently, she is project manager on a National Institute of Health-funded research project on street gangs, motherhood and violence.

Anthony Marcus is a Lecturer in the School of Anthropology, Geography & Environmental Studies of the University of Melbourne. He is an urban anthropologist with research interests in political economy, civil society, the anthropology of the state, poverty amelioration, public policy, and gender, 'race' and ethnicity in the Americas. He is the author of *Anthropology for A Small Planet* (1996, Brandywine Press).

Jon P. Mitchell is Reader in Anthropology at the University of Sussex. He has been researching Maltese culture and society since 1991 and is author of *Ambivalent Europeans: Ritual, Memory and the Public Sphere in Malta* (2002, Routledge), co-editor (with Paul Clough) of *Powers of Good and Evil: Commodity, Morality and Popular Belief* (2002, Berghahn), and editor of *Modernity in the Mediterranean* (special issue of *Journal of Mediterranean Studies,* 12 (1): 2002). He is currently working with Gary Armstrong on a book about football in Malta, and with historian Alex Shepard on a book about Anthropology and History.

Brian Moeran is Professor of Culture and Communication at the Copenhagen Business School. A social anthropologist by training, he has published widely on advertising, aesthetics, art and media in Japan and Asia. Recent edited books include *Asian Media Productions* (2001, Curzon) and *Advertising Cultures* (with Timothy de Waal Malefyt, 2003, Berg). His current research is on women's fashion magazines and on the production and reception of smells cross-culturally.

Cliona O'Carroll is a postdoctoral fellow with the Department of Folklore and Ethnology, National University of Ireland at Cork, Ireland. Her research interests include experiences of migrancy, the creation of meaning in everyday life and the ethnographic interview as a site of collaborative meaning construction.

Josephine Smart is Professor of Anthropology at the University of Calgary. She has conducted research on street hawkers and the informal economy in Hong Kong, the nature and strategies of Hong Kong foreign direct investment in China, Chinese business immigration to Canada, and the impact of NAFTA on three cities (one each in Canada, the USA and Mexico). Her current research is a study of the history of Chinese restaurant food in Canada and its articulation with ethnic and national identity issues. Her most recent book is *Plural Globalities in Multiple Localities - New World Borders* (co-editor Martha Rees, 2001, University Press of America).

Gabriela Vargas-Cetina (Ph.D., McGill University, 1994) has conducted research among Henequen growers in Yucatán, among Plains First Nations in Alberta, with pastoralists in Sardinia and weavers in Chiapas cooperatives and, currently, conducts research on music and identity in Yucatán. Her most recent book (as editor), *De lo público a lo privado: Organizaciones en Chiapas* (2002), was published by CIESAS and Miguel Angel Porrua. She is Professor of Anthropology at the Facultad de Ciencias Antropologicas of the Universidad Autónoma de Yucatán.

Thomas M. Wilson is Professor of Anthropology at Binghamton University, State University of New York. He has conducted ethnographic field research in Ireland, the United Kingdom and Hungary on European integration, international borders and national identity. He is the co-author (with Hastings Donnan) of *Borders: Frontiers of Identity, Nation and State* (1999, Berg), the co-editor (with Irène Bellier) of *An Anthropology of the European Union* (2000, Berg) and the co-editor (with James Anderson and Liam O'Dowd) of *New Borders for a Changing Europe* (2003, Frank Cass).

Drinking Cultures

Sites and Practices in the Production and Expression of Identity

Thomas M. Wilson

Some time ago, on my arrival in Ireland for pre-dissertation research, I was a heady cocktail of confidence and concern. My self-assurance had many sources. I had been well trained in graduate school, in terms of ethnographic methods, theoretical models and comparative ethnology. I had studied Irish history and culture since my under-graduate days, and was reasonably certain that I was not arriving as an ignorant or arrogant American anthropologist, parachuting in to do crisis anthropology and then just as quickly withdrawing, to establish my career and reputation elsewhere. Moreover, I was 'Irish', from Brooklyn, New York, where I was raised as the quintessential hyphenated-American, in ways which I believed not only drew me closer to my counterparts in such places as Chicago, Philadelphia and Boston, but also made me that much closer, in cultural terms I thought (armed with my anthro-pological knowledge and status), to the Irish themselves.

In this ignorant bliss of ethnic pride and anthropological hubris, I felt that I was almost as Irish as the real Irish. Moreover, I was the first one of my family who had been born in America who was coming 'home' to Ireland. In fact, one of my goals of the summer trip was to visit our 'home place', from which my grandparents had emigrated early in the twentieth century. Although it is startling to me now, the fact is that I was not in the least worried about whether I would fit in or be accepted in Ireland. In more contemporary American parlance, I was sure that I talked the talk and walked the walk.

But I was also reasonably sure that I did not know everything that was needed – after all I had not been raised in Ireland, had not learned 'Irish-Irish' culture from birth. I anticipated that there were sure to be many differences in outlook, behaviour and ideologies. Furthermore, I also came complete with untested hypothesis: my goal that summer a generation ago was to find a site for my dissertation research which I expected would commence the following summer. I was looking for a location with a combination of characteristics which would enable me to critically engage the comparative anthropology of Irish society and culture. In my terms this meant that

I wanted a big town in a developed agricultural zone, with local opportunities for off-farm employment. But I had never done ethnographic research, had never tried to find an appropriate site, establish contacts and start my own 'networks', all the stuff of the anthropology of Europe which I had studied for the last seven years. The universal questions of generations of anthropologists nagged me: would my hypothesis stand up? Would I stand up to the challenge?

I had arrived in Shannon airport, and had booked a room in a Limerick hotel, planning to spend the night there before setting off to the cousins' farm. I looked forward to my first night in Ireland, and planned to have my first real pint of Guinness. (At that time it was not exported from Ireland to New York; I had previously only encountered Guinness in small bottles imported from Jamaica.) The bus driver recommended a local pub, which later that night proved to be my first experience of an Irish pub, an institution venerated worldwide as one of the most important in the production and reproduction of Irish culture. The pub was packed, it was noisy and smoky, and I had some difficulty getting close to the bar. But I was happy to be surrounded by the weekend crowd, and asked for my pint with some considerable anticipation. Actually, I had to shout my order to the barman, to be heard over the din of patron interaction. But even at that tender stage of the evening I had already made my first miscalculation, the first of many: I had gone to the pub at 10 p.m., a normal drinking hour back home in New York, but as I was to discover that night, this was only an hour and a half short of the summer closing time in Ireland, when the pace of drinking and discourse picked up considerably.

I handed the barman a five pound note, for the pint which cost 38 pence or so. When he handed the change back to me I promptly put it on the bar. In retrospect I realize that this too was a sign of my cockiness and an example of my ignorance. I had already determined through many travels away from my hometown of Brooklyn, and the wider social space of New York City, that most Americans did not drink in 'rounds', an elaborate system of reciprocity which structured our local drinking practices. I knew that this was an Irish custom (it did not matter to me that it was also a common British practice too), but mistakenly thought that Brooklyn rounds were the same as Irish rounds. As a result I wanted to leave my money on the bar in order to indicate to the barman a number of things: that I was staying for a while, the approximate amount of drink I expected to consume (to be judged by him by the amount left on the bar), to let him know that a tip was in the offing, and to stake a claim to that part of the bar space. But I did not get too far. The barman immediately picked up the money, made a show of giving it back to me, in my palm, and stated in what I thought was too loud a voice: 'Sir, over here, we *never* leave our money on the bar.'

That was my first experience of Irish drinking (i.e., drinking alcohol in Ireland), which made me consider, immediately, what it was that I was assuming about Irish culture. My assumptions were based on my own ethnic heritage in the USA, the ethnographies on Ireland which I had scrupulously dissected over the previous three years, and the drinking practices which I had learned in Brooklyn. This was also my first experience of the bounded and sited nature of what I thought of as an ethnic or a national culture: while 'Irishness', whatever it is and wherever it is found, must have some things in common, it is also just as true to conclude that it is socially constructed and produced differentially, based in part on the circumstances of place, space and social structural context. Irish drinking culture, whether in Brooklyn or in Limerick, is a manifestation of the sameness and differentiation of culture and identity.

Drinking culture in Ireland, at home or in more public domains, has not been a major interest in the ethnography of Ireland, but it should be. The pub, or public house, is a particularly important ethnographic arena, wherein drinking practices and other aspects of Irish culture merge, and where the questions of identity and identification continually matter. In my experiences of over twenty-five years of Irish pub activities, principally but not exclusively in rural areas near Dublin and in Belfast city, the significance of drink, and pubs, in Irish life has been as important and interesting to the people of Ireland as it has been to me. The Irish are aware of their popular, common and distinctive drinking practices, and use these as points of discussion, most often but not only in the pub, but also as differentiating discourses in the construction of socially meaningful identities and identifications. It has been this experience of Irish drinking culture which has been my primary motivation in developing and organizing the book which this chapter introduces.

The anecdote just related, in its mix of ethnographic occasion and context, reveals the principal themes of the following chapters, all of which deal with the intersections of ethnography and ethnic and national drinking practices, and how these practices reflect ethnic and national distinctions and identities. In fact, it is the intention of the contributors to this book to situate drinking within broadly conceived cultural and political frameworks. The places and behaviours of drinking, which in this book refers specifically to the consumption of alcohol,[1] should not be mistakenly conceived as small ethnographic windows on more important structures and actions in the observed social cases. Rather, in the chapters of this book drinking is approached much more sceptically, in order to interrogate whether the places, spaces and practices of drinking play more important roles in the construction of social and political identities than the anthropological literature has heretofore generally suggested.

The cases we present examine something which many ethnographers have experienced, namely that drinking alcohol is an extremely important feature in the production and reproduction of ethnic, national, class, gender and local community identities, not only today but also historically, with little prospect for this importance and the situation to change. In many societies, perhaps the majority, drinking alcohol is a key practice in the expression of identity, an element in the construction and dissemination of national and other cultures. And the roles of drinking, in terms of culture and identity, are not 'simply' (as if such things are simple) aspects of everyday life, that arena of discourse and action so beloved of ethnographers. Drinking is the veritable stuff of any and perhaps every level and type of culture, and is implicated in the behaviours, values, ideologies and histories of these cultures. In essence drinking is itself cultural; it is not so much an example of national and other cultural practices, in the sense that it is a performance of something that runs deeper in the national or ethnic makeup, as much as it is itself a bedrock of national and ethnic culture. As such it is an integral social, political and economic practice, a manifestation of the institutions, actions and values of culture.

This book is a collection of ethnographic case studies in the sites, practices and meanings of drinking, and the various roles which drinking plays in identity and culture. While most chapters focus principally on ethnic and national culture, and all consider such identities, they also explore the intersections of other identities, such as those of gender, age and class, with various drinking arenas, fields, networks, occasions, places and spaces. The anthropology of alcohol and drinking has a long and distinguished pedigree, but some of the major figures in this anthropological tradition have long recognized the need to desist to some extent from theorizing drinking alcohol as a social problem, and to pay more attention to the roles which alcohol and drinking play in historical and contemporary practices and imaginings of the nation and other cultural and political formations (see, for example, the review essays by Heath 1987a and Hunt and Barker 2001). The authors of the chapters in this book seek to contribute to the ways in which the relationships among drinking, culture and identity are perceived and studied by anthropologists and other social scientists. In particular they seek to take the analysis of drinking beyond descriptive notions of performing culture and expressing identity in order to view drinking sites and practices as realizations of national, ethnic, gender and class culture. Before some of the chapters' particular themes are introduced, however, a brief review of the anthropology of drinking alcohol and its relation to studies of national identity and culture is in order.

Leftovers and Main Courses

There is no more important figure in the international anthropological study of alcohol and culture than Dwight Heath, whose historical and ethnographic works have characterized the principal concerns of anthropologists who have studied the drinking of alcohol in every decade since the 1960s (see, for examples of this body of work, Heath 1975, 1976, 1987a, 1987b, 2000). In one of his review essays, Heath (1987a: 113) concluded that 'A special strength of anthropology continues to be its anomalous role as "the science of leftovers." What this means with respect to the study of alcohol is that, unlike many others, we study "moderate" or "normal" drinking – and abstaining – as well as "excessive" or "alcoholic" drinking.' This leftover status has many referents, including those established by the funding institutions in the US and elsewhere, where most money is allocated to those who seek to investigate alcohol in its socially and medically detrimental roles (for a discussion of this funding culture, see Hunt and Barker 2001). But leftover also refers to those behavioural practices which are not seen by anthropologists to be social problems, but rather research problematics, problems in the understanding and configuration of social, political and economic formations. In the terms which most concern us in this book, these are the 'leftover' problems of identity formation and reproduction, the ideas, values and practices of drinking and other cultures. But 'leftover' is a metaphor which still leaves one with the impression that the main concerns are or were elsewhere, 'courses' which are meatier and more substantial. The consumption metaphors are apt: with drinking cultures we are simultaneously examining the consumption of commodities and the behaviours of social and cultural integration and differentiation. In fact alcohol is an excellent example of the commodities which concerned Arjun Appadurai in his examination of the social life of things (1986), guiding us to consider alcohol's role as a commodity and an element in differential regimes of value in the history of our ethnic and national groups. As such, alcohol must be seen as a main course, of food, of action, and of value. It is not a peripheral or easily discarded menu item in the preparation of many identities; what is primarily leftover here is the need to reconsider the importance of drinking to so many social, political and economic institutions, symbols and actions.

One reason why calls for the re-evaluation of studies of alcohol and drinking is a recurrent theme in many anthropological writings[2] is that, while there has been a great deal written by anthropologists about various forms of alcohol and drink-related behaviour, most of these writings are based on research which was not focused principally on them. As Heath concluded in an early assessment, research results which examined drinking and alcohol were a 'felicitous by-product' of other research activities (Heath 1975: 4; see also Hunt and Barker 2001: 167). 'This was because whatever other concerns inspired their ethnographic project they could not avoid taking note of the importance of drinking in the lives of the people they lived among' (Douglas 1987: 3).

In other words many anthropological studies of alcohol-related behaviours were unintended consequences of research and research designs which had other constellations of behaviour and cultural meanings as their principal, and perhaps also secondary, focuses. This is certainly the case with me and my two main research projects in Ireland, the first of which was of agricultural politics in the prosperous eastern Midlands, followed almost a decade later with a study of European Union impact on borderland life in Northern Ireland.

Even given this by-production of anthropological studies of drinking and alcohol, a situation which the authors in this book suggest derives as much from the central role of alcohol in the historical configuration of culture and identity as it does from the interest in alcohol as a social and medical contaminant, since the 1960s there has been a growing but variable interest by anthropologists and other ethnographers in the study of alcohol and culture. This is partly the result of a recognition of the importance of alcohol to so many peoples and cultures, where drinking has increasingly been seen in anthropology as a research subject, object and tool, a means of doing ethnography as well as a focus for it. It is also due to the emotional and intricate relationships which drinking engenders, and the complex ways in which it figures in social structures, political processes and economic and other values. As Heath (1976: 43) has concluded:

> Despite its widespread occurrence, alcohol is almost universally subject to rules and regulations unlike those that pertain to other drinks. Not only are there usually special rules about alcoholic beverages, but the rules tend to have peculiarly emotional charge. This affective quality relates not only to drinking, but also to drunkenness and drunken comportment. Whether predominant feelings about these are positive, negative, or ambivalent varies from culture to culture, but indifference is rare, and feelings are usually much stronger in connection with alcohol than with respect to other things.

The contributions to this volume are ample testament to the emotional and institutional intricacies of alcohol and drinking in many cultures and societies across the globe. But it seems that this growing awareness of alcohol and drinking in anthropology also has a great deal to do with the importance of drink to the ethnographic experience, an eventuality surprisingly unanticipated by many ethnographers, including some of our authors in this volume who reflexively discuss their own relations with alcohol and those who drink it. At one point in my doctoral research I thought it prudent to give up 'the drink', and when in pub situations to ask for a 'soda water and lime'. My field notes improved dramatically, but only in line with some deteriorating social relationships. A few key informants, who had become accustomed to sharing information with me in pubs, simply wondered why I had gone off the drink, and were suspicious of my motives. I like to tell myself that in the interests of science I was forced to go back on the beer, after a three-month hiatus, after which the relationships that had been in jeopardy were quickly restored.

Alcohol is integral to many ethnographic experiences, just as it is integral to many societies and cultures (many of whom might be approached as 'alcohol cultures', to paraphrase Michael Kearney's early notions of life in a village in Oaxaca [1970]). Alcohol is often part of informal and predictable anthropological methodologies and methods. Anthropologists often (and perhaps in the majority of the societies in which we work) gain confidence, trust, information and access to wider networks through and with the use of alcohol, in various drinking locations, within various drinking social and political fields, and on various drinking occasions.[3]

I do not want to imply that ethnographers are using foul or secretive means to ply their trade. Quite the opposite message is intended. Anthropologists often need, and sometimes welcome the chance, to immerse themselves in drinking cultures as surely and as fully as they must be immersed in any other aspect of culture and society among the people they seek to know and study. The one inescapable difference, as suggested by Heath in the quotation above, is that drink is one of the most noticeable, emotional and important ways in which people express and discuss their identities and cultures. Alcohol is one of the ingredients in social cement, but also one of the means to remove such adhesion. As a result, it is a tool of our profession, and one of the key metaphors and practices of the cultures we seek to explicate.

The importance of drink and drinking to ethnographers is clear. We meet informants and share alcohol. We partake of food and drink in ritual and other celebratory events. We use alcohol as gifts and enticements, however meager and unconscious. And we drink for many of the reasons our hosts do: to relax, to laugh, to enhance conviviality, and as an expression of our own multiple and often overlapping, sometimes contradictory, identities.

While much of this increasing research and publishing has focused on alcohol and drinking as socially constituted problems, affecting individuals, families and wider groups in society, a good deal of it has been variously comparative, functional, structural, symbolic and historical, in ways which have provided a necessary complement, perhaps corrective, to broader social and physical science concerns with alcohol and alcoholism's deleterious effects. This is not to say that alcohol is not at the core of some individual and social, psychological and medical, problems. But anthropologists have also produced evidence that drinking alcohol is an important and celebrated aspect of many societies, in ways which beg it to be treated as normal and normative. This new attention to drinking, an attention which has widened and deepened among anthropologists since the 1970s, reflects the simple but important realization that 'alcohol use – like kinship, religion, or sexual division of labor – can provide a useful window on the linkages among many kinds of belief and behavior' (Heath 1987a: 102).

However, not all linkages, beliefs and behaviours have been given equal weight and attention by anthropologists. Foremost among the neglected aspects of the anthropology of drinking and alcohol are the roles which they have played in the historical and contemporary construction of national, ethnic and other cultures and identities, the subject of this book. This neglect is partly a response to new funding constraints, which in the USA at least have favoured the support of social science which sees alcohol and drugs as social and medical problems which need to be fixed. As Hunt and Barker (2001: 171–2) see it, the political war on alcohol and drugs in America has generated new attitudes to alcohol, which in turn has had funding and social policy effects: 'This narrowing of focus means that anthropology is increasingly obliged to forgo one of its most important potential contributions to the field of alcohol and drug research – namely, its charting of the normal and everyday use of these substances, with their attendant rituals, customs, and paraphernalia within social and cultural contexts' (Hunt and Barker 2001: 171).

The relative absence of certain cultural contexts to drinking behaviours may also be the result of new theorizing of ethnography and culture in anthropology, which has shifted the focus of much research away from ethnic groups, nations and states.

Certain wider social and political contexts have receded in ethnographic studies, which often still flirt with alcohol in terms of its evil and detrimental effects. As Hunt and Barker have concluded, 'it is a rare anthropological study indeed which situates problem drinkers in a familial, occupational, economic, social, religious, political, or educational context, especially one that takes gender and age/life stage or ethnicity into serious account' (2001: 169).

Nevertheless, although rare, such studies have been done, and since the 1980s there has been a broader anthropological interest in alcohol and culture, an interest that has explicitly sought to move beyond descriptive analyses in order to contribute to more inclusive and sophisticated theorizing (as in the unified model for the comparative study of ingested substances put forward by Hunt and Barker 2001). According to Heath (1987a: 105–12), in the 1970s and 1980s significant progress was made in the anthropology of alcohol and drinking, when the 'social problem' models became less important to ethnographers, at least in terms of types and numbers of the studies conducted, due to a significant rise in interest in analyses of drinking populations, their cultural contexts, with new attention paid to appropriate methodologies and the relationships among drinking, culture and applied anthropological concerns. These interests have also reflected major shifts in the intellectual and professional concerns of anthropologists.

Since the 1970s, in fact, anthropologists have steadily moved away from what once had been a strict disciplinary focus on non-Western and 'primitive' societies, and in the West on peasants and proletarians, in order to engage issues of culture, power, identity and history at every level and among every group of people, in all of the hemispheres. In these efforts, anthropologists have increasingly encountered the problems of bounding culture and society, problems which were at the core of the revolutionary and reflexive turn in the writing and the doing of ethnography and culture, a transformation which motivates much of sociocultural anthropology today. One of the recurring problems which has affected the anthropology of alcohol and drinking since the 1980s, an effect of this salutary change in the ways anthropologists approach research and writing, has been in the definition of social and cultural entities, communities, ethnic groups, nations and others. While ethnographers still attempt to conduct studies which might have policy appeal, they are finding it increasingly difficult to provide analytical categories, in regard to race, ethnicity, class and nationality, which are of clear comparative utility. As a result, 'social groups and categories are referred to vaguely, inconsistently, and often inaccurately' (Heath 1987a: 106).

Mirroring this fuzzy effect in social and cultural definition, which is an inescapable professional concern among anthropologists today, has been the increasing subversion and transformation in real-world actors' perceptions of their own essential and constructed identities, in a newly reconceived global and transnational world, where ethnic and national identities are not what they once were, and where multiculturalism is matched by multiple citizenships and supranationalism. It is no wonder that there is a dearth of studies of drinking and ethnic and national cultures today, but in fact this situation has been with us for some time. In the early 1980s, in the midst of the sea change in the anthropology of drinking, one of the major forces in that change, Mac Marshall (whose 1979a edited collection, case studies drawn from around the world, was the first major ethnographic collection in anthropological studies of alcohol), called for new research agendas, to redirect his anthropological colleagues away from a focus on alcoholism and ethnic minorities in the USA. towards both the study of drinking and majority populations, and research on alcohol and nations and states (Marshall 1984). The relevance of this call is still apparent, as is the relatively small response to it. The need for more information about the role of drinking and alcohol in the construction and maintenance of identities is one of the calls which this book seeks to answer. The next section explores some of the issues of culture, identity, nation and state that are central themes of the following chapters.

Drinking and the Dimensions of Culture and Identity

While most other social sciences have concentrated on alcohol and drunkenness as social, psychological and health concerns, if not outright problems, anthropology has just as often looked at drinking in its cultural and historical contexts, as part of often acceptable, predictable, encouraged, mainstream, majority and normative behaviour. In so doing, however, anthropologists have had difficulties in recognizing and defining the boundaries of these research populations. These difficulties have many causes, among them: people are more mobile, and culture is a tool and the metaphor of this mobility; globalization relies on many forms of integration and disintegration, including processes of social identification and the production of culture; identities and cultures which seemed relatively immutable in the past have been shown to be quite changeable, historically and today; ethnicity and national identity have receded in academic importance in favour of gender, race, sexuality and class identities; and anthropologists no longer study 'cultures', but culture in practice, process and narrative. For some scholars these changes are exciting challenges. Heath, in his assessment of the state of the art in the anthropology of alcohol (1987a), reviews the complexities of selecting and studying a research population in this new intellectual environment. For others, these changes in the perception and use of culture do not present challenges worth accepting. Many anthropologists today simply choose to avoid making the linkages between respondents, and their local actions and groups. on the one hand, and the larger social formations of which they are a part, such as ethnic groups, classes and nations, on the other. As a result, anthropologists also increasingly avoid studies of 'communities', largely due to the loss of confidence in 'community' as a valuable analytical category, even though many, perhaps most, people in the world use their notion of community daily as an expression of their own group solidarity and personal and group identities.

Overall, in fact, anthropologists have stopped investigating 'culture' as the object, and in many cases as the subject, of their studies. As is well known, in much anthropology there has been a turn away from theorizing culture, in terms of its fixity in place and time to be sure, but also in terms of what it is *in toto*, by definition, and in any socially meaningfully bounded way. The best example of this avoidance of studying culture as a concrete entity, as a thing, which in some elite anthropological circles is approached as if it was *taboo*, is Appadurai's (1996: 12) vexing but compelling notion that 'culture' is troublesome as a noun but attractive in its adjectival form, 'cultural'. Appadurai concludes that culture itself is a differentiating process, a process of recognizing and mobilizing group identities:

> When we therefore point to a practice, a distinction, a conception, an object, or an ideology as having a cultural dimension (notice the adjectival use), we stress the idea of situated difference, that is, difference in relation to something local, embodied, and significant. . . . culture is a pervasive dimension of human discourse that exploits difference to generate diverse conceptions of group identity. (Appadurai 1996: 12, 13)

It is the intention of the authors in this volume to examine the cultural dimensions of drinking, as a practice, as a distinction, as an ideology, and as a conception of individual and group identity. We seek to view drinking as an act of identification, of differentiation and integration, and of the projection of homogeneity and heterogeneity, particularly in the social arenas of ethnicity and national identity. Drinking practices are active elements in individual and group identifications, and the sites where drinking takes place, the locales of regular and celebrated drinking, are places where meanings are made, shared, disputed and reproduced, where identities take shape, flourish and change. To borrow from Keith Basso's (1996) analysis of Western Apache notions of their landscape, where in their terms 'wisdom sits in places', culture not only sits in places, it also journeys on, for it also sits with people, and differentiates them one from the other, and group from group. That is why in this book the contributors view drinking cultures in their wider social, political and economic contexts, as practices of ethnic, national, class, gender, sexual, racial and other identities. As an integral part of this exercise, we also focus on the social fields and political arenas which define and shape drinking places and spaces (whether they be regularized or spontaneous drinking practices and occasions) that serve as building blocks of networks of friendship, work, business and politics, and as elements in these differentiating processes of culture and identity.

We expect that this approach may be less agreeable to anthropologists and other ethnographers who in the past have focused on alcohol and drinking in some of the ways reviewed and critiqued above than perhaps it might be to anthropologists interested in theorizing identity and culture in local, transnational, global and supranational contexts. This is because as culture has waned as the principal object of study in anthropology, it has waxed as the major means to describe and understand configurations of power, social practice, history and identity.

In fact, comparative studies of culture(s) have been all but replaced with *sui generis* as well as comparative studies of identity, as observed by anthropologists in individual and small group interactions, in analyses often given substance by inter-linked narratives of individuals' identifications with groups and institutions, past and present. These identity studies rely almost without exception on the appreciation of the intersections of individual and group performances of culture and identity, and the setting out of cultural constructions of various manifestations of history, politics, economics and society, or the obverse historical constructions of culture. In various and overlapping ways, these studies of identity are often couched in terms of the 'politics of identity' and 'identity politics'.[4]

Culture and identity, including the inventions and constructions of history, values and social practices, are key factors in new theorizing beyond anthropology, that directs the critical eye away from such things as norms, institutions and organiza-tions. This is especially apparent in studies of nations and nationalism, many of which have become bogged down in attempts to support or oppose 'primordial' or 'modernist' interpretations of the nation (for examples of this ongoing debate, consult any volume of the journal *Nations and Nationalism*). Critics of the primordialist position point out that pre-modern or pre-industrial notions of the nation are combin-ations of contemporary social constructions of the past, along with an undue empha-sis on the roles of culture and identity in the origin, organization and spread of the nation. These critics also are sceptical of any notion of the nation that is not linked to the development of the nation- (or national) state. Critics of the modernist position take the opposite view: the nation is a social construction, in that nations are simul-taneously cultural and political, and national differentiation, as a process of individual and group identification with ideas, people and social and political institutions, does not depend on the development of industrially forged nation-states. Their evidence is in the historical records of the cultural awareness of the nation as a process of social differentiation.

While it is not my intention to denigrate the defenders of either perspective on the nation, it is clear that there is middle ground of mutual agreement, perhaps best represented in the works of Anthony Smith (see, for example, Smith 1999) and Walker Connor (see, for example, Connor 1993). In both primordialist and modernist perspectives, the nation is an inherently cultural entity, as cultural as it is political. This is not a surprising conclusion for anthropologists, but it is an important conclu-sion among political scientists, international relations specialists and other social scientists, not least for the emphasis which must then be placed on the differentiating processes of identity. It is no wonder that scholars across the social sciences are theorizing new forms of citizenship, now that culture and other forms of political and social identities are implicated in what was once seen as a relatively unproblematic set of relationships among citizens, their nations and their states. Complicating these efforts to theorize politics, power, culture and history are the various perspectives on globalization, transnationalism and supranationalism, which together have asked us all to reconsider the dimensions and boundaries of past and contemporary nations and states, as well as the people, goods, ideas and capital which flow across them (one manifestation of which is the increased attention to culture and state borders [cf. Donnan and Wilson 1999]).

For many years now scholars globally have benefited from theories on the nation which have asked us to use culture as a tool to understand ethnic groups and nations, and to do so we must focus on ethnic and national identities, those dimensions of differentiation which Appadurai has clarified. In this new theorizing of the nation, culture should not be viewed as a good tool with which to understand the real or true nation; on the contrary, ethnonational values, actions and organizations are the processes of nationalism. When we consider 'invented traditions', 'imagined communities' and 'ethnies', we are demonstrating that culture and identity are not windows on the nation, they *are* the nation. National and ethnic identities are dynamic states of being and becoming, and the values, actions and institutions which make these identities material are differentiating practices which must be of paramount concern to social scientists. Drinking is such a practice: it is a historical and contemporary process of identity formation, maintenance, reproduction and transformation. Its importance to scholars of national identity and ethnicity is not principally in its role in grand state policies and the loftier ideals of the nation (although there too alcohol has played a role). Rather, drinking is the stuff of everyday life, quotidian culture which at the end of the day may be as important to the lifeblood of the nation as are its origin myths, heroes and grand narratives.

Drinking cultures are aspects of other cultures, part and parcel of wider webs of significance, broader fields of affiliation, identification and action. Drinking is itself a practice of differentiation, an example of cultural praxis. And although many anthropologists still seek to avoid definitions, some scholars continue to recognize the value in delineating the characteristics of something so important as 'culture'. In the discussion I have presented here, I have been following Stuart Hall (1994: 527; emphasis in original), who has suggested that culture might be best conceived as '*both* the meanings and values which arise amongst distinctive social groups and classes, on the basis of their given historical conditions and relationships, through which they "handle" and respond to the conditions of existence; *and* as the lived traditions and practices through which those "understandings" are expressed and in which they are embodied'. The chapters in this volume present case studies of drinking, culture, power and identity, in terms of their related practices, traditions, understandings and embodiments.

Drinking Cultures

Given all of this attention to historical and contemporary anthropological accounts of the intersections of drinking alcohol, culture and society, it is worth noting that one of the most durable and influential analyses of the meanings and practices of drinking remains that of Mary Douglas (1987), in her introduction to the second major (mostly ethnographic) collection of case studies in the social constructions associated with alcohol. Douglas sets out in stark terms the principal differences between most anthropologists' accounts of drinking behaviour and those of other social scientists. Anthropological research cross-culturally shows that regular and repetitive drinking is not necessarily perceived as drunkenness or alcoholism, and such behaviours may not be a sign of a breakdown in culture, but rather may be evidence of a strong and supportive cultural framework (Douglas 1987: 4). Drunkenness, when it is recognized as such, is an expression of culture because it is socially learned and patterned, and varies in structure and function from society to society. Douglas (1987: 4) reminds us that all cultures celebrate, and most do so with alcohol, and that 'drinking is essentially a social act, performed in a recognized social context'. She argues that drinking acts to mark the boundaries of personal and group identities, making it a practice of inclusion and exclusion (Douglas 1987: 8–12). In these terms alcohol is an element in social construction, and drinking is a key practice in the social construction of the world as it is and as it should be. As the chapters in this collection demonstrate, this construction has both temporal and spatial components, which provide analytical frames upon which to build more ethnographically rich models of national and ethnic identity.

David Sutton's (2001: 7) intriguing interrogation of the notion that 'we are what we eat', and 'we are what we ate', highlights the roles which food plays in identity formation and reproduction, today and in the past, and the ways in which these are remembered. So too alcohol and drinking are often important elements in such identifications and cultural differentiations. Just as food, in terms of its form and content, needs to be understood in the development of national and ethnic sameness and difference, drink's place in these processes must be clarified and engaged critically by anthropologists. In this sense, the contributors to this volume, in various ways, investigate the extent to which we are what we drink, how we drink, where we drink and when we drink. And what, where and when you drink allows us to make judgments about others and their identities, as Marion Demossier illustrates in her chapter, where she discusses the assertion 'tell me what *you* drink, and I shall tell you who *you* are'. Furthermore, who we are, and the actions which substantiate identity, also give substance to the spatial and temporal dimensions to society, polity and economy.

Drinking Places

Much anthropological attention has been paid to the places where people drink. This emphasis has many sources. People who drink may spend a great deal of time in the places where it is socially appropriate to drink, at least at the times when it is appropriate (for example, one should not drink in a pub after the licensing hours, and one should not have a martini in the den for breakfast). As a result, if drinking is a significant practice, then where you drink also bears some scrutiny. Drinking places are locations where other significant behaviours are evident, where other things of importance occur. For the most part, the data I gathered on local politics in rural Ireland were not collected in government offices and political meetings, but were freely offered and sometimes hotly debated by opposing forces in the pub. Drinking places also have rules and dimensions of their own, which may serve as indicators of structures and actions which are significant beyond their own walls.

In fact, drinking places are often particularly significant and culturally patterned spaces for drinking and other intercourse. As Hunt and Satterlee (1986b: 524) have suggested, we might approach the spatial dimensions of drinking in various ways, depending on the significance of a number of related factors in any one drinking 'arena', where arena is seen to be an allocation of space with a surrounding boundary that acts as both a physical barrier and symbolic border. These arenas can be realized in any 'drinking *space*, which can be created instantaneously and practically any-where and the drinking *place*, with its more elaborate physical structure' (Hunt and Satterlee 1986b: 524; emphasis in original).

All of the chapters in this book examine drinking practices in drinking arenas. Some have placed particular importance on the relations among locality, territory and drinking, with broad perspectives on the roles of alcohol in the construction of the region, the nation and the state. Other chapters focus more on drinking places and spaces. Brian Moeran examines the spaces of drinking in rural Japan, domestic spaces configured around the table and in the garden, but also the public spaces of village and valley. Cliona O'Carroll compares two drinking places in Berlin, the 'Irish' pub and the *Eckkneipe*, the local version of the working-class bar. While these two places might have historical roots in common, in that the local pub in Ireland, especially in the cities, functioned much like *Eckkneipen* continue to do in Berlin, they no longer seem to serve the same purposes or peoples. At least, this appears to be the case with the German Irish pub. As O'Carroll demonstrates, while the Irish pub presents itself as a comfortable alternative to Germans who do not have access to the comforts of the community *Eckkneipe*, it is not in itself a direct substitute. Rather, the pub may be viewed as an arena of contesting identities, of at times disputed and at times uncontested authenticity, where the differentiating processes of local, national and even European identities are as much a part of the make-up of the pub as is the Guinness on tap and the commoditized Irishness. Perhaps due to the mix of pub culture and cultural representations, the pub provides an arena of drinking places and spaces where the transformations of national and transnational identities in a changing Europe are played out.

In the midst of this new Europe, in fact at the heart of the old Mitteleuropa and the new European Union of twenty-five states (as of May 2004), lies Prague, in the Czech Republic. As Timothy Hall reviews in his contribution to this book, beer is at the heart of this heart of Europe; beer drinking is an important and often complicated practice, among a people who define themselves at least in part by what and how they drink. This is especially so among males, and Hall's chapter, like those of just about every author in this collection, relates the constructions of national identity to gender. Masculinity is an important theme in the understanding and practice of beer drinking among Czechs, in ways similar to the Berliners and Japanese, but drinking is also a window on the complexities of gender identity as it intersects with class, ethnic and national identity, and sexuality. As Hall records, in the words of at least one Czech, a man's relationship with a beer is just like a relationship with a woman: when you are enjoying either you should not be thinking of any others.

The important role which drinking arenas can play in local and national senses of the self are also demonstrated in Pauline Garvey's analysis of the *vorspiel*, a home drinking party in Norway. In the town of Skien, among young adults, drinking, whether in the pub or at home, but in friendship groups where some degree of recip- rocity is expected, demarcates time and space, between day and night, work and leis- ure. But drinking practices are also linked to wider notions of individual and group character, notions which in turn are generated by, and are reflected in, state policies. The *vorspiel* acts as agent of both order and disorder: it provides some coherence to groups of people who in other ways and times might reject the values of normalcy in Norway, but who, through the control provided in the informal but regularized cycle of drinking, serve to support broader conceptions of social order. In this way the drinking place, the home, becomes a building block of the national space.

While these chapters, and the others in this collection, show that it is important to consider the physical and territorial context to drinking, such a consideration alone is incomplete. In other words, drinking places and spaces are not themselves intrin- sically special or of a significance that transcends most other forces in the construc- tion of identities. Thus, no matter how socially significant drinking arenas seem, their importance also rests with their roles in the framing of actions, networks and other social relations beyond their own bounds. There is perhaps no more important place where drinking is seen to be a significant social act than in the pubs of the British Isles, yet even in their case Hunt and Satterlee (1986a: 63) conclude that

> although there exists within the walls of the pub a social world which possesses its own rules of behavior and its own practices, these behaviors and practices cannot be fully understood if they are seen as discrete entities. The rituals, practices, behaviors and social groupings found within the pub are inextricably tied to life outside the pub. The 'culture' of the pub . . . has to be seen as a continuation of the culture of social groupings outside.

The obverse is also true: the cultures of the pub, bar, café, *shibeen*, country club and street corner have their own continuations elsewhere. They too are productive forces in the differentiations of identity, in part because they are sites in the making and maintenance of social memory.

Drinking Memories

While the spatial dimensions of drinking, which include drinking places and arenas such as bars, festivals, religious rituals and homes, are important domains in which to begin to understand drinking practices, often and alternatively termed 'drinking comportment' (Marshall 1979b), they are by themselves insufficient if one seeks also to understand the breadth and depth of the roles which alcohol-related behaviours play in cultural differentiation. Drinking places and actions must be seen also within their temporal dimensions, as 'drinking occasions'. As Heath (2000) demonstrates in his book-length analysis, it is all but impossible to separate when we drink from all of the culturally significant behaviours, ideas and values which are associated with alcohol. Consider, for example, the roles which drinking plays in establishing the temporal pattern to the middle-class American's daily life, in which the time of day inhibits or entices particular drinking behaviours, and those actions and times mark the socially significant transformations from work to leisure, the work-place to the home (Gusfield 1987). Also of particular note in this regard are the drinking encounters in the daily, weekly and annual cycles of the Japanese village discussed by Moeran in the chapter which follows this one, encounters which imply happenstance, but which are often predicted occasions of reciprocal and hierarchical exchange, reinforcing historical and contemporary notions of difference and sameness.

The importance of drinking occasions is discussed by many of our contributors, who look at the roles of alcohol and drink as they relate to historical consciousness and constructions, in terms which make us consider that not only are we what we drink, but we are also what we drank. These 'drinking memories' (to paraphrase Sutton's discussion of 'food memories' [2001: 4–16]) are particularly important among people who perceive that their distinctive regional behaviours and values are at the core of what can, and perhaps should, be seen as a 'nation'. Sharryn Kasmir examines drinking sociability among the Basques, who view their drinking behaviours as traditional aspects of the Basque character. Steffan Igor Ayora-Diaz and Gabriela Vargas-Cetina portray the complex relationships among food, drink and music in the creation and duration of the Yucatecan soul. In this intricate mix of consumption and expression, the distinctive nature of a Yucatecan identity, as part of a regional identity and political movement, takes shape, demonstrating yet again that leisure activities are very often seen by people to be the embodiment of who they are as individuals and societies, constitutive of ethnicities and national identities. In the changing relations between the Yucatán and the Mexican state, drinking is one of the motifs in the Yucatecan construction of who they are and who they were, in a projection of their authentic history, dating for some to the Mayans.

It is arguable that no nation on earth is more associated with a particular type of drink, and particular styles of imbibing, then the French, but as Marion Demossier shows in her chapter in this book (see also Demossier 1997, 2000), while the significance of wine and wine drinking may be growing in France, the types and uses of drinking behaviours are the basis for remarkable divergent social and cultural identifications. Wine is a mode of regional differentiation, class distinction and discourse of French national identity. What, when, how and why the French drink wine are increasingly debated topics, in ways which show the twin forces of integration and disintegration at work among the French, long held high as the principal example of the homogeneous cultural and political nation. As a result, wine and its relation to life cycles, of the individual, of the village, of the region, continue to play important roles in the historicity and negotiations of French region and nation, a negotiation which Demossier contextualizes within globalization, the great force of time and space compression.

The processes of globalization, and the configurations of transnational and other identifications of the international migrant, are also changing the ways in which Hong Kong people demonstrate ethnicity, regional identity and class status and mobility. In Josephine Smart's chapter, it is clear that cognac, a symbol of French drinking and regional identity, has taken on significances that could not have been predicted in Hong Kong's colonial and imperial past. Cognac use in Hong Kong today, and in recent memory, serves as an example of how one commodity can provide the code for understanding great changes in local and global economics, the changing culture of class, and the roles of authenticity and nostalgia in local, regional, national and transnational identity formation and transformation. Cognac also is an element in a changing celebratory ritual, in this case that of the wedding banquet, which is as much a product of modernity as it is of tradition. For Hong Kong emigrants, cognac is one of the memories of migration, a practice which allows one to think of home. But Smart also shows us cognac is a commodity, with remarkable linkages in economic production, exchange and consumption, locally and globally.

Drinking Economics

Drinking is an economic relation, linked to the production of alcohol, its marketing, its consumption, and its role, as commodity and symbol, in the wider commodification of society. Mary Douglas has viewed alcohol's production as an 'economic activity of consequence' (1987: 8), which also plays an important role in many informal and illegal economies (see also Crump 1987 and Mars and Altman 1987, analyses of alternative economies which were included in the important constructive drinking collection which Douglas introduced). Drinking is literally a consumptive activity, which figures importantly in many processes and practices in wider fields of social consumption. In his chapter Brian Moeran investigates how one commodity, alcohol, particularly sake, and its related drinking behaviours, can illustrate the regimes of value in rural Japanese economy and society, and the modes and relative significance of interpersonal business, family and generational relations. Ultimately, this is an act of identity and identification, a demonstration of what it means to be Japanese, but it also serves as an example of how one bit of material culture can give substance to a moral order in the midst of its roles in economic and social exchange. In this case we see the same processes at work which William Roseberry (1996) identified in middle-class, 'yuppie' America, where the distinctions of class which overall society protests are not important can be found in the privileged consumption of elite commodities.

Examining consumption as an act of social class distinction has been an important analytical strategy for some time, chiefly influenced by the works of Mary Douglas and her colleagues (see, for example, Douglas and Isherwood 1979), Pierre Bourdieu (see for example Bourdieu 1984), Arjun Appadurai (see, for example, Appadurai 1986) and Daniel Miller (see, for example, Miller 1987). But many of our contributors also present case studies which direct us to investigate exchange as a differentiation process, in some terms which are familiar, such as those of capitalist exploitation and accumulation, and some which are no longer principal interests of anthropologists, as in reciprocal and redistributive economic and social relations. As the chapters by Moeran, Garvey, Smart, Jon Mitchell and Gary Armstrong, and Anthony Marcus show, drinking is an economic relation, as important perhaps as the politics of culture in identity matters. These 'identity economics' are often clearly delineated in the ethnographic investigation of drinking cultures.

Drinking Politics

Drinking is also a political act, whether it be in terms of the grander formal politics of government, party and policy, or in the interpersonal relations of power and authority. In Anthony Marcus's chapter we approach the intersections of civil and political society, on the margins of big-city and small-city life in the United States, in ways which demand that we rethink the roles of social capital in industrial democracies. At least in the situations in which he and his respondents found themselves, in public arenas of drinking and drug use, the political ideologies and social networks which were created and sustained provided the basis for alternative politics to mainstream notions of democracy. These are the not the full-blown politics of national identity, and their attendant constructions of political culture, but the divisive and disputed politics of power, representation and democracy, in a country which seeks to export its reputably homogeneous notions of liberty and democracy, even if that exportation is at the point of a bayonet.

The politics of the street, where violence constructs the boundaries of ethnicity, masculinity and the social and economic roles of gang members in American cities, are the subjects of the contribution by Geoffrey Hunt, Kathleen MacKenzie and Karen Joe-Laidler. They explore the occasions, preferences and expressions of drink and identity among the youth of three ethnic groupings who find solidarity within gangs. They consider ways in which drinking is an important part of being masculine, in the context of both ethnicity and gang dynamics, but also how the expressions of violence and identity vary across the range of ethnic backgrounds. Drinking provides social cohesion to groups whose actions result in an opposite effect for other groups in society. Both gangs and their victims are faced with the violence and dehumanization of the identity politics of the city, where one 'does' drink, drugs and gender in order to gain and keep power.

A number of our chapters in this volume, however, also deal with other small and big politics of the cultural dimensions to politics, especially those of the nation and national identity. Sharryn Kasmir's analysis of national identity in the Basquelands starts with the premise that politics associated with religious and other rituals are real politics, like other rituals elsewhere, which are often as central to political expression in industrial and modern contexts as they are in less developed countries (as so convincingly demonstrated in Kertzer 1988). Kasmir's review of a night of slightly profane actions, revolving around a representation of the Madonna, is but an introduction to the roles which patterns of reciprocal drinking in bars play in differentiating Basques from other nations in Spain and France. This nationalism, among the Basque youth who figure prominently in this chapter and who take pride in the associational life rooted in local bars, is a movement for self-determination, a valued prize for many types of nationalism in Europe and beyond in today's seemingly borderless world. But Kasmir also reminds us that when we think about the politics of the nation in the Basquelands, we must also think about the politics of class (Kasmir 2002), a concern shared by other authors in *Drinking Cultures.*

Jon Mitchell and Gary Armstrong examine expressions of masculinity in the drinking behaviours of urban Malta, where cliques, born from long histories of colonial relations, express their localism and nationalism through feasts, reciprocal rounds of bar drinks and visits, and sporting celebrations. This case study illustrates many of the themes which vitalize the other chapters: the politics of class and national identity, the distinctions represented in beer and wine drinking, the formal and informal economic relations which depend on alcohol and drinking behaviors, and the local and global intersections which give definition to identities, and cause for change in all the drinking arenas which have proved so important to Maltese identity and culture. As Mitchell (2002) has discussed elsewhere, Malta also serves as one of the many places where European identity is a new and important form of cultural differentiation, and one that is sure to have many more comparators in the expanding European Union. As such, Valletta is a crossroads in the politics of the movement of ideas, people, values and goods, where blockbuster film crews, working-class British tourists and European football teams and symbols intersect, creating new dimensions to the 'everyday' and 'extraordinary' drinking arenas of Maltese life, where new and old expressions of identity mix.

Drinking Expressions

Drinking is a communicative act, a performance of identity to be sure, but one which also communicates so much more. As Turmo (2001: 131) reminds us, drinking functions as an almost silent language, 'it is a language that, on many occasions, needs neither words nor expressions'. Even the solitary silent drinker in the bar speaks wonders, in part because drinking 'is a cultural fact on which thousands of years, millions of gestures have accumulated' (Turmo 2001: 130). At other times, however, drink is the elixir of verbiage, the privately understood and publicly sanctioned approval to talk, a lot, and loudly. Sometimes this occurs in the course of festivals, parties and celebrations, as we can see in Mitchell and Armstrong's Maltese case, a celebration of sport and death, and in the religious parody of 'Mary in a Box' in the Basque town which is discussed in Kasmir's contribution to this book.

The convergence in anthropological interest in drinking and communicating takes us full circle, back to the Japanese study by Moeran with which I began this section of my chapter. In his case study, it is clear that exchanging cups in a ritualized drinking occasion is a crucial element in a drinking arena where important information is also exchanged. This information is about business, and the strategies to succeed, but it is also about the less explicit but no less important demonstration of gender, class and local identity. This drinking talk communicates a great deal about the positions and values of status, hierarchy and reciprocity, between men and women, old and young, the dead and the alive. 'Drinking talk' also provides this volume with a good starting point in our joint effort to begin a more comprehensive approach to the roles of drink and drinking in the expression of identity.

Conclusion

This chapter has sought to clarify the themes which run through the contributions to the book which it introduces, and to do so with brief visits to the history of the anthropology of drinking and alcohol, recent changes in ways anthropologists have approached culture and identity, and the relevance of anthropological studies of drinking, ethnicity and national identity to wider scholarly concerns with the differentiating processes of culture. Our chapters review various aspects of drinking places and spaces, memories, economics and politics, and wider expressions of culture and identity. Many other thematic threads run through them, such as gendered drinking (a particular focus of the chapters by Hall, Garvey, Mitchell and Armstrong, and Hunt et al.), consumption and identity (in the chapters by Demossier, O'Carroll and

Smart), religion and identity (as approached in the chapters by Kasmir, and Mitchell and Armstrong), and the interplay of national and regional identities (as examined in the chapters by Ayora-Diaz and Vargas-Cetina, Kasmir, Marcus and Moeran).

Given this range of ethnographic case studies and rich portraits of drinking practices, however, it might be easy to lose sight of the one thread that runs through them all: national and ethnic identities must be understood in the context of other identities and identifications, such as those of class, gender, region, locality and religion, and all of these find important expression in drinking sites and practices. If and when alcohol and drinking are moral and health problems, they may also be, perhaps always are, elements of social and political integration and order, where culture and identity have as much to do with the acceptance of drinking as they do with its avoidance.

While the themes of the individual chapters often overlap and complement each other, in that many of them deal simultaneously with ethnic and national identities and their construction and expression in drinking memories, economies, politics, places and communication, many also engage other issues of identity and differentiation, in terms of age, class, race and locality. These similarities and differences provide a rich environment in which to investigate the intersections of culture and identity and drink. In fact, it is hoped that the ethnographic cases which follow will help to direct anthropologists to further consideration of drinking as an important expression of identity and culture, particularly ethnic and national identity, but one which also influences scholars to construct innovative comparative research designs which are not unduly tied to the nation, the nation-state or the ethnic group as the units for comparison. Rather, this volume's contributions (in concert with de Garine and de Garine 2001a) invite more scholarly attention to the utility of developing ethnographic perspectives on drinking as a socially constructive act. These perspectives should seek to engage cultural differentiation and its intersections with language, economic production, exchange and consumption, and the politics of history, memory, culture and power.

Notes

1. See de Garine and de Garine (2001b) for a broader anthropological approach to drinking and culture that places alcohol within wider fields of production and consumption.
2. See, for example, the recent review of Hunt and Barker (2001), which seeks to provide a new framework for a unified theoretical approach to the anthropologies of drink and drugs, a theme echoed by Marcus in this book.

3. All of which are illustrated in the 'bar culture' of rural Catalonia, as depicted by Hansen (1976), in an article that still stands as one of the best applications of a political economy approach in anthropology to regional and national culture and society. See Health (2000) for a discussion of the utility of concentrating on 'drinking occasions' for comparative analyses of drinking and culture.
4. For a discussion of some of these approaches to culture, power and identity, see Hill and Wilson (2003); see also Hall (1990) for one of the most influential statements on culture and identity, and one of the clearest on the new importance of cultural identity in discussions of culture.

References

Appadurai, Arjun (1986), 'Introduction: Commodities and the Politics of Value', in Arjun Appadurai (ed.), *The Social Life of Things*, Cambridge: Cambridge University Press.

—— (1996), *Modernity at Large: Cultural Dimensions of Globalization*, Minneapolis: University of Minnesota Press.

Basso, Keith H. (1996), *Wisdom Sits in Places: Landscape and Language among the Western Apache*, Albuquerque: University of New Mexico Press.

Bourdieu, Pierre (1984), *Distinction: A Social Critique of the Judgment of Taste*, London: Routledge & Kegan Paul.

Connor, Walker (1993), *Ethnonationalism: The Quest for Understanding*, Princeton: Princeton University Press.

Crump, Thomas (1987), 'The Alternative Economy of Alcohol in the Chiapas Highlands', in Mary Douglas (ed.), *Constructive Drinking: Perspectives on Drink from Anthropology*, Cambridge: Cambridge University Press; Paris: Editions de la Maison des Sciences de l'Homme.

de Garine, Igor, and Valerie de Garine (2001a.), 'For a Pluridisciplinary Approach to Drinking', in Igor de Garine and Valerie de Garine (eds), *Drinking: Anthropological Approaches*, New York: Berghahn.

de Garine, Igor, and Valerie de Garine (eds) (2001b), *Drinking: Anthropological Approaches*, New York: Berghahn.

Demossier, Marion (1997), 'Producing Tradition and Managing Social Changes in the French Vineyards: The Circle of Time in Burgundy', *Ethnologia Europea* 27: 47–58.

—— (2000), 'Wine Festivals in Contemporary France: Reshaping Power through Time in Burgundy', in Karin Friedrich (ed.), *Festive Culture in Germany and Europe from the Sixteenth to the Twentieth Century*, Lewiston, NY: Edwin Mellen Press.

Donnan, Hastings and Thomas M. Wilson (1999), *Borders: Frontiers of Identity, Nation and State*, Oxford: Berg.

Douglas, Mary (1987), 'A Distinctive Anthropological Perspective', in Mary Douglas (ed.), *Constructive Drinking: Perspectives on Drink from Anthropology*, Cambridge: Cambridge University Press; Paris: Editions de la Maison des Sciences de l'Homme.

Douglas, Mary and Baron Isherwood (1979), *The World of Goods*, New York: Basic Books.

Gusfield, Joseph (1987), 'Passage to Play: Rituals of Drinking Time in American Society', in Mary Douglas (ed.), *Constructive Drinking: Perspectives on Drink from Anthropology*, Cambridge: Cambridge University Press.

Hall, Stuart (1990), 'Cultural Identity and Diaspora', in Jonathan Rutherford (ed.), *Identity: Community, Culture, Difference*, London: Lawrence & Wishart.

—— (1994), 'Cultural Studies: Two Paradigms', in Nicholas B. Dirks, Geoff Eley and Sherry B. Ortner (eds), *Culture/Power/History: A Reader in Contemporary Social Theory*, Princeton: Princeton University Press.

Hansen, Edward C. (1976), 'Drinking to Prosperity: The Role of Bar Culture and Coalition Formation in the Modernization of the Alto Panades', in Joseph B. Aceves, Edward C. Hansen and Gloria Levitas (eds), *Economic Transformation and Steady-state Values*, Flushing, NY: Queens College Press.

Heath, Dwight B. (1975), 'A Critical Review of Ethnographic Studies of Alcohol Use', in R. J. Gibbins, Y. Israel, H. Kalant, R. E. Popham, W. Schmidt and R. E. Smart (eds), *Research Advances in Alcohol and Drug Problems*, Vol. 2, New York: Wiley.

—— (1976), 'Anthropological Perspectives on Alcohol: An Historical Review', in Michael W. Everett, Jack O. Waddell and Dwight B. Heath (eds), *Cross-cultural Approaches to the Study of Alcohol: An Interdisciplinary Perspective*, The Hague: Mouton Publishers.

—— (1987a), 'Anthropology and Alcohol Studies: Current Issues', *Annual Review of Anthropology* 16: 99–120.

—— (1987b), 'A Decade of Development in the Anthropological Study of Alcohol Use, 1970–1980', in Mary Douglas (ed.), *Constructive Drinking: Perspectives on Drink from Anthropology*, Cambridge: Cambridge University Press; Paris: Editions de la Maison des Sciences de l'Homme.

—— (2000), *Drinking Occasions: Comparative Perspectives on Alcohol and Culture*, Philadelphia: Brunner/Mazel.

Hill, Jonathan D. and Thomas M. Wilson (2003), 'Identity Politics and the Politics of Identities', *Identities: Global Studies in Culture and Power* 10 (1): 1–8.

Hunt, Geoffrey P. and Judith C. Barker (2001), 'Socio-cultural Anthropology and Alcohol and Drug Research: Towards a Unified Theory', *Social Science and Medicine* 53: 165–88.

Hunt, Geoffrey P. and Saundra Satterlee (1986a), 'The Pub, the Village and the People', *Human Organization* 45 (1): 62–74.

—— (1986b), 'Cohesion and Division: Drinking in an English Village', *Man* 21: 521–37.

Kasmir, Sharryn (2002), '"More Basque than You": Class, Youth and Identity in an Industrial Basque Town', *Identities: Global Studies in Culture and Power* 9: 39–68.

Kearney, Michael (1970), 'Drunkenness and Religious Conversion in a Mexican Village', *Quarterly Journal of Studies on Alcohol* 31 (1): 132–52.

Kertzer, David (1988), *Ritual, Politics, and Power*, New Haven: Yale University Press.

Mars, Gerald and Yochanian Altman (1987), 'Alternative Mechanism of Distribution in a Soviet Economy', in Mary Douglas (ed.), *Constructive Drinking: Perspectives on Drink from Anthropology,* Cambridge: Cambridge University Press; Paris: Editions de la Maison des Sciences de l'Homme.

Marshall, Mac (ed.) (1979a), *Beliefs, Behaviors, and Alcoholic Beverages: A Cross-cultural Survey*, Ann Arbor: University of Michigan Press.

Marshall, Mac (1979b), *Weekend Warriors: Alcohol in a Micronesian Culture*, Palo Alto, CA: Mayfield Publishing.

—— (1984), 'Alcohol and Drug Studies in Anthropology: Where Do We Go From Here?', *The Drinking and Drug Practices Surveyor* 19: 23–7.

Miller, Daniel (1987), *Material Culture and Mass Consumption*, Oxford: Blackwell.

Mitchell, Jon P. (2002), *Ambivalent Europeans: Ritual, Memory and the Public Sphere in Malta*, London: Routledge.

Roseberry, William (1996), 'The Rise of Yuppie Coffees and the Reimagination of Class in the United States', *American Anthropologist* 98: 762–75.

Smith, Anthony D. (1999), *Myths and Memories of the Nation*, Oxford: Oxford University Press.

Sutton, David E. (2001), *Remembrance of Repasts: An Anthropology of Food and Memory*, Oxford: Berg.

Turmo, Isabel González (2001), 'Drinking: An Almost Silent Language', in Igor de Garine and Valerie de Garine (eds), *Drinking: Anthropological Approaches*, New York: Berghahn Books.

–2–

Drinking Country

Flows of Exchange in a Japanese Valley

Brian Moeran

Drink and drinking in Japan are a serious business. On the one hand, the fact that Japanese men (and it is mainly, though not exclusively, men) like to drink together has contributed to the growth of a national alcohol industry that includes such breweries as Suntory, Asahi and Kirin, and a host of sake rice wine manufacturers boasting particular traditional and regional tastes.[1] Of these, Suntory started out by producing wine, but is now the largest and oldest distiller of whisky in Japan (its Suntory Old is the world's best-selling whisky), as well as being a major producer of spirits, beer, wine and soft drinks. It produces and distributes Carlsberg in Japan, and manages a whisky distillery in Scotland, together with wine producers in France and Germany. Consolidated annual sales of the 173 companies in the Suntory Group come to about $12 billion. For its part, Asahi, which owns the Nikka whisky distillery, has annual sales of about $9 billion, brews Asahi Super Dry (Japan's most popular beer), and has a 46.2 per cent share (the largest) of the beer market in Japan. Kirin, which used to be Japan's leading beer brewer, has sales of approximately $10 billion. Like its main rival, Asahi, it runs a group of companies with such diverse interests as soft drinks, foods, restaurants, distribution, pharmaceuticals, engineering and real estate. The consumption of alcohol, therefore, has contributed to the postwar development of giant Japanese corporations employing tens of thousands of people, with worldwide operations in all kinds of related – and seemingly unrelated – businesses. This kind of corporate structure in itself has been seen to mark a particular kind of Japanese capitalism – alliance (Gerlach 1992) or welfare (Dore 2000) capitalism.

The fact that Japanese men like to drink together has also ensured that there are all kinds of places where they can drink – from *akachōchin* red lantern eateries and beer halls, via plain watering holes (*nomiya*) to, frequently expensive, bars that go by such misleading generic names as *club*, *snack* or *stand*.[2] These different kinds of drinking establishments tend to be found together in different parts of every city or country town, catering to different types of clientele. In Tokyo, for example, exclusive Japanese restaurants and bars, frequented by politicians working in and around the nearby Diet, can be found in Akasaka. The area around Shibuya station, on the other hand, has more affordable and more popular places to eat and drink, since it is here that young people gather day and night. Each district's entertainment area (known as *sakariba* [Linhart 1998]) in which its various drinking establishments are found thus takes on a certain characteristic atmosphere, depending on whether it is catering to media professionals (Ginza), young people (Roppongi) or students and academics (Yotsuya). In this respect, too, alcohol as a product of material culture has its social repercussions.

But drinking is also a serious business in a different sense. Very often Japanese drink alcohol in order to pursue and successfully conclude business negotiations of one sort or another. This is by now well known among those Europeans and Americans who have had even indirect dealings with the Japanese. Indeed, it has been cause for wonder and comment since it seems that business consists of two totally different worlds that together form the Siamese twins of Japanese welfare capitalism. One is a public, daytime world of light, in which businessmen meet and enter into formal negotiations. This strictly businesslike association, with little apparent concern for developing long-term ties, the Japanese call 'dry' relations. The other is a more intimate, twilight, 'happy hours' world of darkness, lit by neon signs and the painted smiles of more and less attractive hostesses whose job is to murmur sweet nothings and keep their clients' glasses full, while praising their – often better unremarked – renderings of popular karaoke songs. This world is known, somewhat poetically, as 'the water trade' (*mizu shōbai*), and is said to provide the informal heart that enables formal business negotiations to be concluded. This more intimate approach to business the Japanese appropriately refer to as 'wet' relations.

This division between day- and night-time worlds, as well as between 'dry' and 'wet' forms of social interaction, is also characteristic of many of Japan's rural communities, where, as we shall see, what goes on in the day-to-day lives of local farmers, potters and other craftsmen tends to be discussed over alcohol, and what is said during these evening drinking sessions itself affects the daytime discourse and its outcomes. In other words, a particular kind of commodity flow enables certain kinds of symbolic and social exchanges. In its move from production through distribution and representation to consumption, alcohol (a drink) takes on a 'social life' (drinking) in which participants talk about, negotiate and reclassify their respective positions in a social world, primarily through the exchange of words. The reference point for this social world is sometimes little more than a local community. At other times, however, it extends to embrace the notion of a national identity, in the sense that those drinking in the country valley studied here often felt themselves to be the only people left in Japan who practised a 'truly Japanese' and 'traditional' way of life. In short, country people exoticized themselves almost as much as anthropologists in search of 'the real Japan'.

Under such circumstances, it will hardly surprise my readers if I continue by saying that drinking is a serious business for any anthropologist engaged in the study of forms of social organization in which men are the main protagonists (like a rural community, company, fire station or sumo wrestlers' stable). It is 'serious business' because when Japanese men drink, they tend to let slip pieces of information and gossip that, in the daytime world, they keep to themselves. I say 'let slip', but such knowledge is not necessarily revealed out of indiscretion or inability to control the effects of alcohol. It may very well be consciously imparted and politically motivated, in order for the speaker to see what reaction he gets out of his drinking partner and whether they will be able to build a relationship of mutual trust.

So, too, with the anthropologist himself. On every occasion that I have embarked upon fieldwork, whether in a remote pottery community in Kyushu or a large advertising agency in downtown Tokyo, I have found myself being tested for weaknesses during drinking sessions with informants-to-be. Could I hold my drink? Could I sing? Would I – could I – become a trusted drinking companion? Was I all that I made myself out to be – an anthropologist – or was I, perhaps, a government spy or tax inspector in disguise? What was it that, as an anthropologist, I *really* wanted to find out about them? And what would I do with all the information they gave me?

As I say, in Japan drinking is primarily for and by men. This is not to say that women do not drink. Of course, they do. Many of the hostesses and *mama-san*s I have met over the years hold their drink far better than the men they serve. At least one Japanese woman friend of mine can drink me under the *kotatsu* table at any time of the day or night. But in general the kind of drinking that goes on among businessmen in city bars, or among farmers and potters in country homes, places women in a secondary, subservient role as hostesses or housewives preparing and serving alcohol and the occasional titbit of food for their male visitors. As the local postmaster in the valley where I lived between 1977 and 1982 once – perhaps a little crudely – put it: 'The men, they drink sake, and the women, they gossip. That is our form of entertainment.'[3]

Drinking Occasions

In this chapter, I intend to focus on a particular field of social relations (a country valley), the cooperative networks of people living there, and the frames in which their drinking took place (Moeran 2003).[4] By examining their sake cup exchanges and the stories that they told during drinking encounters, I hope to be able to show how people living in a remote rural valley in Kyushu – the main southern island of Japan that was home to the middle-ranking samurai nationalists who restored the Meiji emperor to power in 1868, and which is still a bastion of 'masculinity' or 'male chauvinism' (take your pick) – used drinking to make sense of the world in which they lived and of the social relationships in which they engaged.

It is now more than two and a half decades since I first set foot in the Ono valley, leading up towards the pilgrimage site of Mount Hikosan, near the border between Oita and Fukuoka prefectures in northern Kyushu. But the drinking that I did with local people during the four years that I lived there remains indelibly etched on both my memory and my liver. This is partly because I quickly learned that, if I wished to find out what was really going on behind the façade of answers that greeted my questions during participant observation fieldwork interviews, I needed to drink with my informants. It was then that they began to reveal some of the less obvious aspects of what they thought about the people they associated and lived with. But I remember the drinking, too, for the sheer fun and hilarity of many of the stories that I was told, as well as for the rather too many, less pleasant, 'second-day inebriations' (*futsuka yoi*) or hangovers that I had to endure.[5]

Perhaps I should have heeded the warning greeting all those who enter the winding valley road that leads out of the enclosed plain surrounding the country town of Hita. 'The Ono valley', reads the calligraphy on a giant roadside bowling pin, 'does not admit drunken drivers.' I later learned that there was ample justification for these words. During my stay there, the Ono valley was designated by the local Hita police as a 'model village' – not because of the tasty *nashi* pears or famous folk crafts that some of its farmers and potters produced, but because its inhabitants as a whole had the highest rate of recorded drunken driving in the whole of the (very broad) area that came under Hita's local government administration.

My drinking companions were in general rather proud of this official recognition of their alcohol-related practices. They joked about how they might be designated a 'super-model village' if the police were to find out about and take into account how much they *really* drove under the influence (that is to say, without getting caught). They also interpreted the designation as indicating that they imbibed more alcohol than any other community in the Hita plain. They were, in short, 'real Kyushu men'.

So, what kind of alcohol did the potters, farmers, foresters, carpenters and other people in the Ono and neighbouring valleys drink? When and where did they drink, and for what purposes? Their alcohol consumption can, I think, be usefully separated into two basic social categories. People either drank Japanese rice wine (sake or *nihonshū*),[6] or occasionally a sweet potato distilled liquor (known as *shōchū*), which was almost invariably shared – in the sense that men drinking would exchange drinking cups among themselves. There were certain occasions when men would not exchange cups while drinking sake, but these invariably had to do with particular festivals that took place in each of the hamlets scattered along the fourteen kilometre length of the valley.[7] For the most part, however, drinking sessions would be limited – in terms of both alcohol quantity and imbibing time – only by the staying power of participants. As such, they might involve a number of different venues, from valley home to city bars (hence the drunken driving).

Alternatively, men in the Ono valley drank beer, whisky and whatever else they could lay their hands on, including wine. This they did out of their own glasses. They would drink together, of course, but not go through the exchange ritual that characterized sake drinking. This shift in drinking pattern occurred most obviously in local Hita bars, where men often turned from sake to beer, whisky or wine. The move from valley to town thus tended to mark a shift from a communal to an individualized drinking pattern, although this was by no means fixed. Men *did* drink beer with friends in their valley homes or local sake shops. They occasionally exchanged glasses. They were also known to drink sake in the downtown bars.

People in the Ono valley used to drink together in a number of differing combinations. For the most part, formal drinking encounters involved one or two representatives of each household making up a particular community or hamlet (*buraku*).[8] Depending on the community, there could be as many as nine or ten regular gatherings of this sort every year – primarily to celebrate local deities. In Sarayama, for example, household representatives met six times a year to celebrate Kōshinsama, three times for the fire goddess Akiyasama, and once for the god of trade, Ebisusama. Each household took it in turn to host the festivity.

In addition, however, all households in a community would send one or more of its representatives for other, non-regular drinking sessions.[9] These special occasions might be to mark a man's forty-first birthday, the raising of the main roof beam (*mune-age*) of a resident's new house, or the purchase of a new car (on the principle that one's good fortune should be shared, if only to avoid unpleasantness). On such occasions, a man might well invite friends and acquaintances from other communities in the valley, so that these gatherings would be more mixed, last longer and, as a result, often be rowdier.

Other large drinking gatherings were usually connected with work or school. The Ono Pear Growers' Association, for example, would hold regular six-monthly meetings that were followed by sake drinking among men who lived for the most part in the lower half of the valley. The Ebisusama festivity in Sarayama, mentioned above, was exclusive to the potters of Sarayama, although one or two local pottery dealers might be invited to participate. The two local primary schools in the valley also provided opportunities for plenty of drinking among parents at their children's sports days, kendo Japanese fencing competitions and other similar occasions.

Smaller gatherings of men, either at home or in a local sake shop, also took place regularly, though with no particular fixed pattern. Foresters might drop by a potter's workshop on their way home from work and go down to the nearby noodle shop for a few bottles of sake (in winter) or beer (on a thirsty day). Someone wanting to buy a piece of land might find himself spending several evenings sharing sake cups with the seller and their two go-betweens during the course of (what might often become protracted) negotiations. Certainly, the conclusion of any kind of business – whether a land deal, kiln contents sale, forest clearing or whatever – would be followed by the sharing of sake among participants. If an agreement between people was in any way involved (like the promise to sell a particular piece of land at a particular price), those concerned would formally clap hands – ideally in front of a witness from the household of the man making the promise – and seal the agreement with sake.

Finally, the general importance of sake in the valley may be seen in the fact that it was presented to different community and household deities, including the ancestors, on special occasions (very often with rice cooked in one form or another). Bottles of sake were also exchanged among households during the two annual gift-giving seasons of mid-summer, *o-bon*, and year-end, *o-seibo*. They also constituted the main gifts given at communal occasions – such as the annual outing of the *sōnenkai* adult men's association, a community archery or other sporting occasion – usually by those especially invited from outside or by inside members unable to attend the festivity concerned. This was primarily because people in the Ono valley, like those living in the village of Suye in nearby Kumamoto Prefecture during the mid-1930s, were always ready for a party. Like Ella Wiswell, I was frequently 'impressed by their seemingly limitless capacity to find occasions for them' (Smith and Wiswell 1982: 73).[10]

Drinking Exchanges

My focus here will be on formal drinking encounters, when a large group of men (and women) would gather for one of the specific purposes outlined above and drink an unlimited quantity of alcohol.[11] Such ceremonial occasions tended to follow a typical pattern. First, representatives from each household in a neighbourhood or work association would gather at the place where the festivities were to take place. If this were – as it often was – a private house, on arrival each guest would make his way to the parlour (or *nando*), an informal living room where family members gather to eat, socialize, or watch television. While awaiting the arrival of other guests, his talk would focus on the host's household members or the outside world – the rapid growth of the former's children, the quality of his pears in the orchard outside, and so on. The neighbourhood or work association itself would never be mentioned.

Once everyone was assembled, the host would ask people to move into the main guest room or rooms (*zashiki*),[12] where low tables were laid out across the top and down the sides of the room(s) in the shape of an inverted horseshoe. I use the words 'top', 'down' and 'inverted' because the *zashiki* is marked by the presence of a 'sacred dais' or *tokonoma* which is built into every country house and is considered to be the most important part of the building. As a result, only the most important people can sit with their backs to the *tokonoma* (and gaze out across the closed verandah into the surrounding garden). Thus, guests would always sit in this position, while their hosts sat facing them in a 'lower' position. In the event of several guests, the eldest man was asked to sit at the 'top' of the room, with the second-eldest placed to his right, and the third-eldest to his left. The fourth-eldest then took up his position at the second-eldest's right, and so on down the two lines of tables to the youngest man present. Then, and only then, were participating women able to take up their places – again theoretically in order of age, although in practice they were much less particular about who sat exactly where. As a general rule, perhaps, it might be said that the older a man or woman was, the more particular he or she tended to be about being seated according to seniority, and that men tended to be more particular than women about seating order.

Once the guests had taken up their positions and were kneeling formally in front of their places, the host formally greeted and welcomed them from the very bottom of the room. The most senior member among those present would then reply to the host's greeting. His formal speech used to repeat, in its highly ritualized series of set phrases, the distinction between host and guest households, but then blurred it by reminding everyone why they were gathered together that day. The rarer the occasion, the more detailed that information, and the greater the stress on the occasion itself. The host would then be thanked for providing a place for everyone to gather, visitors thanked for taking the trouble to come, and a toast proposed. At this point, the women would get up from their places at the bottom of the room and, from the inside of the inverted horseshoe, fill the men's sake cups from the bottles already heated and standing on the table tops. The speaker would raise his voice and shout '*Kanpai!*' ('Glasses dry!'), to be joined by a chorus of voices as those present lifted up their cups and downed their contents of sake in a single gulp.

This marked the end of the first stage of any formal drinking encounter. Immediately after the *kanpai* toast, participants would shift from a kneeling to cross-legged sitting position on their cushions and refill one another's cups.[13] They might well start sipping soup and dipping into the dishes of food in front of them, but drinking was what counted for it was – and to some extent still is – a man's ability to drink and talk or sing which marked him out from among his fellows on such occasions. So, while some of the women might linger in the inner space of the room, each man would pour sake for his neighbours on either side and have his cup filled in return, as they talked – still rather formally – about the weather, food and work, before shifting to more informal conversation about community events and local gossip.

It was at this point that a man would start to exchange sake cups with his neighbour, and the second stage of the party began. By 'exchange' I mean that when his cup was empty, instead of waiting for it to be refilled, a man would pick it up by the foot rim, balance it between the tips of his fingers and offer it to someone sitting nearby. As he did so, he would call out the other person's name, and raise the hand with which he was holding the cup very slightly once or twice – both to attract the other's attention and as a characteristic gesture of humility from someone offering a gift. The receiver would take the cup – usually with an exclamation of (feigned) surprise – bow his head slightly, again raise the cup (this time in a gesture of humble acceptance), and allow it to be filled by the other man from one of the bottles on the table between them. He then downed the sake and almost immediately returned the cup following an identical set of formal expressions and gestures.

As long as a man exchanged cups with his immediate neighbours, the flow of conversation tended not to be affected immediately in any appreciable way. However, the first exchange would be a signal for those concerned to shift from informal gossip to somewhat more intimate exchanges about how events previously touched upon more formally might affect them. Once he had exchanged cups with those on either side of him, a man would pass cups to others sitting further up or down the table, going through the same formalities.

Provided that those with whom he was exchanging cups were within arm's reach, a man tended to remain seated where he was. But as the gathering gained alcoholic momentum, men would find themselves exchanging cups with others several places away from where they were sitting. Since it was rude to drink on one's own without exchanging cups, and since it was also not good form to trouble one's neighbours by asking them to pass one's cups up or down the table, at this stage a man usually got up from his allotted place and took his cup directly to whomever he had in mind. This would involve either making one's way along behind one's neighbours, or stepping across one of the low tables into the empty centre of the room.

This shift from immobility to mobility in participants' cup exchanges can be said to mark a party's third stage and usually occurred about ten to fifteen minutes after the proposal of the formal toast. Why did this happen? Quite simply, it enabled a man to initiate conversations with others not in his immediate age group. It was from this time that the gathering started to become a 'serious' drinking session, and it was usually at this time, too, that women would withdraw to talk, drink and eat among themselves at the bottom of the room. This stage was marked by complete verbal, even physical, informality and there were few, if any, restrictions on who said or did what to whom. Moreover, whereas the first stage of formal speeches was conducted in standard Japanese (or as near an approximation to it as local elders could manage), the second and third stages would be marked by people's reverting to dialect, as they spoke in their 'own' language and not some 'foreign' tongue imposed upon them (through schooling) by outsiders living far away in Tokyo. Country drinking meant country talking, too.

But who initiated this third stage of the party? In the old days, it was an unwritten rule that a man could only exchange cups with someone sitting immediately below him – in other words, with someone younger than him. Protocol forbade him from passing his cup up the table to an older man (cf. Befu 1974: 200). This meant that the shift to the third stage was in large part determined by the elders, since it was they who could get up and move down the room to drink with younger men. Of course, a certain amount of lateral movement was also permitted, since people of approximately the same age used to (and still) sit on opposite sides of the room because of formal seating arrangements. They could cross over to exchange cups with men of their own age. Ultimately, however, it was the old men who controlled sake cup exchanges and thus the shift of any drinking encounter from a formal gathering to wild party.

Drinking Talk

But why do all these cup exchanges take place? As with everyone else in the world who drinks, the men of the Ono valley love to talk. What they talk about is what is of interest here.

As the sake flows, men exchange words on matters that are closest to their hearts or on their minds. This means that conversations with fellow men are potentially political, in the sense that they may well start discussing matters that affect the hamlet, school or work association of which they are a part. In other words, drinking encounters provide occasions for participants to further their intra-community interests. As a result, a man always needs to be alert while drinking, keeping an eye on the rest of the room, weighing up who is talking to whom and putting two and two together from his knowledge of local affairs. This means that cup exchanges are themselves political, for a man will take advantage of the custom to join a conversation in which he senses that he might have a vested interest. If he is a smart strategist, he will ensure that his membership of a drinking group appears both fortuitous and casual. He thus needs to chart his way around the room, working out how best to start drinking with the man he has in mind in as 'natural' a way as possible so that, when they do meet, their encounter will not attract the attention of others. Of course, this is not as easy as it sounds – if only because all the men have strategies of their own at parties and are likely to start moving around the room independently at any moment. Still, it is almost inevitable that they will get together at some stage during the course of this third stage of drinking and discuss whatever matter of common interest it is that they share.

But, again, we have to ask: why is such strategizing necessary? Here we need to go back to the system of age grading that in former times prevailed in this part of Japan. In almost all formal matters, it was the old men (born around the turn of the twentieth century) who had held positions of authority in the valley. It was they who were heads of households, they who were chairmen of village councils, agricultural associations, school committees, and so on. As mentioned above, it was they who sat at the top of the room at every drinking session and they who, until the 1960s, determined the course of drinking encounters.

By the 1970s, however, the 'rule' about not passing a cup 'up' the table to older men had been relaxed. As a result, it was not the elders, but those men aged between 40 and 60 who became most active in exchanging sake cups during the third, informal stage of a drinking encounter. It was they who were first to get up from their seats and move around the room, they who drummed up support from their juniors and took up communal issues with the elders. They were the men who vested themselves with power as they took over control of exchanges at drinking parties.

And what did they talk about that was so important? This depended very much on the kind of gathering that was taking place, but in general their topics of conversation echoed social divisions of one sort or another. These were of age and gender, on the one hand, and of household, community, valley, prefecture and country, on the other.[14]

Household matters within a hamlet or community often brought out a lot of rancour among men drinking in the Ono valley. These are, after all, matters closest to home. So, one household head would be castigated for charging more for his pottery than had been agreed upon by the Cooperative; another lambasted for going back on an agreement to sell a plot of land to a neighbour; a third ridiculed over a clash with a relative that almost led to the cancellation of his daughter's marriage. A fourth would be criticized for postponing a purification ceremony and potentially endangering in some way the lives of his neighbours. As Ronald Dore (1978: 266) has eloquently put it in his description of a mountain village in central Japan: 'The "harmony of the village" has its cost. Underneath the placid landscape there are geological faults – a personal incompatibility, a clash of economic interest, a belief that one has been cheated – along which tensions build up which require occasional release.' In the Ono valley, the eruption of such tensions could even lead to the occasional fisticuffs, with plenty of drunken hands ready to restrain the combatants and make sure that no really serious harm occurred, and drunken heads that, in spite of their inebriation, the next day would recall very clearly who had said what to whom and with what results. Indeed, night-time arguments often formed the unspoken sub-text of daytime activities. This was where the power of the middle-aged men usurped the authority of the elders (cf. Moeran 1998b [1986]: 253–7).

Community talk, however, tended to be more jocular. There was often less at stake. One story that inhabitants of Sarayama liked to tell was about a neighbouring pottery community, in which a tree juts out rather incongruously into the middle of a brand new road. People said that three generations ago there had been an argument between the heads of two households over a piece of land. One of them, who felt cheated, planted a tree in such a way that its shadow would eventually fall over his neighbour's yard and prevent his pots from drying there. And so it came to pass, until the local authority decided to widen the road through the village to enable tourist buses to pass by more easily. This meant cutting down the offending tree, which the current head of the house who owned it absolutely refused to allow. As a result, at this one point only, the road narrows and the neighbouring potter still does not have all the sunshine he needs to dry his wares.

This kind of story was intended to show how good the storyteller's community was in comparison with all others, and thus marked a division between in-group and out-group within the Ono and neighbouring valleys. Similar stories occurred whenever a hamlet resident died, and men gathered round at the back of the kitchen to prepare rice for the funeral feast. In due course, alcohol made its necessary appearance and they would start comparing their own community customs favourably with those of neighbouring communities. As part of the identification with the community, as well as of individual households in which they lived, men also liked to tell stories of the past: of how they used to have to dig graves and got frightened by skeletons that they unearthed; of how they went together on a communal outing and got so drunk that they could hardly remember what they did or where they were. Nostalgia in drinking stories thus also played an important part in sustaining community identity.

Another kind of story contributing to this sense of being 'country people' was that contrasting a local community with those who lived down in the nearby town. One tale that was repeated quite frequently during my stay in Sarayama was one in which tax inspectors came up from Hita to check how much rice was being harvested and, at the same time, search all the houses in the hamlet to ensure that nothing illegal was going on. This meant that everyone had to rush home and hide things under the floorboards, behind the ancestral altars, and anywhere else they felt was safe. On this particular occasion, the local residents decided to serve the inspectors some food and drink, but one of the live chickens they were plucking slipped out of their hands and fell into a cesspool. Instead of washing it, the men just cut it up and served it raw (with ginger and soy sauce) to the inspectors, while they themselves ate a different bird. Their victory became the sweeter when the inspectors dispatched two men to buy more sake from the brewery at the bottom of the Ono valley and one of them managed – with two deft strokes of a brush – to change the inspectors' hand-written demand note for three bottles into five. They thus got free of charge two extra bottles for their next party. The local community had totally outwitted members of the local government.

By playing on a nostalgia for the past, and yet by including people who were still alive, stories like this very often subtly praised the elders. The man who changed the tax inspectors' demand note for sake had, in 1977, just retired as head of the Potters' Cooperative, but was still chairman of the Ono Valley Local Council and had plenty of say in both hamlet and valley matters during the next half dozen years. In some important respects, he was resented by younger household heads, but their clear admiration for what he had done for them over the years was obvious in the way that they told this story (and other tales about other older men).

Another story illustrating the superiority of an Ono valley community over Hita residents concerned the local bus company and incidences of 'night crawling' (or *yobai*) into the room of the conductress who – in the days when it seemed more economical not to send an empty bus down the valley late at night and up again in the early morning – stayed overnight in the hamlet at the top of the valley.

Here gender became an unstated theme. Night crawling was a fairly common topic of conversation and laughter among men who took both pride and pleasure in instructing a foreign anthropologist in how best to open a wooden shutter noiselessly at night (urinate on it first), and then walk soundlessly on tatami rice straw mats (unroll the *obi* sash that tied one's *yukata* sleeping robe and tiptoe along it) (see Moeran 1998a: 20). They also liked to boast of their own purported prowess at *yobai* and tell of certain funny incidents (like failing to wake up in the morning and being obliged to have breakfast with the girl's parents). This particular story related how a young conductress was taken off into the night by a young man who tried to make love to her in a disused charcoal-burning kiln nearby. At some point, it seemed, they were overheard. The alarm was raised and a fruitless search for the culprit ensued.

The bus driver, who also stayed overnight (but in a different house) in the same community, threatened to report the matter to his employer, but was dissuaded from so doing by the hamlet headman, who pointed out how such an incident would bring dishonour upon the girl's family, the bus company and the driver himself. It would therefore be better if he, the headman, approached the bus company to suggest that the bus no longer remain in the hamlet overnight (as the driver wanted). The driver agreed to this, but the headman did nothing and it was only when a second conductress was molested that action was taken by the driver.

The main issue taken up by this story was the maintenance of the community's integrity in the face of the outside world – especially when it involved officials of a transport company based beyond the Ono valley in the town of Hita. This was achieved by sound argument (plus devious practice), which in itself led to further trouble. The fact that virtually no consideration was given by my companions to the women involved in this story reveals how men in the valley were firmly convinced that women were socially irrelevant (see Moeran 1998a: 186). This issue of gender was, however, not limited to men in the valley, but characteristic of men from Kyushu, who were – and still are – firmly convinced of the validity of the commonly heard phrase: 'Honour men. Despise women' (*danson johi*).

In a way, stories involving the local bus company might be seen as rural farmers' and craftsmen's symbolic victory over urban business and, by implication, over Japanese corporate capitalism and the social change it had inevitably wrought in the lives of people inhabiting the Ono valley. One tale, for example, focused – with great relish – on how the bus driver would be entertained by his hosts from time to time during his overnight stay in the hamlet and later be persuaded to drive everyone down the valley in his bus for a second drinking session (*nijikai*) in the bars of Hita. On one occasion, so the story goes, the driver was so drunk that the bus ended up in a rice field and all the villagers had to clamber out and heave the vehicle back onto the road.

In this way, stories told during sake drinking in the Ono valley established a series of Chinese boxes or Russian dolls with which men variously identified. The smallest doll was the household, which fitted into a group of work specialization dolls (like potters and non-potters in Sarayama [Moeran 1997: 159–64]), which itself fitted into a community doll, which then fitted into the valley doll, and so on, into ever larger dolls comprising country town, prefecture, the island of Kyushu and, finally, Japan itself. Even though stories might set household against community, valley against town, or Kyushu against Tokyo, these shifting arcs of identity – not unlike the political allegiances of the Nuer so famously described by Evans-Pritchard (1979 [1940]: 142–50) – were not necessarily exclusive. A man was always a member of household *and* occupational group *and* community *and* valley *and* town (of which Ono was an administrative unit), and so on. Different circumstances would affect *which* of these identifications would be emphasized at any given point.[15]

Ultimately, such identification focused on my drinking companions' sense of being 'Japanese' – the largest Russian doll that enclosed all others when faced with my own foreignness and their need to explain why they behaved in the ways that they did. Exchanging cups, for example, or singing were things that 'we Japanese like to do'. Past practice like *yobai* 'night crawling', together with the implicit gender discrimination that *yobai* involved, was portrayed as a 'traditionally Japanese' lifestyle that may no longer have existed in the valley, but which was still recent enough in men's memories to make it 'real' and 'authentic' in comparison with the perceived surreal nature of contemporary urban lifestyles.

Flows of Exchange

This description of drinking practices in a Japanese valley probably strikes my readers as interesting – possibly even entertaining – but may leave them wondering what it has to offer by way of theoretical analysis. So, let me look at sake from the point of view of material culture – the point, indeed, with which I began.

The first point that we should note about people's use of things is that they enable the social. Sake is a drink that is produced, talked about (as well as in its cups) and consumed. As such, it has a 'social life' and, during the course of its movement from production through circulation, and representation to consumption, enters into various 'regimes of value' (to use, in the plural, a much favoured phrase from Appadurai 1986). Sake manufacturers, for example, think and talk about what makes a 'good' sake in a manner that is rather *technical* – focusing on ingredients used, the combination thereof, and what they should do to get the 'right' blend of the five flavours of sweetness, sourness, pungency, bitterness and astringency.[16] Some of their findings might be taken up by marketers' advertising material for particular brands, but this is likely also to include other elements of appeal to consumers – like romance, nostalgia or tradition, for example – which are not of immediate concern to the manufacturing *per se* of sake.

Those consuming sake probably talk about their drink in a mixture of these two *appreciative* languages ('I like my sake like I like my women: not too sweet and not too astringent'). But they also bring to such discussion a *social* dimension of the kind described here. This is found in the content of the stories they tell while drinking, and in the manner in which sake drinking is used to strengthen friendships, seal agreements, pick arguments, welcome the gods, honour the ancestors, and so on. In this way, through exchanges, sake as a material object takes on a 'social density' (Weiner 1994)[17] that is not necessarily apparent in other alcoholic drinks (like beer and whisky), but which can be found in the social use of certain foods (like whale meat [Kalland and Moeran 1992: 141–57]).

Although, in the long run, sake is always consumed, it is put to all kinds of different *use* – as seasonal or one-off gifts, libation, purification, offering, and so on

– and it is the particular way it is consumed and the resulting effects that have been the focus of my account. Together these four different kinds of value – technical, appreciative, social and use or utility – give sake a *symbolic exchange* value that enables drinking encounters of the kind described here to continue to take place. The fact that people are prepared to pay a certain fixed amount of money for a bottle or barrel permits sake to have a *commodity exchange* value.[18]

Having said this much about the different values that people bring to bear on sake at the different stages of its production, circulation, representation and consumption, we need to ask just how specific the system as a whole is *vis-à-vis* other commodities. Is there any major difference between the social lives of sake the liquid, the individually crafted *sakazuki* cup from which it is drunk, and the mass-produced glass bottle in which it is sold? In other words, is there anything particular about sake and its drinking in Japan that sets it apart from other objects or commodities in general?

In many ways, the answer to these questions has to be no. In Sarayama itself, for example, pottery was often the idiom in which potters there discussed and coped with social change (Moeran 1997: 171–5). Like pottery, sake has no 'intrinsic' nature, but is embedded in what Alfred Gell (1998: 7) has called 'a social-relational matrix'. This matrix includes fellow drinkers in the Ono valley, as well as 'Japanese' at large. Thus, on the one hand, sake is as much a part of a (constructed) national identity as is an architectural heritage, art form or music style (which, in the case of Japan, would include *shinden* and *shoin* building styles, *ukiyoe* woodblock prints and *enka* popular songs). On the other hand, just as taste has been shown to depend on class position (Bourdieu 1984), so does sake drinking in the Ono valley depend upon and reinforce men's conviction that they are part of a (threatened) underclass rural population, which continues to practise a traditional and 'truly Japanese' way of life that is distinct from both urban lifestyles and Western customs and practices.[19] No wonder, then, that the word '*sake*' can be used generically for all alcoholic drinks, on the one hand, and that, on the other, many like to refer to what we have been talking about here as 'Japanese alcohol' (*nihonshū*).

Secondly, the ingredients of the drink itself may be unusual, but no more so than those of other forms of alcohol produced and consumed around the world. As a material object in a bottle, sake circulates more or less like other material objects – from *kula* to artworks.[20] Like other alcoholic drinks, too, it induces inebriation. And drunkenness itself creates a shared sense of unity with others – a unity which, like art, signifies an alternative set of values to that found in everyday life, where the 'human spirit' or 'family of man' reigns supreme.[21]

This unity is premised on a sense of egalitarianism among men drinking in the Ono valley – an argument likely to raise the eyebrows of those old 'Japan hands' who are accustomed to talking about Japanese society in terms of hierarchy. But it is precisely this sense of being egalitarian induced by drunkenness that permits men who do *not* have authority in everyday life to argue with their elders about different aspects of household, community and valley life. In that the latter's authority is not questioned during men's daytime activities, sake drinking also permits the *re*-establishment of a social hierarchy that situates elder men above younger men, and men above women. In so far as men rarely forget who has said what during the course of drinking encounters, and seek to incorporate the results of drinking exchanges into their everyday lives, the flows of sake exchange may be seen ultimately to balance social differences and similarities.

Thus sake can be said to be constitutive of certain social relations (Miller 1987: 122). On the one hand, it acts as a fundamental platform for political organization. On the other, it involves an enormous amount of hard work on the part of those concerned to keep it flowing, and to know when to withhold it (cf. Annette Wiener in Myers and Kirshenblatt-Gimblett 2001: 297). Moreover, through its very flow of exchanges, sake obliges a renewal of social relationships, by means of which various processes of social distinction take place. We see such forms of impression management at work in people's purchase of a Porsche car, Impressionist painting or Nike athletic shoes, each of which enables different kinds of people to enhance their social and cultural capital in different ways.

But there is something else about sake that brings it in line with other objects of material culture. It contributes to and reinforces *certain kinds* of social relationship: men's domination over women in public affairs; the public authority that accompanies age; the interlocking institutions of household, hamlet and village (or valley); reciprocity between this and other worlds – between the living and their household ancestors (in other words, relations through time); and between people and gods (*kami*), located in and around the household and community (relations in space). Identities are produced and consumed in sake exchanges (witness the naming that accompanies a cup exchange). Sake thus produces exchanges that build up and mediate relations in ways that are not dissimilar from (though clearly not identical to) other objects of material culture that have attracted anthropological attention over the years. In other words, people produce and consume both alcohol and the social relationships that such alcohol facilitates. In their exchange of drinks, people drink exchanges.

Notes

1. There are about 3,000 manufacturers of refined sake in Japan today. Many of these are local brands (*jizake*) and produced all over Japan, outside the main manufacturing districts of Kyōto and Hyōgo prefectures in the centre of the country.

2. Takada (1980: 130) classifies drinking places into 4 different types, according to the functions they fulfil (which include specialized drinks, food, sex, information exchange and music).

3. A remarkable description of women and drinking is given by Ella Wiswell in her diary of life in the Kyushu village of Suye in the mid-1930s (Smith and Wiswell 1982). Although women in the Ono valley did drink, and once or twice got unashamedly drunk in the process, they hardly ever did so on their own. Rather, they acted as a foil to the local men, providing cupped breasts or a folded cushion, for example, for the empty beer bottle used to simulate a man's penis in one of the many dances that took place during parties. In general, they were there for the important purpose of flirtation.

4. This approach strikes me as rather more helpful than the more customary exotic and Orientalist strains in the general anthropology of Japan which still tends to see issues of structure and agency, for example, in terms of 'group' and 'individual'.

5. My first visit to the Ono valley (1977–9) was occasioned by what became two years of fieldwork among the potters of Sarayama (Onta) as part of my study of the Japanese folk craft (*mingei*) movement (Moeran 1997). During the third and fourth years of my stay there (1980–2), I carried out post-doctoral fieldwork research on the ceramic art market in Japan (Moeran 1987). A slightly fictionalized account of my stay in Ono and of the people who shared their lives with me there may be found in Moeran (1998a).

6. Sake is an alcoholic drink made from fermented rice, with an alcohol content of about 32 proof. It is usually served hot, at a temperature of about 50°C in a small earthenware bottle called a *tokkuri*, from which it is poured into small cups known as *sakazuki*.

7. In the pottery community of Sarayama, for example, the gathering held annually for the mountain god (*yama no kami*) stipulated that only one *go* (0.18 litres) of sweet sake be drunk by the fourteen household heads present. On New Year's Day, they drank just one *shō* (1.8 litres) of cold sake.

8. Each community consisted of somewhere between eight and twenty households.

9. I have here adopted, for better or for worse, a combination of 'ethnographic present' and past tenses, since I have no reason to believe from more recent brief visits to the Ono valley that the kinds of drinking patterns and forms of exchange described in this chapter have changed substantially.

10. Admittedly, I never saw people taking the opportunity of a visiting vaccination clinic to start drinking, but most of the other occasions described by Wiswell might just as easily have taken place in Ono.

11. This section follows the outline of an argument made in an earlier paper that I wrote on sake drinking (see Moeran 1998b [1986]).

12. The *zashiki* often comprised two rooms, separated by sliding screens that could be removed when there were many guests.

13. It is considered extremely impolite to pour one's own drink in Japan. When drinking with others, one must ensure that their glasses are never empty. This, as we shall soon see, involves a lot of topping up.
14. A slightly fictionalized account of some of the stories that follow may be found in my ethnographic diary of life in the Ono valley (Moeran 1998a).
15. This was particularly clear in local people's support of teams during the annual high-school baseball competition, in which one team from each prefecture participates in a series of knock-out games over a two-week period. Once the local Oita team had been eliminated, people's allegiance would shift to neighbouring prefectural teams in Kyushu, then to Okinawa and the western part of Honshu or to Hokkaido and prefectures in the far north (whose inhabitants were seen to live in the same state of remoteness from the capital as people in the Ono valley). Once all these teams had been eliminated, support would shift to any team left from the Osaka or Nagoya region. Tokyo teams were never supported.
16. A similar kind of approach may be found among wine scientists studied by Lehrer (1983: 113–48).
17. As I understand her, Weiner's concept of density is a little different from that used here, since she refers to the density of an object while I am applying the idea to social relations.
18. I have elsewhere outlined more fully the different values that people bring to things (Moeran 1996: 281–97).
19. Not surprisingly, then, we find that the first four decades of a Western anthropology of Japan focused predominantly on the study of rural communities in its pursuit of exotic and Orientalist fantasies.
20. As Miller (1987: 89) reminds us, in spite of the large body of anthropological literature devoted to discussions of art, 'art and unique objects are . . . only a minute proportion of the material world'.
21. The similarities cited here for the most part follow Myers (2001: 29–30), who uses the same categories to argue, to my mind unconvincingly, that 'art is not just another example of material culture'.

References

Appadurai, A. (ed.) (1986), *The Social Life of Things*, Cambridge: Cambridge University Press.

Befu, H. (1974), 'An Ethnography of Dinner Entertainment in Japan', *Arctic Anthropology* XI (supplement): 196–203.

Bourdieu, P. (1984), *Distinction: A Social Critique of the Judgement of Taste*, London: Routledge & Kegan Paul.

Dore, R. (1978), *Shinohata: Portrait of a Japanese Village*, London: Allen Lane.

—— (2000), *Stock Market Capitalism–Welfare Capitalism*, Oxford: Oxford University Press.

Evans-Pritchard, E. E. (1979) [1940], *The Nuer: A Description of the Modes of Livelihood and Political Institutions of a Nilotic People*, Oxford: Oxford University Press.

Gell, A. (1998), *Art and Agency: An Anthropological Theory*, Oxford: Oxford University Press.

Gerlach, M. (1992), *Alliance Capitalism: The Social Organization of Japanese Business*, Berkeley and Los Angeles: University of California Press.

Kalland, A. and B. Moeran (1992), *Japanese Whaling: End of an Era?* Scandinavian Institute of Asian Studies Monograph Series Number 61, London: Curzon Press.

Lehrer, A. (1983), *Wine and Conversation*, Bloomington: Indiana University Press.

Linhart, S. (1998), '*Sakariba*: Zone of "Evaporation" between Work and Home?' in Joy Hendry (ed.), *Interpreting Japanese Society: An Anthropological Introduction*, London: Routledge, pp. 231–42.

Miller, D. (1987), *Material Culture and Mass Consumption*, Oxford: Basil Blackwell.

Moeran, B. (1987), 'The World of Japanese Ceramics', *Journal of Japanese Studies* 13 (1): 27–50.

—— (1996), *A Japanese Advertising Agency: An Anthropology of Media and Markets*, London: Curzon.

—— (1997), *Folk Art Potters of Japan*, London: Curzon.

—— (1998a), *A Far Valley: Four Years in a Japanese Village*, Tokyo: Kodansha International.

—— (1998b) [1986], 'One over the Eight: Sake Drinking in a Japanese Pottery Community', in J. Hendry (ed.), *Interpreting Japanese Society: An Anthropological Introduction*, London: Routledge, pp. 243–58.

—— (2003), 'Fields, Networks and Frames', *Global Networks* 3 (3): 371–86.

Myers, F. (2001), 'Introduction: The Empire of Things', in F. Myers (ed.), *The Empire of Things: Regimes of Value and Material Culture*, Santa Fe: School of American Research Press, pp. 3–61.

Myers, F. and B. Kirshenblatt-Gimblett (2001), 'Art and Material Culture: A Conversation with Annette Weiner', in F. Myers (ed.), *The Empire of Things: Regimes of Value and Material Culture*, Santa Fe: School of American Research Press, pp. 269–313.

Smith, R. J. and E. L. Wiswell (1982), *The Women of Suye Mura*, Chicago: University of Chicago Press.

Takada Yasutaka (1980), 'Bunka to Shite no Sake', *Jūrisuto Zōkan Sōgō Tokushū – Nihon no Taishū Bunka* 20: 127–33.

Weiner, A. (1994), 'Cultural Difference and the Density of Objects', *American Ethnologist* 21 (2): 391–403.

−3−

'Cold Beer, Warm Hearts'
Community, Belonging and Desire in Irish Pubs in Berlin

Cliona O'Carroll

Two Stories and a Question

Kilkenny: Referent on the Run

In the early 1990s in Ireland I started working as a tour guide for a school that taught English as a foreign language to businesspeople. Each Wednesday I would pick up a new group of continental European businesspeople and take them to the greyhound races, and then on to an evening in the pub. Each Wednesday, one or more German students would tell me that at home in Germany, he drinks Kilkenny. On the first night, I didn't quite know what the student was talking about, partly due to his basic level of competency in English. Nodding and smiling frantically (I was new to the job), I attempted to find out: Had he been to Kilkenny? Had he drunk a drink there? What exactly was he (nodding and smiling, making drinking motions, repeating the word 'Kilkenny') trying to communicate to me? My confusion stemmed from the fact that I was unaware that a drink called 'Kilkenny' existed, and so was trying to locate this man's statement in the context of the only Kilkenny I knew, a city of 18,000 people on the banks of the river Nore in Ireland. All the while, he was trying to communicate with a language made available to him by the context of consumption of 'Irishness' in Germany. However, the red ale produced by Guinness, which had been popular on the German market for around four years, was virtually unknown to the general drinking public in Ireland.

Where's the Guinness? The Irish Pavilion, Expo 2000, Hanover, Germany

Two members of the pavilion staff stand outside the pavilion, welcoming visitors and handing out leaflet guides. Every hour or so, a visitor (usually German) addresses the following to the welcomers: 'Where's the Guinness/whiskey?', 'I've come for my Guinness/whiskey', 'Here you will give us Guinness/whiskey.' The welcomers explain that actually there isn't a bar in the pavilion and direct the visitors (who have reacted with varying degrees of playful or more heartfelt incredulity and disappointment) to the Irish pub, which, they explain (with varying degrees of regret or concealed glee), is a few kilometres away on the far side of the Expo site.

These examples serve to show how alcoholic brand names or their consumption can become an element of the language being used by members of one national group to talk to or about others. Often this communication is problematic. The image of a language student attempting to communicate with a tour guide who is unable to even recognize what, for him, is the face of Irish ale shows us that the language is some-times not mutually intelligible, with meaningful forms not carrying anything approaching consistent meaning. Sometimes, as in the second example, this 'lan-guage' becomes part of a stylized dramatic interface, with participants articulating and responding to expectations with differential affective investment in the fulfil-ment or confounding of those expectations.

Sometimes the communication is less with or about the other than it is about the self. In this chapter I would like to look at how meanings bound up with the con-sumption of 'Irish' alcoholic beverages in Berlin, Germany, are sometimes conversa-tions or narratives which are more concerned with the performance of one particular kind of urban 'Germanness' than with the generalized, unitary 'Irishness' that forms a large part of the discursive language.

With this case study, I would like to illustrate the fact that the narrative or com-municative processes of identification that are central to social action (Cohen 1994; Somers and Gibson 1994; Melucci 1996) involve interaction with an increasing range of available meaningful forms, which are by their very nature multivocal. One cannot tell at first glance what meanings have been invested in these meaningful forms by different actors: these meanings are temporally and geographically specific, informed both by the existing 'habitats of meaning' (Hannerz 1996) of the actors and by the framing and creative interpretation of 'new' meaningful forms. This aspect of the nature of meaning-formation and identity-formation in everyday life alerts us to the value of regularly engaging in ethnographic fieldwork in order to gain an analy-tical appreciation of the dynamics of these processes, and of the importance of the spatio-temporal specificities of the expression, negotiation and constitution of identities in daily lives.

The watching, listening and 'being in a place and time' of ethnographic fieldwork sometimes confronts the researcher with unexpected motifs which provide clues to the operation of economies of desire, hopes, fears and longing all bound up with self-identification and the business of existence. In this chapter I want to examine one such clue which emerged in the answers to one question. In the course of carrying out fieldwork in Irish pubs in the mid-1990s,[1] I regularly questioned German customers about why they spent time there (as opposed to any other bar or café). An over-whelming proportion gave the sense of community in the Irish pubs as a reason. For some, this was facilitated by the informality of the pubs; for others, by their 'special atmosphere'. A theme which was an unexpected component of over three-quarters of answers was expressed as follows: 'Because it isn't an *Eckkneipe*.'

In this sense Irish pubs were, for many of their German clients, defined by what they were not, the ambivalently regarded *Eckkneipe*. In this chapter I examine the imaginative materials, including representations of the *Eckkneipe*, available to customers in Irish pubs in Berlin, along with the representational conventions of modes of 'Irishness' and modes of 'Germanness', which are used to articulate a need for and to actively create a sense of contemporary urban community in the city.

Habitats of Meaning and the Increased Role of the Imagination in Social Life

Examining the implications of transnational cultural flows for lived experiences and the study thereof, Ulf Hannerz draws on Zygmunt Bauman's (1992) conception of agency interacting not with system, but rather 'with a flexible sense of habitat; a habitat in which agency operates and which it also produces, one where it finds its resources and goals as well as its limitations' (Hannerz 1996: 22). Hannerz introduces the concept of 'habitats of meaning' (associated with individuals or groups), which expand and contract, and overlap to different extents. Everything we experience, and all the influences and meanings to which we are exposed, become part of our habitats of meaning to a greater or lesser degree. How much and what kind of impact the things we are 'physically' exposed to will have on our habitats of meaning depends on the competencies we possess in dealing with them meaningfully and knowledgeably: 'the languages we understand, write or speak, our levels of literacy with respect to other symbolic forms, and so on' (Hannerz 1996: 23).[2]

Arjun Appadurai, addressing the cultural dynamics of what is now called deterritorialization, introduces the term 'ethnoscapes': the landscapes of people 'who make up the shifting world in which we live: tourists, immigrants, refugees, exiles, guest-workers, and other moving groups and persons' (1991: 192), landscapes of people and identities which are in continuous interaction with each other. This interaction, and the proliferation of the mass media, has had a profound effect on the role of the imagination in social life, presenting people with a varied and mutable store of, and creating space in their imaginations for, 'possible lives' other than their own, 'some of which enter the lived imaginations of ordinary people more successfully than others'[3] (Appadurai 1991: 197). This role of the imagination is not just escapist, 'for it is in the grinding of gears between unfolding lives and their imagined counterparts that a variety of "imagined communities" (Anderson 1983) is formed, communities that generate new kinds of politics, new kinds of collective expression, and new needs for social discipline and surveillance on the part of elites' (Appadurai 1991: 198). I argue that some participants[4] in Berlin use the categories available to them through tourist marketing representations of Ireland (and through available positive narratives of the *Eckkneipe*, examined below) in collaborative performances and interpretations not only of 'Irishness', but also of a 'Germanness' which strives towards the local community of the *Eckkneipe* while wishing to distance itself from intimidating or from negative aspects.

This increased role of the imagination changes the nature of the local (and, of course, the non-local) and demands attention from the social sciences. In order to understand the meanings and agency in people's lives, we must have some appreciation of their imagined lives, and cannot ignore the myriad forms of inspiration for these imaginings. Neither can we ignore the political potential of 'imagined communities' that arise in the interaction between 'real' lives and the central categories of imagined ones. We shall now examine two such categories: the *Eckkneipe* and the Irish pub.

The *Eckkneipe*

Translated as 'corner pubs', these institutions are small bars, often situated on street corners in cities, which cater to a local and regular clientele, mainly but not exclusively men. *Eckkneipen* are usually quite small and a lot cheaper than the more common café-bars, and tend to be somewhat dingy and grubby, with interiors more closed off from the outside world. The customers are predominantly working-class or underclass, and they are usually the only hostelries where there is overt drunkenness or alcohol abuse. There is far more interaction between different groups of customers (and between the customers and the bar staff) in *Eckkneipen* than in the café-bars, where the former is rare. *Eckkneipen* are some of the few places in Berlin where sitting at the bar is normal, and where one hears people singing. The atmosphere and the regulars' descriptions of *Eckkneipen* I have experienced suggest the idea of the 'local' pub where the drinkers know each other and meet regularly. They have the same system of table service (although less formalized), tabs and opening hours as the café-bars. In many cases, the members of mainstream German society do not approve of *Eckkneipen* and what goes on there. Many Germans would not consider drinking in them; they are frequented by old men, undesirables, alcoholics and 'people not like us'.[5] The main experience that Germans I questioned associated with *Eckkneipen* was that of *angemacht werden* (being accorded unwanted and persistent attention: this phrase can mean anything along the continuum of being buttonholed to being harassed, by either sex).

In what follows, we shall examine the possible nature of the link that exists for German participants between the *Eckkneipe* and the next category to be discussed, the Irish pub.

But, ah, a lot of them wouldn't really be for me a real Irish atmosphere. But it seems just, you put a name outside the door 'Irish Pub', a Guinness sign outside and then for an awful lot of pubs it **works**. Now beyond that you would sort of say 'Well, they're not the real Irish pub, they're not the real country pub where a good old session is in Ireland or in **Clare** or in **Galway** or so, it lacks a lot of the atmosphere.' But there's such a ring about, ja, Irishness, Irish friendliness, Irish liveliness, that it's quite **amazing** when you think about fifty Irish pubs here and I think there's one English pub. (An Irish musician in Berlin)

C: And what do you think of the Irish pubs in Berlin?
N: Great, but the prices are too dear.
K: Is that Irish spelt O.I.R.I.S.H.?
(Irish construction workers interviewed in an Irish pub)

In 1995–7, the number of Irish pubs in Berlin was in the fifties and increasing. Irish language, music and dance classes were fully subscribed, Irish shops (whose customers were predominantly German) were being established. Irish drink, music, dance and 'culture' were all selling well. The building boom was at its peak, with thousands of Irish construction workers living in and passing through the city.

The central location for the conspicuous production and consumption of Irish cultural forms were the Irish pubs, which ranged from the huge chain pubs to small family-run affairs. As with many 'themed' pubs, the décor consisted of collections of fairly standardized items of 'traditional' material culture: churns, reed baskets, earthenware pots, old books. They had a range of food and drink, including a core menu of recognizably Irish meals, invariably Irish stew and smoked salmon. The pubs sold a range of German beers, spirits, juices and tea, coffee and hot chocolate in addition to their more exotic wares.[6] They stocked one stout, either Guinness or Murphys, Kilkenny ale or Murphy's Red ale, cider (mainly Cashel's), and a range of Irish whiskeys and Scotch whiskies. Every pub had a drinks menu, usually in both English and German, giving the range of drinks available, the price and the volume in litres. Some included descriptions of the drinks and their place in Irish society, nomenclature (e.g. 'pint') and pronunciation tips.

These spaces of consumption were inhabited by different groups of people[7] who interacted to varying degrees. The first were German *Irland-Fans* (Ireland-fans). *Irland-Freunde* (Ireland-friends) and *Irland-Freaks* (Ireland-freaks). This is the labelling used by some Germans to describe increasing levels of interest in and love for all things Irish. They came to Irish pubs to relax, to enjoy the atmosphere and the music, and because they like to sit at a bar and drink Guinness, some in order to be reminded of happy visits to Ireland. Then there were the (predominantly Irish) people who made a living out of Irish culture and traditional forms: musicians, dancing teachers, Irish language teachers, the pub staff, and so on. Another large group were the Irish and British construction workers who used the pubs as a space for networking, finding jobs, arranging accommodation, eating, drinking and socializing. The majority of German customers were professionals and white-collar workers in their thirties to fifties. The majority of Irish customers were construction workers, with the balance representing a range of other trades and professions. Men were slightly better represented than women among the Germans, and, apart from students and barmaids, the Irish presence was almost exclusively male.

The success of Irish pubs in Germany may stem from the fact that there is no one institution which carries out the same social function or acts as the same kind of focus for social life for so many sections of the population there. Generally speaking, urban Germans tend to socialize in a number of different contexts: eating together (at home or in a restaurant: this may include *Frühstücken*, or breakfasting sociably), going to the cinema, concerts, the theatre, or meeting in cafés. The emphasis on alcohol consumption as a focal point of social life is not as pronounced as it is in Ireland. Places serving alcohol tend to provide a wider range of non-alcoholic alternatives than would be found in Ireland, and alcohol is freely available in many settings that Irish people would find surprising: the cinema, snack outlets and stalls, hostels and cafés. The most common Berlin 'watering-holes' are café-bars which serve a wide range of teas, coffees, juices, hot chocolate and snacks as well as bottled and tap beers, liqueurs and spirits, and where, also unlike Ireland, table service and tipping are the norm. Cafes and bars in Berlin tend to have a relatively homogeneous clientele. One rarely finds a broad mixture of ages, social classes or lifestyle choices on one premises: the 'successful young things' socialize elsewhere to the manual workers, and the executives socialize somewhere else again.

I will examine below how tourist advertising constructions of Ireland, which privilege pubs as sites of meaningful experience and contact, are drawn upon by promoters in the portrayal of the settings, activities and people associated with Irish pubs as contexts of transformation for German customers.

Performing Ireland

Ethnographic examination of 'Irish' cultural production and the Irish pubs in Berlin showed the centrality of tourist representational conventions of Ireland in these contexts. Irish culture producers (musicians, teachers of language, dance or music, event organizers) tended to limit cultural performance to a fulfilment of their appreciation of the expectations of the 'tourist gaze' (Urry 1990), presenting a unified 'traditional' Irish culture, and avoiding the innovation, change or hybridity sometimes associated with new contexts. Likewise, the Irish pubs in Berlin engaged in a system of signification that resonated with the tourist symbolic complex through their décor, wares and publicity. I would like to draw attention to some of the facets of representation involved, in order to trace how they have been engaged with by German customers to create a safe space for face-to-face community within the city.

Tourist advertising selectively highlights certain aspects in its construction of an area. Central motifs identified in constructions of Ireland as a tourist destination for European and North American visitors include the following:

- spectacular natural beauty, open space and uncrowded nature;
- a leisurely pace of life;

- the Irish people as 'friendly folk' (Schulze 1994: 93);
- 'tradition' as unbroken linear connection with the past, and Irish culture as unified and traditional (Byrne et al. 1993; O'Connor 1993; Péchenart and Tangy 1993; Schulze 1994; Slater 2000; O'Carroll 2001).

The object of the 'tourist gaze'[8] is frequently constructed in terms of opposition to the everyday lives of the target audience[9] (Urry 1990), often in contrast to alienating, disenchanted, impersonal city life, where *Gemeinschaft* is a thing of the past. I suggest that the last three categories above present Ireland as a physical and psychic space full of possibilities of transformation and self-realization, and that promoters of the Irish pubs in Berlin make use of the symbolic complex developed by tourist constructions of Ireland to present them as transformative spaces.

Under the title 'Am I ready to enjoy the peace?,' a German-language Irish Tourist Board brochure promises: 'You will also quickly grow to appreciate the relaxed way in which the Irish enjoy life' (Bord Fáilte 1998: 5; my translation). An examination of the content of tourist advertising materials available in Berlin reveals a consistent portrayal of Irish lives as free from the negative impact of alienating work practices. Irish people are predominantly pictured as 'at leisure', and the lack of alienating influences in everyday life leads to an impression of an integrated, non-fragmented and unproblematic sense of personal and community identity, where all the 'locals' know each other and 'belong'. They have much to offer: their relaxed lifestyle ensures that they always have time to talk and are interested in the visitor. They are open, socially and emotionally, and are ready to take strangers to their hearts.[10] Meaningful contact with strangers occurs 'naturally' in Ireland: the visitor may actually become part of the community on some level, as well as engaging in the act of gazing. The people themselves are a link with unbroken tradition and the past:

> Ireland. . . is known for its natural beauty, for its cultural tradition which reaches far into the past, for its unmistakable music and above all for its helpful, welcoming and talkative inhabitants. . . . The 'Ireland experience' sets in over the evening drink in the pub: the search for the 'easy way of life [*sic*.]' ends here. How better to experience and learn the culture and language of another country than in person-to-person conversation? (English language learning holidays brochure. My translation)

> On this trip we will make a bridge from yesterday to today, not least because of the openness and hospitality of the Irish people, who are happy to get into conversation with travellers over a glass of Guinness (Studiosus Studienreisen 1997: 96; travel company brochure, my translation)

Here meaningful communication with the friendly locals and the fostering of face-to-face relationships is situated squarely in the pub and is inextricably linked with the consumption of alcohol/drink. It is 'over' a drink that the 'Ireland experience' is consummated. Drink, pubs and a sociability that may have transformative possibilities for the visitor are all bound up together, and the act of consuming the drink is the gateway to the sociability and to the magic secret of 'the easy way of life'.

It is interesting to note, however, that the 'glass of Guinness' referred to in the advertisement is, speaking figuratively, in a German hand, and reflects a particular relationship to an 'Irish' meaningful form which has become encoded for many different groups. Although women are no longer expected to take their chosen beer in the more 'feminine' half-pint glass in Ireland, the glass, as opposed to the pint, is comparatively rarely used by men and sometimes is seen to be effeminate. A glass of Guinness, gateway to conviviality, has become a badge of 'Germanness', a marker of German tourist behaviour for Irish people. The description of the tableful of German tourists sitting in a pub for an evening, over one glass of Guinness each, listening to the music and soaking up the atmosphere, abounds. The widespread use of this motif by Irish people says much about both groups' attitudes towards the 'proper' use of this transformative object. Sometimes this is taken one step further in the game of 'them and us', and used by some Germans to talk about other Germans, as with a couple I witnessed 'German-spotting' in a pub in West Cork: they were using markers such as clothing, close attention to the traditional music session, and the glass of Guinness to playfully identify other Germans present. This is just one example of how certain categories propagated by tourist advertising are engaged with, invested with meaning, and inhabited differently (at different levels of creative engagement) by different participants. In what follows, I will argue that this system of symbolism is adopted and customized in the Irish pubs in Berlin, providing rich ground for the planting of symbolic action and self-definition.

'Cold Beer, Warm Hearts': The Pubs and the People

The promoters of Irish pubs in Berlin tap into the symbolic complex of tourist-orientated representations of Ireland as part of a narrative that explicitly promises an affective leisure experience equivalent to that of being in Ireland, through the consumption of drink, food, 'Irish' culture, ambiance and people. They prioritize tradition over modernity and the rural over the urban, and also foreground Irish people as an essential part of the 'Irish pub' experience. These pubs are transformative spaces that hold a promise of belonging in a community of locals, spaces which facilitate metaphorical travel away from the everyday, from stress and from formal social convention, to a liminal experience of community, friendship and acceptance.

This association occurs on many levels: layout and décor, wares and public relations. Either the façades or the signage on the pubs are painted green, a suggestive colour coding which continues inside with the walls and menus, and with movable markers such as leaflets and advertising. Links with the past and with traditional culture and agriculture are emphasized through the use of sepia-toned photographs of rural scenes and 'traditional' farm implements and household objects. Tableaux such as the 'Irish village' with a 'typical Irish street scene' advertised by one pub resonate with the ideal of the small-scale, integrated community life to be found in Ireland, the shop-fronts locating it in a time when individual and quality goods were produced in the context of face-to-face relations and non-alienated skilled labour. The musical instruments displayed around the walls are unambiguously 'traditional' instruments, which simultaneously evoke the 'traditional' in Irish music and the category of spontaneous creativity. Objects offered for consumption are presented in terms of being traditional, high-quality and 'natural'. However, people are also offered as central to the package: Irish pub advertising echoes tourist advertising in foregrounding Irish people and their hospitality, friendliness and charm as an essential part of the Irish pub experience.

The advertising motto of a chain of five pubs in Berlin is 'Cold beer, warm hearts'. There is more on offer here than just the physical commodity, the beer: in this case the physical activity of drinking satisfyingly cold beer is coupled with the affective promise of 'warm hearts'. This resonates with the construction of Irish people as warm and open, always willing to accept strangers into their community. But whose are these promised 'warm hearts'? If Irish, are they the staff's and musicians' hearts? Or are Irish customers who may be there also implicated? I would argue that a generalized claim is made which advertises the Irish staff and customers in the pubs (directly or by implication) as legitimate objects of the gaze, and as a central part of the package which offers friendship and acceptance into a community as well as food, drink and atmosphere.

The 1999 poster for one pub's St Patrick's Day party exhorts people to 'meet friendly Irish people, taste real Irish cooking, quench your thirst with Irish beer, enjoy fun and music all the day'. The friendly people promised are most certainly customers as well as bar staff, people living as short- or long-term migrants in Germany who are nevertheless cast as objects of the tourist gaze: 'locals abroad'.[11] Their safe, friendly presence is perhaps offered in recognition of a thirst for something over and above Irish beer: a sense of locality and belonging. One pub's brochure claims: 'In [the pub], you can experience a real Irish welcome/real Irish hospitality, just like in Dublin. . . . Enjoy the charm of the Irish over a Guinness, a Kilkenny or a Harp beer' (my translation). Irish charm and beer are both offered for consumption, and they promise an experience of Irish hospitality 'just like in Dublin'. The pub seems to be displaced through this assertion, moving away from Germany and towards Ireland. Customers no longer need to go to Ireland: they can escape their everyday life and be transported just by walking into the pub.

Another pub's menu bears the legend: 'You might come as a stranger – you will leave as a friend.' This pub's promise of a mystical transformation from stranger to friend plays on the phrase 'a stranger is a friend you haven't met yet', and promises the ready inclusion into the 'community', which may contrast starkly with the visitor's (own perception of his or her) urban German life experiences. Here the pub is portrayed as a site of travel: a 'tardis' of transformative experience (not unlike Dr Who's telephone-box-shaped space-time vehicle in the television science fiction series) where the visitor embarks on an affective and personal journey, entering as a stranger (one among many alienated urban subjects) and leaving as a friend (having developed face-to-face community bonds). The pubs' low level of physical interface with the outside world and lighting contribute to this experience; in this they are similar to *Eckkneipen*. The space inside is dim and almost womb-like, separate from the outside world, a place for private, affective development in the midst of an accepting community.

The use of symbolism redolent of the tourist constructions of Ireland by Irish pub promoters, coupled with the explicit promises which build on possibly pre-existing expectations, construct the pubs themselves as a 'free space': a transformative and liminal space, where it is possible to form interpersonal and community links, and where strangers can become friends with the 'locals' and with each other, freed up from the formalities of German social interaction in this new (metaphorically distanced) emancipating atmosphere. The category of the 'local' is particularly multi-vocal in this case: the visitor to the pub is welcomed into the community of 'locals'[12] and changes his or her role and status; there are enticing possibilities of being accepted, of moving towards 'local' status by becoming a 'friend'. The pubs become a locality where belonging and community can occur: we can all be friends, and perhaps even locals, here. They are a 'local' place in the anonymous city.[13]

We have seen how the consumption of Irish alcoholic products has been con-structed by Irish pub promoters in terms redolent of tourist advertising as part of a transformative experience bound up with friendship, relaxation and the consumption of 'charm' and atmosphere, perhaps also involving emancipatory travel away from the everyday. We might ask: do German customers in Irish pubs go there in an attempt to travel towards the Ireland of tourist advertising, an Ireland that never was, an Ireland that is but a dream, in a rather non-critical effort to escape or hide from the everyday? This would be a too superficial reading of the situation, relegating these participants, who inhabit the pubs and also construct them in the light of their own desires and meanings, to the status of uncritical pawns of a ubiquitous advertising machine. A large amount of fieldwork data would, on superficial examination, seem to point in this direction. However, this is largely because participants use the language of the tourist symbolic complex to communicate and construct their own meanings.

Construction from the Other Side: How German Participants Express Things

The 'special atmosphere' which is often quoted by German customers as a reason for frequenting Irish pubs has four main components: it is relaxed, open and friendly, spontaneously creative and welcoming. These descriptions have an uncanny similarity with the categories central to the Irish tourist package, and indeed Irish pubs are treated as spaces of difference to the German everyday by both promoters and German customers, spaces where people can do things that they wouldn't normally do, just as if they were on holiday and 'free'.

Many people described to me the happiness afforded to them by (as I would see it) the exposure to and involvement with new habitats of meaning and meaningful forms that came about through trips to Ireland or Irish pubs. A large number remarked that they enjoy sitting at the bar in Irish pubs, ordering their beer in English and engaging in 'chat' with the bar staff: all modes of engagement with a setting of spatial relations and social interaction which allow them to travel away from the everyday and 'to relax'. Relaxation through sociability was promoted as an antidote to the stress, strain and high levels of formality of everyday urban German life. The act of relaxing was sometimes described to me as a journey away from both stress and the excessive formality of German social convention (sometimes even 'Germany'). Through engaging in 'Irish' activities, customers can escape the everyday and even the perceived traits and constraints of their own nationality: they can not only sit at the bar and drink Guinness; they can relax, talk to strangers, and engage in or listen to inconsequential, phatic chat and spontaneous cultural production. Going to Irish pubs is, for them, about much more than the consumption of alcohol. However, the consumption of Irish beer and whiskey is portrayed by pub promoters and German customers alike as serving as a gateway to relaxation, sociability, spontaneity, intensification of social relations, and informal, face-to-face human contact.

Do the pub promoters dupe Germans into uncomplainingly paying well over the odds for their wares by giving them a distorted, 'inauthentic' version of Ireland? Irish customers tended to name four or five Irish pubs in Berlin as 'real', and reject the rest as inauthentic, lacking the correct atmosphere or 'feel'. Does this mean that the less selective German customers are somehow being fooled because they 'don't know any better'? I suggest that the German customers are anything but passive consumers. Their agency comes to the fore when we examine the other category mentioned as a reason for frequenting Irish pubs: community.

The German customers are making use of a number of aspects of the Irish pubs which function as vectors, facilitating movement away from everyday life. This movement is not, however, towards Ireland, but towards a desired sense of community,[14] a community in locality. The pubs provide a range of imaginative materials with which to work, and participants are planting desire in the rich imaginative ground provided, using these resources to engage in symbolic self-definition and the building of 'imagined communities'.

Engaging in 'different' physical and cultural consumption (that of Guinness and Kilkenny, traditional music and dance), production (developing and using a competency in music or dance) and social interaction (sitting at the bar, talking to the barman and others not in one's immediate circle) all serve to distance people from negatively perceived aspects of their everyday lives and to enable them to enter into different and more 'community'-based social relations. The objects in Irish pubs (and sometimes the people) could be seen as 'transitional objects', objects that 'contain in themselves a transformational quality' (Curtis and Pajaczkowska 1994: 204); through interaction with or consumption of these objects, subjects may transform themselves, perhaps incorporating desired aspects of the 'other'. The ultimate focus, however, is on the self and its immediate surroundings: these particular lifestyle and consumption choices transmit particular messages about a person, and lead to the construction of a cultural repertoire which becomes integrated into a perspective, a particular 'self' (Hannerz 1996).

Owing to the multi-vocal and multi-referential quality of symbols, each person engages differently with the imaginative materials at his or her disposal, and invests a particular meaning/set of meanings in his or her engagement with that material. Fieldwork indicated that common meanings associated with the frequenting of Irish pubs might paint a thumbnail sketch of such a 'self' as rejecting German bureaucracy and excessive formality, culturally aware, discerning, thoughtful, not interested in cheap thrills or products (rather in high-quality culturally embedded and meaningful goods), and willing to invest the time and money necessary in order to have rewarding and culturally rich experiences.

Attending Irish traditional music sessions, learning to play Irish music, drinking Guinness and sitting at the bar in a pub are all acts of production or consumption which speak without using words, appropriating symbols associated with the cultural tradition of another nation.[15] The 'little communities' that participants assert exist in the Irish pubs arise through the grinding of gears between their perception of their own lives and of the imaginative alternatives provided to them through representations of the *Eckkneipe* and of the Irish 'easy way of life'. They are participating in the (safe) space provided by the Irish pubs to construct themselves and their 'imagined communities', operating in a 'subtle complicity with the discursive and representational conventions' (Appadurai 1991: 207) of the Irish tourist symbolic complex.

The 'reality' or 'authenticity' of the representations of 'Irishness' in the Irish pubs is wholly immaterial (although an interest in 'getting it right' may function as part of the process); it is a language being used primarily by Germans to talk to Germans about their own lives. Those who do not use this language sometimes point out its inconsistencies when viewed within a continuum of 'authenticity' which privileges the habitats of meaning of those who are 'from' Ireland', as in the last statement from an interview with construction workers and a barman (F) in an Irish pub.[16]

C: How do you get on with the Germans in the Irish pubs?

M: Fergal'll answer you that one. She's asking how we get on with the Germans in an **Irish** pub! [directed at F] [*laughter*]

F: No, actually they mix quite well. There's never any **hassle** between German and Irish anyway.

M: Mostly. If you don't speak German, they keep to themselves, you keep to yourself.

F: And the ones who can speak English want to get into conversation.

K: Just bother you.

M: Ah, they're all right, they were never no trouble.

F: They just want to **talk** to you and **talk** to you and **talk** to you.

K: Get your problems out, son! [*laughter*]

M: Most of the Germans that come in here have been to Ireland. And they like talking to you about it.

F: Yeah, you know them; they all drink Guinness and we all drink German beer. [*General laughter, including barman and waitress*] That's always funny.

K: It is yeah. That's all you need to see, is a guy drinking Kilkenny and having a Tullamore Dew: 'Ah, yeah, you're Irish, **aren't** you?' Both are so **plentiful** in **Ireland**![17]

To K and others, the consumption of these goods is a marker of an 'aspiring-towards-Irishness' which has no intersection with the majority of habitats of meaning of the Irish 'locals'. However, very often the Kilkenny or Tullamore Dew is being drunk less as part of a conversation about 'Irishness', and more as part of a conversation about what kind of a contemporary German city-dweller the drinker chooses to be, how he sees his own life and its alternatives, and how he chooses to pursue his desire: it has taken on a new meaning and is embedded in a collaborative construction of community. In its use as a transitional object, it doesn't really matter that it may not have the same meaning as that which Irish people accord it. The act of drinking Kilkenny or Guinness is not about replicating 'Irishness', it is about interacting meaningfully with its available representations.

Irish Pub and *Eckkneipe*: Conflated Categories of Desire?

The question arises, why does the *Eckkneipe* come up so often, in contrast with the Irish pub and in conjunction with the phrase 'Here [in the Irish pub] one is not bothered/harassed'? Why mention the *Eckkneipe* at all? Why were café-bars never mentioned? It is fitting to examine the categories associated with *Eckkneipen* in order to explore the connection between the two constructs.[18] Many positive categories are associated with *Eckkneipen*:

- a sense of community in a city;
- long-term, stable social relationships;

- real, salt of the earth people;
- *Treffpunkt*: a regular meeting-place: a 'local';
- knowing and being friends with the staff;
- a protected space;
- an 'extended family';
- openness towards others;
- an authenticity which may be vanishing.

These positive elements are offset by the undesirable:

- *angemacht werden*;
- intimidating: a closed community;
- pollution, both physical (dirt and contamination: sticky tables, smoke) and social, including:
  - unemployment;
  - a working-class or underclass clientele;
  - alcoholism, or excessive drunkenness.

The remarks of Stefanie, a German ethnographer, translated by me from German, are in confluence with and best sum up fieldwork findings.[19] Here she speaks of the positive associations that *Eckkneipen* have, even for people who do not frequent them:

> But there is a positive element with which they are connected, the Eckkneipen are the loci which hold an area together, the meeting-places [*Treffpunkten*], they're also something very romantic, ideal, where one meets **good** people: rough diamonds with hearts of gold, who really have a good heart and care for the neighbourhood, who were always there and also will always be there, and there's a feeling of 'long-term-ness' – in a kind of community. There's also the element that people can't see in from outside, they have curtains, one is shut away in a kind of a protected space. I would expect that it's a bit like an extended family, that people meet each other there and discuss each other's problems and what has happened, and you can open up with regard to the others who are in there and are a part of this sworn-in community [*eingeschworne Gemeinde*].

When talking about her own expectations of what her experience would be like if she walked into an *Eckkneipe* off the street, she noted

> that I wouldn't feel comfortable there, that I wouldn't feel like in a café, where I could sit down alone. Instead I would assume that I would be somehow bothered [*angemacht*] before two minutes were up, that's not just sexually, but also in a stupid way [*auch blöd angemacht*], in any case I'd be noticed because I wouldn't fit in.

As we can see, there is an ambivalence to these remarks. On the one hand, a desirable sense of 'a community in the city' is associated with *Eckkneipen*: the *Eckkneipe* (or membership of this group) is an object of desire. On the other hand, the group is closed, exclusive, not open to outsiders, and its non-inclusive difference elicits both apprehension and distaste. The community is closed, and there are elements of social pollution present that make the *Eckkneipe* undesirable to many outsiders.

I would suggest that *Eckkneipen* were mentioned so often, not because they are the only alternative to, or even the 'opposite' of Irish pubs, but because both categories are loci of desire, a desire for community in a city, informal 'family-like' human interaction, a feeling of belonging and locality, and an elusive quality which I will dub 'heart'. Irish pubs could be seen to possess the positive aspects of *Eckkneipen* without the negative. Indeed, it may well be asked whether the 'imagined communities' in Irish pubs represent or are the enactment of a re-mapping of desire from the *Eckkneipen* to a more open and safe alternative. To some German customers of Irish pubs, the pub promises what denizens of the *Eckkneipe* are seen to have: stable face-to-face relationships in a nurturing environment. Those who mention *Eckkneipen* in contrast with Irish pubs may do so because they are drawn to the positive elements of the *Eckkneipen*, but feel that the community there is closed to them because of difference. The Irish pub promises a warm welcome, clean tables and an absence of social pollution. The 'community of locals' in the Irish pub provides a promising starting point and/or backdrop to the creation of community in the city.

Although the collaborative construction of community and locality often obscures possible tensions, some sources of tension undermine this process on more than one level. The rupture caused by the marked presence of construction workers in the Irish pubs of Berlin for five or six years in the mid-nineties served to alert us to some aspects of the processes occurring in those spaces, and to how these processes are part of a negotiation with issues of class, tourism and self-identification.

Fieldwork has indicated that some social pollution that exists in the Irish pubs (for example, lone drunken Irish 'locals' buttonholing German customers and talking at them, and low-level inappropriate physical contact) is in many cases reinterpreted as friendliness, spontaneous cultural production, conviviality and an acceptable fondness for 'the black stuff'. In this way, social pollution, which might otherwise cause rupture within the community, is reframed and accepted: the undesirable image or action is transformed into the exotic and desirable by its refraction through the lens of the tourist gaze. On the other hand, many German customers indicated that they felt uncomfortable with the presence of large numbers of Irish and English construction workers in what were sometimes referred to as 'their' pubs, and some changed their choice of venue or timing to avoid them. It cannot be denied that the presence in one's social space of large groups of men, who often drank a lot and were sometimes associated with (predominantly in-group) violence, could be intimidating, in what may be seen as overt social pollution. However, I would suggest that an important part of the damage done by the presence of the construction workers, and the reason why this social pollution cannot be reconstructed, was on a symbolic level. It was damage to the symbolic construct that is the Irish pub.

The fact that these Irish men are current-day urban workers (immigrant workers, *Gastarbeiter*, at that) cannot be ignored, for it causes damage to the construction of the Irish locals as at leisure and unalienated by modern-day work, and of Ireland as a somehow classless society,[20] with its associated ideal of conflict-free community relations. The construction workers inhabit the pubs in ways that are largely independent of other pub users, making the space their own. They eschew contact with German customers in the main, and, unlike those who make a living out of being Irish, they have no reason to be complicit with a role as legitimate objects of the gaze, often playfully refusing the gaze by making fun of the gazers (O'Carroll 2001). Their social interaction is often exclusive: verbal playfulness and allusion to locality and shared habitats of meaning are not very open to participation by German customers. In a way, they are perhaps 'locals' in a sense similar to *Eckkneipe* locals. They are a community inhabiting a space in which they are 'at home': a closed community, which may not welcome outsiders and may in fact make fun of them or 'bother' them by causing social pollution, whether that be drunkenness rowdiness, or the fact of being workers.

Conclusion

This chapter has approached some of the meanings associated with Irish pubs that are used by customers to talk about, and construct, themselves and others. We have seen how the pubs are constructed spaces, both physically and socially. They are sites of consumption where food, drink, Irish culture and 'Irishness' are consumed. They are also inhabited spaces, sites of sense and meaning to those who inhabit them, which sometimes function as vectors that facilitate travel towards a desired community. The pubs, and the tourist representations of Ireland into which they tap, provide some of the imaginative materials used by German customers in order to engage in ways of imagining and performing the self, and to construct safe spaces for the performative creation of community in the city.

In this way, an ethnographic examination of Irish pubs in Berlin in the mid-1990s provides an illustration of the role of the imagination in social life: of how people engage with imaginative materials at their disposal, using the representational conventions of tourist representations of Ireland and the international marketing strategies of the 'Irish Pub' to articulate a felt need for, and create a sense of, contemporary urban community in the city. Through their engagement with 'Irish' material culture, drinks, modes of sociability and habitats of meaning, certain German customers evoke and raise questions about particular 'modes of Germanness' (articulated through ideas of inflexibility, excessive formality, lack of spontaneity and small-scale community interaction, and the category of the *Eckkneipe*), rejecting or re-imagining them in the creation of a sense of community in locality.

Different 'modes of Irishness' and 'modes of Germanness' are engaged in order to create and celebrate collective identities, yet these identities are presented as having locality rather than nationality at their core. If this is a form of what Jonas Frykman (1995: 9) terms 'the informalization of national identity', where '[t]he national is used to formulate new collective identities which do not necessarily have to do with the nation', it is a variation facilitated by increased international flows of meanings and meaningful forms, where imaginative materials specifically associated with another nation are made available, through tourism, trade and migration, and used as imaginative resources in processes of collective identification.

An ethnographic study alerts us to other aspects of this process, such as the experience of migrants who find themselves faced with a mirror of 'their' national culture, the rupture that occurs when the 'real' threatens symbolic constructs, and the manner in which actors may be aware of and playful about inconsistencies in the symbolizing of a nation. The manner in which different groups in the Irish pubs engage differently with drinks, ways of drinking, cultural production and modes of sociability reminds us of the desirability of regular engagement with the multi-vocality of meaningful forms in social scientific research. When actors utilize symbols of national identification to articulate personal or local concerns, the multi-vocality of symbols simultaneously enhances possibilities of freedom and effectiveness of expression (as new and different meanings and emotions can be invested in the symbols), and of misinterpretation by others for whom the symbols have other meanings and affective associations. As constructions of various nations are increasingly available as imaginative materials to social actors worldwide through travel, tourism, migration and the media, the implications of differential use of systems of symbolism must be taken into account. The different possible meanings and uses of the pint of Kilkenny and the glass of Guinness are relatively straightforward reminders of complex processes of identification and construction of meaning that take place every day and are intrinsic to social action.

Acknowledgements

The research for this piece was carried out with the help of the German Academic Exchange Service (DAAD), and the author was in receipt of a HEA Irish Council for Research in the Humanities and Social Sciences scholarship for the year 2000–1 and a Government of Ireland Post-doctoral Fellowship in 2002–3. Thanks are also due to the staff and students of the Institute of European Ethnology, Humboldt-Universität zu Berlin, particularly Stefanie Everke, and to those who gave me their time in the field.

Transcription conventions

C: Interviewer.
K:, M:, D: Each letter is the abbreviation of a separate respondent's alias.
talk to you   Use of emphasis represented in bold type.

Non-verbal noises or my own commentary, including key concepts in the original German, are included in the transcript between square brackets.

Notes

1. The research was carried out from 1995 to 1997 as part of a doctoral thesis. Through it I explored the migrant experiences of Irish-born people living in Berlin in order to examine the effects of movement and existence within that particular, somewhat new context on 'Irish' cultural forms and people, and to examine the processes involved in flows of people and meaningful forms in an intersection of migrancy and tourism.
2. Meaningful forms can, of course, be incorporated into people's habitats of meaning and accorded different meanings to those the originators of the forms invested in them. Contrasting Irish and German approaches to Irish alcoholic beverage serving sizes illustrates this.
3. This does not mean that people everywhere actually have more choice in improved lives, but that imagination plays a more important role in the constructions that are the lives of ordinary people.
4. By 'participants' I mean the individuals who constitute the landscape of people in the Irish pubs in Berlin, who all participate in the everyday performance and construction of identities within this context.
5. This assertion is only part of the picture. The positive and negative attributes of *Eckkneipen* as seen by participants will be discussed in greater depth below.
6. It should be noted that more and more German cafés and bars now offer either Guinness or Murphys as part of their range of beverages.
7. This is a gross oversimplification for the sake of descriptive clarity. The 'groups' are not discrete, with some individuals moving from one to another (as in the case of the construction worker who taught Irish and took part in music sessions as a musician), and with individuals identifying themselves as a member of a particular 'group' to greater or lesser degrees. People frequenting Irish pubs, however, will generally find themselves spending more time and/or identifying more closely with members of one particular 'group', such as culture producers, musicians, audience, construction workers, etc.

8. Urry's privileging of the gaze and of visual consumption does not adequately deal with the increasing centrality of discovery, experience and contact in tourism (Franklin and Crang 2001), yet the concept of the 'tourist gaze' is nevertheless a useful one.

9. In this case members of the managerial/professional and white-collar population categories AB and C1 (Bord Fáilte 1999).

10. This is strikingly represented by the widespread use of the 'old Irish saying', 'Strangers are friends you haven't met yet', in tourist materials.

11. The impact of this objectification on staff, musicians and customers is examined in O'Carroll (2001).

12. These people may be 'locals' because they are Irish, because they are part of the 'community' of people who use the pub as their 'local' watering-hole, and sometimes because they are both.

13. Here the word 'local' is a category of affective aspiration, rather than of geographical provenance. A large number of regular customers in Irish pubs travel through the city, sometimes for miles, to get there.

14. I wish to make no grand claims about this desire for community. I feel, however, that I can refer to its generalized existence because of its centrality to customers when talking about Irish pubs ('we're a little community here', 'there's a great sense of community here', etc.) and because of the close, if contrastive, association by participants of Irish pubs and *Eckkneipen*.

15. The question, 'Why of another nation and not of one's own?' is outside of the scope of this chapter. A reason presented to me very often during fieldwork was that National Socialistic engagement with aspects of German 'traditional culture' resulted in subsequent generations regarding that culture as 'tainted', forcing those in search of an alternative to mainstream culture to turn the gaze outwards. It must also be noted, however, that a model of small-scale urban social relations which does exist within Germany, within the social space of the *Eckkneipe*, is explicitly rejected because of reasons which are bound up with class consciousness.

16. This extract touches on many themes relevant to this chapter: the role of tourism; the relationship and interaction between staff, construction workers and German customers in the pubs; the differential approaches to meaningful forms; and the well-developed awareness, among these participants, of symptoms indicating the multifaceted processes at work in the pubs.

17. At that time, Kilkenny was still not widely available in Ireland, and Tullamore Dew is a whiskey associated with the export market.

18. These are categories associated with *Eckkneipen* by outsiders, those who do not drink there. I derived these categories from interviews with German people, all of whom were middle-class. The *Eckkneipe* 'locals' with whom I spoke emphasized the positive categories, particularly that of long-term stable face-to-face relationships based on locality of habitation or provenance.

19. Observations made during a tape-recorded interview with Stefanie Everke, May 2001.
20. Tourist promotion has been careful not to disprove Heinrich Böll's (1971) remarks to this effect.

References

Anderson, B. (1983), *Imagined Communities*, London: Verso.

Appadurai, A. (1991), 'Global Ethnoscapes: Notes and Queries for a Transnational Anthropology', in Richard G. Fox (ed.), *Recapturing Anthropology*, Santa Fe, New Mexico: School of American Research Press, pp. 191–211.

Bauman, Z. (1992), *Intimations of Postmodernity*, London: Routledge.

Böll, H. (1971), *Irisches Tagebuch*, Munich: Deutscher Taschenbuch Verlag GmbH & Co.

Bord Fáilte (1998), *Irland – Das Leben neu erleben*, Frankfurt am Main: Irische Fremdenverkehrszentrale.

—— (1999), *Tourism Facts '98*, Dublin: Bord Fáilte.

Byrne, A. R., Edmondson and K. Fahy (1993), 'Rural Tourism and Cultural Identity in the West of Ireland', in Barbara O'Connor and Michael Cronin (eds), *Tourism in Ireland*, Cork: Cork University Press, pp. 233–58.

Cohen, A. P. (1994), *Self Consciousness: An Alternative Anthropology of Identity*, London and New York: Routledge.

Curtis, B. and C. Pajaczkowska (1994), '"Getting There": Travel, Time and Narrative', in G. Robertson, M. Mash, L. Tickner, J. Bird, B. Curtis and T. Putnam (eds), *Travellers' Tales*, London: Routledge, pp. 199–216.

Franklin, A. and M. Crang (2001), 'The Trouble with Tourism and Travel Theory?', *Tourism Studies* 1 (1): 5–22.

Frykman, J. (1995), 'The Informalization of National Identity', *Ethnologia Europaea* 25(1): 5–15.

Hannerz, U. (1996), *Transnational Connections*, London: Routledge.

Melucci, A. (1996), *Challenging Codes: Collective Action in the Information Age*, Cambridge: Cambridge University Press.

O'Carroll, C. (2001), '"We Go There and They Come Here": Migrancy and Dislocation Through the Looking Glass of the Tourist Gaze', Unpublished Ph.D. thesis, NUI Cork.

O'Connor, B. (1993), 'Myths and Mirrors: Tourist Images and National Identity', in B. O'Connor and M. Cronin (eds), *Tourism in Ireland*, Cork: Cork University Press, pp. 68–86.

Péchenart, J. and A. Tangy (1993), 'Gifts of Tongues: Foreign Languages and Tourism Policy in Ireland', in B. O'Connor and M. Cronin (eds), *Tourism in Ireland*, Cork: Cork University Press, pp. 162–83.

Schulze, B. (1994) "'The Greenest of All Summers". . . ? Tourism and Tourist Imagery in Ireland', unpublished final year thesis, Department of Sociology, University College Cork.

Slater, E. (2000), 'When the *Local* Goes Global', in E. Slater and M. Peillon (eds), *Memories of the Present: A Sociological Chronicle of Ireland, 1997–1998*, Dublin: Institute of Public Administration, pp. 247–59.

Somers, M. R. and G. Gibson (1994), 'Reclaiming the Epistemological "Other": Narrative and the Social Constitution of Identity', in C. Calhoun (ed.), *Social Theory and the Politics of Identity*, Oxford and Cambridge, MA: Blackwell, pp. 37–100.

Studiosus Studienreisen (1997) *Mittel-, Nord- und Osteuropa 1997*, Munich: Studiosus.

Urry, J. (1990), *The Tourist Gaze*, London: Sage.

–4–

Pivo at the Heart of Europe
Beer-drinking and Czech Identities

Timothy M. Hall

A Czech never says that he's going out to have 'a few beers', and he never counts the beers while he's having them. You go out for *a beer*. A beer is like a woman: when you're with a woman, you never think of women that you've been with before, and you never think of the next woman. It would be disrespectful. It's the same with a beer. You go out and you have *one* beer. . . and maybe, when the unfortunate time comes that you reach the end of your relationship with your beer, then *maybe* you'll have another.[1]

Such was my first introduction to the importance of *české pivo*, at the start of a long night of drinking and pub-hopping in Prague in 1998. As I learned, beer provides a useful point of entry to many of the core features of Czech culture. Beer itself is an emblem of Czech national identity as well as a major mediator of sociality and a key element in recreation and leisure time. For the last decade, Czechs have maintained their position as the largest per capita consumers of beer in the world, nearly 165 litres per person in 2002. Along with several Czech liqueurs (including Becherovka and *slivovice*), beer plays a key role in Czech folk ideas of illness and health, while the etiquette around bar behaviour highlights Czech attitudes towards money, hospitality and reciprocation, and also acts as a forum of contention between Czech and Slovak ethnic identities and values. Though few Czechs abstain from drinking alcohol, beer and the pub in particular are gendered as masculine and play a significant role in the construction of male–male interactions.

Beer is such a common beverage among Czechs that many do not consider it a form of alcohol: 'It's just beer.' (The Czech word for beer, *pivo*, comes from the same root as the verb 'to drink', *pít*, and is cognate with the English word *beverage*, from Latin *bibere*, 'to drink'.) The normative values of heavy beer consumption and lenient attitudes towards inebriation both demonstrate some basic Czech values, such as the importance placed on relaxation and comfort (*pohoda*), and contribute to the substantial medical and social problems caused by alcoholism.

This chapter examines several ways in which beer and beer drinking figure in the construction of Czech identities, principally in national and masculine identities. In an era of increasing globalization and with the accession in 2004 of many former

Communist countries to the European Union, anthropologists and other social scientists have turned their attention to the negotiation and reinvention of national and local symbols of identity (Gellner 1983, 1987, 1998; Hobsbawm and Ranger 1983; Goddard et al. 1994; Berdahl et al. 2000). As one of several European cultures brought back from the verge of language death and reinvented during the nineteenth and twentieth centuries, the Czech Republic presents a particularly intriguing case study in the formation of national identities (Holý 1996; Sayer 1998; King 2002), and beer is one of the central elements in both Czechs' and foreigners' conception of Czechness. In fact, Czechs have long been recognized as a drinking culture, with concomitant and increasing problems with alcohol (Škála 1970; Bútora 1979, 1980a–c, 1995). Anthropologists have often documented the relationship between local cultural meanings of alcohol consumption or abstinence and the various problems associated with drinking (Hamer and Steinbring 1980; Segal 1990; O'Nell 1996), and have long noted how drinking institutions structure sociality, shape gender and sexual identities, and in turn are elaborated and shaped by local cultural forms (Cavan 1966; Schwartz and Romanucci-Ross 1974; Marshall 1979; Read 1980). This chapter speaks to all three of these discourses.

Beer at the 'Heart of Europe'

Czechs describe their country as lying in the 'heart of Europe' (*srdce Evropy*) but émigré Czech journalist Benjamin Kuras's image is perhaps more accurate: a bridge between East and West, trod upon by both sides (Kuras 1996: 9). Certainly the Czech people have existed in an ambiguous state, geographically at the centre of an ethnically mixed and politically contested Europe. The Czech lands (Bohemia, Moravia and part of Silesia) were politically and culturally united during the Middle Ages under the Přemyslid and Luxemburg dynasties, but the Czechs lost their political independence to the Austrian Habsburgs beginning in the sixteenth century. After the Protestant Hussite defeat at the battle of White Mountain (*Bílá hora*) in 1621, most of the Czech intellectuals and much of the aristocracy went into exile (Sayer 1998: 45–50).

By the time of the National Revival (*národní obrození*) in the nineteenth century, the Czechs had nearly lost their linguistic and ethnic identity under centuries of Habsburg rule. Prague itself, the historic capital of the Czech lands, was called the 'city of three cultures': Czech peasants and bourgeoisie, German aristocrats and Jewish artisans and intellectuals. When the country achieved independence in 1918, little remained in the cosmopolitan cities of Prague and Brno, or the Czech-speaking countryside, from which to build the symbols of a new Czech nation, and after the devastation of the Holocaust and the subsequent expulsion of the Sudeten Germans in 1945, two of the three cultures were gone. Aside from historic sites and the language, one of the single best-recognized Czech products abroad was beer. In his history of Czech identity, sociologist Derek Sayer quotes a passage from Czech historian Josef Pekář on the ancient roots of beer and language as two of the main emblems of Czechness: 'Writing to Ladislav Pohrobek after his coronation in 1453, the Pope suggests that the Czechs will not let their new boy-king go "until he masters Czech [language] – and beer-drinking"' (Pekář 1992 [1927] cited in Sayer 1998: 42).

Beer making has a long history in the Czech lands, and the quality of Czech beer and hops are recognized by beer drinkers around the world (*Brewers Journal* 1903: 692). Most Czech beers are lagers (*ležák*) rather than ales. Lagers are brewed at lower temperatures with yeast that lies on the bottom of the vat during fermentation. The product is usually lighter than ales, which are brewed at higher temperatures with a yeast that rises to the top. Czechs like their beer highly hopped, with a clean, bitter taste. Czech beers are slightly higher in alcohol than most Western European and North American beers and are almost exclusively made with barley, in contrast to North American beers, which often have a high content of rice or corn.

Two of the most popular types of beer in the world today originated in Bohemia and are still sought out by Western tourists. The recipe for pilsner-style beers originated in the West Bohemian town of Plzeň (Pilsen in German). In 1842, the then newly incorporated Burgeliches Brauhaus (now Plzeňský prazdroj, a.s., a division of SABMiller, the world's second largest brewer) adopted a Bavarian style of lager brewing and modified it by increasing the content of hops and allowing it to undergo a secondary fermentation called *krausening*, which produced the foamy head desired by Czech beer drinkers (*Brewers Journal* 1903: 692; Hernon and Ganey 1991: 36). The Pilsen model was later copied by other brewers and exported from both Germany and Bohemia to Western Europe and North America. It has come to indicate any light, lager-type beer, and pilsner beers are among the most popular in the world. The town of Plzeň has been brewing beer at least since it received a charter from Václav II in AD 1290. Its Pilsner Urquell (the German form of the name, used for export, or Plzeňský prazdroj in Czech; both mean 'Pilsner Original Source') is the single most popular beer in the Czech Republic and the most recognized Czech beer abroad.

The town of Ceské Budějovice (German Budweis) in South Bohemia gave the world the original Budweiser-style beer. Brewing in the town dates at least to AD 1265. By the mid-nineteenth century, several breweries in the town had been producing a particular style of slightly sweet lager for a number of years, marketing it under the Czech name Budvar and the German name Budweiser and exporting it to Western Europe and even to North America. The name in the United States, however, was first registered as a brand name by one Carl Conrad, an American importer of wine and liquor. In 1875, German-American immigrant and brewer Adolphus Busch bought the rights to use the name from Conrad and began large-scale production. Anheuser-Busch ran into problems in 1907 when they attempted to trademark the name in the United States; they were challenged by a German brewer on the grounds that it was a geographical name and had originally been used in Europe. In 1911, Anheuser-Busch reached a settlement with both the German brewer and Budějovický Budvar, under which Anheuser-Busch received the rights to use the name in North America but agreed not to market their product in Europe; the Czech brewer retained the rights to sell Czech Budvar in the US under the label 'Imported Budweiser'. In 1939, this agreement was modified and Anheuser-Busch obtained the exclusive right to market Budweiser in the United States (Hernon and Ganey 1991: 35–8).

Since the end of Communism in Czechoslovakia in 1989, the two companies have again been engaged in international trademark battles, updates from which periodically feature in the Czech news. The American version of Budweiser is the single best-selling brand of beer in the world and one of the world's most recognized trademarks. It currently accounts for one-fifth of the US beer market. Anheuser-Busch is the single largest brewer in the world, with an output several times larger than that of all the breweries in the Czech Republic combined and nearly one hundred times that of Budějovický Budvar (Reuters 2001). On the other hand, Czech beers are famous throughout Europe and many connoisseurs believe that Bohemia produces the best hops in the world. Anheuser-Busch has attempted to resolve the matter by purchasing a stake in Budvar, but the Czech government has so far refused all offers. Budvar is one of the most profitable Czech companies and the government are understandably reluctant to sell it to a foreign investor and long-time competitor. The Czech government petitioned the European Union to designate 'Budweiser' and 'Budvar' as geographically specific names, like 'champagne' and 'Roquefort'. This would have been the first time that a beer has been so recognized, but in December 2004 the EU ruled that Anheuser-Busch could receive a registration for 'Bud' throughout the entire European Union. Starting in 2001, Budejovický Budvar began marketing its beer in the US under the name 'Czechvar', an unwieldy portmanteau of 'Czech' plus *pivovar*, which means 'brewery'.

Czech beer is measured by 'degree' (*stupeň*), which tends to confuse foreigners. Degrees do not measure percentage of alcohol directly; rather, they indicate the amount of malt used in brewing.[2] The degree does correlate with the amount of alcohol, a higher degree indicating a higher percentage of alcohol within the same brand of beer, but 12° beer from one brand can have a lower alcohol content than a 10° from another brand, depending on the strain of yeast and the brewing process. A higher degree beer also commands a higher price within a given brand of beer. The most common degrees are 10° (*desítka*) and 12° (*dvanáctka*), but the full range extends from 6° to 19°. Czech brewers produce both light (*světlé*) and dark (*černé*, literally 'black') beers, but the international repute comes from the light lagers. In Britain, Ireland and North America, dark beers are usually more strongly flavoured, heavier, more caloric, and are perceived to be higher in alcohol content – typical men's drinks. Among Czechs, the gender stereotypes are reversed. Though the darker beers are still more caloric, they are much sweeter than the highly hopped lighter beers, and are often dismissed by men as 'women's drinks'.

Beverages of Choice: Beer and the Marking of Local Identities

Beer and other forms of beverage alcohol are deeply imbricated in Czech notions of local and ethnic identity, both in Czechs' awareness of their local specialties or brands and in the ways that local beverages and their associated customs mark off Czechs from neighbouring nations or mark distinctions among local groups. Bohemians, inhabitants of the northern and western two-thirds of the Czech Republic, are the most prodigious beer consumers in the world, and Bohemia produces some of the world's best hops. The climate, however, is generally too cool and damp, with too short a growing season, to boast much in the way of wine. Slovakia, on the other hand, produces and consumes more wine than beer, while Moravia, the eastern third of the Czech Republic, lies somewhere in between. One can often identify the Moravians and Slovaks in a pub in Bohemia merely by looking for the wine drinkers.

Before Communism, multitudes of small breweries supplied each locale with its own distinctive brews. Most of these small breweries were consolidated or eliminated in the process of collectivization. Some have re-opened since the revolution in 1989, but modern economic realities and the lack of available capital prevent the re-emergence of such local diversity. Nonetheless, there remain regional differences in beer preferences, supported in part by explicitly stated local loyalties. Everyone knows that Staropramen and Krušovice are from Prague, Starobrno from Brno, and of course Budvar and Prazdroj from their famous towns. Inroads are being made by the newcomers Radegast and Velvet, but imported beer remains an oddity, confined to the tourist-orientated bars of Prague.

The most basic Czech drinking establishment, central to Czech leisure time, is the *hospoda* or pub, usually a fairly casual, neighbourhood tavern whose customers drink mainly beer, though some may have wine or hard liquor. A basic *hospoda* serves some beer food as well, usually at least *párky* (steamed or boiled sausages like frankfurters), *tatranky* or *oplatky* (sweet wafer cookies with cream filling), pretzels and nuts. Many also have other traditional 'beer foods': *nakládaný hermelín* (a brie-type cheese marinated in oil with onions, bay leaves, allspice and other flavourings), *utopenci* ('drowners' – small sausages marinated in vinegar with onions and spices) or *sekaná* (thick slices of forcemeat, similar in taste and texture to baked or fried bologna). All of these are served with slices of brown rye bread flavoured with caraway (*kmín* – one can hardly escape the flavour of *kmín* in Czech cooking), and if you're lucky, the *párky* or *sekaná* will come with horseradish-enhanced mustard and a sweet gherkin. Higher quality *hospody* have more extensive offerings of food, though still tending toward the fairly basic – sausages, soups and goulashes – and the kitchen often closes long before the last call. At the upper end, *hospody* shade into low-end *restaurace*.

Many of the traditional Czech bar foods are threatened by EU regulations. *Utopenci* and *nakládaný hermelín* in particular are both marinated foods which are normally kept at room temperature. Even though both are pre-cooked and pickling is a traditional means of food preservation, they do not meet EU standards for food safety. New regulations that were passed in anticipation of EU accession require all establishments serving food to maintain certain standards, including refrigeration and a stainless steel food preparation environment. Most small pubs and even some restaurants cannot afford to purchase new equipment and retrofit their kitchens. In the end, many will probably stop serving food altogether or go out of business, while others will probably attempt to bypass the regulations by removing the offending food items from the menu but still providing them to regular customers who know to ask for them.

The typical *hospoda* is a ground-floor or basement establishment with a number of long tables and benches, occasionally having smaller tables and chairs. Ceilings are low and the air is smoky except in summertime, when windows and doors are opened to admit cooler air. Regulations call for separate non-smoking areas in places that serve food, but this is rarely enforced and comes as news to most Czechs. Approximately 70 per cent of the adult population smoke and the others are largely used to it. Seating, as in all but the fanciest Czech establishments, is more or less do-it-yourself. The pub world has both a certain camaraderie and a certain Czech pragmatism: empty seats at the long tables are available to all comers, so long as they are not being saved or reserved. If the table is not reserved, one simply asks whether the seat is available, '*Je tady volno*?', and sits down. Czech society experienced one of the most effective wage-and class-equalizations within the Soviet Bloc, a fact which persists in the relative informality of the pub. Individuals of the same age rapidly progress to the informal *ty* (rather than the formal *vy*), and a pub is a place where men, at least, from all classes can socialize.

Accounts in most pubs are kept on tallies of paper (*lístek* or *učet*), usually left on the table. Beers are marked at the bottom of the tab with a 'P' for *pivo*, and other items are listed at the top by their cost. In fancier night clubs, one receives an individual *konzumační karta* or consumption card which one pays before exiting. Waiters assume that men will have half-litres of the light beer, and usually only ask whether one wants 10° or 12° – '*Desítku nebo dvanáctku*?' Women will sometimes be asked if they want a one-third litre 'small beer' (*malé pivo*) or dark beer.

Most pubs have an exclusive contract with a single brewer for their draught beer, which provides them with a discount but restricts them from offering other brands; to order a *pivo* thus means a half litre of the draught beer from the brand that a given pub serves. Sometimes other beers are available in cans, but Czechs rarely order them and sometimes appear puzzled when foreigners ask for a non-draught beer. This exclusivity is changing slowly as the brewing industry is privatized and restructured. During the period of privatization and consolidation since the end of Communism, some breweries have merged. Their customers can now offer several brands of beer on draft, but a wide selection of beers remains the mark of a somewhat over-priced tourist bar.

The camaraderie of the pub is somewhat mitigated by Czech conventions of exact payment, however, a point about which Slovaks often complain. Ethnographers in Britain, Ireland and North America (Cavan 1966: 112–35; Scheper-Hughes 1979: 54–5) have noted the practice of 'standing rounds' – buying a round of beer for everyone at the table, or for everyone in the group of friends. Similarly, in singles bars in Western countries, buying someone a drink may be seen as a gesture of flirtation and buying drinks for one's friends is a minor statement of solidarity. The Czech situation is rather different. Except between extremely close friends, or late in the night when someone is very drunk, or when someone is celebrating a birthday or name-day, Czechs rarely buy rounds of drinks for the table. This reflects a broader pattern of precise accounting in restaurants and pubs, in which tabs are divided at the end of the evening down to the single crown (*koruna*, the unit of Czech currency). Buying a round for other than very good friends can engender some anxiety until the recipient has the opportunity to repay the buyer's largesse. Even switching pubs in the course of an evening can bring on some tension between acquaintances if one has bought a round of beers, because the beer in the next pub could cost more or less than the beers in the first pub, thus obviating exact repayment.

Slovaks comment on this point quite unfavourably when the topic comes up. While Czechs are quite hospitable to their personal guests, hospitality holds a much higher ranking in the pantheon of Slovak values, particularly in regards to generosity with food and drink. Slovaks do each stand their round when drinking in a pub, and small items such as snacks or cigarettes are freely, even ostentatiously, shared among the drinking buddies. The greater emphasis that the Czechs put on individuality and account-keeping strikes the Slovaks as cold and calculating, and they often contrast it with Slovak generosity.

At the end of the evening, one of the headwaiters (*vrchní*) comes and tallies up the marks on the card. Individuals keep track of what they have, and waiters in pubs and in more casual restaurants typically assume that customers will be paying separately, though they usually ask: '*Dohromady nebo zvlašt'*?' ('Together or separately?'). Although people in pubs do not normally buy rounds for the table, each person usually drinks about the same amount, which makes it easier to keep track. It is fairly unusual simply to divide the bill equally in a Czech pub, unless the parties involved are quite good friends or the bill involves many items and individuals all consumed roughly the same amount.

Beer and Leisure

While Czechs' consumption of Becherovka or rum by the shot-glass does not match the Russian or Polish consumption of vodka (Segal 1990), the most common forms of leisure activity usually involve or end with the consumption of alcohol, whether in a pub, in a private home or at the weekend cottage. '*Dáš si panáka?*' ('Will you have a shot?') is a common gesture of hospitality when visiting someone's home. In the pub, meanwhile, it is permissible to drink wine (especially if one is Moravian or Slovak) or to order a non-alcoholic beverage (if one is known as a non-drinker, presumably someone who had personal or familial problems with alcohol), but generally nearly everyone has beer.

Under Communism, Czechoslovakians enjoyed a higher average standard of living than the inhabitants of most other Soviet Bloc countries, continuing their previous position as the industrial heart of the former Austro-Hungarian Empire. While the inhabitants of the Baltic states were deported to Siberia or killed outright, Czechoslovakia was in part bought off with a tacit social contract. Although they were effectively forbidden to travel abroad or to purchase foreign-made consumer goods, and even staple foods were often of low quality or in short supply, Czechs and Slovaks could always count on inexpensive and available beer and liquor, and most Czech and Slovak families had a cabin or cottage (*chata* or *chalupa*) to retreat to on the weekends. During the Communist period, Czechs and Slovaks were subtly (and sometimes not so subtly) encouraged to change their patterns of recreation to use minimal materiel, confine their social activities to the family and a circle of close friends, and to avoid activities with political ramifications. During the work week, the pub served as a neutral venue in which one could meet friends and relax without the need of consumer goods such as expensive electronics or sporting equipment, and without risking invidious evaluations of one's home (in a period of chronic housing shortages) or inadvertently exposing one's reading choices or correspondence, for instance, to unwanted scrutiny. On weekends and the numerous state holidays, one would retreat with the family or friends to the cottage, where the main forms of entertainment were hiking, board- and card-games, singing songs and drinking high-quality, government-subsidized beer.

Bútora (1995) reports that beer prices in Czechoslovakia remained practically unchanged from 1955 to 1980. Even with the reduction of government subsidies in the post-Communist period, beer has usually been the least expensive beverage by volume in Czech bars and restaurants. In a society where free water is practically unknown except in a handful of tourist-orientated restaurants and where food prices are slowly but steadily increasing to approximate EU norms, the continuing low price of liquor and specifically of beer demonstrates the government's reluctance to end subsidies for such a culturally valued commodity. Some beer and alcohol prices have risen recently in the wake of EU accession, and Czech consumers are already complaining.

There are several other venues for drinking in addition to the basic *hospoda*. In summer, many restaurants have outdoor seating (called a garden or *zahrada*, though often more like a patio or sidewalk seating). The Czech Republic does not have the sort of well-developed Biergarten culture that Germany has refined, but independent beer gardens operate in some of the larger parks during good weather. Other types of establishments include the *vinárna* or wine bar (often advertised as 'Moravian', implying a better quality wine) and the *vinný sklep* or *vinný sklepík* (literally 'wine cellar' or 'wine cellarette', usually smaller than a *vinárna*). A *herna* is a small gambling joint or casino, often open late or non-stop, with slot machines and possibly other games such as darts. A *herna* is rather seedier than a normal bar; while it may act as a neighbourhood bar, it often serves as a stop-over for drunks whose bar has closed for the night. Beer in a *herna* is often only bottled or in cans, and comes with a higher price tag. The disco or *diskotéka* is a dance club, where people may drink beer but also wine, spirits and mixed drinks. A *kavárna* is nominally a café, but nearly all of them also serve alcohol and a substantial number of men in a *kavárna* in the afternoon or evening will be drinking beer. All of these can be described as *podníky* or establishments.

The one establishment which does not serve alcohol to most of its customers is the *čajovna* or tea room, which also provides one of the few smoke-free public venues in the Czech Republic. *Čajovna* patrons tend to be a younger, somewhat alternative crowd, who smoke marijuana and listen to various kinds of alternative music when they are not in the tea room. The *čajovna* scene itself represents the current Czech (and more generally Central and Eastern European) fascination with elements of 'Eastern' mysticism – astrology, ayurvedic and traditional Chinese medicine, vegetarian and other diets – as a replacement for both Marxist ideology and organized, Western religion in a post-Communist, post-Catholic world.

Drinking Gender: Beer and Male Sociality

While Czechs in general often relax with some form of alcohol, beer drinking and the pub are particularly central to male sociality. Most Czech males begin drinking with friends in mid-adolescence, around the age of 15 or 16, and are regularly spending time with friends in pubs by the age of 18 or so. The drinking age is only loosely enforced, and 16- and 17-year-olds are often served if they are with a group of older friends or are not obviously under age. (For comparative data on teen alcohol consumption across Europe, see European Commission 1995; ESPAD 1997.) Certainly by adulthood, drinking alcoholic beverages and especially beer has become the normal mode of socializing, and attitudes towards alcohol consumption and even frank inebriation are quite tolerant.

Within Czech society, beer drinking provides a unique opportunity for *communitas* across lines of class and hierarchy. Czech society is perceived to be one of the least class-differentiated in Europe. While some identifiable class differences remained even at the end of the Communist period (and are slowly re-emerging today), these are largely muted by the camaraderie of the pub. In the Czech Republic, pubs are largely neighbourhood affairs, drawing their clientele from the immediate surroundings, and some class and occupational differences are naturally reflected in the make-up of the pub's regular customers. Within the pub, there is a notion that we are 'all Czechs together'. This is a trope that is gendered both by the nature of the Czech language (in which the masculine form stands for both) and by the practical consideration that the majority of the regulars in a Czech pub are males. The camaraderie and *communitas* of the pub explicitly cut across lines of hierarchy, uniting males in their collective maleness and appreciation of male interests and activities. Czech men frequently drink in pubs with their colleagues and superiors from work, either at a lunch break during the day or after work has finished. Unlike some other instances of drinking with colleagues, as among Japanese businessmen where the hierarchies of work are explicitly and somewhat laboriously negated in such a way as to underscore the predominant ethic of hierarchy (Allison 1994), Czech drinking with colleagues instead draws on the images and praxes of camaraderie within the space of the pub or the action of drinking beer which have been built up in multiple experiences since adolescence, and reinforces instead the highly valued egalitarian ethic of Czech culture – an egalitarian ethic which assumes a basic equality among all Czech men.

Czech women drink substantially less than their male counterparts, though still a considerable amount. Women are more likely to drink wine than are men, are less likely to drink hard liquor, and drink smaller amounts in a single episode of drinking (ÚZIS 2002b). Women often drink with their male partners, husbands or boyfriends, but are less likely to go to a *hospoda* alone. An important exception to this can be found among young women in cities, especially young, single women, who do go alone or more often in groups of female friends to dance clubs where they drink wine or mixed drinks. The pub, however, is gendered as masculine territory to the extent that one will only rarely see groups of women in a pub by themselves. The typical crowd in most pubs comprises groups of men, or, in pubs which attract a younger crowd, groups of men and mixed groups of young men with their girlfriends. In fact, the advertising campaign in 2002–3 for Staropramen beer bore the slogan '*chlapi sobě*' ('guys for themselves') and showed groups of obviously working-class men enjoying themselves with cold half-litres of Staropramen (for further discussion of gendered aspects of Czech drinking, see Bútora 1995; Hall 2003a; Kubicka et al. 1993, 1995; ÚZIS 2002b).

The Etiquette of Beer

Beer is a metonym of relaxation and leisure (*pohoda*), but it commands a certain respect and formality, and also points up a number of peculiarities in Czech drinking behaviour. The general rules of beer drinking all express respect for the beer and for one's companions. Beer is not wasted, it is not mixed, and the good feeling and even the next day's hangover mark a certain sense of *communitas* with one's drinking fellows. It is, in a sense, both a sacral drink and a medium of liminality. One of the first rules that you learn in the Czech lands is that you never leave a beer, though while this persists some time into full adulthood, this is perhaps more common drinking behaviour among young men, comparable to the 'rule' among some young men in the United States that a party cannot end until the keg is finished. Nonetheless, to leave a beer glass with a noticeable amount of liquid in it is to say that something is wrong with the beer. Perhaps it has gotten warm, or the glasses have not been adequately rinsed and have been contaminated with soap. Either way, it is a statement that the beer was not up to par.

Beer is treated differently than other beverages. If possible, it is normally put on a coaster or mat (*podložka*), usually provided by the brewer and bearing various advertisments for that brand of beer. Sometimes the coaster is omitted if the beer is placed on a tablecloth, but even then a coaster is typical. The first round of beer of an evening, or in a given establishment, normally calls for a toast (*připítek*). It also requires that one wait until everyone in the group is present and seated; to start without toasting or without waiting for someone else in the group is to show disrespect. To make a toast classically means to raise one's glass while looking into the eyes of one's companion, clinking the glasses together lightly and saying *'názdraví'* ('to health'). Rather more informally, one can simply use the various salutations, most commonly *'čau'* but also the old Sokol slogan *'nazdar'*,[3] which means much the same thing, or the informal greeting *'ahoj'*. A somewhat humorous pun is to say *'nádraží'*, which sounds like *'názdraví'* but means 'train station'. (Zíbrt 1910: 65–71 *et passim*, describes a number of Czech toasts and drinking lore from the sixteenth through nineteenth centuries.)

A few rules must be followed: one must look into the eyes of one's partner while clinking the glasses together, and clink the glasses one at a time rather than in a group. To do otherwise is to be insincere, not to give the other person the attention or respect they deserve (see Zíbrt 1910: 49 for the antiquity of this custom). Several neighbouring cultures also require looking into one another's eyes while toasting: Austrians and Slovaks do, but Germans apparently do not, and failure to make eye contact is sometimes described as a 'German' habit. Neither is eye contact required while toasting in Britain or the United States. Part of this general rule of toasting with a single person at a time, each in succession, states that one may not reach under or over another person's glass in order to clink glasses with someone else. (At the other extreme, Hungarians never clink when toasting. The clink of glasses during a toast was once the signal for a coup, so the story goes, and today no Hungarian patriot will touch glasses while toasting.) As is often the case when culture is understood as a set of prescriptive rules, many Czechs think that foreigners take some of the toasting a bit too seriously. Failure to look into someone's eyes directly while toasting is grounds for reproach, but Czechs sometimes say that foreigners' concern for toasting with every last person is excessive. And then they proceed to do precisely that, and to express offence when they are overlooked.

Among students and young men, there are more elaborate forms of clinking glasses. The simplest elaboration is to tap the glass on the coaster or a on wooden table top after clinking glasses and before taking the first drink. A slight variation on this is to clink the glass additionally against an ashtray or any other item on the table that is glass or ceramic so long as it is not another drinking glass. The idea in this is that it makes a different quality clink than either the glasses together or the tap against the table, but clinking one's glass against another glass sitting on the table is either rude (to the person whose glass it is), or distasteful, and in any case runs the risk, especially as the evening progresses and the tally marks on the tab increase in number, of breaking the target glass. The fullest variation is to clink the glasses together first top, then bottom, then angled to one side and the other, then to rub the glasses against one another, tap them firmly on the table top or coaster, and then to take a long drink. People see this as a deliberately humorous caricature of the toasting tradition and usually smile while doing so. As a near-burlesque, it practically demands either the most formal '*názdraví*' in a tone of mock gravity or suppressed laughter, or something silly like '*nádraží*'.

Czech beer is ideally served cold, with about two centimetres of foam (*pěna* or *smetana*, 'cream') on top. A holdover from the Communist era is that all glasses are marked with a measuring point which should be reached by the meniscus of the liquid.[4] Bartenders can short their customers somewhat by serving greater amounts of foam; ideally, the beer should be level with the mark when the foam is nearly dissolved, and to fall short of this is to give bad measure. Bartenders learn a complex art of drawing beer from the tap in order to achieve the right amount of foam on the beer, involving several glasses and pouring foam off from the main glass into others, where it will settle into a few centimetres of liquid beer which is then topped off from the tap to serve a later customer. This process is most necessary for the first several litres of beer to come out of a newly tapped keg.

The bartender, however, like handlers of sacred substances in other cultures, is the only person permitted to mix beer or pour it from one glass to another. Once a beer has arrived in its final glass and been placed on the table, it should not be poured into another glass or mixed with anything. Neither do Czech pubs serve pitchers of beer; beer is always served in individual glasses straight from the tap (though sometimes people will carry home beer from a local pub in litre bottles if a party at home runs short – essentially beer take-out). On my first trip to Prague, I discovered this rather painfully. I was sitting in a pub with a group of Czech men, drinking and talking. The waiter had already brought the next round of beers, though we were only about halfway through our half-litres, but he had brought small beers. I thoughtlessly poured my small beer into my large beer, to cool down the large beer and clear some space on the increasingly crowded table as I might do in a bar in Boston or San Diego. Conversation abruptly stopped and my companions looked at me as though I had spat into the beer. I have seen Czechs occasionally split or consolidate beers, but this usually occurs late in the evening, among close friends, and rather surreptitiously below table level, as it is considered more than a little gauche.

There do exist a few mixed drinks involving beer, but none are common. Though some Czechs claim not to have heard of them, I have seen all of them served in bars at some point during my time in Prague. One is beer with Sprite, at a mixture of about half and half. Most informants responded that this sounded like an abomination and was probably a German drink. (Later research found that this is in fact a German and Austrian drink called a *Radler*, though some Czechs drink it on rare occasion and call it *pivo se sprajtem*.) Beer can also be mixed with Fernet or Becherovka, analogous to the Japanese-American 'sake bomb', but this is equally rare. Czechs generally demonstrate disgust at mixing anything else with beer, like lemon slices in German Hefeweizen or lime wedges in Mexican Corona. Wine, however, which most Americans would balk at mixing, is often drunk mixed with soda or cola. There is one legitimate exception to mixing beer, and an exception to the rule that men do not normally drink dark beer. The so-called 'cut' beer (*řezeno pivo* or *řezák*) is a 50-50 mix of light and dark beer (see description in Hrabal 1993 [1976]: 87). This is not like a Black and Tan, in which Guinness is floated on a lighter beer, but is in fact blended. One is not supposed to mix beers from different breweries in making this drink, but given that most pubs have contracts with a single brewery, that concern is more hypothetical than practical.

The Healing Powers of *Pivo*

Beer and various Czech herbal liqueurs also play a major role in Czech folk medicine. Many Czechs swear by the healing powers of *pivo*. They say that it has 'a lot of vitamin B' and that it's very nutritious.[5] The belief in alcoholic beverages as medicine extends to several liqueurs peculiar to the Czech lands and Slovakia which have reputations as 'digestives' and 'medicinal'. Absinthe is a popular liqueur that was banned for some time in most countries of today's European Union, except the Czech Republic, Slovakia and Spain. It is a decoction of herbs in grain alcohol, prepared from a combination of wormwood (*Artemisia absinthum*), licorice, angelica and other herbs, and has an alcohol content of some 70–80 per cent. Less potent but still strongly herbal and fairly alcoholic are Becherovka, from the Jan Becher distillery in the spa town of Karlovy Vary (Carlsbad) in Western Bohemia, and Fernet, from the Stock Plzen-Božkov distillery in Plzeň. Both belong to the same Central European family of bitters, herbal liqueurs such as the German *Jägermeister* and the notoriously bitter Hungarian cordial *unicum*. Becherovka and Fernet are drunk straight as shots or mixed with tonic (*beton* is Becherovka with tonic, *bavorák* is Fernet with tonic).

Also common with local variations throughout Central and Eastern Europe, *slivovice* or plum brandy carries a reputation for general but unspecified medicinal powers. (Less common variations are made from a number of fruits and flavourings: *jablkovice* from apples, *borůvkovice* from huckleberries or bilberries, *hruškovice* from pears, *merunkovice* from apricots, and even *borovice* flavoured with pine needles). Although *slivovice* is produced and drunk from Poland to Bosnia and from Bohemia to Romania, it is nonetheless construed as pre-eminently traditional, old-fashioned and local. Everyone's grandfather, father or uncle makes his own. In parts of the Czech Republic and Slovakia, the government, realizing that it cannot suppress domestic manufacture of *slivovice* and hoping to avoid deaths from improperly home-brewed stuff, has enacted a programme whereby individuals can bring in their home-grown plums or other fruits, have it brewed and distilled in a local distillery, and receive a proportion of the resulting liquor. Veteran home-distillers complain that it does not taste quite the same as what their fathers and grandfathers used to make, but most go along with the new programme as a compromise between the authenticity and localness of the 'real' home-made stuff and the safety and relative convenience of modern mass-production techniques. In any case, devotees of *slivovice* advocate it as a sovereign remedy for nearly any minor illness or upset, though they also believe that the home-made stuff, particularly their own home-made stuff, is a better curative than the commercially produced liquor.

Czechs believe with almost superstitious fervour that 'mixing' drinks – in the sense of switching from one category of alcohol – beer, wine or liquor – to another in the course of an evening is bad. This does not stop them from doing it, of course, but doing so will often draw comment from someone in a group, especially if the understanding is that the group is just out for a couple of beers. Some Czechs will actually show some nervousness – as in warning that 'you really shouldn't mix different kinds of drinks' – and sometimes will even comment on switching different brands of beer if one is switching pubs. I have heard this given as a mild reason not to switch pubs; presumably this excuse was actually motivated by something else, but the fact that it could be given as an argument at all is suggestive. It was not that they disliked the brand of beer at the proposed pub, but rather that we had been drinking brand X all evening already and should not 'mix' our drinks. Slightly more common is the comment, if changing between pubs with contracts to the same brewer, 'Such-and-such a pub even has the same kind of beer, so we won't be mixing.'

A final consideration in the folk medical beliefs around alcohol strictly prohibits drinking while taking antibiotics. This warning is given in other countries of course, and has two major justifications from a medical viewpoint. Alcohol can increase the risk of various side-effects of antibiotics, including toxicity and carcinogenicity. It also can increase clearance of the antibiotic from one's body and reduce its effectiveness, either by increasing urination or by stimulating metabolism of the drug by the liver. The Czech folk belief holds a peculiar horror for mixing alcohol with antibiotics, however, as distinct from all other categories of medicine which might have interactions with alcohol, and also distinguishes two categories within the Western category of antibiotic – 'true antibiotics' (*antibiotikum*) and 'chemotherapeutics' (*chemoterapie*). Western medicine draws a technical distinction between bactericidal antibiotics, which actually kill bacteria, and bacteriostatics, which merely impede their growth and allow the body's own immune system to clear them. This does not seem to be the exact distinction represented by that between *antibiotikum* and *chemoterapie*, and the absolute prohibition on alcohol consumption in the public consciousness is reserved for *antibiotikum* alone.

The Dangers of Drinking

Czechs consume more beer per capita than anyone else in the world, and have consistently maintained one of the highest rates of general alcohol consumption over the last century, a fact which Czechs regard with a mixture of pride and anxious embarrassment. Total alcohol consumption has increased nearly threefold since the 1930s, from 3.6 litres per person per year in 1936 to 9.9 litres per capita in 1999. Beer consumption has increased two and a half times over the last seven decades, from 64.8 litres per capita in 1936 to 165 litres per capita in 2002.[6] Most authorities suspect that reported alcohol consumption underestimates the true numbers (ÚZIS 2001, 2002b).

Many Czech thinkers have discussed the problem of alcoholism in their writings and speeches. Tomáš Masaryk stated that 'a nation which drinks more will undoubtedly succumb to one that is more sober. The future of each nation and especially of a small nation depends on . . . whether it stops drinking. Each nation destroys itself by drinking and drinking injures everyone who does not resolve himself against it' (Masaryk 1905; see also Masaryk 1938 [1912]; Beneš 1915; Čapek 1995: 238). Recognition by the general public, however, has been slow in coming. A more typical attitude is that expressed in the most famous Czech opera, Bedřich Smetana's (1824–84), *Prodaná Nevèsta* (*The Bartered Bride*). Smetana (1982 [1866]: Act II, Scene 1) praises beer with the following lines: 'Beer's no doubt a gift from heaven, it chases away worries and troubles and imparts strength and courage to men . . . Without beer we should cut a poor figure; there's so much trouble in the world – that foolish is he who cares too much!'

Bútora describes how the phenomenon of alcoholism, like many other social and psychological ills, was either hidden or caricatured under Communism. The Communist press portrayed alcoholism as a degenerate behaviour of the bourgeoisie, alien to the authentic, right-thinking, socialist Czechs and Slovaks (Bútora 1995: 39–40; 1980a; Škála 1970). The image of a wild-eyed, dissipated counter-revolutionary clearly did not fit the more insidious problems of ordinary Czechs: missing work or arriving late because of a hangover (*kocovina*), fights with spouses and neglect of children, or an untimely death from cirrhosis.

Heavy drinking behaviour and frequent consumption of alcohol are supported by cultural norms of drinking beer in most social situations and a concomitant tolerance for drunken behaviour. Alcohol is easy to obtain and there are few if any sanctions for alcohol consumption in itself. It is in fact the abstainer who stands out in Czech society (Škála 1970). Drunkenness and its effects are also treated with a fair degree of leniency. Czechs feel little guilt at calling in sick or showing up late to work when they have a hangover, and feeling under the weather due to heavy drinking the night before at one's own or a friend's birthday or name-day celebration is fairly common. In contrast to the United States or Britain, where intoxication is *de facto* evidence of culpability, Czechs consider that overindulgence in alcohol reduces one's responsibility for neglect of duties, at least up to a point. A colleague of mine spent a wintry weekend teaching English to businessmen on a study retreat at a hotel in the mountains. Both nights, the caretaker stayed up late drinking with some of the businessmen. As a result, he allowed the furnace to go out both nights, leaving the hotel cold and without hot water, and was too hungover to prepare breakfast. Not only did none of the Czechs complain, but when my colleague remarked on this the second cold morning without breakfast, several of the businessmen defended the caretaker: 'But he'd been up drinking all night.'

Similarly, several prominent celebrities and politicians are known to drink heavily on a regular basis, with minimal criticism in the press. Data from the Czech Ministry of Health (ÚZIS 1998a, 1998b, 2002a) reveal two trends in drinking behaviour: relative numbers of individuals hospitalized for alcoholism have increased over the last two decades among both men and women, and the number of women showing problems associated with drinking has increased at a faster rate than the comparable number of men. A consistent finding is that women's drinking patterns, particularly among younger, more educated and urban women, are slowly coming to resemble those of their male counterparts (ÚZIS 2002b).

Actual rates of alcoholism are difficult to measure, and in a cross-cultural situation particularly must be considered against the prevailing social norms and the local effects of alcohol consumption. However, it is clear even from the society-specific data that Czechs do experience relatively high rates of alcohol-related problems.

Czechs: A Culture of Drinking

If any culture in the world qualifies as a beer-drinking culture, it is the Czechs. Images of beer and beer drinking pervade Czech literature and film, from Hašek's (1930) drunken anti-hero Švejk or the brewery which dominates Hrabal's *Little Town Where Time Stood Still* (1993 [1976]), to the scenes from the popular musical *Starci na Chmelu* (*The Old Folks in the Hops*) (1964). Beer acts as a major mediator and occasion of sociality, and Czechs are among the greatest beer drinkers in the world. This set of associations and values, however, has a dark side. Czechs suffer from elevated rates of alcoholism and other health and economic consequences from their prodigious and pervasive alcohol consumption.

Images of the pub and of beer figure prominently in the construction and practice of local, national and gendered identities. Most forms of sociality between males from late adolescence onwards involved drinking beer (or, more rarely, one of the local Czech liqueurs), and the *communitas* of the pub reinforces both the distinction between the genders and the egalitarian ethic which attempts to deny differences of class or hierarchical status outside the workplace. Local beers, local wines, home-made *slivovice* and the preference for beer (generally Bohemian) or wine (Moravian or Slovak) all symbolize the local in tangible, potable, emotionally charged form. More broadly, the tropes of the pub – from the slowly disappearing game of *mariáš* to the bar foods threatened by EU regulations – figure in individual minds and in public discourse as icons of venerable, local traditions fading in the face of a new and more global (post)modernity. Behaviours and beliefs around beer and other alcoholic beverages also provide an entrée to many Czech values.

So what happens now, as Communist government subsidies disappear, as young Czechs increasingly have opportunities to travel and study (Nash 2003), and the Czech Republic increasingly opens itself to European and international influences? Will the camaraderie of the *hospoda* go the way of *mariáš*, lingering only among pensioners in villages, or will beer and alcohol more generally maintain their hold on Czech social life? It remains to be seen what will happen to Czechs' relationship with their beer now that the nation has 'returned to Europe'.

Acknowledgements

This chapter would never have been possible without the help of Karel Vrbenský, my first guide to the world of *české hospody* and someone who takes his *pivo* quite seriously. Many thanks also to Vojtěch Kostiha, Dušan Quis, Bohdan Ševčík, Margaret Rance and the staff of Stella bar, Alcatraz and Angel. This chapter is based in part on the author's dissertation research in Prague, Czech Republic (July 1999–November 2002), which was supported by the Jacob K. Javits Fellowship, US Dept. of Education; the MST Program at UC San Diego School of Medicine (NIH grant #5T32 GM07198); a language training fellowship from the Rotary Foundation; the Center for Gender Studies and the Committee on Human Development at the University of Chicago; and the Melford E. Spiro Fieldwork Grant from the Department of Anthropology, UC San Diego. The dissertation (Hall 2003c) examines the relationship among Czech cultural values, the experience of Communism and its aftermath, and alcoholism, depression and dysthymia among the Czech population. Methods included semi-structured and unstructured interviews, the administration of a questionnaire and a depression screen to 144 Czech men, and participant observation with several dozen Czech men (and a few women) in bars, at home and in leisure settings. An earlier version of this essay appeared as Hall (2003b), and an expanded version can be found in Hall (2003c: 336–66).

Notes

1. Karel Vrbenský, 'hospoda U medvídků', Prague, June 1998.
2. The degree system was developed by Carl Joseph Napoleon Balling in England, based on earlier researchers' work on density measurements and saccharometry. It was introduced into British and German brewing in the 1840s. Each 'degree' in the Balling scale represents 1 per cent sugar content by volume (in the mash, for brewing contexts) at $14°$ R (63.5 °F or 17 °C). The Balling scale uses the Rankine temperature measurement, an absolute temperature scale using Fahrenheit degrees. The system has since been replaced in brewing by the Plato scale and in wine making and confectionery by the Brix scale, which were developed later and calibrated to degrees Celsius (*Brewers Journal* 1903: 48–9, 80–1; Goldammer 2002).
3. Sokol is an athletic organization which began in the nineteenth century and played a significant role in the Czech and Slovak nationalist movements. '*Nazdar!*' was one of its slogans and passed into the vernacular as a greeting. The organization still exists.
4. Ordinarily 0.33-litre or 0.5-litre glasses for most beers. Velvet, a relatively new beer with a wheat-beer taste, semi-opaque consistency and small, descending microbubbles like Guinness, is served in special 0.4-litre glasses. Some expensive tourist-orientated bars also serve beer in 0.4-litre glasses.
5. Beer probably constituted a relatively healthful beverage in a pre-industrial setting. Turning barley into beer preserves the calories through the winter, reducing the chance of spoilage or loss from mould and rodents, and also provided a source of sterilized liquid in an era when most water was probably contaminated with bacteria. Beer does contain small amounts of B-complex vitamins, but its overall nutritional significance is unknown. A study by Mayer et al. (2001) suggests that moderate intake of beer (less than 7 litres of beer weekly, or less than two half-litre beers a day, calculating from their data) may provide a significant source of folate, pyridoxine and cobalamin, in diets otherwise lacking these nutrients. See also Kellner and Čejka (1999) and Walker and Baxter (2000).
6. For more detailed discussion and statistics, see Bútora (1979, 1980a–c, 1995); *Statistical Yearbook of Czechoslovakia*; ÚZIS (2001, 2002a); Hall (2003b); and FAOSTAT – United Nations Food and Agriculture Organization's Statistical Database, *World Drink Trends*, regularly published by Produktschap voor Gedistilleerde Dranken, the Netherlands.

References

Allison, Anne (1994), *Nightwork: Sexuality, Pleasure, and Corporate Masculinity in a Tokyo Hostess Club*, Chicago: University of Chicago Press.

Beneš, Eduard (1915), *Problém Alkoholové Výroby a Abstinence*, Prague: Nakladate-lství československého abstinentního svazu.

Berdahl, Daphne, Matti Bunzl and Martha Lampland (eds) (2000), *Altering States: Ethnographies of Transition in Eastern Europe and the Former Soviet Union*, Ann Arbor: University of Michigan Press.

Brewers Journal (1903), *One Hundred Years of Brewing: A Complete History of the Progress Made in the Art, Science and Industry of Brewing in the World, Particularly During the Nineteenth Century. Historical Sketches and Views of Ancient and Modern Breweries. Lives and Portraits of Brewers of the Past and Present. A Supplement to the Western brewer, 1903*, Chicago and New York: H. S. Rich and Co.

Bútora, Martin (1979), 'K Sociologickým Dimenziám Alkoholizmu a Jeho Terapie I', *Československá Psychiatrie* 75 (4): 243–49.

—— (1980a), 'K Sociologickým Dimenziám Alkoholizmu a Jeho Terapie II', *Československá Psychiatrie* 76 (1): 47–54.

—— (1980b), 'K Sociologickým Dimenziám Alkoholizmu a Jeho Terapie III', *Československá Psychiatrie* 76 (2): 115–22.

—— (1980c), 'K Sociologickým Dimenziám Alkoholizmu a Jeho Terapie IV', *Československá Psychiatrie* 76 (4): 256–63.

—— (1995), 'Alcoholism in the Czech and Slovak Republics in the last 30 Years: An Uneasy Legacy for the Reformers', in Rumi Kato Price, Brent Mack Shea and Harsha N. Mukherjee (eds), *Social Psychiatry across Cultures: Studies from North America, Asia, Europe, and Africa*, New York: Plenum, pp. 39–50.

Čapek, Karel (1995), *Talks with T. G. Masaryk.* [Czech original: *Hovory s T. G. Masarykem.* 1935.], trans. Dora Round, ed. Michael Henry Heim, North Haven, CT: Catbird Press.

Cavan, Sherri (1966), *Liquor License: An Ethnography of Bar Behavior*, Chicago: Aldine.

ESPAD [The European School Survey Project on Alcohol and Other Drugs] (1997), *The 1995 ESPAD Report: Alcohol and Other Drug Use among Students in 26 European Countries*, Stockholm: The Swedish Council for Information on Alcohol and Other Drugs, CAN. Council of Europe. Cooperation Group to Combat Drug Abuse and Illicit Trafficking in Drugs (Pompidou Group).

European Commission (1995), *Drug Demand Reduction in the Central and Eastern European Countries – Second Regional Report*, Barcelona: Intersalus and ABS.

Gellner, Ernest (1983), *Nations and Nationalism*, Oxford: Blackwell.

—— (1987), *Culture, Identity, and Politics*, Cambridge: Cambridge University Press.

—— (1998), *Language and Solitude: Wittgenstein, Malinowski, and the Habsburg Dilemma*, New York: Cambridge University Press.

Goddard, Victoria A., Josep R. Llobera and Cris Shore (eds) (1994), *The Anthropology of Europe: Identity and Boundaries in Conflict*, Oxford: Berg.

Goldammer, Ted (2002), *The Brewers' Handbook: The Complete Book to Brewing Beer*, Herndon, VA: Apex Publishers.

Hall, Timothy M. (2003a), 'Czechs', in Melvin Ember and Carol Ember (eds), *Encyclopedia of Sex and Gender: Men and Women in the World's Cultures*, Dordrecht: Kluwer/Plenum Press, pp: 380–8.

—— (2003b), '*Pivo* and *Pohoda*: The Social Conditions and Symbolism of Czech Beer-drinking', *The Anthropology of East Europe Review* 21 (1): 109–38.

—— (2003c), 'Social Change, Mental Health, and the Evolution of Gay Male Identities: A Clinical Ethnography of Post-Communist Prague', Ph.D. dissertation, University of California, San Diego.

Hamer, John and Jack Steinbring (1980), *Alcohol and Native Peoples of the North*, Lanham, MD: University Press of America.

Hašek, Jaroslav (1930), *The Good Soldier Švejk and his Fortunes in the World War* [Czech original: *Osudy Dobrého Vojáka Švejka za Svetové Války*], trans. Paul Selver, illus. Josef Lada, Garden City, NY: Doubleday.

Hernon, Peter and Terry Ganey (1991), *Under the Influence: The Unauthorized Story of the Anheuser-Busch Dynasty*, New York: Simon & Schuster.

Hobsbawm, Eric and Terence Ranger (eds) (1983), *The Invention of Tradition*, Cambridge: Cambridge University Press.

Holý, Ladislav (1996), *The Little Czech and the Great Czech Nation: National Identity and the Post-Communist Social Transformation*, Cambridge: Cambridge University Press.

Hrabal, Bohumil (1993), *The Little Town Where Time Stood Still* [Czech originals: *Postřižiny*. Prague: Československá spisovatel, 1976, trans. as *Cutting it Short*; *Městečko, Kde se Zastavil Čas*. samizdat, 1973; Innsbruck: Austria, 1978; Toronto: 68 Publishers, 1989. trans. as *The Little Town Where Time Stood Still*], trans. James Naughton, London: Abacus.

Kellner, Vladimír, and Pavel Čejka (1999), 'Kladné Účinky Piva na Zdraví Populace', *Yearbook of the Research Institute of Brewing and Malting* 1999: 134–42, Prague: Research Institute of Brewing and Malting.

King, Jeremy (2002), *Budweisers into Czechs and Germans: A Local History of Bohemian Politics, 1848–1948*, Princeton, NJ: Princeton University Press.

Kubička, Luděk, Ladislav Csémy, Jirí Kožený and Karel Nespor (1993), 'The Substance Specificity of Psychosocial Correlates of Alcohol, Tobacco, Coffee and Drug Use by Czech women', *Addiction* 88 (6): 813–20.

Kubička, Luděk; Ladislav Csémy and Jirí Kožený (1995), 'Prague Women's Drinking before and after the "Velvet Revolution" of 1989: A Longitudinal Study', *Addiction* 90 (11): 1471–8.

Kuras, Benjamin (1996), *Czechs and Balances: A Nation's Survival Kit*, Prague: Baronet.

Marshall, Mac (ed.) (1979), *Beliefs, Behaviors, and Alcoholic Beverages: A Cross-cultural Survey*, Ann Arbor: University of Michigan Press.

Masaryk, Tomáš Garrigue (1905), *Prednáška ve Vídni*, and *Přednáška ve Vsetíně*, reprinted in Jaroslav Dresler (ed.), *Masarykova Abeceda: Výbor z Myšlenek Tomáše Garrigua Masaryka*, Prague: Melantrich, 1990.

—— (1938), *I. O Alkoholismu. II. O Ethice a Alkoholismu* [Part II originally published as: *O Ethice a Alkoholismu*, Prague: Tiskem A. Reise, 1912], Prague: Nakladatelství ČIN, and Brno: Moravskoslezské zem. ústředí Československého abstinentního svazu.

Mayer, O., J. Šimon and H. Rosolová (2001), 'A Population Study of the Influence of Beer Consumption on Folate and Homocysteine Concentrations', *European Journal of Clinical Nutrition* 55: 605–9.

Nash, Rebecca J. (2003), 'Re-stating the Family: Reforming Welfare and Kinship in the Czech Republic', Ph.D. dissertation, University of Virginia.

O'Nell, Theresa D. (1996), *Disciplined Hearts: History, Identity, and Depression in an American Indian Community*, Berkeley: University of California Press.

Pekář, Joseph (1992) [1927] , *Žižka a Jeho Doba*, vol 1. Prague: Odeon.

Read, Kenneth (1980), *Other Voices: The Style of a Male Homosexual Tavern*, Novato, CA: Chandler & Sharp.

Reuters (2001), 'Czech Brewer Budvar Picks New Name for U.S. Exports', 28 March.

Sayer, Derek (1998), *The Coasts of Bohemia: A Czech History*, Princeton: Princeton University Press.

Scheper-Hughes, Nancy (1979), *Saints, Scholars, and Schizophrenics: Mental Illness in Rural Ireland*, Berkeley: University of California Press.

Schwartz, Theodore and Lola Romanucci-Ross (1974), 'Drinking and Inebriate Behavior in the Admiralty Islands', *Ethos* 2 (3): 213–31.

Segal, Boris M. (1990), *The Drunken Society: Alcohol Abuse and Alcoholism in the Soviet Union*, New York: Hippocrene Books.

Škála, Jaroslav (1970), 'Czechoslovakia's Response to Alcoholism', in Elizabeth D. Whitney (ed.), *World Dialogue on Alcohol and Drug Dependence*, Boston: Beacon Press, pp. 90–115.

Smetana, Bedřich (1982) [1866], *Prodaná nevesta* [*The Bartered Bride*], libretto by Karel Sabina, programme notes by František Bartoš in English, French and German and libretto in Czech with translations, Prague: Supraphon.

Starci na Chmelu (1964), feature film, Czech Republic, director: Ladislav Rychman, screenplay and lyrics by Vratislav Blažek, © 1964 Filmové studio Barrandov, distributed by Filmexport Home Video, s.r.o.

ÚZIS [Ústav zdravotnických informaci a statistiky České republiky – Institute of Health Information and Statistics of the Czech Republic, URL: *www.uzis.cz*] (1998a), *Aktuální Informace (AI) č. 67: Psychiatrická Péče v Psychiatrických Lůžkových Zařízeních ČR v Roce 1995 a 1996*, Prague January.

—— (1998b), *Aktuální Informace (AI) č. 67: Psychiatrická Péče v Psychiatrických Lůžkových Zařízeních ČR v Roce 1997*, Prague, 7 December.

—— (2001), *Aktuální Informace (AI) č. 41: Zdravotně Riziková Konzumace Alkoholu v ČR (Srovnání Šetření HIS CR 1999, CIDI 1999 a Studie SZÚ 1996)*, Prague, 10 July.

—— (2002a), *Aktualní Informace (AI) č. 57: Hospitalizování v Psychiatrických Lůžkových Zařízeních CR v Roce 2001*, Prague, 3 December.

—— (2002b), *Aktualní Informace (AI) č. 9: Šetření Zdravotního Stavu České Populace (EUROHIS 2001) Díl XI.: Spotřeba Alkoholu*, Prague, 22 February.

Walker, Caroline and E. D. Baxter (2000), 'Health-promoting Ingredients in Beer', *Technical Quarterly, Master Brewers Association of the Americas* 37 (2): 301–5.

Zíbrt, Čeněk (1910), *Řády a Práva Starodávných Pijanských Čechu a Družstev Kratochvilných v Zemích Českých (Příloha Časopisu "Sládek" Neodvislého Týdenníku Pivovarského, Ročník Druhý)*, Prague: Knihtiskárna V. Kotrba.

–5–

Drunk and (Dis)Orderly
Norwegian Drinking Parties in the Home

Pauline Garvey

Alcohol is traditionally a salient category in defining state intervention in Norwegian public life and provides an interesting case study to question the ways in which individual transgression becomes normative. This chapter focuses on how state measures regarding alcohol are appropriated by a group of young working-class adults in the Norwegian town of Skien. Taking an example of state literature and policy, and a case study of a drinking party (or *vorspiel*), I find an emphasis on healthy drinking as being underpinned by ideas of collectivity and by group responsibility for individual consumption. I start by examining a local assumption that drunkenness is characterized by introspection, fantasy and alternate ways of being, which, when taken to extremes, can lead to social pathologies: for example the alcoholic is frequently portrayed as the lone drinker. What this perspective overlooks is the social role of transgression.

The chapter begins by giving an overview of the issue of alcohol in Norway before examining the more detailed case study of drinking behaviour in Skien. This is then followed by a discussion of strategies undertaken by county and state agencies in combating the threat of youth drinking and responsible retailing, and concludes by drawing parallels between Durkheim's analysis of social influences as the lynchpin of extreme individualized action, such as suicide (Warde 1994), and individualized consumption, such as drunkenness. As in other forms of consumption, drunkenness is characterized by individualized choice but is frequently found to be constrained by group pressures and 'indicative of high levels of integration into collective cultures' (Warde 1994: 884). Drunkenness plays on these same qualities in defining normative transgression, and bolstering group equality through a play on individualism.

There is a tenacious link between alcohol consumption and the forms of sociality it engenders. This has largely to do with the framework through which alcohol is perceived and the relatively strict conventions that surround its consumption. In Norway alcohol provides the interface for both social and anti-social behaviour. It is accepted as a social lubricant and a ubiquitous presence at house parties. Conversely it is concomitantly perceived as a channel for social disarray and disorder. Saglie and Nordlund (1993) argue that underpinning the political debate surrounding alcohol in

Norway lies a tension between liberalism and restriction, or balancing individual freedom and collective responsibility. The main principle in Norwegian alcohol policy is that the state will have chief responsibility for the importation, production and trade of alcohol, although individual provinces have a certain autonomy in being able to decide what alcoholic drinks are allowed to be sold. The active, political discouragement of alcohol is also attempted through heavy taxation and local and national sales restrictions (Saglie 1996: 309), the ban on advertising strong beers, wines and spirits since 1975 (Hauge 1986), and, in common with American experience, a period of Prohibition in the early twentieth century. Nordic Protestantism and the Temperance Movement actively campaigned against alcohol consumption, and Gusfield argues that only in Finland, Norway and Sweden have anti-alcohol movements been as politically salient as in the United States, where alcohol has remained a 'dangerous commodity' (1996: 62), a medium of social control and resistance. When legitimate consumption norms are breached, he argues, the resulting behaviour is cause for 'disapproval, ridicule, and more punishing sanctions' (Gusfield 1996: 62).

In the Norwegian public sphere alcohol is heavily patrolled in state licensing restrictions and availability, as well as limited exposure to alcohol advertising. Through this medium, therefore, one finds a particular relationship posited between the citizen and the Norwegian state in which the state takes an active role in regulating the collective effects of alcohol consumption. One finds this regulation in numerous examples ranging from actual restriction of alcohol to directives and policies informing the public of drinking's inherent dangers. Informants respond to these measures with both support and condemnation. For example, Saglie and Nordlund (1993: 44) report an increasingly liberal attitude towards the sale of wine and, to a lesser degree, spirits in supermarkets rather than in the state Vinmonopol (monopoly), but this attitude shows a strong correlation with factors such as age, gender and education. Also small-scale production of home-brewed liquor is still a long-standing practice in many communities, despite its illegality.

In keeping with MacAndrew and Edgerton's (1969) point that the experience and enactment of drunkenness is culturally learned, and that drinking practices are contextually embedded, drinking in Norway involves a consideration of the marked separation between public and private spheres. Gullestad (1991a: 488) argues that 'the intimacy of the home contrasts sharply with the impersonality of the outside world'. It is the place where many people feel they can exercise control and is the last bastion against the bureaucracy and lack of personal engagement which characterize the public sphere (Gullestad 1991a: 488). Alcohol consumption enhances this distinction because it is temporally and spatially framed. My informants drink little during the week, and then usually at home and in the evenings. In contrast to this domestic restraint, socializing on Friday or Saturday nights is more uproarious, starting often with heavy drinking in a private home, and then moving from there to a pub or night club. Conventional minimal lingering in public spaces is often reversed when drunken socializing overflows into the town centre. In addition to individual sauntering from pub to pub, groups of young people chat and linger on street corners. Drunken teenagers congregate at unlikely spots such as the local bus station, and male youths circuit the town in loud vehicles. Of the various night-spots in Skien. most are defined by the generational differences of their clientele. My informants go to one or two pubs, their parents and parents' friends to others, some with live music or disco. The movement and progression of people from the private to public sphere enhances the impression of drinking as spectacle. Strangers are more easily approached and the transition from the disciplined behaviour of the home to the greater freedom of the social arena is underlined. In such a setting Gullestad notes that the common Norwegian code of modesty is not the norm. Conventional expectations of sameness and reticence do not apply in exceptional circumstances involving, for example, sport competitions and heavy alcohol consumption. 'Intoxicated Norwegians become louder and more generous than they are when sober; they also become more bragging and quarrelsome' (1991b: 11). Sobriety, by contrast is more usually characterized by a 'central value' of equality, convention and integration in which 'Norwegians are no less interested in recognition than others, but for them an initiative to attain recognition must be inscribed in the ideal of sameness' (1991b: 10). Social boundaries – which influence with whom, where and why one socializes – often play on these values of being equal and being the same.

In the Nordic countries, we are told, there is a perception that individuals are citizens because people are similar to each other socially, ethnically and religiously (Stenius 1997: 161). Egalitarianism takes this route in Norway because it represents a mix of consensus and sameness. Yet 'equality' is not incompatible with independence, nor is freedom incompatible with conformity (Gullestad 1991b; Stenius 1997). Under the rubric of equality lie values of conformity and individualism that are maintained through 'social boundaries' (Gullestad 1991b). Emphasis on equality has implications for social distancing, for being the same or drawing distinctions between difference. But symbolic boundaries appear to get blurred with alcohol consumption, where normative expectations of modesty or order are contradicted. Berggreen (1989; cf. Cohen-Kiel 1993) has suggested that sameness achieves its salience through its visibility. I argue that the same emphasis on visibility applies to drunken comportment. For my informants to be drunk is to be seen to be drunk. The question posed therefore is to what degree do state measures that emphasize the importance of parental and peer influence, thereby bolstering social values of sameness, find expression in drinking parties amongst a group of young people in Skien?

Anthropological scholarship has illustrated that 'alcohol can be fundamentally important in producing and maintaining cohesion within a community', but that 'at the same time that it enhances social solidarity, it produces social demarcation and division' (Hunt and Satterlee 1986: 523). As a medium portrayed by the state as dangerous and disruptive, drunkenness might be expected to challenge normative categories of sameness and equality; however, I found the means by which alcohol is consumed or intoxication performed to be of greater relevance to my informants.

Exposure to alcohol is subject to state patrol, yet there appears a greater public acceptance of drunken behaviour. One can see this at weekend house parties; as guests prepare to leave and make their way to Skien night clubs, they gather coats and shoes and reassemble their belongings, hurriedly consuming unfinished beer before leaving the house. A few stray bottles might be taken and finished during the walk into town: 'Drink it on the way,' I'm told, 'it'll keep you warm.' As we approach the centre, the bottles pose a problem and are deposited in dark corners along the way. 'You can get as drunk as you like,' one laughs, 'but hide the bottle – you might get a ticket.'

The Ethnographic Context

Sørhaug (1996: 184) argues that in Norwegian society alcohol is most commonly employed to mark times as special: weekends, festivals, holidays, parties and other occasions such as the beginning of new love or friendship. But when confined to these forums, drinking can be both heavy and intense and almost ritualistic in its departure from the profane routines of daily life. In this respect my informants are no different. The material on which this chapter is based is the result of sixteen months fieldwork during 1997/8 in the town of Skien, in south-east Norway. The region in which Skien is situated, Grenland, is host to the largest concentration of industry in Norway and has a population of 100,000 – half of whom reside in Skien. Vike (1996: 4) describes the town as characterized by a 'relatively high dependence on industry, a proletarian social structure and a comparatively high rate of unemployment'. With a population of 49,000, Skien is considered the capital of Telemark and is the eleventh largest town in Norway.

The people I describe live in the town centre or on its outskirts; they are in their mid-twenties, and are predominantly childless. Employment responsibilities in shops, services and factories around the town confine socializing in the public sphere to Friday and Saturday nights, when heavy drinking is the norm. This pattern of behaviour is, I am told by informants, rare for individuals with children, and for that reason is more characteristic of teenagers or twenty-somethings. Consumption of alcohol and drunkenness have temporal and spatial qualities for my informants, separating work from leisure, and day from night. Similarly, weekend drinking is highly regularized and is salient in marking the boundary between ordinary weekday routine and the specialness of the weekend. Because alcohol consumption is characterized by drinking on occasions that are delimited from work and everyday life, irregular drinking is perceived as unusual or even threatening (cf. Sande 1996: 302). The importance of conforming to normative drinking habits may have some connection with predictability as an idiom for social action. In different forms predictability is demanded of the social and material world and was continuously stressed by my informants throughout my fieldwork. This observation equally applies to drunkenness. Sande (1996: 302) argues that irregular intoxication is often perceived as a sign of illness or social problems. Amongst my informants it is unusual to socialise during the week, and casual visits to the pub during the day, as one might find elsewhere in Europe, are unheard of. The *vorspiel* or drinking party is one of few occasions to meet friends on a weekly basis and it thus represents an important opportunity to foster social ties.

While work has been conducted on school-leavers (Sande 2000, 2001), youth (cf. Henriksen and Sande 1995) and marginalized groups in Norway (Sande 1996), my interest lies in a more 'ordinary' body of individuals who illuminate both the particular and the general in Norwegian society. The regular participants in the *vorspiel* I studied numbered fifteen in total, although during sixteen months of fieldwork I interviewed fifty-eight people.[1] My informants predominantly live in a working-class part of the town; they are largely unmarried and childless, yet have permanent jobs in local factories or the service industry. Whilst representing specific tastes of individuals, their experience is more mainstream than marginal and illustrates not only age-specific, class-based practice but also how general processes in Norwegian society are manifest in a sector of that society. All fifteen were interviewed in their own homes during the course of my fieldwork, but it was through the weekly drinking parties that household predictability and disorder came under focus. 'Drinking' is not the only source of transgression in Norway, but it does provide a medium for a particular genre of behaviour which is both controlled and understood. One site where this play on routine and disorder, on private and public behaviour and introspection versus collective abandon, takes place is through the drinking party – or *vorspiel* – in the home.

Alcohol and Anomie

Alcohol drives a particular and frequently contradictory social dynamic. Whereas in moderate measures it is seen as fuelling and facilitating social relationships, drunkenness, on the other hand, is often equated with anti-social behaviour: with individualism, narcissism or anomie. This perspective is illustrated, Gusfield (1996: 4) argues, in the corpus of social research that has traditionally approached alcohol use as a 'social problem'. Similarly, in his analysis of the anthropological study of alcohol use, Heath (1987) points to 'cross-cultural' issues relating to 'power-theory', 'anomie' and 'dependence'. He notes that, up to the 1980s, studies of alcohol were dominated by biological and medical specialists who were more interested in the effects rather than the uses of alcohol (1987: 36). In the social sciences the emphasis has changed, however. Douglas (1987) claims, for example, that the value of an anthropological approach is that the discipline brings several new challenges to assumptions made about alcohol. For instance, anthropologists might dispute the view that alcohol leads to anomie, or suggest that a state of anomie leads to alcoholism rather than stems from it. Similarly, Douglas suggests that anthropologists find no clear relation between the use of alcohol and a tendency to aggressive or criminal behaviour. Instead of codifying it as deviance, she argues that drinking is essentially a social act. She thus expounds the merits of assuaging 'the perspective of sociological and medical writers, whose focus is so strongly upon personal degradation of individual alcoholics' (1987: 14).

While Douglas may contest academic assumptions made about the causes and effects of drunkenness, informant descriptions often imply that alcohol consumption encourages certain behaviour, or that rational capabilities and inhibitions are dulled to give imagination, desire and fantasy free reign. Drunkenness is frequently linked with certain forms of anti-social behaviour. As Gullestad (1991b: 11) argues, 'Norwegian drinking patterns traditionally imply no drinking most of the time, but very heavy drinking once in a while, usually during the weekends.' And while she characterizes sobriety as premised on an ideal of sameness, heavy alcohol consumption elicits a different form of interaction. When discussing their experience of drunkenness, my informants describe being 'weepy', overly sentimental, excited, happy or giddy when drunk. Others become belligerent and argumentative, while others again behave in a 'crazy' way. Descriptions centre on behaving in an uncharacteristic fashion, or alternatively in a manner that is more akin to one's 'true' self. The *vorspiel* represents a time and space given to abandon, play or possibly transgression, and provides an appropriate outlet for this form of expression. In addition to its temporal and spatial separation from routinized daily life, a parallel connection is also often drawn between drunkenness as a departure from the community of drinkers into the consciousness of oneself, focusing on uninhibited self-expression. The Norwegian anthropologist Tian Sørhaug, for example, contends that drunkenness is a medium through which one explores alternative identities. It provides a means of moving into a community while also moving out of it (1996: 185). Weakening inhibitions, nausea, diminished personal control, aggressive or violent behaviour or changes in personality are cited as symptoms of over-consumption according to the Directorate for Health and Social Affairs, Department for Alcohol and Drugs.[2] The chief medical officer of the Blue Cross Centre advises of the transformative qualities of alcohol that may be drawn upon as an excuse or buffer to deflect criticism: a talkative person might become more talkative, a controlled person may become impulsive, and an individual who shows verbal aggression while sober might permit himself violence (Fekjær 1994: 4). In cases such as these, he argues, blame is often more lenient as a result of the mitigating factor of alcohol. Fekjær warns that this way of thinking is based on the supposition that when inebriated, one is not fully aware or in control of one's actions and therefore is not entirely responsible. In studies of deviant behaviour, therefore, guilt is frequently attributed to intoxication for a variety of actions; often the more stigmatized the behaviour, the more guilt is attributed to the influence of alcohol. It is therefore no surprise that alcohol may be framed as an 'alibi' for action (Fekjær 1994: 2). Alcohol here is presented as a substance that relaxes social or personal inhibitions and enhances ways of being that are otherwise subdued.

In agreement with this position, participants in the *vorspiel* repeat similar ideas of alcohol-induced behaviour. Crimes of passion have been explained, if not justified, by the contributing factor of alcohol that unleashes a volatile nature, undeterred by social confines or cognizance of consequences. This perspective is evident in a conversation I had with Eva and her friends about a case where a 15-year-old boy had killed a 17-year-old at an unsupervised party. We will return to Eva and her friends for a fuller discussion below, but it is noteworthy that when the women were talking about the episode, they imagined how the boy might feel: 'at that age they don't know what they are doing when they are drunk. Think how he feels now, sitting in jail and realizing that he has killed someone,' argued one. The others agreed and speculated that jealousy had something to do with the incident. A third woman commented: 'If he wasn't drunk I wouldn't have any sympathy for him, but if he was drunk it wasn't in cold blood like, it is probably only now that he realizes what he did and feels guilty about the guy he killed and the family and everything.'

State sources place emphasis on the 'individualization' of alcohol consumption, primarily framed as 'losing control', but also inherent in the danger of drinking alone. I would rather perceive individual performances as inspired and driven by collective action. To illustrate this point, I draw on the work of Émile Durkheim. Durkheim's (1951) discussion of suicide is a classic text on the connection between individual acts and social regulation. Based on an analysis of the way in which social bonds become weakened in modern societies, his work has immediate relevance to the study of deviance and social pathology. According to a Durkheimian perspective, a transgressive act driven by exaggerated introspection can find its source to a large degree in external social causes. Similarly, alcohol in its destructive role represents social disorder, in which 'all proscribed actions are threats to the existence of the norm' (Gusfield 1996: 174). Not only does drunkenness represent norm violation, but it also carries some of the stigma associated with the modern age, in which social solidarity is broken down by individual impulses. Accordingly, egoism and anomie signify for Durkheim the relative absence of social goals and social regulation, but are actually themselves products of modern forms of society and modern belief systems (Lukes 1985: 218). Alcohol consumption as an individualistic exercise holds some analogies with Durkheim's analysis of suicide. Like other forms of consumption, drinking is risky (cf. Warde 1994 for discussion). It is particularly risky because consumers are acting as individuals; they are exercising choice and expressing freedom. Of specific interest here is the connection between Durkheim's anomie as a socially induced state, and anomie as a state induced by heavy drinking. Like other forms of consumption, excessive drinking is often associated with excessive individualism but differs in the respect that it is subject to particular social restrictions monitoring its availability and visibility. This is particularly the case in Norway, where it has been argued that 'stable norms which all citizens share and for which all citizens have a similar responsibility' stand as a basic ideal of society (Gullestad 1991b: 14). This emphasis on 'stable norms' not only describes a social morality, but also contrasts with an American view of society which eulogizes 'mobile competition between equal individuals' (Gullestad 1991b: 14). Alcohol is a medium through which state intervention and regulation, consumer freedom versus citizen responsibility, come into focus. Norwegian national policy on alcohol remains one of the most restrictive in Europe (Saglie 1996: 309), and while advertising alcohol and drinking in public (in non-licensed premises) is banned, and therefore preferably 'unseen', drunkenness is very visible.

Although alcohol in the public sphere is heavily patrolled, in the private domain it is defined in terms of its sociality. Drinking alcohol is laudable, permissible or understandable depending on how it is framed, whether it is an amelioration of an intimate atmosphere or sense of fun rather than drinking for its own sake. The first signal for worry is the occasion of anti-social drinking. As it is understood and experienced by my informants, correct or healthy drinking is consumed in the company of friends. In addition to crossing from order to disorder, drunkenness marks an inversion of conventional group dynamics. Behaviour increasingly flies in the face of domestic etiquette as individual antics compete for attention. Routine gives way to rupture and impulse, and compliance gives way to challenge. Modesty or reticence may be replaced with flirtation and sexual innuendo. However, in order to appreciate the significance of drunken behaviour in the home, one must first place it in the context of sobriety.

Control and Disorder: The 'Club' and the *Vorspiel*

In Skien one finds a highly developed public sphere where both men and women are active in procuring employment outside the home and young children are accommodated through a network of state-run and private kindergartens. In addition to this, one finds a heightened form of home-centredness, one expression of which is found in the maintenance of domestic boundaries and through stated values such as privacy and predictability. In the following section I will compare two highly differential modes of domestic sociality in order to throw the latter, the *vorspiel*, into relief. The first represents one method of negotiating boundaries of domestic seclusion and access through the organization of 'clubs'. 'Clubs' – comprising, for example, sewing clubs, wine-tasting clubs, baby clubs – refers to a group of individuals who meet monthly on a prearranged evening. The club meets in a participant's home and eats small snacks while catching up on the latest news, or sharing common interests. These meetings often take place on weekday evenings and do not generally include alcohol or late nights, except for exceptional circumstances such as Christmas celebrations. Traditionally needlework might have been a focus for 'sewing-clubs', but more recently meetings can focus on any pastime. Clubs can vary, and one might be involved in several simultaneously, one for staying in touch with old friends, another for hobbies, craftwork, and so on. According to Skien informants, clubs are female-dominated but are relevant for most age groups and may, unusually, include children. Tine, a single mother of a young child, relies heavily on this arrangement and explained it thus: 'People like to keep a certain distance and when we arrange to meet once a month, it is easier than ringing two weeks in advance before calling in. Otherwise it would be too difficult to come into contact, we wouldn't meet otherwise . . . .' The club represents an occasion for group socializing that takes place in the home and is usually alcohol-free, unless it is a wine-tasting club. This system allows participants to meet and socialize within the home without the fear of imposing on or interrupting family life, and each member shoulders the responsibility for hosting the meeting in turn.

The popularity of such arrangements vary but in Skien this mode of socializing is widely popular. Eva, whom we will describe more fully in the following section, was occasionally involved in clubs of this type that included old friends from the neighbourhood. She had a small flat that occupied the upper part in a privately owned house, and consisted of one bedroom, a kitchen, a bathroom and living room which she kept immaculately clean. During these meetings she professed to be extreme in her maintenance of order – everything has to be in its place. Even when eating from a box of chocolates, she hates to see the gaps in the tray: 'if there is a space in the middle, I keep looking at the gap and it gets on my nerves.'

The club provides a convenient way of controlling access to the home without appearing to do so. Membership of a club allows both social and private needs to be facilitated: the householder maintains control of home socializing without being impolite or denying the needs of others as well as one's own. The club is an efficient socializing tool for Eva, and one that also conforms to her need for order and predictability. 'I hate disorder, I couldn't take mess even if it was just for a weekend while I was redecorating. I know I am paranoid, I think it is untidy now because there is a jumper on the chair and some books on the chest of drawers.' Eva is extreme in her maintenance of domestic order, yet she accentuates features that are articulated to varying degrees by others. However, perhaps surprisingly, she also participates in the *vorspiel*, a social milieu that is the inverse of the routine, order and gender exclusivity that characterize club socializing.

The *Vorspiel*: Eva

The *vorspiel* takes place ideally on a Saturday night, and as a rule is followed by a trip to a pub or night club. Occasionally the party continues through the night and is termed the *nachspiel*. The general routine of the vorspiel is to start drinking in the early evening, approximately 7.00 p.m., until one is 'ready' to go into town at 11.00 or 11.30 p.m. The next venue is, as a rule, a familiar designated place, although arrival there is commonly punctuated by several breaks in the journey to check that one is not missing anything (or anyone) more exciting somewhere else.

Eva was 25 years old, lived alone and was unemployed when I first met her. Usually up to fifteen people attended her parties, depending on the importance of the occasion and the availability or inclination of her friends. Her flat, however, lacked seating for more than twelve people. To describe one such evening, when I was present, Eva had invited six friends. Most of these were settled in the town, working in local factories or state services. One couple present had children (who were with a childminder at home that evening), the rest were single and childless and the ages of those present ranged from early twenties to early thirties. Without the responsibilities of children, couples were able to socialize together, whilst for others, individuals could negotiate childcare with partners.

The *vorspiel* is usually preceded by considered calculation as to how much one will drink during a party, followed by a trip to the supermarket to purchase mainstream beers (up to 4.76 per cent alcohol content) or to an outlet of the State Wine-Monopoly for strong beers (5–7 per cent alcohol), wine or spirits. A price catalogue is available on entering and one queues in line to reach a counter. Smartly dressed men and women behind the counter fetch the bottles one chooses from the catalogue, one pays and the line moves up. One must be aged 18 to buy beers and wines and 20 to purchase spirits. Later, on arrival at the party, people first find some room in the refrigerator for their beer, carefully distinguishing their own from the others, while small savouries are placed in bowls and spread on the coffee table. Drinking is highly individualized; there is no pooling or sharing of drinks in parties, no 'round' system in pubs and bars. Each individual caters for his/her own consumption. My expectations of pooling drinks in *vorspiels* and dinner-parties initially led to embarrassing mistakes on my part when I first arrived in Norway.

The drinking starts immediately, the chatting is excited but calm and candles are lit. Most guests talk quietly in twos and threes and catch up on the latest events which have occurred during the week. After a short period people begin to get lively, the small tête-à-têtes break down to include everyone present. Common joking and singing gradually replace the former whispered conversations. As the group becomes livelier, the mood changes dramatically; guests get restless and occasionally group dancing adds to the atmosphere. The music is changed and the volume increased while small light-hearted quarrels break out regarding music preferences. 'War' is declared over the music differences and bottle tops and corks are aimed at the 'enemy'. Folk music might be played to add to the hilarity of the occasion and people get up to strut to it. Equally popular is Norwegian party music; animation reaches a peak with songs such as 'I'm Gonna Make Money from My Body', accompanied by more strutting and dancing.

During the party, humour breaks boundaries. Eva is known for the strict orderliness which she maintains in her flat but, nevertheless, bottle caps may be thrown around the room. Dancing marks the climax of the party and often this is used as an excuse to exhibit oneself in front of the others. A few might stand in line and parade their impromptu dance routines to the cheers and directions of the others. Hilarity is fostered by drawing on familiar objects and making the ordinary seem suddenly strange and impulsive. Guests vie for attention, with animated bravado, such as performing for the group, who cheer them on.

The *vorspiel* allows the display of certain behaviour which is not permitted during 'normal' life. Former shyness and self-consciousness are traded in for gregariousness and attention-seeking. People begin to speak English to me, which is significant as I was often told by informants 'I can speak English, I choose not to in front of my friends as I would feel stupid and I don't want them to witness it.' The changeover occurs with intoxication and insistence on speaking English, which suggests to me an enhanced self-confidence. In distinction to the everyday, guests compete for attention and revel in collective abandon. The influence of alcohol allows both men and women some lee-way which might be less acceptable in different circumstances. However, despite small indiscretions, and the transgressive antics described above, control is maintained within the group. Drinking is not mixed with driving, for example, and even at the height of the *vorspiel*, drunken driving or drug use is not countenanced.

Small misdemeanours become more frequent with a weakening of inhibitions and social restraints. Social boundaries are crossed with relative impunity. Strangers who might be unapproachable can suddenly share a joke or engage in a laugh; party-goers might don wigs or joke-shop masks while Eva's friend Per might walk into town in his girlfriend's high heels. This licence is often contained through the collective environment, and that which is unconventional is rendered safe or unchallenged. Per was known for his erratic drunken behaviour, but was excused and managed within the protective arena of the *vorspiel*. This protectiveness frequently fell apart after the party and on arrival in the town centre, however, where he frequently wandered aimlessly, and was often unaware of his movements the next day.

Drinking parties are organized along a relatively defined set of expectations of how the evening should unfold. The consumption of alcohol and the experience of some form of abandon is common. In losing control, the individual is seen as sharing part of themselves with those present, they are turning themselves 'inside out' (Sørhaug 1996: 184). To become drunk in company therefore demands or creates a bond of trust between the participants, even if this is of a temporary or superficial nature. In turn, social drunkenness is patrolled by the group. This is evident in the group dynamics of the drinking party.

The *vorspiel* is organized with a central focus in mind. Chairs are placed around a large central coffee table, usually with a sofa on one side, and participants sit in a circle. Bottles of beer are placed in the refrigerator or wine bottles are put on the table, while the host or hostess provides glasses and snacks. As drinking proceeds, the group faces one another and talking moves from the individual to the group. The volume of alcohol consumed is visible – one can count the empty beer bottles in front of each person or gauge how much wine is left. As the evening progresses, one can calculate roughly the number of bottles consumed by each person. On one occasion

Kari, a friend of Eva's, complained because she was tricked as to how much another guest, Tor, was drinking. On this occasion Tor seemed sober, but, when questioned, he claimed that he was drinking 'spirits'. The bottle of mineral water in front of him therefore was considered to be a cocktail he had mixed earlier. Later, when it was found that he had left the party and driven home, it was realized that he had lied about his drinking earlier. Kari complained bitterly about this deceit.

As a certain point in the evening, the group inevitably prepares to move on to a night club or pub in the town centre and guests absentmindedly search for coats and shoes. Friends and siblings arrive suddenly in cars to ferry party-goers to town night-spots. Soon after leaving the house the group dissipates, as individuals move to their favoured destination and occasionally, almost by chance, meet up with the *vorspiel* company later during the evening. A group of friends drifts to a popular night-spot. Soon after, one might say 'come on we're going for a walk', and we proceed to make a brief reconnaissance tour of nearby pubs and clubs. Such venues, numbering fewer than a dozen, were all within a short walking distance and the explanation for this excursion was 'to look for the others'. 'The others' meanwhile eventually drift and wander to conduct their own tours. We pass each other on the street, wave and continue, eventually retracing our steps back to the original location.

Sexual innuendo may become more explicit with drunkenness. Romantic over-tures are initiated and negotiated or relationships terminated during such evenings. Flirtation too is frequently foregrounded. Tor and Jenny, for example, are a married couple who are employed in a local hotel. Both work long hours, and are teased by their friends for Tor's exacting organization of their home routine. During weekend evenings, however, they have a lively social life and attend many of Eva's parties. And on Saturday nights, after an evening party, both are known for flirtatious behaviour, with Tor playfully checking out his female companions, while Jenny boasts of exchanging numbers with barmen, bouncers or DJs in local night clubs. Friends comment on this but excuse them: '[Tor] does things like he might feel my ass, or if he was giving me money he would try and put it in my bra and I would threaten him, in a funny way', one explains. Tor and Jenny only flirt when they are drunk, it is pointed out, and a certain degree of risqué behaviour – within recognized limits – is accepted. And while flirtation is codified within the same parameters as stepping outside routine, or as a sign of how Tor and Jenny would like to 'really be', the couple maneouvre around their small indiscretions by teasing each other when amongst friends, and routinely socializing separately.

The vorspiel can be interpreted as a cathartic exercise whereby individuals are provided with a channel for abandon or play. Central issues here include those of disorder, challenge and collective transgression as situated within a domestic setting. Conventionally the public sphere is associated with excitement and danger (Gullestad 1984). Through the performance of drunkenness, many values pertaining to home, such as control, security and order, are inverted. This process of 'inversion', however, can be interpreted in differing ways. First, inversion can be seen as a form of transposition whereby the norms of domesticity are overturned in an act of rebellion. As we see in the case study, domestic order can be thrown into disarray during parties. Daily routine becomes domestic clutter as participants become increasingly animated. A second interpretation disentangles associations of control and order and suggests that while disorder is the rule for parties, it is mediated through control by the host/hostess, and surveillance by the group. Drinking alone, on the other hand, has very different connotations. We can see this when we compare the example of the *vorspiel* with a previously mentioned member of the group, Per, who is often anti-social in his drinking habits and consequently perceived as having a 'drinking problem'.

Per was 25 years old and lived alone when I first met him. He was part of Eva's social circle and, as fieldwork progressed, concerns about him mounted. Per's socializing typically revolved around drinking parties and night clubs, and while this was accepted by his friends, it was when he began to drink heavily while alone at home that his circle started to allude to his 'drinking problem'. For example, during Christmas festivities he was accused of a run of missed appointments and abrupt changes of plans. On Christmas Day he responded to a party invitation by suggesting that he would drink at home first and wait to sober up before he arrived. It was no surprise when he didn't appear that evening. This predilection for lone drinking not only distinguished Per from his friends but also represented a crucial difference between 'normal' and 'abnormal' drinking practices. As we have seen in the case study, the consumption of alcohol carries with it an accepted anticipation of action and behaviour. Consequently Per's anti-social drinking suggested 'uncontrolled' and 'uncontrollable' to his friends. The individualism exhibited by Per is qualitatively different from that of the drinking party, where individual exhibition is paraded, and celebrated by group recognition. Per's rejection of social consumption in preference to solitary intoxication was sufficient to cause concern for his perceived problem and fears that his drinking habits were spiralling out of control.

Drinking in company is a double-edged sword. Although issues of control and the importance of peer or parental influence emerge in state policy regarding alcohol consumption, one also finds that individual behaviour welcomes imitation, that drinking, in short, is contagious. It is to this that I turn next.

Alcohol Policy, Drinking as Performance and Being Seen

As I have argued, conventional emphasis on healthy drinking frames alcohol as a collective medium; it is most usually enjoyed as an appurtenance to socializing with its effects extending beyond the individual in reaching a variety of social spheres. So while informants talk of drunkenness as an illustration of relaxed inhibitions, abandonment or confident self-expression, nevertheless sameness, consensus and equality emerge in unexpected ways. In much the same way as correct drinking takes place in a group, state measures proffered to contain consumption are also codified in terms of the collective and normative.

The most important tool in the control of alcohol is the A/S Vinmonopol(et) or State Wine-Monopoly, which was first established in 1922. This State Wine-Monopoly imports and controls the sale of spirits, wine and strong beers, while beers of a lesser alcohol content are available in supermarkets. In addition to controlling the availability of spirits and wines, these beverages are subject to high taxes in order to further discourage consumption. The A/S Vinmonopolet is one of three agencies dedicated to alcohol research and intervention, the remaining two being the Rusmiddeldirektoratet (Norwegian Directorate for the Prevention of Alcohol and Drug Problems) and the Statens Institutt for Alkohol og Narkotika-Forskning (National Institute for Alcohol and Drug Research). These agencies come under the aegis of the Ministry of Health and Social Affairs, which is responsible for national alcohol policy (except taxation) and has general responsibility for the secondary prevention and treatment of alcohol- and drug-related problems. According to this body, the sale of alcohol in Norway is low in comparison with other European countries: the annual registered *sales* of alcohol in Norway per inhabitant (pure litres of alcohol) in 1994 was 4.74 litres of alcohol. By comparison, in Ireland the estimated average *consumption* of alcohol for those over 15 years old was 11.23 litres of pure alcohol (National Alcohol Policy, Ireland). Nonetheless, consumption of alcohol in Norway has been increasing since 1993. In addition, large quantities of non-registered alcohol are consumed, such as alcohol illegally produced or imported from trips abroad. To counter this, and to assuage the rising evidence of drug abuse, the government issued White Paper no. 58, 'Plan of Action for Reducing the Use of Intoxicating Substances' in 1998 (Policy on Intoxicating Substances, Sosial- og Helsegdepartment). The intention of this initiative was to reduce the total consumption of alcohol and to minimize the use of illicit drugs. It also aimed to help integrate a number of measures, the most important of which are to establish a 'Drug and Alcohol Advisory Council' in order to make society more knowledgeable about the use and abuse of various intoxicants and to increase collaboration with schools and parents. In order to accomplish this objective, it draws on agencies such as the National Directorate for the Prevention of Alcohol and Drug Problems, which is concerned with the coordination of governmental work on alcohol and drug matters, and the promotion of education and information activities, including advisory activities to public authorities. As well as granting licences for the import, export and trade of alcohol, the directorate is responsible for 'initiating countrywide information measures and campaigns to influence peoples' attitudes and behaviour towards the use of drugs and alcohol'. This includes production and distribution of information material (*Social- og Helsedirektoratet*). Their most recent campaigns include a project in the city of Bergen involving the cooperation of local restaurants, hotels and night-spots in a campaign to target alcohol-related violence through 'responsible retailing'.

A second national campaign targeted parents and the home in order to intervene in teenagers' access to alcohol, as a way to delay the debut age of alcohol consumption. Posters displayed in public centres (e.g. train stations) during the winter of 1999 advised postponing children's alcohol debut and claimed that 'Youths who get alcohol at home, drink more outside' (Rusmiddeldirektoratet). Others illustrated a young teenage girl, and imitating an Absolut Vodka advertisement, stated instead '*Absolutt For Ung*' (Absolutely Too Young) The poster warned:

> The earlier children begin to drink, the more they drink later as teenagers. Those who begin at 13 years old drink on average a half bottle of spirits by 19. That is three times more than those that start at the age of 17. A half of all young people have begun drinking before the age of 15. Do your children belong to this half?

This poster is accompanied by another in which an older woman is illustrated, and is entitled *Absolutt Godtroende* (Absolutely Gullible). In this poster a similar message is recommended:

> During adolescence children experience greater freedom. Ideas of friends and peers become more important. Parents meanwhile continue to have a big influence as role models and norm setters for dealing with adulthood. Drinking alcohol is something that many young people associate with becoming an adult. An early alcohol debut leads to greater consumption later in teenage years. It also increases the danger of using narcotic drugs. Liberal attitudes and easy access increase the possibility of an early debut. Research Youth-Time in the city by Anders Bakke shows a clear connection between parents' practices and adolescents' own habits.

It continues:

> The more liberal the attitude, the greater the possibility that young people drink every week, that they drink a lot, that they start early and that they end up in difficult situations connected with drinking. Especially high is the consumption of those who often get alcohol at home, even if only for special occasions.
>
> Adults who take a clear stand against alcohol amongst minors are delaying children's alcohol debut. The age restrictions which are applicable in society – 18 years for beer and wine and 20 years for spirits – should be the key guide also at home.

Rather than speaking exclusively to individual consumers, information published by Oslo's Agency for Alcohol and Drug Problems (Oslo Kommune Rusmiddele-taten) emphasizes how an individual has the ability to influence the alcohol habits of others and the obligation to do so. In view of the fact that nine out of ten bottles of beer are drunk in the company of others, it recommends that alcohol consumption is 'contagious'. Posters suggest:

If you drink less, the others will also drink less. In a 'wet' environment there are a lot of big drinkers. IF YOU DRINK LESS, THE OTHERS WILL ALSO DRINK LESS. In a 'drier' environment there are fewer big drinkers. (emphasis in original)

By controlling alcohol, one is patrolling the barricades which confine the menace of social disorder. Recalling Fekjær above, what one does while drunk might bear little correspondence to normal patterns of behaviour, and for this reason alcohol is seen as the catalyst which unleashes this menace. Social conscience is thus threatened by the effects of excess, which increase individual disregard for others. Although drinking parties are not condemned outright, the home is specified as having particular responsibility in framing attitudes to alcohol. The Norwegian Directorate for the Prevention of Alcohol and Drug Problems advises parents on the role of the home in curbing youth consumption, while during Christmas festivities one might see notices in local newspapers warning adults of the disarming effects that inebriation might have on their children. Framed through the eyes of their offspring, the reader is encouraged to empathize with a child who is troubled and confused by the loud, boisterous and excited behaviour of otherwise sedate, responsible adults.

A party and the feelings of expectation and fun which it generates does not begin with the absorption of alcohol into the blood-stream but peaks much earlier, with the purchase of beer or the first sip of wine. Much as drinking practices are contextually embedded, so too is drunkenness. Intoxication in Norway is perceived as the outcome of sociality (Henriksen and Sande 1995: 184), and drinking 'well' has certain performative requirements. The *vorspiel* is defined along certain, predictable criteria. While the state defines alcohol consumption in terms of contagion, a version of this sentiment is played out in the collective antics of my informants. Performance and demonstration act as a kind of containment. Despite the introspective nuances of abandonment, sameness is crucial to the group dynamic. 'Being drunk' implies a certain mode of behaviour in the *vorspiel* that holds a tenuous relation to volumes of alcohol. On a number of occasions, the driver (and non-drinker) of the group would be as obstreperous as the others. On other occasions when Eva or her friends were in a difficult financial situation they explained that they 'could get drunk on very little'. However, while structured or routinized disorder is the norm for the *vorspiel*, lack of control is not. Designated drivers are not pressurized into drinking, and often the number of guests is maintained by the host or hostess. Therefore an essential consideration in defining alcohol as a 'good thing' or a 'bad thing' depends on how it is consumed. As we have seen above, drinking in company, in particular, is emphasized.

Contagious Consumption

Drunkenness in the *vorspiel* is not merely a state of being but a way of interacting; the abandon and gregariousness that expresses this behaviour would be meaningless if not conducted in a group situation. One gets little impression that lone drinking would be accompanied with similar antics of dancing and strutting. The cure for contagion is not isolation but rather its opposite. Whereas drinking in certain public places might be read as resistance, drinking in company is legitimation. Drinking alone, on the other hand, has very different connotations in suggesting that the consumption of alcohol is an end in itself, and, as an extension of that, a form of escapism.

Underpinning Durkheim's work lies a question of normativity, which is equally of relevance in explaining drunken action amongst my informants. For the first part, drunkenness as described above is often characterized as a drift from group aware-ness to an internal introspective state. Durkheim saw that forms of social behaviour are more highly constrained by group pressures than might be immediately recog-nizable. Social bonds can relate the individual to the group or to 'society' in two ways: attaching one to socially given purposes and ideals, and regulating individual desires and purposes (Lukes 1985: 206). Egoism and its opposite, altruism, highlight that which ties an individual to socially given ideals and purposes; anomie highlights that which holds an individual's desires in check, regulating and moderating them. In the example of egoism and anomie one finds society's insufficient presence in individuals, one involving a lack of 'object and meaning in genuine collective activity', the other leaving 'individual passions . . . without a curb to regulate them' (Lukes 1985: 207). Anomie is characterized by being lost in an infinity of desire or passion, no longer recognizing any group bonds. It results from a weakening of an established and accepted normative framework, a weakening which can be affected by economic or conjugal causes. When an individual's social context fails to provide requisite sources of attachment and regulation, then psychological or moral health is impaired (Durkheim 1951: 215).

Drunkenness is perceived as harbouring some of the dangers of anomie. It repre-sents either individual transformation (according to state literature) or intensified personality traits (according to informants), both of which, when taken to extremes, harbour the potential for social disorder. As we have seen, not only does the state seek to check alcohol consumption through various measures, but it also recommends that social patrol should take place on a local level, in the home or during the drinking party. Alcohol-induced passions can have dire consequences, either immediately (as in the case of youth) or later on in life. Therefore social regulation by the group ensures 'healthy' consumption and combats the negative potential of lone drinking. On the face of it, both suicide and drunkenness represent a disengagement from the social body in an exercise of will or 'an individual action' (Lukes 1985: 194). As individualized action, drunkenness is a prime example of 'sticking out' (Gullestad 1996). Cohen-Kiel (1993: 65) suggests that Norwegians prefer to be 'faceless in a crowd' because of their fear of 'doing something embarrassing in public', suggestive of losing control or being different. The person is defined socially with how one 'fits in' with others. Gullestad (1996) equally refers to the fear of 'sticking out' as a common worry in former decades, but less so today. Contrasting with the ambivalence that surrounds public attention, however, drunkenness appears to court and revel in it. Individualism, or 'sticking out' in terms of intensified personality traits, high-spirited antics or heightened feelings, is ascribed to drunkenness, but at the same moment measured and controlled by its performance. As such, drunkenness holds similarities with suicide in representing the individual antithesis of social solidarity, but one in which various social measures can be seen to be at play. In the example of alcohol, we have seen numerous measures advised or imposed by the state and enacted by the group which strive to contain the transgressive aspects of drunken behaviour. Drunkenness represents a form of social interaction and performance through which disorder is routinized, controlled and structured.

Conclusion

Alcohol in Norwegian politics is a controversial issue, and one which draws on a variety of social perspectives. While the state intervenes in the exposure that one has to alcohol, there are nevertheless relatively efficient social networks which manoeuvre around these restrictive mechanisms. As drunken behaviour is framed as socially threatening and thus requiring social regulation, it is perhaps not surprising that it gives rise to themes of both challenge and abandon. But while Gusfield (1996) argues the case for challenge being a facet of drinking in the United States, and while it may be the case for other types of drunken behaviour in Norway, the example of the *vorspiel* points to its opposite. By violating conventional rules of normality, and by transgressing social codes of behaviour, the group redefines itself, assessing its solidarity and forming a coherence. This form of abandon, which is defined, structured and immediately recognizable, is in itself controlled. Through processes such as this, alcohol reaffirms the values of the group. In this way 'licensed' rebellion or rejection of the system can act as the harbinger of its inversion, in a celebration of the existing order (cf. Gluckman 1963).

Disjuncture is exhibited through drunkenness, and therefore could be taken as an inversion of the normative and a challenge to social equality. This is the perspective of state regulation which highlights the destructive influences of alcohol. However, from the study of a group of specific informants, one can see how this medium of transgression reaffirms the normative, rather than challenges it. If, as Gullestad (1991b, 1992) argues, equality as sameness and self-sufficiency are overarching cultural categories in Norwegian social interaction, then it comes as little surprise to find these values underpinning sociopolitical measures to combat alcohol which are mirrored in group activities. The play on disorder is particularly perspicuous in the home, where routine, control and predictability are the norm. However, to look only at conventional living is to present a partial picture of the Norwegian home; the ethnographer must compare what people state as 'normal' living with the actual practice of it, which includes as important features drunkenness and other forms of rule violation. For this reason, while some might readily condemn the antics which I describe, these antics would at least be, to some degree, familiar. Alcohol creates distance and disjuncture, as in the example of the *vorspiel*. These effects are not in defiance of personal and group control but rather bolster it through textured forms of 'not going too far'. This expanded sense of the normative experience of domestic life enables a wider consideration of the relationship between strategies of self-definition and group behaviour, which in Skien span the private and public fields.

Notes

1. All names cited here are pseudonyms.
2. *www.rusinfo.no*

References

Berggreen, B. (1989), *Da Kulturen kom til Norge*, Oslo: H. Aschehoug & Co.

Cohen-Kiel, A. (1993), 'Confessions of an Angry Commuter: Or Learning How to Communicate the Non-Communicating Way', in *Continuity and Change: Aspects of Contemporary Norway*, Oslo: Scandinavian University Press, pp. 55–69.

Douglas, M. (ed.) (1987), *Constructive Drinking: Perspectives on Drink from Anthropology*, Cambridge: Cambridge University Press.

Durkheim, E. (1951), *Suicide: A Study in Sociology*, London: Routledge.

Fekjær, H. O. (1994), *The Psychology of Getting High. www.bks.no*.

Gluckman, M. (1963), *Order and Rebellion in Tribal Africa*, London: Cohen & West.

Gullestad, M. (1984), *Kitchen-table Society: A Case Study of the Family Life and Friendships of Young Working-class Mothers in Urban Norway*, Oslo: Scandinavian University Press.

—— (1991a), 'The Transformation of the Norwegian Notion of Everyday Life', *American Ethnologist* 18 (3): 480–99.

—— (1991b), 'The Scandinavian Version of Egalitarian Individualism', *Ethnologia Scandinavica* 21: 3–18.

—— (1992), *The Art of Social Relations: Essays on Culture, Social Action and Everyday Life in Modern Norway*, Oslo: Scandinavian University Press.

—— (1996), *Everyday Life Philosophers: Modernity, Morality and Autobiography in Norway*, Oslo: Scandinavian University Press.

Gusfield, J. R. (1996), *Contested Meanings: The Construction of Alcohol Problems*, Madison: University of Wisconsin Press.

Hauge, R. (1986), *Alkoholpolitikken i Norge*, Oslo: Statens Edruskapsdirektorat.

Heath, D. B. (1987), 'Anthropology and Alcohol Studies: Current Issues', *Annual Review of Anthropology* 16: 99–120.

Henriksen, Ø. and A. Sande (1995), *Rus: Felleskap og Regulering*, Oslo: Kommune-forlaget.

Hunt, G. and S. Satterlee (1986), 'Cohesion and Division: Drinking in an English Village', *Man* (N. S.) 21 (3): 521–37.

Lukes, S. (1985), *Émile Durkheim: His Life and Work*, Stanford: Stanford University Press.

MacAndrew, C. and R. B. Edgerton (1969), *Drunken Comportment: A Social Explanation*, Chicago: Aldine.

National Alcohol Policy, Ireland, see www.eurocare.org/profiles/irelandsect2.html

Oslo Kommune Rusmiddletaten (Oslo's Agency for Alcohol and Drug problems) *www.rusmiddeletaten.oslo.kommune.no*

Rusmiddeldirectoratet (Norwegian Directorate for the Prevention of Alcohol and Drug Problems), see *www.rusdir.no*

Saglie, J. (1996), 'Attitude Change and Policy Decisions: The Case of Norwegian Alcohol Policy', *Scandinavian Political Studies* 19 (4): 309–27.

Saglie, J. and S. Nordlund (1993), Alkoholpolitikken og Opinionen, *SIFA – National Institute for Alcohol and Drug Research* – Rapport 3/93, Oslo.

Sande, A. (1996), 'Rus som Sekularisert Rituale', *Norsk Antropologisk Tidsskrift* 4: 302–11.

—— (2000), 'Den Norske Russefeiringen: Om Meningen med Rusmiddelbruk Sett Gjennom Russefeiring Som et Ritual', *Nordisk Alkohol- & Narkotikatidskrift* 17 (5–6): 340–53.

—— (2001), Rusens Betydning i Feiringen av Nasjonale Fellesskap', *Dugnad* 27 (1): 43–58.

Sørhaug, T. (1996), *Fornuftens Fantasier: Antropologiske Essays om Moderne Livsformer*, Oslo: Universitetsforlaget.

Sosial- og Helsedepartmentet (Directorate for Health and Social Affairs), Policy on Intoxicating Substances, see *www.odin.dep.no/hd/engelsk/publ/veiledninger/ 030091-120003/index-hov005-n-f-a.html*

Sosial- og Helsedirektoratet, avdeling for rusmidler (Directorate for Health and Social Affairs, Department for Health and Drugs), see: *www.rusdir.no*. For 'responsible retailing' campaign, see *www.rusdir.no/nyhetsarkiv/2001/ansvarlig_ vertskap_bergen.html*

Stenius, H. (1997), 'The Good Life is a Life of Conformity: The Impact of Lutheran Tradition on Nordic Political Culture', in O. Sørensen and B. Stråth (eds), *The Cultural Construction of Norden*, Oslo: Scandinavian University Press, pp. 161–71.

Vike, H. (1996), 'Conquering the Unreal: Political Bureaucracy in a Norwegian Town', unpublished Ph.D thesis, University of Oslo.

Warde, A. (1994), 'Consumption, Identity-Formation and Uncertainty', *Sociology* 28 (4): 877–98.

–6–

Cognac, Beer, Red Wine or Soft Drinks?
Hong Kong Identity and Wedding Banquets

Josephine Smart

A recent survey reports that fewer than four in one hundred people (4 per cent) in Hong Kong drink regularly (New Beverage Publication, Inc. 1998). This finding concurs with the long-standing observations that Chinese are light consumers of alcohol and Chinese populations in China and overseas are relatively free of alcoholism and other forms of alcohol abuse and the associated negative consequences (Singer 1979: 317–20; Legge and Sherlock 1990–91: 632). This low rate of alcohol consumption provides a startling backdrop for the extremely high consumption of cognac in Hong Kong at 15.2 bottles per capita in the mid-1990s, compared to 1.2 bottles per capita in the United States (India Today 1997). Furthermore, the Chinese express a very high rate of acceptance of alcohol consumption for both sexes, at 69 per cent (drinking by women) and 98.2 per cent (drinking by men), respectively (Legge and Sherlock 1990–1: 637–8). These various findings paint a picture of the drinking practices among the Chinese that is seemingly inconsistent and contradictory.

A general objective of this chapter is to show that drinking is 'part of a larger cultural configuration' (Mandelbaum 1979: 15). Using wedding banquets in post-1949 Hong Kong as a focus, it hopes to show that, given the proper cultural contextualization and historicization, the seemingly inconsistent and contradictory patterns of drinking behaviour in Chinese societies have their internal logics rooted in global consumption, regional development, cultural symbolism and identity politics. Of particular significance is the accepted status of cognac, an imported French liquor, as the proper and appropriate drink at wedding banquets in this historical and localized context. By tracing the history and localized formats of cognac consumption in post-World War II Hong Kong, this chapter makes a contribution towards the ongoing debates about the outcomes of globalization. Many have argued that the world is becoming increasingly homogeneous at the expense of cultural diversity, a process often equated with Americanization or Westernization and the dominance of consumerism (see Sklair 1991; Klein 2000). Others emphasize the proliferation of new hybrid or creolized cultural forms (Hannerz 1992; García Canclini 1997). Global products – Coca Cola and McDonald's are just two examples among many – are commonly consumed with local modifications and infused with new meanings that are not characteristic of the same product and its consumption in the country of origin (see Howes 1996; Watson 1997; Scholliers 2001). Globalization is not a simple process with simple outcomes (Rees and Smart 2001; Smart and Smart 2003).

Another highlight in this chapter is its anthropological focus on the cultural dimensions of consumption – in particular those related to issues of identity and social meanings – which often receive rather superficial attention in the literature on global marketing and consumption despite their centrality in the patterning of consumer behaviour (Bretherton and Carswell 2001). In other words, the success of the introduction of a new product, cognac in this case, is highly dependent on its appeal to the consumers in a culturally appropriate manner so that its 'foreign-ness' can be moderated or localized to fall within the established social norm of consumption. Unfamiliar food and alcoholic beverages (or any other consumer products by extension) are likely to invoke sentiments of threat and even crisis because they fall outside established 'culinary norms' that are rooted in our identification of self and our comprehension of our social universe. Fischler (1988:275) points to the centrality of food in identity and identification by suggesting that in the act of eating/drinking

> people *absorb* food, they seize the opportunity to demarcate their own and the other group. People eating similar food are trustworthy, good, familiar, and safe; but people eating unusual food give rise to feelings of distrust, suspicion and even disgust. Food taboos formalise to an extreme the position with regard to particular foods, hence the existence of a culinary classification and norms, which attributes to food and its eaters a given place in the world. (italics in the original)

Fischler's idea convincingly explains people's common aversion to unfamiliar food, but it bypasses entirely the very important question of why and how people try and often adopt new types of food and drinks (Mennell 1985: 5). It is this latter issue of *how* unfamiliar and novel items and practices become integrated into people's 'culinary classification and norms' in cross-cultural contexts that constitutes the core of international business know-how, an area of knowledge and analysis to which social anthropology has much to offer. The existing emphasis on marketing campaigns of consumer goods and services is premised on the belief that brand recognition is directly related to purchase and consumption. There is little doubt that brand recognition affects consumer behaviour in product selection, but brand recognition alone is insufficient to convince potential consumers to buy or consume a new product. A case in point is a 1996 survey in Qingdao (north-east China) which found that the most recognized brand of food or beverage was Rémy Martin (Jussaume 2001: 227). The French company's high profile in this part of China may have something to do with the fact that Rémy Martin set up the first joint venture winery in China in May 1980 (Bretherton and Carswell 2001: 24). Yet, despite the brand recognition, it is quite certain that for both economic and social reasons only a very small portion of the local citizens have actually tried Rémy Martin products. Economically speaking, the imported cognac carries a price tag that is beyond the means of most people in China, given that the average per capita income there is still around US$500 per annum. Socially speaking, most regular drinkers are men who consume alcoholic beverages at meal time, and their traditional beverage is one of the varieties of *jiu* (see below). Even among the Chinese who can afford imported cognac or wine, they may stay with the familiar Chinese products by choice, a choice rooted in their culturally mediated taste and preference. It cannot be assumed that high brand recognition necessarily leads to greater consumption of the brand products, because the acceptance of a new product and its continued consumption must be supported by the appropriate economic and social-cultural contexts (Ferraro 1998:27).[1] The economic and cultural processes that mediate between product introduction, recognition and consumption are the key issues that this chapter will explore through a case study of cognac in post-World War II Hong Kong.[2]

Chinese Drinking Culture: A Historical Overview

Alcohol Production

The making of alcoholic drinks, known as *jiu*,[3] is believed to date as far back as the Neolithic (Huang 2000: 245–7). Written records in the Shang Dynasty (1600 BC) indicated a sophisticated understanding and application of the biochemical technique involving yeast cultures and controlled conditions in alcohol production (Zhang 1982: 12). *Jiu* is a generic term for alcoholic beverages regardless of alcoholic strength, production method or ingredients. Differentiation of different types of alcoholic beverage is achieved by using a prefix based on colour, transliteration of the name of the drink in another language, place of origin, content or function, as in *hong jiu* for red wine, *bi jiu* for beer and *yao jiu* for medicinal alcoholic potions. The Chinese term *jiu* is confusing for non-Chinese readers because it has a very different epistemological root. The English language carefully distinguishes alcoholic beverages by their alcoholic content. The terms 'wine', 'liquor' and 'beer' convey to the reader a clear shared understanding of their alcoholic content at 9–13 per cent, 40–50 per cent and 3–7 per cent, respectively. In the Chinese usage of the term *jiu*, it conveys nothing more than the idea that the drink contains alcohol; whether it contains 5 or 50 per cent is irrelevant. For reasons of accuracy and clarity, I will use the Chinese term *jiu* throughout this chapter instead of following the common but misleading practice in the English literature to substitute it with either wine or liquor.

Three major varieties of *jiu* are readily available and consumed in Chinese culture:

1. *Huang jiu* or amber drinks are usually made from rice, millet, barley, sorghum, soy beans and other grains; the alcoholic content is usually in the range of 10–25 per cent (Zhang 1982: 12). These are fermented grain beverages that are technically 'ales' or 'beer' (*Cambridge Encyclopedia of China* 1991: 373).

2. *Bai jiu* or white drinks are distilled spirits made from rice, sorghum, sweet potato, corn, and some starchy roots; the alcoholic content is usually in the range of 30–50 per cent (Zhang 1982: 12). Technically the *bai jiu* are vodkas (Zhang 1982: 12; *Cambridge Encyclopedia of China* 1991: 373).

3. *Yao jiu* or medicinal *jiu* is a fusion of herbs, animal parts, insects, fruits and seeds, flowers and distilled liquor; the particular configuration of ingredients are recorded in medical texts and annotated with their effectiveness in regard to specific ailment or symptoms (Huang 2000: 255–7). *Yao jiu* are known to have restorative and curative functions that can improve appetite, enrich the blood, improve circulation, ease hypertension, relieve symptoms of rheumatic pains and colds, contribute to longevity, and reduce depression (Zhang 1982: 12; Lee 1999: 255–8). There are specific *yao jiu* designed for men and women to treat their respective life-cycle problems (Singer 1979: 317; Lee 1999: 217).

Wine, made from grapes, was known and produced in China by the early Han (202 BC–AD 220). It became a popular drink within the imperial court and among scholar-official elites, but its production remained small and its distribution limited (Zhang 1982: 252–5; Huang 2000: 252–5). During the Yuen Dynasty (AD 1276–1368), a food shortage forced the court to prohibit *jiu* consumption and production in order to ensure that grains were reserved for subsistence purposes. Even though grapes were not considered a subsistence staple, wine making and consumption diminished under this period of prohibition and contributed further to its insignificant role in traditional Chinese drinking culture (Man 1998: 60). There was an attempt to re-establish wine production in China in 1892, with limited success, but the wine production industry received a new injection of capital and technology after 1979 when the Chinese government welcomed foreign investment as part of its economic reform. Rémy Martin, Allied-Lyons, Pernod Ricard, Seagram and other European and American investors are involved in wine production joint ventures in China (Bretherton and Carswell 2001: 23–4).

Beer was not known in China until about 100 years ago. The Chinese name for beer (*bi jiu*) is a transliteration from the German word *bier*. The first foreign beer brewery was German and was set up in Qingdao in 1903, followed by Russian investment in Harbin, Japanese investment in Shenyang, and British and French investment in Shanghai. A Chinese-owned beer brewery did not come into being until 1915, with the founding of the Double Prosperity Beer Brewery. Today, there are over 850 beer breweries in China with an annual production volume of over 14 million tonnes; China ranks second in the world in beer production, after the United States (Man 1998: 98).

Over time, various foreign wines and liquors were introduced into Chinese societies within and outside China. These foreign drinks are known by the generic term *yang jiu* or 'ocean' drinks to symbolize their foreign origin outside of China. In Hong Kong, the British presence since 1841 can be expected to have had an impact on the introduction of *yang jiu*, yet it is not the drinks favoured by the British – such as gin, scotch whisky and beer – that have made the greatest inroad into the Chinese drinking culture in Hong Kong. French cognac emerged in the second half of the twentieth century to become the ultimate symbol of prestige, status and conspicuous consumption in Hong Kong society. In order to understand this spectacular integration of cognac into the Hong Kong Chinese drinking culture, we must first look at the social context of drinking in Chinese culture.

The Social Context of Drinking

Drinking has great ritual significance in Chinese culture, and while the elaborate traditional rules governing the proper rites associated with drinks and drinking are not part of most people's everyday life in Hong Kong today, the cultural premises of drinking that emerged several thousand years ago still have a bearing on the normative codes associated with drinking in contemporary Chinese societies. From very early on in Chinese history, *jiu* and drinking were considered essential components of every major ceremony that merits celebration or memorial – the major rites of passage (birth, marriage, death); all the major events in the Chinese calendar such as Chinese New Year, *Ching Ming* grave visits, the Ghost Festival, and others; and social occasions such as a dinner banquet, a farewell party and the reunion with a friend from afar (Zhang 1982: 13–14; Man 1998: 111; Zhang 2000: 59). Drinks are offered to living guests as well as gods, ancestors and ghosts. Depending on the occasion and the social ranks of the guests, there are specific rules regarding the size of the drinking vessel used, the spatial positioning or seating of the guests, the order of serving and drinking (who is served first, who should drink first or last), the number of accompanying food dishes at the occasion, and the quantity of drinks served to each guest. These complex rules are formalized in the Book of Rites[4] and the imperial court employed 'drink masters' to oversee the proper drinking rituals at all state dinners (Man 1998: 111). Over the passage of time, these formalized and ritualized rules governing drinking in social occasions became enshrined as normative codes that are practised with some regional differences and subjected to individual modifications to accommodate personal preferences and desires. In general terms, the normative code on drinking is as follows (Zhang 1982: 13–14; Man 1998: 111; Lee 1999: 213):

1. Drinking is a social activity in the company of others; it is considered inappropriate and suspicious if one drinks alone.

2. Drinking is a blessing and pleasure when consumed in moderation; excessive consumption is both disgraceful and harmful. Drunkenness in general is looked upon with contempt and considered a disgrace and a face-losing indulgence.
3. Drinking etiquette is governed by social hierarchy. If an elder has not raised his/her cup to drink, nobody younger or of junior rank should do so. When a person of senior generation/rank pours wine for you, you must stand up to show proper respect. Do not drink non-stop and do not put too much food in your mouth at one time. When serving, hold your breath so that you do not breathe on other people's food or drinks.
4. Snacks or meals should accompany drinking.

It should be noted that drinking in the Chinese context has certain particular characteristics. First, drinking is a cultural performance intended to reinforce social hierarchy and contribute to social solidarity. Second, the focus or intended purpose in drinking has little to do with the alcoholic content or the effects of alcohol; rather, drinking is an integral component in the proper administration of a ceremony or ritual. In other words, one drinks at a wedding banquet to celebrate the occasion and to complete the necessary rituals associated with the occasion; one does not drink to get drunk. Third, drinking *per se* is not condemned in Chinese culture. On the contrary, it is considered an integral part of the culture and is considered to be beneficial to health as long as the consumption is undertaken in moderation. Last, there is no explicit exclusion of women from drinking. On the contrary, the repertoire of *yao jiu* is orientated very much to women and their specific needs at different life-stages. Despite the widely shared contemporary impression that youths, women and students usually are not expected to engage in drinking, and that drinkers are mostly men from the lower stratum of society (Zhang 1982: 14), drinking as a ritual and proper social behaviour in specific situations is observed by all regardless of gender, class and frequency of alcohol consumption in one's daily life.

Consumption Patterns in Contemporary Hong Kong

Alcohol is sold in supermarkets, corner stores and all retail outlets at convenient locations close to consumers. In traditional old-fashioned grocery shops, rice *jiu* is stored in large ceramic urns and measured out in specialized ladles. The lack of restriction on the sale of alcoholic drinks in specialized stores as practised in North America and elsewhere[5] means that alcoholic drinks ranging from beer to liquor, of both import and local origins, are readily available anywhere in Hong Kong. This accessibility may be viewed with apprehension by some readers as a potential problem encouraging alcoholism, but the reality is that alcoholism is not common in Hong Kong and the proportion of the population who are regular consumers of alcohol is very low, at less than 4 per cent according to one study (New Beverage Publication, Inc. 1998).

Comprehensive data for alcohol consumption patterns in China and other Chinese societies are hard to come by in both Chinese and English publications. The exception is Singer's (1979) article, in which he provided the figures for alcohol consumption in Hong Kong by volume (imperial gallon) and type (Chinese, Western) for the period 1960–9 (1979: 320, table 3). His figures showed that the average per capita consumption of absolute alcohol in Hong Kong was around one imperial gallon or 4.546 litres per annum. This roughly translates into fourteen 750 ml bottles of liquor at 50 per cent alcohol by volume, or seventy bottles of 750 ml wine at 10 per cent alcohol by volume. This consumption level is much lower than the average for the United States, at 1.6 imperial gallons per adult per year in 1953–7 (Singer 1979: 321).

I do not have the current figures of alcohol consumption in Hong Kong; my personal impression is that the average per capita consumption per year probably is not very different from the level indicated by Singer. Published 1998 figures showed Hong Kong to be a light consumer of alcoholic drinks at 22 litres per person per year, compared to 100 litres per person in Germany, 73 litres per person in the United States, 60 litres per person in Canada and 57 litres per person in Japan (*Economist* 1999). The relative proportion of Chinese-type and Western-type alcohol since the 1960s is likely to have changed to show a much higher proportion of Western-type alcohol in the total consumption. Singer's figures indicated a clear upward trend for Western-type alcohol from 0.13 per cent in 1960 to 0.28 per cent in 1969 (1979: 320, table 3). He also made the observation that the rate of alcoholism in Hong Kong was extremely low, an observation shared by other researchers of Chinese in North America and elsewhere (Legge and Sherlock 1990–1; Wall et al. 2000). My own interviews ($N = 25$; 14 male, 11 female) confirm the widely held impression of the general pattern of drinking behaviour among the Chinese:

1. The majority of interviewees are light consumers of alcohol whose occasional consumption of beer with a meal is the extent of their 'drinking habit'. Chinese tea and soft drinks are the most common beverages served with a meal at home and in restaurants.
2. Women tend to drink less than men by quantity as well as frequency. Men are more likely to be regular consumers of alcohol.
3. People usually drink in the company of others in a social setting such as a dinner party or a banquet. Consumption of alcohol at home usually takes place at meal time.
4. Excessive consumption of alcohol at special occasions is common. For example, at a year-end party in Taipei in the early 1990s, four cases of cognac (36 litres) were consumed in one evening involving only forty-eight guests. This kind of extreme drinking is said to have diminished in recent years throughout Hong

Kong and other Asian countries due to two main factors: first, there is a growing health consciousness that encourages lower consumption of alcohol; and, second, the economic downturns since the late 1990s have cut into people's disposable income and consumption of expensive items like cognac.

5. Chinese living in cold or marginal regions, and those who work in manual work, are said to have a tendency to drink more often and prefer liquor with higher alcoholic contents. The drinking is believed to generate bodily warmth and strength.

There are two main explanations of the tendency towards low alcohol consumption and the relative lack of alcoholism among Chinese in China and overseas. The first is a sociological one that points to the stabilizing effects of family configuration and the strong cultural norms against excessive consumption (Lin and Lin 1982). The other is a biological-physiological explanation based on the observation that a portion of the Asian population suffer from a genetic defect that completely or partially blocks the production of the ALDH2 isoenzyme which oxidizes acetaldehyde (toxic product of alcohol) to acetate. When this isoenzyme is absent or produced at a reduced rate, the effect of a hangover[6] becomes severe and extended, thus acting as a deterrent to drinking. In a recent study of 123 subjects of Asian origin in Los Angeles, 3 per cent of the subjects were found to suffer from the inability to produce ALDH2, and 27 per cent were found to suffer partial inability to produce this isoenzyme (Wall et al. 2000: 15).

Of particular relevance to this chapter is the fact that an expensive imported product like cognac successfully establishes itself in a highly competitive and open market dominated by a population of light drinkers and non-drinkers. It is a tough market on which to gain a foothold, yet cognac succeeded very well. For many years, Hong Kong was one of the top consumers of French cognac by value and volume in the world. Many factors contribute to the effective entrenchment of cognac in post-World War II Hong Kong, including the economic transformation of Hong Kong since the 1960s, the rapid rise of a class of *nouveau riche* whose conspicuous consumption set the local trends, and the effective integration of cognac into the social fabric of Chinese culture in the context of wedding banquets. These various economic conditions and social processes enable the localization of cognac to become part of the culinary norm in Hong Kong. The consumption of cognac is tightly entwined with issues of identity, cultural rituals, symbolism of status and prosperity and class.

Chinese Wedding Banquets, Cognac and Modernity

Weddings are major social events steeped in cultural symbolism, conspicuous consumption, transformation of status and roles, and family/community politics. The union of two families in the traditional thinking about marriage is rapidly being replaced by the modern notion of marriage as a union of two individuals, and there have been many other changes over time regarding the rules and protocols of the wedding ceremony. One thing that remains unchanged, however, is the core belief that weddings are joyous occasions that call for collective celebration. One common form of marriage celebration is the wedding banquet. The serving of alcoholic drinks at wedding banquets has a long history in Chinese culture. The Book of Rites describes the sharing of *jiu* between the bride and groom in a wedding ceremony (Lee 1999: 63). On the wedding day, the newlyweds must share food and drink three times in unison to symbolize their commitment to a life together (Man 1998: 127). In Southern China, there was a documented tradition of making rice *jiu* after the birth of a daughter to be used upon the daughter's marriage at the banquet (Li 1995: 95; Lee 1999: 63). This particular brew is known as *Nuerhong* (Red Daughter) or *Nujiu* (Daughter's Wine). Traditionally this special daughter's brew was not sold; each family made it according to their secret recipe. Today, however, *Nuerhong Jiu* are commercially produced and are readily available in supermarkets and stores in China and Hong Kong.

In contemporary Hong Kong, wedding banquets are almost always held in major international hotels and restaurant chains. There is a hierarchy among these venues based on cost and perceived prestige. These wedding banquets are lavish affairs with specialized menus and formal decorations in Chinese- and/or Western-style provided by the hotel or restaurant. These are major money-making occasions for the service provider and there is fierce competition to market these wedding banquet packages. In the past wedding banquets were not always staged in hotels and restaurants in Hong Kong. The use of commercial outlets for wedding banquets only became common after the 1970s when Hong Kong attained substantial economic development. As the local population became more affluent, the level of conspicuous consumption rose accordingly.

In the old days, wedding banquets were held in the village square, the lineage ancestral hall or in one's home. In urban Hong Kong in the 1950s and 1960s, many people held wedding banquets at neighborhood community halls and hired catering companies to do the cooking and serving on site. One informant describes his wedding in 1964 as follows:

> We were living in Shek Kep Mei then, we lived in the public housing estate. My wedding banquet was held at a local community hall. We hired a catering company to do the cooking. Three-star brandy was served . . . I got a very good price through the liquor retail store I was working for. I drove a truck and did the deliveries and pick-ups. The three-star brandy retailed for $20 or $22[7] in those days; I got it for $16 a bottle. Serving brandy at a wedding banquet then was a big deal . . . [*Did you look into the hotel or restaurant wedding banquet package at that time?*] . . . No, it was not common to hold a wedding banquet in a hotel or a restaurant in my days. Such wedding packages did not

exist then, and only the very rich could afford to host a banquet in a restaurant. (Male, aged 60–5, interviewed in Hong Kong in February 2002; original in Cantonese, translation by the author)

With the exception of the case mentioned above, five other marriages in my sample that took place in Hong Kong or China in the 1950s and 1960s did not involve the use of foreign liquor. When asked if cognac was served at their children's wedding banquets in Hong Kong (in the 1980s and 1990s), most of my respondents replied in the affirmative. When pressed to identify the brand or name of the cognac served at wedding banquets, many could not do so. One couple's reply was, 'We got the same kind of cognac [for our youngest daughter's wedding in 2001] that our eldest daughter used in her 1992 wedding.' In fact, the eldest daughter does not drink cognac; it was her husband who decided to serve Rémy Martin Club at their wedding banquet, which was held at one of the international hotels in Hong Kong. At home, neither of them drinks cognac. The husband drinks scotch, beer and wine, while the wife prefers cocktails like margaritas (tequila and lime juice) and grasshoppers (crème de menthe and cream). However, the husband would drink cognac at social occasions when offered.

The recognition of cognac among non-drinkers is often guided by visual cues such as the shape of a bottle or the brand logo. Dr Tong[8] is a Hong Kong- and British-educated sociologist who holds a faculty position in one of the universities in Hong Kong. When he married in 1974, he hosted the wedding banquet at Maxim's (one of the major restaurant chains in Hong Kong). Cognac was served at his own wedding banquet but he could not remember the brand. Quite recently, he attended a nephew's wedding banquet. When asked if he remembered the brand of cognac served at this occasion, he replied, ' Well . . . mmm . . . it is the one that comes in a bottle like a fan.' What he described may be Rémy Martin XO, which retails for about HK$1,000 a bottle, or it is equally likely to be Martell XO or Bisquit XO. They all come in a flat bottle with fan fold lines.

It should be noted that most consumers in Hong Kong know the cognac brands by their Chinese names, and not their original names in French. Cognac is known in Cantonese[9] as *gon yap*, which is a close reproduction of the sound of the word in French. This is a Hong Kong-created linguistic label that is not recognized by Chinese outside Hong Kong, unless they have been exposed to its usage in advertisements or by other Hong Kong residents. Brand names, however, are translated in diverse ways. Rémy Martin is known as *yan tau ma* ('human head horse'), based on the motif (a centaur throwing a spear) on the label. Hennessy is known by its transliteration in Cantonese, *hin nei si*. Similarly Martell is known as *ma dek lei*. The Denis M. FOV comes in a bottle that is long and slender and it is known in Hong Kong as *cheng gen* ('long neck').

The pairing of cognac with wedding banquets in the Hong Kong context has a fairly short history. It probably originated in the 1970s and gained momentum throughout the 1980s and early 1990s as the economic situation in Hong Kong experienced an uninterrupted upward spiral (Chiu and Lui 1997). Since 1997, Hong Kong has suffered real deflation every year, climbing unemployment that reached 8 per cent in 2003, and downturns in property value (*South China Morning Post* 2001a, 2001b, 2002; Kwong and Miscevic 2002: 24). The post-1997 economic downturn in Hong Kong caused a general decline in consumption, and the sales of luxury goods suffered. But a random survey of twenty-two published banquet menus from thirteen restaurants in Hong Kong[10] indicates that the association of cognac with wedding banquets remains strong despite the economic downturn (see table 6.1). Red wine is showing up regularly in banquet packages and the trend suggests that it will continue to gain the ground lost by cognac.

Table 6.1 A comparison of beverages included in the published set menus for three types of banquet in Hong Kong, 2002

Number of restaurants that offer listed beverages*/description of beverages	Wedding	Birthday	Chinese New Year
Cognac	5	2	2
Red wine	3	2	1
Beer	8	8	5
Soda pop	8	8	5
Non-alcoholic punch	1	0	0
Champagne	2	0	0
Total number of menus surveyed	8	8	6

*Several beverages are usually included in each set menu.

There is a clear differential in cost among the three types of banquets, with the wedding banquet menus being the most expensive at HK$2,300–5,000 per table of ten. The common inclusion of cognac in wedding banquet menus (63 per cent) is probably one of the factors that contribute to their higher cost. Most restaurants include one bottle of cognac for every two tables, and the brand of cognac is always identified clearly on the menu. In this particular menu survey, two restaurants offer Courvoisier VSOP or XO, two offer Rémy Martin VSOP and one offers Bisquit VSOP. It should be noted that the VSOP is a superior-quality cognac and considered a high-value product, retailing for HK$300–400 each. The XO cognac is excellent quality and is correspondingly very expensive at over HK$1,000 each. A bottle of wine, when offered, is included for each table, and usually six cans each of beer and soda pop are also included for each table. Unlike the Western emphasis on champagne as the drink of choice at weddings and other celebrations, only two Hong Kong restaurants include champagne in their wedding banquet menu. One requires a minimum order of eighteen tables to qualify for two bottles of complimentary champagne, the other requires a minimum order of fifteen tables for one bottle of complimentary champagne.

It is a custom at Chinese wedding banquets that guests are invited to arrive several hours before the feasting begins. A typical invitation reads, 'Your honourable presence is expected at 6 p.m., the banquet begins at 8 p.m.' Unlike the Western format, which precedes the banquet with a reception where alcoholic drinks and snacks are served, the Chinese pre-dinner reception offers *mahjong*,[11] and those who are not part of a *mahjong* game sit and chat. Children play and run around. Chinese tea and soft drinks are served; alcoholic drinks (including beer) are rarely served. Melon seeds (dyed red to symbolize good luck and happiness) and candies are also served.

During the banquet, guests are given a choice of drinks by the waiting staff. Children usually have soda pop, women mostly opt for tea, and most men and some women will have cognac, wine or beer. Wine is a newcomer to the scene, becoming quite popular on the strength of its 'proven' benefit to health. However, cognac remains the signature drink at wedding banquets in Hong Kong. It is served from the beginning of the feast in water tumblers or highball glasses and usually in generous servings. Most people drink their cognac straight and it is consumed steadily throughout the meal, as is done with wine in a Western setting. Some people add ice or soda pop to their cognac (sometimes also to wine and scotch). Unlike the Western etiquette of consuming dinner wine at one's own pace and without fanfare, the drinking etiquette at a Chinese banquet usually involves the entire group's raising of glasses for a toast at the initiation of a fellow guest at the table, or when a new dish arrives, and done with much gusto when the newlyweds and their parents come to the table to thank the guests for coming. Guests may also have drinking competitions during the banquet, a game common among friends, especially men.

The supply of cognac at a wedding banquet is usually the responsibility of the hosts; the restaurant may or may not charge a corking fee. The decision of which label to serve at a banquet is guided by several principles. First, there is the economic factor. Cognac is an expensive item; some cost as much or more for a single bottle as the cost for a banquet for ten settings.

Second, there is the brand recognition factor. The Hong Kong market is very open and competitive and many labels are offered at a wide range of prices. A cursory survey of advertisements[12] by three major supermarkets in Hong Kong – Wellcome, ParkNShop, CRC Shop – identified a total of twenty brands of cognac on sale at discount prices for Chinese New Year in 2002. The VSOP cognac was the most commonly advertised brand of superior quality brandy and it retailed at around HK$300–400 each (750 ml). Of the six brands of XO cognac listed in these advertisements, the most expensive was Courvoisier (HK$1,400), followed by Hennessy (HK$1,300) and Rémy Martin (HK$1,260). Even though Martell Cordon Bleu is not an XO cognac, its retail price range was comparable at HK$1,100. For the general consumers in Hong Kong, most of whom are not connoisseurs of cognac, their knowledge about cognac either comes from their peers or from advertisement. The major labels – Hennessy, Martell, Rémy Martin and Courvoisier (together they accounted for 70% of worldwide sales of cognac in 1995–6 according to Cognac Torula News Market Data 2002) – all have healthy advertising budgets and they are widely covered in the mass media and bill-boards throughout Hong Kong. What is popular or perceived to be well known is usually taken as an indication of its superior quality *vis-à-vis* other lesser known products. If your friends all consider Martell Cordon Bleu to be *the* brand, you will go for the same if you can afford it. If you serve a lesser-known brand, your personal reputation and prestige may suffer on the suspicion that it is an inferior product.

Third, decisions regarding the brand of cognac for a wedding banquet are influenced by the symbolic value factor. While most people are not knowledgeable about the industry-regulated grading of cognac into numerous categories such as VS, VSOP, XO, three-star, heritage and Napoleon, they are quick to pick up the simple equivalence of quality with cost. Since XO is more expensive than VSOP, it is generally accepted as superior. This simplistic acceptance is reinforced by the consistent feedback from drinkers regarding the superior quality of XO over VSOP, which in turn is superior to brandy. The quality of cognac is judged on the basis of flavour and smoothness. A smooth cognac is a better product than another brand or other liquor which 'burns the throat' or which is harsh. The marketing industry is well aware that export markets have less consumer loyalty than home markets. Consumers in export markets are less able to identify with the historical and cultural basis of imported products, and less informed about the quality distinctions. Attraction to imported products is based on image rather than knowledge of the product (New Beverage Publication, Inc. 1998).

Finally, decisions regarding the choice of cognac are influenced by previous exposure to products and recommendations by friends and relatives. In a case mentioned above, a couple served Rémy Martin Club cognac at their youngest daughter's wedding in 2001 because it was the brand served at their eldest daughter's wedding in 1992. In many instances, people made their choice based on the recommendation of a relative or friend who is in some way connected to the food industry, or can get them certain brands of cognac at discounted prices. Sometimes, customers go along with the restaurant's recommended brand which is included in the banquet package. It should be noted that the brands of cognac in these banquet packages are all well-known labels in Hong Kong.

Consumption, Identity and Globalization

Cognac is a brandy aged in oak barrels for a minimum of thirty months under tight guidelines and quality control by the Bureau National Interprofessionnel du Cognac (New Beverage Publication, Inc. 1998). It is known as a 'symbol of luxury, refinement and art de vivre' (India Today 1997). The production of cognac is restricted to the town of Cognac and its vicinity in western France. While this distilled liquor is said to have been 'discovered' by travelling Scandinavians who chanced upon the town of Cognac in the eleventh century, the naming of the liquor as 'cognac' only came about in the eighteenth century (*Funk and Wagnall's Encyclopaedia* 1996: 407).

It is not clear when exactly cognac was introduced to the Chinese market. What is known is that brandy was part of the repertoire of 'foreign drinks' in China by the early twentieth century and possibly earlier. An informant who now lives in Calgary recalled his young adult days in Shanghai in the 1930s and 1940s when Johnny Walker whisky (Red Label) and Hennessy brandy were the drinks of choice among the young and rich crowd. Brandy was known and consumed in Hong Kong in the post-World War II decades. The Asian market accounted for just over 30 per cent of the market share of the global sales of cognac by volume at 45 million bottles in 1996 (Cognac Torula News Market Data 2002). When it comes to revenue, the Asian market is extremely important to the cognac makers because it is the only region in the world where most of the products sold are the high-end 'superior-quality' products. The Asian market accounted for 59.7 per cent of cognac exports by value in 1996 and 47.3 per cent in 1997 (New Beverage Publication, Inc. 1998). As indicated in table 6.2, the Asian market continued to be a loyal consumer of superior quality cognac in 2000–1 despite the traumatic economic downturn throughout the region since 1997.

While it is not clear when and how cognac became a symbol of affluence and sophistication in Hong Kong, there is little doubt that its sales volume in Hong Kong and other parts of Asia is closely tied to local economic conditions (Stein 1997). Table 6.3 documents the importation of cognac to Japan, Singapore and Hong Kong for 1981–2001. Three points of interest are worth noting: first, by 1981 cognac consumption was well established in these countries; second, the per capita sales of cognac were the highest in Hong Kong until Singapore took over in 1997; third, both

Table 6.2 Worldwide cognac sales in millions of bottles, 2000–1

	Cognac bottles sold in 2000–1 (million)	% superior qualities
United States	40.7	25
Britain	11.3	15
France	8.6	33
Germany	7.2	38
Japan	6.0	100
Singapore	5.0	100
Hong Kong	4.5	100
Finland	3.3	33

Source: Bureau National Interprofessionnel du Cognac 2002

Table 6.3 Sales of cognac by country in millions of bottles, 1981–2001.

Year (population, 1997)*	Japan (125 million)	Singapore (2.9 million)	Hong Kong (6.3 million)
1981–2	7.8	2.6	8.4
1982–3	8.2	3	8.3
1983–4	10.5	2.6	8.7
1984–5	9.8	2.9	6.6
1985–6	11.9	3.2	7.8
1986–7	13.7	3.3	9.7
1987–8	17.9	4.1	12.3
1988–9	24.2	4.6	10.7
1989–90	27.9	4.5	13.5
1990–1	26.9	3.6	13.3
1991–2	25.2	3.7	13.1
1992–3	22.3	3.1	18.1
1993–4	17.4	3.7	16.7
1994–5	19.5	7	14.8
1995–6	17.6	6.7	12.2
1996–7	14.6	6	9.5
1997–8	11.7	6	4.3
1998–9	8.2	3.7	5.1
1999–2000	6.7	4.4	5.2
2000–1	6.0	5.0	4.5

Source: Bureau National Interprofessionnel du Cognac 2002.
*Canadian Global Almanac 1997.

Japan and Hong Kong experienced a height of cognac consumption in the period 1988–96, to be followed with a drastic drop after 1997 due to declining local economic growth.

Closer examination will show that these surges and declines in cognac consumption correlate quite closely with the economic fluctuations in these Asian countries. However, while these macro-level correlations provide general information, they tell us very little about who the consumers are and how this consumption is conducted. The following ethnographic vignette may provide some answers to the who, where and how questions concerning cognac, and highlights the tight interrelationships between consumption, global commodity distribution, identity, class, gender and cultural symbolism.

Mr Fong is 72 years old and his introduction to and subsequent 'love affair' with cognac is quite typical of a segment of Hong Kong men of his age cohort, who constitute a significant market share of cognac consumption in this city of seven million (2001 figure). Mr Fong was born and raised in Kaiping, a rural region in the province of Guangdong in southern China. He came from a poor family and had very little formal education. He came to Hong Kong by himself in the late 1940s and lived from hand to mouth for years. By the 1960s, he had his first shoe-manufacturing factory in a residential building in Mongkok, one of the most developed commercial areas in Hong Kong. Shortly after, he also became a partner in a shoe retail outlet in the same district. It was during this period of his improved economic situation that he learned to drink cognac from his business associates. He took to it because other people drank it at business dinners. Mr Fong cannot read English or French, and he has never visited Europe. Before he learned about cognac, his drink of choice was rice *jiu* produced in Hong Kong or China. Over time, he became a regular consumer of cognac throughout the 1970s and 1980s. At one time he was drinking a bottle in two to three days. His favourite to this day is Martell Cordon Bleu, which retailed for over HK$1,000 in 2002.

Mr Fong married a young woman chosen by his mother in Kaiping in 1954. It was an arranged marriage. His wife remained in Kaiping and raised two children, mostly on her own until the family moved to Hong Kong to join Mr Fong in 1985. When his son married in 1986, Mr Fong hosted two wedding banquets: one in Macau, where the majority of guests were relatives and family members from both the bride and groom's sides, the other in Hong Kong, which was a bigger affair involving mostly his own business associates. At the Macau banquet, Mr Fong served Martell Cordon Bleu. In his own words, 'These are relatives, we must serve the best.' At the Hong Kong banquet, he chose a slightly cheaper cognac, the Denis M. FOV (it retailed for around HK$400 in 2002). Mr Fong's personal consumption of cognac was cut down after his retirement in 1991, and he now drinks it only on special occasions. His son-in-law, a cook in a Chinese restaurant in Toronto, stocks up on Martell Cordon Bleu for Mr Fong when he visits. Mr Fong and his wife immigrated to Canada in 1995 to join their daughter. Now they spend half a year in Toronto living with the daughter and her family, the other half-year in an apartment in Kaiping which Mrs Fong bought in 1999. Mr Fong does not have Martell Cordon Bleu in his Kaiping apartment. He drinks the local rice *jiu* with his daily meals, a reversion to his habit in his younger years as a struggling immigrant in Hong Kong.

Conclusion

The rising affluence in Hong Kong since the 1960s created a market for consumer goods and provided the necessary conditions to support conspicuous consumption. However, that in itself does not go far in explaining the success of cognac in Hong Kong *vis-à-vis* other imported or local products. Advertising campaigns may contribute to greater brand and product recognition but this does not always translate into actual consumption behaviour. A necessary mediating factor that bridges imported product recognition and actual consumption is the proper and culturally appropriate integration of the imported product in the local context. My understanding of the success of cognac in Hong Kong points to two major levels of integration that are closely linked to identity issues. The first is the inclusion of cognac in Chinese wedding banquets since the 1960s. My research for this chapter could not go far enough to delineate the exact circumstances under which this inclusion arose - whether it was by design with the aid of cognac producers, or whether it was by accident through the personal innovation of one or more restaurant managers in their effort to create a more competitive image for their wedding banquet packages. Whichever way it might be, the end result is a highly successful integration of an imported product in a local cultural ceremony. Cognac, by its association with wedding banquets, is firmly consolidated in its image as a symbol of extravagance and luxury, a symbol that resonates with the image of wedding banquets as a form of conspicuous consumption. In one interviewee's words, the whole thing about serving cognac at wedding banquets is for 'show' (i.e. to show others how much money you have or how sophisticated you are). The coupling of cognac with wedding banquets has worked to mutual benefits at this symbolic level.

Second, the use of cognac at Hong Kong wedding banquets is a unique phenomenon. Other affluent Asian and Chinese societies do not share this practice. In Japan, sake is still the preferred and most common drinks at wedding banquets. In Taiwan, cognac is rarely served at wedding banquets. In China, in its current post-1978 phase of rapid economic development, conspicuous consumption has escalated by leaps and bounds and directly supports the rising importation of French wine and cognac. Still, the use of cognac at wedding banquets is rare in China. The uniqueness of the use of cognac in Hong Kong has become one of the common identity markers that Hong Kong residents use to distinguish themselves from Chinese in other localities. They think of it as being symbolic of their greater affluence and worldly sophistication than their counterparts in China, Taiwan and elsewhere. Two interviewees in Taiwan, each in their late fifties to early sixties, comment that many Taiwanese Chinese look up to Hong Kong Chinese in fashion, hairstyles and other modes of modernity. Those in Taiwan who drink cognac, in their view, are probably emulating the Hong Kong Chinese, who are well known throughout Asia to be big consumers of the product. These comments further support Friedman's (1994) notion that Hong Kong is being upheld as a model of Chinese modernity by Chinese worldwide.

Cognac consumption in Hong Kong has taken on local colours in multiple ways. As many studies have shown, imported food and foodways are modified and transformed in diverse ways to reflect and create new local meanings and reality (Howes 1996; Watson 1997; Scholliers 2001; Wu and Cheung 2002). The success story of cognac as a prestige item in the Hong Kong market must be understood in the context of its effective integration in local society. More specifically, the coupling of cognac and wedding banquets provides an appropriate cultural context for the integration of an imported French product in a Chinese society and a main reason behind its strong penetration into the everyday life of Hong Kong citizens despite the generally low level of alcohol consumption at home and in other private settings.

The recent marketing strategies to entice the younger generation in Asia with a new image of cognac as a 'long drink' – a drink for any occasion, a cognac cocktail to be served with ice and mixes (juice, soda, sparkling water) – is a brave effort to move the product away from its established image of prestige and formality (India Today 1997; New Beverage Publication, Inc. 1998). In a society like Hong Kong where the younger population is not showing the same affinity to drinking as their counterparts in North America, this strategy emphasizing individualist consumption for personal gratification may not work that well, however. In fact, I would argue that it might not be effective at all in gaining new markets among the younger generation, and it might actually run the risk of further eroding its market share in the future. My speculation is based on my understanding of the strength of cultural symbolism in the rise of cognac as a symbol of luxury in the Hong Kong market. Cognac consumption is greatly boosted by its association with Chinese wedding banquets, and its associated image as a luxury product for special occasions. By creating a new image of cognac as a cocktail for *all* occasions, it may very well endanger the foundation of its past success, a foundation that has great cultural continuity and relevance regardless of economic conditions and global trends.

Notes

The data for this chapter are based on several sources: first, I draw upon my nearly two decades of research involvement in the Hong Kong–South China region, supplemented by my childhood experience in Hong Kong, to provide a long lens of scholarly and personal observations about drinking. Second, I draw upon publications in English and Chinese to provide a historical background and sociological discussion about drinking in Chinese culture in general. I also draw upon many resources on the internet that provide invaluable information about alcohol production and consumption. Finally, I conducted a series of interviews with a total of 25 Chinese subjects (14 male, 11 female) in Hong Kong, Taipei (Taiwan), Los Angeles (USA) and Calgary (Canada) on their experience with wedding banquets and their own drinking behaviour. These subjects were drawn from an opportunistic sampling method connected to my past research links and personal social networks. The interviews were conducted mostly in the subjects' home during two separate trips to Asia in February and March 2002. All interviews done in Hong Kong were conducted in Cantonese, the interviews in Taipei and North America were conducted in English.

1. According to Ferraro (1998: 27), whether a new product or innovation is adopted or not is governed by five major variables: relative advantage, compatibility,

complexity, trialability and observability. While culture permeates every variable, it is particularly central for 'compatibility', which is described as 'the extent to which an innovation is perceived to be congruous with the exiting cultural values, attitudes, behavior patterns, and material objects'.

2. Hong Kong became a British colony in 1841. It was returned to Chinese sovereignty in 1997 and renamed Hong Kong Special Administrative Region (HKSAR). The British colonial legacy distinguishes Hong Kong from China and other overseas Chinese societies in multiple ways. Since its economic take-off in the 1960s to become a major manufacturing and financial centre, Hong Kong has become a model of Chinese modernity (Friedman 1994). The Hong Kong Chinese consider themselves to be worldly citizens of sophistication, a self-image that is widely uphold by Chinese outside of Hong Kong. The high level of cognac consumption is a much publicized and widely accepted unique trademark of Hong Kong affluence and sophistication.

3. Otherwise specified, the Chinese terms used in this chapter are based on Putonghua (Mandarin) pronunciation. *Jiu* is an alcoholic brew made from grains or fruits with an alcoholic content of 10–40 per cent by volume.

4. The Book of Rites is a recording of Confucian and neo-Confucian teachings regarding the proper behaviour and interaction between individuals at specific occasions according to their relationship based on generation, social status, gender, age and kinship.

5. In Canada, only government-approved liquor stores can sell alcoholic drinks; in Australia these are known as 'Bottle Shops'.

6. Symptoms of hangover include thirst, fatigue, insomnia, tachycardia (irregular heartbeat), headache, nausea and vomiting.

7. As of October 1983, the Hong Kong dollar was pegged against the US dollar at a fixed rate of HK$7.8 to US$1. The exchange rate in 1964 was HK$5.7143 to US$1 according to information extracted from the Pacific Exchange Rate Service (2003).

8. All names have been changed and certain personal details modified to ensure informant anonymity.

9. Cantonese is the most common dialect used in Hong Kong. It is very different from the official spoken language in China, which is Putonghua. The two are mutually incomprehensible. The Cantonese pronunciation used here follows the system developed by Lau (1977).

10. Three of the thirteen restaurants surveyed are part of chains. The largest chain has over fifty branches throughout Hong Kong. Of the remaining ten independent restaurants, five are in Kowloon and five are in the New Territories. These published menus are set menus for ten persons at each table. Prices are per table as listed in 2002 and all the drinks listed were included in the price.

11. *Mahjong* is commonly known as Chinese dominoes, and four players are required. It is a very popular game in Hong Kong.

12. These advertisements were collected in Hong Kong from *Oriental Daily* and *Apples Daily* over a period of two weeks in February 2002. Both papers are Chinese dailies published in Hong Kong.

References

Bretherton, P. and P. Carswell (2001), 'Market Entry Strategies for Western Produced Wine into the Chinese Market', *International Journal of Wine Marketing* 13(1): 23–35

Cambridge Encyclopedia of China, new edn (1991), Cambridge: Cambridge University Press.

Canadian Global Almanac, The (1997), Toronto: Macmillan.

Chiu, S. W. K., K. C. Ho and Tai-Lok Lui (1997), *City-States in the Global Economy: Industrial Restructuring in Hong Kong and Singapore*, Boulder, CO: Westview Press.

Economist The (1999), 'Weekly Indicators: Alcohol Consumption', 16 December.

Ferraro, G. P. (1998), *The Cultural Dimensions of International Business*, 3rd edn, Upper Saddle River, NJ: Prentice Hall.

Fischler, C. (1988), 'Food, Self and Identity', *Social Science Information* 27: 275–92.

Friedman, E. (1994), 'Reconstructing China's National Identity: A Southern Alternative to Mao Era Anti-imperialist Nationalism', *Journal of Asian Studies* 53(1): 67–91.

Funk and Wagnall's Encyclopedia (1996), New York: Funk and Wagnalls, Inc.

García Canclini, N. (1997), 'Urban Cultures at the End of the Century: The Anthropological Perspective', *International Social Science Journal* 153: 345–54.

Hannerz, U. (1992), *Cultural Complexity: Studies in the Social Organization of Meaning*, New York: Columbia University Press.

Howes, D. (ed.) (1996), *Cross-cultural Consumption: Global Market, Local Realities*, London: Routledge.

Jussaume R. A., Jr (2001), 'Factors Associated with Modern Urban Chinese Consumption Patterns', *Journal of Contemporary China* 10 (27): 219–32.

Klein, N. (2000), *No Logo: Taking Aim at the Brand Bullies*, Toronto: Knopf Canada.

Kwong, P. and D. Miscevic (2002), 'Globalization and Hong Kong's Future', *Journal of Contemporary Asia* 32 (3): 323–37.

Lau, S. (1977), *A Practical Cantonese–English Dictionary*, Hong Kong: The Government Printer.

Legge, C. and L. Sherlock (1990–1), 'Perception of Alcohol Use and Misuse in Three Ethnic Communities: Implications for Prevention Programming', *The International Journal of Addiction* 25 (5A & 6A): 629–53.

Lin, T.-Y. and D. T. C. Lin (1982), 'Alcoholism among the Chinese: Further Observations of a Low Risk Population', *Culture, Medicine, and Psychiatry* 6: 109–16.

Mandelbaum, D. (1979), 'Alcohol and Culture', in M. Marshall (ed.), *Beliefs, Behaviors, and Beverages: A Cross-cultural Survey*, Ann Arbor: University of Michigan Press, pp. 14–29.

Mennell, S. (1985), *All Manners of Food: Eating and Taste in England and France from the Middle Ages to the Present*, Oxford: Basil Blackwell.

Rees, M. and J. Smart (2001), *Plural Globalities and Multiple Localities: New World Borders*, Lanham, MD: University Press of America.

Scholliers, P. (ed.) (2001), *Food, Drink and Identity: Cooking, Eating and Drinking in Europe since the Middle Ages*, Oxford: Berg.

Singer, K. (1979), 'Drinking Patterns and Alcoholism in the Chinese', in M. Marshall (ed.), *Beliefs, Behaviors, and Beverages: A Cross-cultural Survey*, Ann Arbor: University of Michigan press, pp. 313–26.

Sklair, L. (1991), *Sociology of the Global System*, Baltimore: Johns Hopkins University Press.

Smart, A. and J. Smart (2003), 'Urbanization and the Global Perspective', *Annual Review of Anthropology* 32: 263–85.

South China Morning Post (2001a), '70 Percent Felt Pinch of Hard Times, Survey Shows', 2 October.

—— (2001b), 'Alarm Sounded on Poverty', 24 September.

—— (2002), 'SAR's Jobless Figure Suffers by Comparison', 17 July.

Stein, P. (1997), 'Asia's Financial Ills Spill into Cognac Market', *The Wall Street Journal* 19 December: B9A.

Wall, T. L, S. M. Horn, M. L. Johnson, T. L. Smith and L. G. Carr (2000), 'Hangover Symptoms in Asian Americans with Variations in the Aldehyde Dehydrogenase (ALDH2) Gene(*)', *Journal of Studies on Alcohol* 61: 13–17.

Watson, J. L. (ed.) (1997), *Golden Arches East: McDonalds in East Asia*, Stanford: Stanford University Press.

Wu, Y. H. D. and S. C. H. Cheung (eds) (2002), *The Globalization of Chinese Food*, Honolulu: University of Hawaii Press.

Zhang, F.-P. (1982), 'Drinking in China: The Drinking and Drug Practices', *Surveyor* 18: 12–15.

Internet Sources

Bureau National Interprofessionnel du Cognac (BNIC) (2002) *www.bnic.fr/web_bnic/htm/Economie/2000_2001/eco_com_vente_pays.html#ho*

Cognac Torula News Market Data (2002) *www.swfrance.com/torula/torulamarket.htm*

India Today, Fourth Quarter (1997) The Reinvention of Cognac. *www.inida-today. com/iplus/41997/cognac.html*

New Beverage Publication, Inc. (1998) *www.beveragebusiness.com/art-arch/ bnesta01.html*

Pacific Exchange Rate Service (2003) *pacific.commerce.ubc.ca/xr/*

References in Chinese

Huang, L. H. (2000), *The Evolution of Chinese Food and Drinking Culture*, Beijing: Chinese Academy of Social Sciences.

Lee, Z. G. (1999), *Drinking Culture, Medicinal Wine and Health*, Taipei: One Bridge Pub.

Li, Hua Hsu (1995), *Chinese Drinking Culture*, Shanxi, People's Republic of China: Shanxi People's Publications.

Man, G. K. (1998), *Chinese Alcoholic Beverages*, Taipei: Sook Hing Pub.

Zhang, Y. (2000), *Chinese Culture and Traditions*, Shanghai: Shanghai University Press.

–7–

Consuming Wine in France
The 'Wandering' Drinker and the *Vin-anomie*

Marion Demossier

In two of the most important publications in the anthropological approach to the drinking of alcohol (Douglas 1987; de Garine 2001), it has been argued that drinking has to be studied in a comparative context and that anthropologists have a distinctive perspective to offer on this social act. For Mary Douglas (1987: 3), the specificity of the anthropological perspective is to examine drinking as a 'constructive' activity, a way of life, one element of a given culture, while, for de Garine (2001: 2), drinking endorses a negative as well as a positive activity. According to these authors, anthropologists have traditionally turned their attention to the issue of drinking as a 'social act performed in a recognized social context' (Douglas 1987: 4). Yet few studies have focused on drinking as a marker of national and regional identity and as a complex field for asserting and negotiating questions of competition, power, identity and social ordering, that is to say, as a 'field for action' (Douglas 1984: 30). It is also true that most of the studies presented in these multi-authored volumes have employed traditional ethnographic methods which focus upon a specific fieldwork or locale. However, the complexity of the national or regional character of drinking or even the issue of changes affecting it has been largely ignored by anthropologists.

This chapter aims to explore the complex position of wine in France. A single national alcoholic drink, French wine, has been defined as 'a national treasure' (Ulin 1995: 524). At the same time, as a plural drink, French wines express a whole range of social relations that refer to a complex and dynamic set of meanings and values. As Loubère has noted, 'all the regional wine economies were strongly influenced by geographic, economic and cultural ties to the Nation' (1990, as quoted in Ulin 1995: 523). By employing the technique of a multi-sited ethnography as defined by Douglas Holmes (2000), it is possible to analyse different cultural perspectives on drinking as a place for the production, performance, expression and reception of drinking cultures. The practices of wine drinking provide a space for the renegotiation of social ordering and define the changing relationship between national and regional identities in France. In this context, ethnography offers a fruitful way to explore the dynamic and fragmented character of this complex social act embodying attributes of social organization and general culture.

This chapter is based upon ten years of participant observation[1] of wine production in France and uses a fragmented and multi-sited ethnography encompassing
wine festivals, wine fairs, wine clubs, wine expertise and extensive interviews with
professionals in the wine trade. The intention is to explore different aspects of the
diversity of meanings, discourses and actions encountered in relation to the concept
of 'wine-drinking culture' as a cultural object as defined by Gusfield (1987: 75). This
is understood as a 'cultural production' (in the sense underlined by Ulin 2002), as 'a
medium in which other levels of categorisation become manifest' (Douglas 1984:
30), and as a national and regional emblem that is expressed through both the media
of literature and scholarship and patterns of consumption. Using a series of detailed
ethnographies of wine culture, including the composition of the *Guide Hachette*, the
spring fair of *Caves Particulières*, the wine festival of the *Saint Vincent tournante*
and a multi-sited ethnography of drinking places, this chapter will address the
complex and dynamic nature of wine drinking in France by discussing the ambigui-
ties raised by a declining wine-drinking culture, as set against the background of the
constant work of 'cultural production' led by specific national and regional social
actors to construct drinking wine as 'an ideal world' (Douglas 1987: 11). In consuming wine, there are a number of values and social representations which act as
cultural markers indicating the main elements that define French national and
regional identities. It could be argued that when consuming wine, the drinker imbibes
tradition, time, space and authenticity, a core of common values which helps to
define common identity. What is at stake here is the balance of power between
producers and consumers, experts, connoisseurs and what I shall define as 'wandering drinkers', and, last but not least, national and regional identities in the context of
French society. French national identity, which could be identified by the consumption of a single ordinary type of wine, has seen its sphere of influence challenged by
the increasing consumption of quality wines attached to specific wine-growing
regions. In this context, the concept of regional identity has come to the fore through
this new type of consumption, a new medium for social differentiation and identification. Drinking is often central to French senses of individual identity, beliefs and
collective representations. I would argue that through the consumption of wine and
by choosing which wine to buy, when and how or with whom to drink it, individuals
are actively engaged in a process of identity building.

Wine-drinking Culture in France

Through its soil, its people, its history, its culture, customs, daily life, literature or
songs, France is inextricably linked to the vine and to wine.

Durand 1994: 820; author's translation

Wine drinking and the culture associated with it are for many an essential part of what it means to be French. According to no less an authority than Theodore Zeldin (1977: 755), 'the part wine played in life – at the end of the nineteenth century and the beginning of the twentieth century – was indeed as considerable and as complex as that of political and social ideas'. Roland Barthes (1973) has reached similar conclusions, defining wine as a 'totem drink' and underlining its seminal importance to French culture. Drinking wine remains a national technique with its associated sociability, self-control and culture of moderation defining an important part of what it means to be French. For French people, wine, or, more precisely, the love of good wines, characterizes Frenchness in much the same way as being born in France, fighting for liberty or speaking French.[2] The cliché of the French people as a nation of wine connoisseurs remains widespread within France and abroad. This image of a strong national wine-drinking culture still prevails in the national imagination despite the changes affecting wine production and consumption. Most of the French literature on wine has, until recently, been written by historians, social scientists, experts, connoisseurs and politicians who continue to repeat the traditional story.[3] Yet the seemingly impregnable position of the 'civilisation' of wine has started to come under attack, and it is time to ask if the existence of a distinctive French wine culture is a myth,[4] and if it is not, whether it still serves as a medium for the preservation and transmission of cultural and national memory.

In Pierre Nora's fêted *Les Lieux de mémoire* (1994), Georges Durand devoted a chapter to the three main types of memory associated with wine – personal, national and cultural – arguing that wine has become a place of memory. French wine-drinking culture as it was traditionally constructed acted as a repository of memories underlying major changes affecting French society, such as the rural/urban divide, the growing fragmentation of French society and the changing nature of social classes. These social changes illustrate the transformation of wine as an element of French national identity, and the reshaping of regional and local identities attached to wine production and consumption. As Nora pointed out (1994: 1011, author's translation), 'the past no longer guarantees the future, memory which is continuity enables the reshaping of a fragmented national identity'.

In order to explore the changes affecting wine consumption and culture and their relationship to expressions of national, regional and local identities, it is important to recall that wine drinking has become increasingly detached from the act of eating, representing a unique act of consumption in its own right. By shifting from an integrated element of diet into an intrinsically hedonistic food, it has gained a highly complex set of meanings. Attached to these new representations, wine tasting has also become an *affaire de goûts*, or a place of social discernment, hierarchy and power. Wine drinking has become drinking wines. Bourdieu (1979) has argued that taste is socially constructed and that, traditionally, the hierarchy of wines became identified with the social hierarchy. The consumption of quality wine was historically

attached to the emergence of the bourgeoisie and restaurants, which have transformed the act of eating and drinking into a highly cultural and social occasion. As
Bourdieu has pointed out, among the bourgeoisie, foods are also sources of pleasure,
but with less emphasis on the physical character of food than on its commensal and
taste-symbolizing aspects. The symbolic dimension of wine drinking has been the
apanage of the bourgeoisie. With the democratization of eating out and with the
recent and growing importance of the middle class, new strategies were needed to
differentiate groups of individuals from each other and wine offered a means of
expressing this differentiation: 'I love Bordeaux . . . I do not like Burgundy . . . I
prefer vins de pays.' The varied patterns of consumption are illustrated by the many
discourses embedded in the cultural object of wine, and, very often, the consumer
finds him/herself lost in the profusion of expertises. The access to oenological/
scientific discourse is thus, in part, a question of power, as very often people who are
able to describe wine position themselves in relation to that knowledge, distinction
and social domination.

Consequently, there are various tensions between different types of consumers,
the connoisseur and the wandering drinker, who increasingly define their identities
through wine drinking and through a complex set of consumption and cultural
patterns. The connoisseur is defined as the classic example of the educated drinker
for whom wine culture is much more than drinking wine, while the wandering
drinker might be defined as the average wine drinker who knows little about it and
is experiencing a *vin-anomie*, in a social world of wine with too many norms and
rules that make some people confused and anxious. There are also numerous examples of people making their careers out of the publication of this knowledge, and each
wine-producing region can boast its own local culture and experts who seek to
disseminate it. New wine cultures have emerged at both local and national level in
response to the decline of a traditional and national wine-drinking culture.

These developments have taken place against a background of changing French
and European patterns of food and drink consumption which are heavily influenced
by a growing concern for healthy eating. As eating and drinking and the pleasures of
the table have always loomed large in the French perception of what constitutes the
good life (Zeldin 1977: 725), the effects have been particularly dramatic. According
to the French sociologist Claude Fischler (1990), French dietary patterns have been
transformed since the 1970s. He has argued that a new model of consumption has
emerged combining traditional and modern practices, something he describes as
gastro-anomie. Put simply, this can be defined by the lack of norms and rules
defining food consumption. For example, a growing number of French people will
prefer a snack during lunchtime hours instead of a meal. However, recent studies[5]
have argued that the only element which has survived modernity is the emphasis
placed on sharing a meal together, with commensality still structuring daily life.

The same social phenomenon of *vin-anomie* has revised the position of wine in
French culture and has altered its consumption patterns, but it could be argued that

commensality remains here the principal element of wine consumption. Several anthropological studies have argued that 'drinking brings pleasure and could act as a social lubricant in many gatherings' (de Garine 2001: 2). Yet it could also be used as a space for expressing tensions between individual and collective identities, between the emerging figure of the wandering drinker and the declining national figure of the connoisseur. If we look at the official statistics, alcohol consumption decreased by a remarkable 25 per cent between 1970 and 1990.[6] While declining in popularity, wine is still the dominant beverage. Beer consumption remains stable and the consumption of spirits has increased slightly.[7] Since 1981, the percentage of regular drinkers of wine has decreased continually, while the proportion of occasional drinkers continues to rise as a specific social and cultural phenomenon. The growing number of wine clubs illustrates this recent trend. However, according to Badouin (1990: 41), the proportion of non-consumers appears to have stabilized following a period of increase (23.6 per cent in 1980 to 38.2 per cent in 1990). It is worth noting that in 1990, the number of people who declared that they never drink wine was as high as 50 per cent, which demonstrates a huge change in alcohol drinking culture. The norm has shifted from a collective alcohol-drinking culture to a non-alcohol-drinking culture. If these statistics reveal profound changes in French society, they also suggest that drinking wine has become a strong social and cultural marker and therefore a sign of social differentiation. Drinking even more than eating provides a vehicle for a conferring or displaying of status in which prohibitions and preferences operate (de Garine 2001: 6). To question them enables us to understand to what extent drinking as a biological need and as a social act is intrinsically an element of social identity in action.

The principal change affecting wine consumption is related directly to the nature of wine itself, in which a product once appreciated for its nutritional qualities has been transformed into a beverage loved for its taste. Wine has been replaced by water as the staple drink consumed during the family meal. The consumption of alcoholic drinks, and especially wine, is now closely related to the nature of the meal, whether or not it is a special social occasion. The phenomenon of eating out has also influenced the separation of ordinary family meals from more festive and occasional events, with a greater emphasis upon drinking for social occasions. As consumption has declined, wine has increasingly become a noble drink and a sign of 'distinction'. In the process, it has been transformed into a highly ritualized and 'cultural' object. Connoisseurship in the matter of wine is in itself a field for competition and it has the power to identify the person as well as the wine (Douglas 1987: 9). Taking possession of wines and 'all the manners' involved in their use grants the person a certain status and a certain identity. Good wine and the culture attached to it has become a symbol of a middle-class lifestyle, and more so than food its consumption acts as a social marker or a sign of belonging to a dominant social class (Grignon and Grignon 1980: 533). According to Holt (1997: 113), those with high cultural resources construct what they perceive to be a unique style through the consumption of objects and through authenticity and connoisseurship. Today, however, with more individuals adopting modern lifestyles, the core of wine-drinking culture as a cultural, symbolic and material object has come under attack.

As Douglas has argued (1987: 12), the economic dimension of wine culture plays a major role in the way the product is used as a commodity. Wine production has always been a protected economic sector, and France still ranks amongst the largest wine-producing countries worldwide, which helps to safeguard the domestic market. However, since the 1950s, France has had to redefine its position, owing to its membership of the European Union and the resulting competition from major wine-producing nations such as Italy and Portugal. More recently, the emergence of New World wines has offered further competition and it is likely to pose a serious challenge to French wines in the future.[8] Consequences of this competition have been a significant improvement in the quality of wine produced in France and a concentration of the major companies in the wine sector. These developments have increased the range of wines available to the consumer, responding in part to the growing diversification of drinkers and their desires, and contributing in turn to changes in tastes. Another major influence has been the role of the wine industry and Anglo-Saxon experts in standardizing tastes and advising producers to create wines with oak flavours (which are perceived as more stable and reliable from one vintage to another). Accompanying these changes, a large number of local producers have progressively taken control of the commercial side of their activity and have developed a direct contact with the consumer. As a consequence, regional and national markers of identity have been renegotiated. French people consume fewer wines and are no longer as attached to their local or regional beverage, but are instead prepared to explore other French regions or even other countries through their wine consumption.

Despite the impressive and wide-ranging literature on wine and wine-drinking culture in the arts, humanities and social sciences, few authors have challenged the conception that wine culture and consumption have become fragmented. Two works have, however, adopted a more critical approach, identifying some of the major issues for consideration by any study of wine consumption. In the first, *Drinking in French Culture* (1965), Roland Sadoun, Giorgio Lolli and Milton Silverman raised a number of important issues. First, drinking wine and eating, which are very closely associated in French culture, were defined as two related elements of the process of nutrition. Secondly, wine was not consumed by all their respondents but it was drunk more often than any other alcoholic beverage and in the largest volumes. The authors also concluded that most wine was consumed at home. The largest percentage of wine consumers was found amongst those with an 'average education'. Sadoun et al.'s survey also pointed out the pronounced regional differences in wine consumption, with the lowest percentage of wine drinkers in France living in the Northwest (49 per cent in Normandy and Brittany) and the North (56 per cent in Artois and Picardy), and the highest found in the South (the Midi), where, not surprisingly, wine production was a major industry. The authors' findings clearly challenged the traditional stereotype of the French as knowledgeable and eclectic wine drinkers, but they are rarely cited by French scholars, who have continued to argue for a more united, coherent and national wine-drinking culture.

In the second work to offer a revisionist perspective, *Le buveur du XIXème siècle* (1990), the historian Didier Nourrisson argues that French drinking culture evolved over the course of the nineteenth century. According to his analysis, the French went from consumers of a single type of drink – wine – who varied by age, social class and region, to consumers of many types of drink, whose affluence offered more opportunity for choice at a time when the number and quality of beverages was increasing. In Nourrisson's analysis, the dynamic and geographic character of drinking culture, as a reflection of social, cultural and economic changes, is presented as an essential aspect of any serious study of patterns of alcohol consumption. With this historical context in mind, the contemporary situation can now be explored.

Wine Culture, Writings and Power

> In other words, the social group which has sufficient knowledge to control the quality of wine declines dangerously compared to the declared group of connoisseurs.
>
> Guille-Escuret 1987: 93; author's translation

Episode 1: Ethnography of the 1990 and 1999 Guide Hachette Classification in Burgundy

In January 1990, I participated in a workshop on wine tasting organized by the BIVB (Interprofessional Office for Burgundian Wines), during which I was invited to join the wine-tasting committee of the *Guide Hachette*, which met some weeks later. Several roundtables of 'experts' were formed and we were given the task of tasting specific samples of wines and then discussing them. My panel was composed of a famous female oenologist from one of the big 'wine merchants' in Burgundy, three wine growers from the local area, one courtier[9] and a businessman. The results of our deliberations had to be written up and submitted to the organizer of the panel. Intense discussion followed each tasting, and very often the judgement of the oenologist, seen as an expert, dominated the debate.

Years later, on 14 January 1999, I was invited again, this time in my capacity as an anthropologist, to a wine tasting organized by the *Guide Hachette* for the sixteenth edition of their wine guide. On this occasion, the editor of the guide, Mme Montalbetti, was present to inaugurate the first wine-tasting session. In her speech,[10] she announced, 'I would like to thank you for coming again this year, as it is our seventeenth year together and I would like to thank all the tasters who have worked with us over this period, tasters who come again and again for the pleasure of tasting and also for the rigour of the exercise.' The wine tasting lasted for three months and a local expert technician, M. Bianchi, was appointed to organize this highly 'professional' and orchestrated event. In two of the wine-tasting rooms of the new BIVB, forty-three people, including six women, gathered together to taste fifteen wines from the village of Gevrey-Chambertin. They included sellers, wine merchants, wine growers, wine journalists, chefs and a small number of connoisseurs who had been recruited from all over Burgundy. According to Mme Montalbetti, the quality of the guide derives from the high level of expertise of the professionals involved. She emphasized the relative absence of connoisseurs, with many judged as not sufficiently competent to participate. Tasters are given a place with a separate desk, two Institut National des Appellations d'Origine (INAO) glasses and a technical slip which they have to fill in. In front of them, a sink and a tap enable them to drink water and to spit during the tasting. Each of the forty-three committee members taste blindly (i.e. the bottles are presented with a black cover masking their origins); after the samples are given to them they try to put into words their sensorial experience.

These two ethnographic episodes separated by a period of ten years illustrate how professional wine culture has changed since the 1990s. While wine consumption has declined continuously, a new wine culture – at national and regional level – has proliferated in a variety of ways, from television programmes and specialised literature to wine experts and wine bars (Albert 1989: 117–24). Most libraries now have a specific shelf devoted to drinks as part of the cultural activities on offer, from travel guides to cookery books. In 1994, a specialist wine library was launched by Hachette in collaboration with a Burgundian wine merchant. Accompanying this trend, the wine expert has become one of the main actors in the commercial sphere, and his or her expertise has been legitimized and recognized by these various publications, which present the wine expert as an 'objective taster'.[12] The proliferation of guides and books devoted to wine are a good indication of this movement. The *Guide Hachette* sold 150,000 copies in 1999, while the guide produced by the American wine guru Robert Parker sold 60,000 copies in 1999 (Garcia-Parpet 2000: 151). According to Mme Montalbetti,[13] 'They aim at different audiences. Parker's book is the work of a man with a school of thought and a very personal approach to wine. It is what we called an "art book", while the *Guide Hachette* does not have a "*esprit d'école*" [school of thought].' Another characteristic of the *Guide Hachette* is the diversity of consumers it wishes to embrace: 'to prescribe a search for diversity of taste is how I see its main role', insisted Mme Montalbetti on several occasions during the interview. The great diversity of guides and wines covers nearly all of the editorial market, and it is in part a response to the increasing fragmentation of consumers (Garcia-Parpet 2000: 150). In the case of the *Guide Hachette*, the wide range of experts reflects the diversity of consumers. The success of both guides is also an indication of wider processes affecting drinking tastes in French society.

The world of both wine guides and connoisseurs in France is, however, constructed upon the foundations laid by the ideology of the AOC (Appellation d'Origine

Contrôlée or Denomination of Origin), which was created after the First World War and has now spread to foodstuffs and other traditional products, both in France and elsewhere in Europe. If we take the example of the *Guide Hachette*, it is organized in line with the regions and denominations authorized by the AOC. During the tasting in Beaune in 1999, the wines from different AOCs were sampled together. The whole exercise was controlled by professionals and the experts, who aimed to classify and rank the various producers within the same AOC, which underlines the fact that competition remains constructed at a local rather than at a national level. Their judgement, which is presented as being as 'objective and professional' as possible, is rarely unanimous. In France, the quality of wine could be defined as 'an affair of specialists', and recent studies have argued that quality is often a subjective issue (Casabianca and Saint-Marie 1999; Morrot 1999) and that the legitimacy of the process of decision-making in the wine-tasting committees relies upon a consensual and negotiated process more than an objective evaluation of the product.[14] The interviews that I have conducted over the last ten years with various actors of the wine industry confirm this analysis. They also show very clearly that different professions in the wine industry, from wine waiters to oenologists, use different languages to describe the same product. The growing wine literature underlines this lack of a unified and collective language as far as wine tasting is concerned; it also confirms the fragmented nature of wine-drinking culture. Through the use of a certain language, rituals and practices, specific groups of individuals seek to dominate others. As argued by Giddens (1981: 4), power is regarded as generated in and through the reproduction of structures of domination. Clearly, in an area where the French state is still very active, new groups have sought to empower themselves and to create a new order.

During the meeting held in 1999, the work of the wine-tasting committee, including the definition of the type of wine (red, rosé or white/dry, medium or sweet/ still or sparkling), was followed by the description of the sight/eye (foam/robe if coloured, intensity, colour, legs), the smell/nose (intensity, aromas, bouquet, flaws) and finally the taste/mouth (first impressions, dominant tastes, body, flavours, intensity and flavours, length and flaws, balance). All of these parameters enabled the evaluation of the product based on whether or not it was already drinkable and which dish could best complement it. A special recommendation or *coup de coeur*, which is, according to Mme Montalbetti, seen as the most interesting element of the evaluation, was left to be marked in the bottom right-hand corner. Finally, a mark was given out of five to complete the evaluation, zero being a wine with serious faults which was rejected and five being reserved for an exceptional wine. Each group of three tasters shared the same samples, and from their judgement, the local organizer, M. Bianci, had to produce 'a coherent and technical wine-tasting note', a task that was extremely challenging when the three tasters did not agree on the wine's qualities.

Once the tastings were complete and the technical note had been agreed, a local 'expert' was asked to rewrite each of the notes in a poetic and anecdotal manner. In this case, the 'expert' was a journalist and local politician (a previous head of the regional council) who is the author of a series of best-selling books on the wine-growing villages of Burgundy in which he adopts a literary stance, positioned between folklore and ethnology. Mme Montalbetti briefly mentioned his contribution, praising the highly professional character of the guide.[15] Her comments emphasized the objective context of the wine tasting, which is clearly explained in the guide's introduction. The guide offers a vast panorama of each wine-producing region, and through the editorial work conducted by the local 'expert' or mediator, its publication integrates changes at a micro-socio-economic level, recognizing good producers from one year to the next and shaping their reputations as a result. Its essential role is to transform through its writings the technical evaluation of a wine into a literary description, which in turn contributes to the reputation and revival of a gastronomic regional identity.

This literature is also part of a wider movement associated with a new form of gastronomic regionalism based upon economic regeneration and local identity (Blowen et al. 2001) which contributes to the region's reputation beyond its own administrative boundaries. It could be argued, following Robert Ulin's study of the South-west wine-producing regions (2002: 696), that a similar process of 'cultural production' and invention has taken place in the majority of French wine-growing areas. The guide is a fundamental tool in constructing reputations, and, consequently, in consolidating economic positions. By 'democratizing wine consumption', as Mme Montalbetti has pointed out, the *Guide Hachette* provides a national framework for the expression of local and regional identities through a well-established national and regional politics of taste. This politics of taste is, according to the head of the *Guide Hachette*, a question of 'everyone expressing his or her difference. We live in a society which must be diverse. Each one has to tell his or her difference.' Wine has therefore become a commodity through which to express differences and 'distinction', and in this respect, the expert who can decode this complexity occupies a powerful position in the diffusion of culture. Its consumption, however, relates back to social differentiation, questions of exclusion, and questions of local and regional identity. It confirms the hegemonic position of some wine producers compared to others in this highly competitive sector.

Wine Consumption and Social Differentiation

Wine is a food for hierarchy and consequently it contributes to the hierarchization of society.

Guille-Escuret 1987: 63; author's translation

Episode 2: Ethnography of the Spring Wine Fair of the Caves Particulières in 1997

On 11 April 1997, I was invited to interview M. Jean Ezingeard, the president of the spring wine fair of the *Caves Particulières* (the head office is situated in Orange, South of France) in Paris (where they had organized their spring fair). The spring wine fair of the *Caves Particulières* (private cellars) is a public event organized by wine producers from all of the main wine-producing regions of France, enabling visitors to buy wine directly from the producer. It is part of a wider economic change by which producers have taken a direct control of the commercialization of their products. The wine fair has attracted growing interest over recent years. In 1994, 25,000 visitors attended, and by 1997, this figure had risen to 45,000. Most of the visitors are from cities and the majority of them from Paris. Twenty-two wine growers participated in 1994, a figure that rose astronomically to 910 in 1997, attesting to the growing presence of individual wine growers in the commercial sphere and to their need to sell directly to customers. The modern building, with its glass and aluminium structure, was in stark contrast to the internal decoration of the fair, where artificial grapes, oak barrels, green and white displays, INAO glasses and a large red carpet dominated the scene.

At the reception, I asked for M. Ezingeard and I was sent to his stand.[16] A stocky vigneron welcomed me with a warm handshake and then proceeded to announce that he was 'the president of a place for authenticity and conviviality, and definitely not a fun fair'. The beginning of our discussion focused on the historical development of the wine fair, and his discourse emphasized the importance of a collective organization of Southern French producers, established in the 1970s, with the aim of taking over the commercialization of their wines. Their influence still dominates the organization of the fair, and from the various displays it is easy to guess where each producer comes from. Each region and each producer tries to impose their own image through such techniques as the displays of bottles and labels on the stand, their wine boxes or the presentation of the *Guide Hachette* conveniently opened to reveal their own personal entry. The sense of diversity and the informal nature of the fair, which is organized in a very haphazard fashion (it was easy to get lost because of the lack of a clear layout between the wine-growing regions), confirms the heterogeneous nature of both production and consumption.

In this open space, visitors wandered about in pursuit of their wine pleasure and passions. Some people already had a clear idea of what they sought, announcing that, for example 'we want to buy twelve bottles of Château-Margaux', while others were more curious and were searching for something new: 'White or red? Which AOC?' asked a producer. The publicity for the wine fair illustrated this tendency: 'Behind each of the bottles that you will meet on your travels, you will see a face, hear a personal story, taste a specific and unique savoir-faire.' Most of the visitors were Parisian men, but during the weekend more wine lovers arrived from all over France, especially for this occasion. The masculine nature of the crowd denoted that wine tasting remains a male collective activity, yet very often, groups of men and women or couples come together to buy the wine. What strikes the anthropologist is the sharp contrast between urban (consumers from the cities) and rural worlds (the wine growers).[17] The fair provides a social space for the urban dwellers in quest of their rural roots. However, any clear sense of social differentiation between the visitors becomes very difficult to read. The profile of the connoisseur of wine[18] in particular dominated the various conversations I had with those present. The wine producers interviewed during the fair confirmed that the connoisseur was their favourite customer and that during this event they had made some interesting and memorable contacts. The producers made the point that the connoisseur was the customer they were looking for, a person of discernment who knows about wine and is not obsessed with labels and 'big names'. There was, however, a strong sense that wine tasting had to be controlled and limited. This distinctive pattern of moderation was encouraged by the organizers, and throughout the exhibition there were posters displaying a single half-empty glass of wine.[19] Security guards were on the scene to assure cohesion and social order in the event of anyone failing to heed this subliminal message.

The success of such events, which have multiplied over the last thirty years, illustrates only one aspect of the changes affecting wine consumption. This is part of a new attraction for popular tastes or 'vins de pays' which illustrates again this new type of consumption dominated by occasional and urban drinkers. Recent surveys have confirmed the increase in the consumption of quality wine, which rose from around 4 million hectolitres in 1960 to 13 million in the 1990s (Badouin 1990: 38). In response to this demand for good wines, the INAO has seen the number of applications for the official status of AOC (denomination of origin) soar dramatically over the last ten years. A growing social differentiation has accompanied this trend. According to Boulet et al. (1991: 24), demographic differences associated with gender and age predominate today. Men and women drink differently: 10.9 per cent of women consumed wine every day in 1990 as against 28.1 per cent of men. To put these figures into perspective, it is interesting to note that the proportion of women drinking every day has declined by 54.8 per cent since 1980, while the comparable figure for men is also a dramatic 32.3 per cent. On the other hand, the proportion of non-consumers has grown from 34.5 per cent in 1980 to 58.5% in 1990 (male non-consumers represented 26.5 per cent in 1980 and 43 per cent in 1990). The 'occasional' category remains stable amongst women, while it has increased slightly amongst men. In terms of age, the rise of non-consumers has affected all age groups and a similar pattern underlies the decline of regular wine consumers. A certain degree of social disordering is going on, reshaping social positions and issues of power. In this new social context, the figure of the connoisseur as a regular consumer emerged as a powerful voice, in contrast to the new occasional drinker, which seems to be used as a symbolic figure in the new wine-marketing campaigns.

Young people are also targeted by marketing campaigns of the wine industry. It is clear that from the 1980s wine was no longer such an integral part of the culture and consumption patterns of young people. This shift has affected most of the Southern European cultures of the wine belt, especially France, Italy and Spain. These tendencies have been confirmed by ONIVINS-INRA's 2002 report.[20] However, these statistical surveys tend to ignore regional variations and focus instead upon a typological approach to an increasingly differentiated and fragmented type of consumption. Drinking has become a marker for an increasing social differentiation, and its analysis defies any strict and straightforward sociological explanation. This is why only a multi-sited ethnography can enable us to grasp drinking as a complex object of analysis. However, for governmental and professional bodies, the consumer's needs have to be anticipated in the context of the already declared crisis of French wines (Berthomeau 2001).

My ethnography of a wine club situated in the urban area of Chalon-sur-Saône offers an excellent illustration of the middle-class nature of the new wine culture. The majority of the members of the club are male professionals, many of whom are retired, including doctors, civil servants, teachers and businessmen, with a small minority of women accompanying their husbands or partners. From the various meetings organized by the group, it is clear that wine is perceived as a special, rather mysterious product and most of the members have joined the club to learn more about it. Their meeting provides the members with an introduction to different wine-producing regions, and the samples tasted are chosen in collaboration with the local oenologist, following a trip to the chosen wine-producing area. Each participant is given a card explaining the main characteristics of the wines tasted. The organizers are devoted to exploring the variety of wines in France and to sharing this knowledge with the club members. In their discourse, they claim that, contrary to the traditional wine club, they are open to all those interested in joining the club, and they cite the example of Jean, a black factory worker, who is a member. That they should feel the need to justify their social openness does, however, raise suspicions about its true extent.

If wine consumption has been democratized, as has been argued by Gilbert Garrier (1994: 249), it has also been transformed into a quest for individual identity in an increasingly fragmented and postmodern society. In this context, the study conducted by Boulet et al. (1991) is stimulating, as it argues for three distinctive types of behaviour related to wine consumption. Their analysis, which is based upon a socio-economic typology of consumers, confirms the fragmentation of social groups in relation to wine consumption and this pattern is illustrated in our wine club. The authors have identified three specific groups of consumers. First is the regular consumer who drinks every day and who is represented by the categories of 'retired people', *ouvriers sportifs* (active working-class men) and 'farmers'.[21] The occasional consumer, on the other hand, tends to be drawn from the middle classes and seems to be the appropriate label for the majority of wine drinkers encountered during this study. And finally, the last group includes 53.2 per cent of the non-consumers and is represented by young women, *modestes complexés* and 'young couples living together'. Occasional wine consumption is, therefore, the increasingly typical behaviour of a specific type of individual, often young, with a comfortable economic position and possessing some cultural capital. The figure of the wandering drinker corresponds to this emerging pattern of *vin-anomie* that is illustrated by the two last categories. The regular consumer is to some extent the personification of certain types of connoisseurs. It could, however, be argued that the wide range of consumers reflects to some extent the social disorder and the increasing fragmentation of the drinkers.

The figure of the connoisseur, often cited, but rarely met, remains emblematic of French wine culture and consumption, but his pre-eminence disguises the lack of a national oenological culture and the relative decline of regular wine consumers. Is the connoisseur another mythical creature? The profile of the connoisseur which is prominent in the vast literature on wines is seen as crucial to understanding the social processes and the values embedded in wine consumption and culture. Yet defining the connoisseur is not an easy task, as social diversity and differentiation affect wine-drinking culture and consumption. The recent upsurge of wine culture in France has, to some extent, contributed to the construction of the connoisseur as a repository of collective memory, who shares his time between drinking wine and buying books, guides and maps of French wine-producing regions in order to make sense of a complex world. The emergence of this curious creature is connected to a wine culture which has been democratized, professionalized and diffused through literature and the media. On the other hand, the figure of the average drinker provides us with a different image of wine-drinking culture. For some drinkers, wine has become an object of social tensions and its consumption has been transformed into a search for identities and differentiation. From a private and domestic activity organized around the family meal, wine drinking has been transformed into a social, public and ritualized act around which the individual is constructing an 'ideal world'.

The 'Wandering Drinker'

> Today, drinking takes place at home. Before that (in the nineteenth century), individual or collective drinking took place above all in a public sphere.
>
> Nourrisson 1990: 9, author's translation

Episode 3: Ethnography of the Saint Vincent tournante. January 1991, Puligny-Montrachet (Burgundy)[22]

The *Saint-Vincent tournante*, the principal regional wine festival of Burgundy, takes place on the first weekend following Saint Vincent's day, 22 January, in honour of the patron saint of wine growers. The right to host the *Saint Vincent tournante* rotates amongst the wine-growing villages of Burgundy and returns every thirty years to its point of departure. The village chosen for the event by the Confrérie des Chevaliers du Tastevin[23] organizes a procession attended by representatives of the seventy-five mutual aid societies in the region, followed by a church service held in parallel with a free wine tasting and, finally, three banquets of honour. Over the years, the festival has been transformed from a family and village gathering into a vast celebration which is open to the public for two days. In 1961, two Americans were invited by the local wine merchant to follow the small procession going to the church. In 1991, more than 100,000 people turned up, including visitors from Switzerland and America. Thirty thousand bottles of wine were drunk, three banquets were organized and the village made a profit of around 4 million French francs. By buying a glass for 25 francs, visitors were able to taste the wines for free. The festival is the occasion to drink good wines which are normally confined to prestigious wine tastings, without specific ritual and *mise en scène*. Three types of wine are consumed during the festival itself. The wine of the *cuvée* Saint Vincent, which is drunk in a public space, was served from the bottle to the glass and was offered directly to the consumer without the ritual accompaniment traditionally attached to this type of wine. This wine is intended for the thousands of visitors who can consume without limits a famous and normally not affordable wine. On the other hand, a hierarchy of bottles of good wines with labels is consumed in the more private and social space of the three banquets, organized by the Confrérie, the local priests and finally the wine growers of the host village. The latter includes the wine growers' clients and focuses on an emblematic and highly ritualized type of wine consumption which accompanies the elaborate meal prepared by a distinguished Burgundian chef. The *Saint Vincent tournante* thus provides an excellent example of how different social situations produce markedly different types of wine consumption for different drinkers and how the festival offers a medium for the expression and reception of a wide range of social identities.

The historical development of the festival illustrates the emergence of a new type of wine consumption. In 1961, wine consumption was privately organized and structured by each family around the Sunday meal. By 1991 it had became a festive, public, less institutionalized and more fragmented type of consumption, shedding light on a new social hierarchy of drinkers. This development could be explained by the wine growers' increasing experience of the commercialization of their wines and the need to attract more customers by promoting the village's name. It is worth noting that as wine consumption has become more public, festive and separated from eating (wine shops and wine bars have given a more visible and social status to wine consumption in French society), differentiation has also become increasingly visible (as revealed in the 1999 festival when compared to 1961). The public and private dimensions of wine drinking have had to be renegotiated. In line with this change, the more public it has become, the less it has been controlled. In 1961, nobody in the village was seen to be drunk during the festival and most of the wine consumption was organized as part of a family meal. By contrast, the organizers of the most recent festivals have complained about the increasing problem of excessive drinking. There were several cases of alcoholic comas in 1991,[24] which is something the Burgundian wine growers do not want to see associated with their product. This problem illustrates the difficult relationship of young French people with alcohol. As one twenty-something visitor from Dijon commented to me, 'Wine is not as much a part of our culture; we are a different generation from our parents, a generation that consumes more than any other, but wine is not part of it.' Excessive consumption also underlines the extraordinary and festive character of the event. In this sense, festive also means occasional. Another important development within the festival of the *Saint Vincent tournante* has been the opening of the wine cellars. Instead of a family gathering, the tasting has become an opportunity to advertise the AOC and to publicize the name of the village and that of the region.

The organization of the festival emphasizes this aspect, giving the wine's name to different wine cellars, from the Folatières to the Clavoillon. The menus of each of the three banquets held during the festival also highlight the various AOCs belonging to the village and enhances the position of each wine in the local hierarchy of wines: 'Lobsters go well with Bâtard-Montrachet (grand cru, white wine)'. For most diners, moderate consumption is encouraged by the combination of distinction with taste. First and foremost, it becomes a stylish exercise of your tastes and a proof of your 'distinction'. Again by becoming public, wine consumption has become more ritualized and sophisticated under the increasing power of the connoisseurs (and not the wine growers). It is worth noticing that in the process, the group represented by the wine growers has declined, becoming marginal as wine tasting is increasingly recognized as a professional art. In this respect, Mary Douglas (1987: 9) has argued, connoisseurship also has its own power for social domination.

The *Saint Vincent tournante* thus reveals a wider phenomenon. Visitors now come from all over France and many take the opportunity to visit the region and combine buying wine with tourism. The leisure culture, of which tourism is an important element, has recently been given a boost in France by the lowering of the retirement age and the new 35-hour week (Demossier and Milner 2000: 76). The emergence of a new wine tourism has accompanied this trend and almost every wine-growing region has its own wine route, and has encouraged the publication of regional guides about gastronomy and wines. The wine tour has contributed to the modernization of local infrastructures and tourist accommodation (Plichon 1996: 131). Numerous examples could be given to illustrate the general efforts of local governments and of the French state to promote French wines, both at home and abroad.

In this voyage of discovery of French wine-producing regions, the wine grower and his wife have emerged as the main intermediaries. In contrast to the supermarkets or the chains of wine merchants such as Nicolas, the wine grower offers an alternative type of consumption based upon a more personalized and authentic approach.

The client has to contact him to make an appointment and the meeting is always organized around the tasting of new wines in barrels followed by bottles of the most recent vintages. Their relationship is based upon a regular and personal contact that each partner tries to maintain. The wine growers are well aware of the ephemeral nature of their modern clientele, who in general demonstrates the following features: occasional in his/her consumption, looking for a new discovery, a *coup de coeur*, passionate in his/her quest and basing the quest on the consumption of others. This approach, incarnated in the wine grower, is a surviving emblem of a rapidly disappearing rural France. However, wine consumption is often more than a simple passion. For many individuals, wine drinking has also become a means of defining their identity in an increasingly modern and fragmented world.

Tell Me What You Drink and I Shall Tell You Who You Are: I Drink Wine Therefore I Am French?

Without wine, France would probably not be France.

Sadoun et al. 1965: 48

Episode 4: Consuming Wine in Different Places

When working as an anthropologist with producers and wine growers, very often a collective wine consumption takes place that it is presented as compulsory for all the members of that group. In the context of a wine club tasting such as that in Chalon-sur-Saône in 1999, on the other hand, consumption is an individual matter and is non prescriptive, in the sense that the anthropologist is very often left to observe rather than being obliged to participate. Specific features differentiate the very structured organization of the professional wine tasting from the less organized space of the wine club. In the first case, the tasting takes place in the cellar, in the morning or in the evening, each individual standing and walking from one barrel to the next, commenting briefly on the wine, but focusing more on the technical aspect of the wine grower's work or on the climatic characteristics of the vintage. The wine club and its members, on the other hand, put great emphasis on the social dimension of the tasting: the wine tasting takes place in the evening, before dinner, and each *dégustation* of the wines selected for the occasion is accompanied by a verbal and emotional description which focuses on sensations, feelings and tastes. Each member enjoys the sharing of his or her experience with the person next to him/her. The silent and quasi-religious atmosphere of the first setting contrasts vividly with the noisy and hedonistic ambiance of the wine club. This consumption could be characterized in the first case as moderate, technical and hierarchically organized – from the youngest to the oldest vintage and from the lowest denomination to the more emblematic one. However, its second context is more accurately defined as a question of pleasure, freedom and a quest for identity: 'I really like this wine, how would you describe it? It reminds me of . . . .' Members of the wine club use the occasion as a means to maintain social relations or to establish new ones. Tasting the wine offers a way of communicating with others and of recalling memories. Moreover, drinking wine is a social act which re-creates a lost sociability in the context of our modern society, creating timeless moments which are perceived as separated from the ordinary.

Between producers and consumers, another group of actors plays an essential role which positions them both literally and figuratively in fields of power which should be seen as socially mediated (Ulin 2002: 694). Wine culture in France is defined by the role of intermediaries, whose ranks include oenologists, wine waiters (*sommeliers*), wine merchants, *cavistes* and chefs,[25] who play a major role in the upsurge of a gastronomic regionalism. However, their field of power is rather fragmented, especially when wine is concerned. Interviews which I conducted in 1999 with these different professional groups soon revealed very different perceptions of wine. For oenologists, the technical nature of the product is central to their description and to their relationship to the wine they drink. Therefore, a specific and highly technical discourse often accompanies their judgement. Their comments refer to basic elements of nature and reveal that wine could be, according to them, objectively grasped. Many of the oenologists I interviewed were very critical of the role performed by the *sommeliers*, who were perceived as being at the other extreme of the spectrum, as 'the eulogists of wine'. The *sommeliers*, on the other hand, refer to a symbolic and cultural approach to wine and very often their approach focuses on its literary and poetic construction.

Fischler (1999) argues that there are two distinct drinking cultures, illustrating the divisions underlined above: the *boire froid*, characterized by a technical approach which dissects, analyses and searches for defects, and the *boire chaud*, which dreams, imagines, fantasizes, remembers, feels and eventually gets intoxicated with sensations. This dichotomy illustrates the range of discourses surrounding wine from a nature/culture perspective, and it must be argued that the consumer is much more aware of the cultural than of the technical dimension. Ulin (2002: 700) has used this dichotomy between artisans and scientists when analysing power as a differentiated cultural production of work and self-identity amongst the South-West wine growers. It could also be argued that both sides of this spectrum are embedded in the *Guide Hachette*, incarnated, on the one hand, by the jury of professionals, and, on the other hand, by the local expert. While the scientific and technical dimension of wine drinking dominates the social arena, most French people are interested in the cultural element. Surveys of French opinion frequently produce observations such as 'Wine is and must be an authentic and symbolic product' (Ipsos-Insight Marketing 1999).

Despite the increasingly fragmented wine-drinking culture, there are a number of other specific values enhanced during the process of consumption which act as cultural markers, indicating the main elements that define individual identities. First, we could argue that the process of non-consumption is still perceived in France as an exclusive act, as alcohol consumption is an integral part of the process of integrating into a group. By contrast, drinking wine in its multiple forms immediately classifies the drinker as part of a group, a community or as one who subscribes to the specific ideology of *bonne chère* (a hearty meal) and passions. It relates to the process of integration, values of happiness, collectiveness and emotions. The humanist conception dominates drinking, despite the quest for hedonist values. In fact, throughout the fieldwork and interviews that I have conducted over the last decade, wine drinking has nearly always been described as a collective practice enabling individuals to test social cohesion through the control of drunkenness and the emotions attached to it. When the tourist travels around France, he or she is invited to visit a country where friendship, taste, wine and local specialities dominate. His/her quest is about reviving memories of places, people and tastes, a feeling of belonging to an 'imagined community', of a common sociability, an original *communitas*, thus an identity (Demossier 2000: 150). The consumption of wine offers the prospect of an intimate relationship with the wine grower and with a culture that is now separate from his/her own experience as a modern urban dweller. It is also part of the new process of regenerating social bonds and re-creating a sense of community between individuals at a local level.

Another value which underlines the inclusiveness and the sense of belonging to wine-drinking culture is the emphasis put upon authenticity and tradition. Philippe Chaudat (2001) shows how supermarket chains refer to concepts of authenticity, *terroir*, tradition and regional identity to promote local wines from the Jura. The *mise en scène* of these products makes sense for consumers as they refer to their specific local and cultural context, and Chaudat notes that the publicity materials used by the supermarkets rely extensively upon the sense of belonging both to a national French heritage and to a regional identity. The same comments could be applied to the spring fair of *Caves Particulières*, where regional identities coexist with each other to form part of a wider French identity, that is, what it means 'to be French'. Authenticity and tradition are cultural markers which fix specific conceptions and imaginary values to the concept of the present. 'Consuming authenticity will enable the consumption of the imaginary and of the past in order to produce the present, but will equally enable the creation of one's own identity, the appropriation of a geographical space, the interiorization of the image of what he/she drinks and the ability of becoming this image in return' (Chaudat 2001: 722, author's translation). Moreover, consuming authenticity and tradition when drinking wine refers to the concept of time, in the context of a constantly changing society. When drinking wine, it could be argued that consumers reinvent time in a different manner, as immortalized by the poetic expression of Lamartine: 'O Time, cease your flight, and you, o friendly hours, cease passing.'

French consumers are very much attached to the idea of authenticity and to the notion that products have to be more natural and less industrialized and processed.

In a survey on the oenological knowledge of French consumers, conducted by Ipsos-Insight Marketing (1999), it was pointed out that consumers are aware of the technical changes affecting wines, but that they are against any complete modernization of the process of wine making: 'The idea of blending wine seems suspicious to them. . . .' Another aspect discussed in the survey is the attachment of French people to the notion of *terroir*. The concept of *terroir* is almost untranslatable, but it refers to a traditional food or to the agricultural produce of a specific geographical, historic region. It has become a term charged with meaning for French urban dwellers in search of their roots. Wine is at the core of this recent upsurge of interest in *terroir* as it provides for some people a support for the expression of social and economic divisions. For French consumers, *terroir* and AOC wines encapsulate two elements. First, they connote the qualities of the soil and the natural characteristics which made the wine and which classify it within the hierarchy of French wines. Second, they are also about social distinction and economic position, as wine prices depend partly on their ranking. Various factors contribute to the position of each wine within the vast range on offer. Consuming wine, therefore, remains an act of differentiation, in which individuals position themselves in relation to others. In this quest for identities, old and traditional values coexist and it is possible to say that wine has never been so modern.

Conclusion

Through this multi-sited ethnography of French wine-drinking culture, it has been possible to question a number of assumptions concerning the complex and contradictory position of wine culture and consumption in France. The chapter has aimed to treat drinking as a medium for constructing the actual world (Douglas 1987: 9), but also to negotiate some of the changes affecting it. I have shown that a certain amount of social reordering has taken place, challenging notions of French national and regional identities. For French people, despite the modernization of their society, wine remains a 'cultural exception' (Ipsos-Insight 1999), and in this context it is part of the French specificity. Wine as a culture and as an object of consumption has always been used in different ways, and in French culture its emblematic position remains the landmark of a cultural specificity as it still underlines Frenchness. However, it also defines a culture of exclusion. Today, consumption in France could be seen as a way of reshaping old ideologies, and contradictory values are undoubtedly embedded in French wine-drinking culture. The national dimension of wine culture no longer relies on consumption, but has more to do with specific emblematic values which are today in danger of disappearing. Attempts are constantly being made to restore, re-create or invent communities (Warde 1997: 183). The changing political, social and economic context has given rise to new expressions of local, regional and national identities based upon differentiation and competition in the social sphere which are negotiated between individuals, groups and society as a whole. In this process, wine offers, through sociability and exchange, a collective and cohesive way of defining declining collective identities in the context of a changing society. Following Warde's argument (1997: 184), the aspiration to culinary or drinking communion is exhibited in the language of tradition, the appeal of regional cuisines or regional wines, the validation of home cooking and home drinking, nostalgia for high-quality locally produced ingredients and wines, and endless reflection on the authenticity and coherence of national cuisines or wines. It also provides a means of expressing differentiation in the context of a democratization of wine-drinking culture and the emergence of a mass consumption headed by the middle class.

As the middle class started to enjoy drinking, new strategies of social distinction were needed to cultivate this 'distinction'. Individuals are now free to choose what they want to drink, and, in this regard, complex processes of differentiation have taken place. There is a real tension between 'the wandering drinker', who reflects the fragmented type of wine consumption, and the 'connoisseur', who is seen as a dominant and perennial figure in wine culture and who likes a personal and loyal contact with the wine growers. The tensions between these two types of individuals illustrate the difficulty of grasping the concept of a national wine-drinking culture as a homogeneous object. Through wine consumption, individuals compete and construct their identity. The source of identity is the lifestyle image that individuals purposively appropriate or construct and the shared normative orientations underlying their consumption. As regional identities have come to the fore and cease to rely on the consumption of local and regional wines, an intense process of regeneration has taken place at regional level supported by the state. At the same time, the values embedded in wine consumption illustrate the attachment of French people to space, time, rural society, commensality and sociability which are today challenged by globalization, modernity and multiculturalism. These values could be read as the traces of a surviving agrarian ideology or they could be seen as an alternative type of consumption in an increasingly global society. I would like to conclude on a positive note by citing the example of a Muslim Algerian in Montmartre (Paris) who some years ago opened a wine shop despite the unease of his own community. Interviewed in summer 2003 on the French radio, he explained that French wine had helped him to discover France, its regions, its diversity and its people, and he concluded that this was what he wanted to transmit to others.

Acknowledgements

I would like to thank the Department of European Studies of the University of Bath, which granted me with study leave in 1999, and the British Academy, which awarded me a larger research grant to complete this study in 2003–4.

Notes

1. Since 1991, I have conducted extensive fieldwork in Burgundy on the wine-growing community and on wine culture. Much of this research consisted of four intensive years of participant observation and ethnography of different parts of the wine production process. Participant observation was my main line of enquiry and I locate my work in the French anthropological tradition. This has resulted in the publication of *Hommes et vins: une anthropologie du vignoble bourguignon* (Demossier 1999). Since then I have been engaged in a new research project on wine-drinking culture and consumption, the results of which are presented in this chapter. This research project has combined ethnographic fieldwork and interviews of professionals in the wine sector (in Paris and wine-growing regions) and it has been inspired by the work of British and American anthropologists and the structuralist and developmentalist sociology of food.

2. See the survey conducted and analysed by the historian Jean-Pierre Rioux (1987).

3. There is a large literature devoted to wine and its history and culture in France. Much of this aims at preserving the mythical status of wine-drinking culture. Amongst the better recent publications are Garrier (1994) and Fischler (1999).

4. Most of the literature analysing the transformation of wine culture comes from national institutes, collective organizations of wine producers or the media in general. However, some historical studies have also focused on wine consumption and culture (Nourrisson 1990; Garrier 1994), but they rarely discuss the decline of wine culture.

5. See the conference proceedings of 'Food in the Future 1993–1997', published by the Ministry of National Education, Research and Technology in collaboration with the Ministry of Agriculture and Fisheries (Research Programme R 94125 by G. Masson and P. Moscovici).

6. *www.eurocare.org/profiles/franceeupolicy.htm*. For a more precise statistical account of the recent evolution of wine and alcohol consumption in France, see Badouin (1990), Boulet et al. (1991, 1997), and the quinquenial reports produced by the ONIVINS-INRA research team.

7. *www.eurocare.org/profiles/franceeupolicy.htm*

8. For details about the economic situation of French wine, see Jacques Berthomeau's report published in 2001.

9. The courtier is the intermediary between the wine producer and the wine merchant. He or she usually negotiates the transaction between the two actors and is paid a percentage of the overall transaction. He or she also has to ensure that the deliveries will take place in accordance with the agreement between the wine merchant and the wine grower.

10. Mme Montalbetti, interview conducted during the *Guide Hachette* wine tasting, 14 January 1999.

11. These glasses are traditionally used by wine producers to taste their products.
12. From the *Guide Hachette* to the *Parker Guide*, the idea of an objective expertise is always tacitly emphasized, and despite their different styles, the guides tend to construct quality as a consensual and scientific category of perception and taste.
13. Interview, 14 January 1999.
14. For more details, see Casabianca and Sainte-Marie (1999) and Morrot (1999). My ethnography of the *Guide Hachette* confirms their conclusions.
15. Similar comments have been made by Marie-France Garcia-Parpet (2000) about wine expertise in Touraine.
16. The entrance fee includes the right to taste the wines for free. A glass with the logo of the wine fair was given to each visitor.
17. French society in the last census of 1999 is characterized by a growing urbanisation.
18. The connoisseur is recognizable by the way he holds his glass and by his extensive knowledge of wine culture, as opposed to the snob, who is obsessed with labels and prices. Many professionals working in restaurants and shops have confirmed this representation attached to the connoisseur. It is also worth noting that for the professionals the connoisseur is usually perceived as a man.
19. Several French public information campaigns have taken place since the 1980s recommending moderate consumption: from 'one glass is OK, but three is too much' to 'how do you look when you are drunk?' targeting young people, the family, the elderly and companies. The social control over alcohol consumption has increased over the years, but in the debate on alcohol consumption wine still occupies a specific position where it is not perceived like any other alcoholic beverages. The discussion around the *Loi Evin* demonstrates the symbolic and political power of wine in French society and economy. The *Loi Evin* (Evin Law No 91-32 of 10 January 1991) effectively bans direct or indirect TV advertising for beverages whose alcoholic content exceeds 1.2 per cent. The French authorities put in place in 1995 a Code of Conduct which sets out detailed rules as to how this ban applies to TV broadcasts of overseas sports events, where drinks branding may be visible on ad hoardings, players' shirts, etc. In 2004 the law was softened by recognizing wine as a food in order to ease the position of French wine producers.
20. Personal communication with Christian Mélani, ONIVINS, Paris.
21. Of these categories, 64.9 per cent drink wine every day while they represented only 38.1 per cent of the French population. The various categories underlined in their survey are part of the typology constructed by the authors of the report. For more details, see Boulet et al. (1991).
22. For more details on the festival, see Demossier (1997).
23. The Confrérie des Chevaliers du Tastevin was created in Burgundy in 1934 by two local notables, Camille Rodier, the chairman of the tourist office, and

Georges Faiveley, a wine merchant in Nuits-Saint-Georges. It serves as an example all over France, and similar *confréries* now promote the wines of regions such as the Loire or the Bordelais. Since the 1970s, the Confrérie has issued its own special commendation for Burgundian wines called *tastevinage*. For a wine grower to be accorded the *tastevinage* label is a source of professional prestige and potentially of advantage when it comes to the commercialization of his or her vintage. The *Saint Vincent tournante* was part of the commercial operation launched by the Confrérie in the 1930s to provide an economic boost and cement social divisions between wine growers and wine merchants in the context of the crisis.

24. During the *Saint Vincent tournante* of 1991, I counted forty alcoholic comas in two days, with most occurring by 10 o'clock in the morning. The wine producers were very anxious that we did not film this part of the festival.

25. It is interesting to note that the French language dominates the vocabulary attached to wine.

References

Albert, J.-P. (1989), 'La nouvelle culture du vin', *Terrain* 13: 117–24.

Badouin, R. (1990), 'L'évolution de la consommation de vin en France', *Compte-Rendu de l'Académie Agricole Française* 76 (7): 33–42.

Barthes, R. (1973), *Mythologies*, London: Granada.

Berthomeau, J. (2001*), Comment mieux positionner les vins français sur les marchés d'exportation?* Report submitted to Jean Glavany, Minister for Agriculture and Fishing Industries, 31 July.

Blowen, S, M. Demossier and J. Picard (eds) (2001), *Recollections of France: Memories, Identities and Heritage in Contemporary France*, New York, Oxford: Berghahn.

Boulet, D., J-P. Laporte, P. Aigrain and J. L. Lamberti (1991), 'La consommation du vin en France: Évolutions tendancielles et diversité des comportements', *Revue d'Economie Méridionale*, 39 (155–6): 19–52.

Boulet, D., J-P. Laporte, P. Aigrain and C. Mélani (1997), 'La transformation des comportements alimentaires: Cycles de vie et effets de génération. Le cas du vin', *Economies et Societés*, série AG, 23 (9): 47–67.

Bourdieu, P. (1979), *La distinction: Critique sociale du jugement*, Paris: Editions de minuit.

Casabianca, F. and C. Sainte-Marie (1999), 'L'évaluation sensorielle des produits typiques: Concevoir et instrumenter l'épreuve de typicité', The Socio-economics of Origin Labelled Products in Agro-food Supply Chains: Spatial, Institutional and Coordination Aspects, 67th EAAE seminar, Le Mans, 28–30 October.

Chaudat, P. (2001), 'In imagos veritas: Images demandées, images produites', *Ethnologie Française* 4: 717–23.

de Garine, I. (2001), 'For a Pluridisciplinary Approach to Drinking', in I. de Garine and V. de Garine (eds), *Drinking: Anthropological Approaches*, New York: Berghahn, pp. 1–11.

Demossier, M. (1997), 'Producing Tradition and Managing Social Changes in the French Vineyards: The Circle of Time in Burgundy', *Ethnologia Europaea* 27: 47–58.

—— (1999), *Hommes et vins: Une anthropologie du vignoble bourguignon*, Dijon: Presses universitaires de Dijon.

Demossier, M. (2000), 'Culinary Heritage and Produits de Terroir', in S. Blowen, M. Demossier and J. Picard (eds), *Recollections of France: Memories, Identity and Heritage in Contemporary France*, New York: Berghahn, pp. 141–53.

Demossier, M. and S. Milner (2000), 'Social Difference: Age and Place', in S. Reynolds and W. Kidd (eds), *Contemporary French Cultural Studies*, London: Arnold Publishers, pp. 60–81.

Douglas, M. (1984), *Food and the Social Order*, New York: Russell Sage Foundation.

—— (1987), 'A Distinctive Anthropological Perspective', in M. Douglas (ed.), *Constructive Drinking: Perspectives on Drink from Anthropology*, Cambridge: Cambridge University Press, pp. 3–15.

Durand, G. (1994), 'La vigne et le vin', in P. Nora (ed.), *Les Lieux de mémoire, III. Les France, 2. Traditions*, Paris: Gallimard, pp. 785–823.

Fischler, C. (1990), *L'omnivore*, Paris: Éditions Odile Jacob.

—— (1999), *Du vin*. Paris: Éditions Odile Jacob.

Garcia-Parpet, M.-F. (2000), 'Dispositions économiques et stratégies de reconversion: L'exemple de la nouvelle viticulture', *Ruralia* 7: 129–57.

Garrier, G. (1994), *Histoire sociale et culturelle du vin*, Paris: Editions Bordas.

Giddens, A. (1981), *A Contemporary Critique of Historical Materialism, Vol. 1: Power, Property and the State*, Berkeley: University of California Press.

Grignon, C. and C. Grignon (1980), 'Styles d'alimentation et goûts populaires', *Revue française de sociologie* XXI: 531–69.

Guille-Escuret, G. (1987), *La souche, la cuve et la bouteille: Les rencontres de l'histoire et de la nature dans un aliment, le vin*, Paris: Editions de la Maison des Sciences de l'Homme.

Gusfield, J. (1987), 'Passage to Play: Rituals of Drinking Time in American Society', in M. Douglas (ed.), *Constructive Drinking: Perspectives on Drink from Anthropology*, Cambridge: Cambridge University Press, pp. 73–90.

Holmes, D. (2000), *Integral Europe: Fast-Capitalism, Multiculturalism and Neo-Fascism*, Princeton: Princeton University Press.

Holt, D. (1997), 'Distinction in America? Recovering Bourdieu's Theory of Taste from Its Critics', *Poetics* 25: 93–120.

Ipsos-Insight Marketing (1999), *Les Français et le Vin*, survey conducted for the ONIVINS.

Loubère, L. (1990), *The Wine Revolution in France*, Princeton: Princeton University Press.

Morrot, G. (1999), 'Peut-on améliorer les performances du dégustateur?', *Vigne et Vin publications Internationales*: 31–7.

Nora, P. (ed.) (1994), *Les Lieux de mémoire, III. Les France, 2. Traditions*, Paris: Gallimard.

Nourrisson, D. (1990), *Le buveur du XIXieme siècle*, Paris: Albin Michel.

ONIVINS-INRA (2002), *Enquête ONIVINS-INRA sur la consommation du vin en France en 2000*, no. 91, March.

Plichon, J.-P. (1996), 'Les mutations du tourisme viti-vinicole en Bordelais', in C. Legars and P. Roudié (eds), *Des vignobles et des vins à travers le monde: Hommage à Alain Huetz de Lemps*, Collection Grappes et Millésimes, Maison des Pays Ibériques, 66, CERVIN, pp. 127–32.

Rioux, J-P. (1987), 'Être Français?' *L'Histoire*, 100, May (43), 11–17.

Sadoun, R., G. Lolli and M. Silverman (1965), *Drinking in French Culture*, New Brunswick, NJ: Rutgers Center of Alcohol Studies.

Ulin, R.-C. (1995), 'Invention and Representation as Cultural Capital: Southwest French Wine Growing History', *American Anthropologist* 97 (3): 519–27.

—— (2002), 'Work as Cultural Production: Labour and Self-identity among Southwest French Wine-Growers', *The Journal of the Royal Anthropological Institute* 8 (4): 691–712.

Warde, A. (1997), *Consumption, Food and Taste: Culinary Antinomies and Commodity Culture*, London: Sage.

Zeldin, T. (1977), *A History of French Passion 1848–1945. Vol. 2. Intellect, Taste and Anxiety*, Oxford: Clarendon Press.

–8–

Romantic Moods
Food, Beer, Music and the Yucatecan Soul

Steffan Igor Ayora-Diaz and *Gabriela Vargas-Cetina*

In 1993, after seven years abroad, we both returned to Mexico to work in the southern state of Chiapas. At a gathering with our new friends and colleagues, they learned that during our stay abroad we only returned home once, for two weeks. They asked us whether we had missed tequila, *pozole* or mariachi music. We answered that we had not and they accused us of 'having turned into gringos'. We explained that, being from the Yucatán peninsula, we had really missed Yucatecan beer, *cochinita pibil* and *panuchos*, and *trova* music (see the glossary at the end of the chapter). Although anecdotal, this experience is similar to those shared by other Yucatecans outside Yucatán. Foreigners travelling to Mexico find Yucatán short of their expectations regarding Mexican food, alcohol and music, three things that often go together in most of Mexico. In this chapter we discuss, in the context of global flows of people and commodities, the role of food, alcoholic drinks and music as markers of regional identity in Yucatán, Mexico.

As Heath (1987, 2000) has pointed out, anthropologists have the opportunity to describe and analyse the ways in which the consumption of alcohol, in different regions and various contexts, cements and lubricates social interaction (see also Douglas 1987; Rehfisch 1987; Ayora-Diaz 2000; Chatwin 2001; de Garine 2001a). In fact, alcoholic beverages have often played an important role in the construction of national, regional, class and gendered identities (Bennett 1996; Cantarero Abad 2001; Guy 2001; Martin 2001; Milano Borruso and Lerín Piñón 2001; Sarasúa 2001; Patico 2002). However, alcohol by itself does not suffice to ground a regional cultural identity. Historians have focused on the socially and culturally disruptive effects of alcohol production and consumption in Mexico and the Americas (Taylor 1987 [1979]; Viqueira Albán 1987; Corcuera de Mancera 1991; Mancall 1995). Most of the anthropological literature on alcohol in Mexico also centres on alcoholism and the health and family problems derived from it (e.g. Menéndez 1990; Menéndez and di Pardo 1996). Here we deal with culturally accepted, and even encouraged, forms of alcohol consumption as they are found in the Mexican state of Yucatán. We look at the consumption of alcohol as it is articulated with other cultural markers so that, together, they contribute to signify practices and preferences as deeply ingrained elements of local culture. We examine the relationship of food and music to alcohol and sociability, all of which contribute to a strong sense of Yucatecan regional identity. However, we wish to stress that *Yucatecan* is never a fixed identity but, rather, a shifting one that changes with the contexts in which identity must be performed.

In this chapter we first describe the historical context in which Yucatecan identity, often referred to locally as 'the Yucatecan soul', is grounded and often displayed in opposition to a 'Mexican' identity. Locals use sociability customs, music preferences, food and alcoholic beverages to establish the contrast and sometimes opposition between Mexican and Yucatecan moral values. We will discuss four forms/instances of sociability where different identity affiliations are displayed: the *hora cristal*, an informal and unstructured form of brief social gathering to drink and be with one's friends; 'Happy Hour', the regular occasions when friends meet to socialize after work; the annual festivity of Mexican Independence Day; and, last, informal meetings where we have seen Yucatecan values and taste affirmed as opposed to Mexican ones. We conclude by focusing on the importance of social drinking in the construction of a sense of Yucatecan identity.

Fragments of the Nation: Yucatán and Mexico's Cultural Differentiation

In 2000, after having spent almost seven years in Chiapas, we moved back to Yucatán.[1] It was a time of political effervescence. The then opposition party, PAN (Partido de Acción Nacional), questioned the legitimacy of PRI (Partido Revolucionario Institucional), the party that had put the then state Governor, Victor Cervera Pacheco, in power. PRI demanded respect for, and promoted, state political autonomy. To that end, the Governor and his party revived long-standing regional symbols such as the Yucatecan flag and anthem. Cars bore stickers, and many men and women wore shirts and baseball caps with the Yucatecan flag and the legend 'Republic of Yucatán'. At that time one could also find Yucatecan flags hanging from the windows of apartments and houses or by the doors of local businesses. In opposition, PAN stressed the duties of the state toward the federation and emphasized the affirmative value of seeing Yucatán as an integral part of Mexican culture. In response, some Yucatecan restaurateurs decided that visitors should eat 'food as we eat it in Yucatán' and began to refuse concessions in flavouring or in the presentation of dishes to foreign clients. The state government promoted Yucatecan music, particularly *trova* music (a regional musical form usually played by guitar trios who sing romantic songs), while PAN (which then ruled the city of Mérida) promoted a 'Mexican Night' on Saturdays; an event in which visitors and immigrants could watch the performance of musicians from other Mexican regions.

The triumph of PAN in the state elections of 2001 was followed by the dissolution of the Band of the State of Yucatán, which had been an important local musical institution for over a century. Local musicians attuned to the musical roots of the region were displaced by professionals from other regions of Mexico and abroad who did not necessarily find regional music to their personal taste. While *trova* music remains an important part of night-life in Mérida, now *trova* associations must renegotiate their position within the state government's funding priorities. Also, Yucatecan restaurateurs are less radical now and more willing to present local gastronomy within the aesthetics and flavours of central Mexican cooking or even *haute cuisine*.

This was just one among the recent manifestations of a long-standing ambivalence in the state of Yucatán toward the central government. After Independence from Spain, in the early nineteenth century, the Yucatán peninsula and Mexico began to negotiate the terms of their relationship. A number of Yucatecans were willing to join Mexico as long as regions were granted an autonomous administration and government. Other Yucatecans were less interested in joining Mexico; some wanted outright independence, and still others petitioned the US government for the annexation of Yucatán to the northern Union (Aliski 1980). For their part, successive Mexican governments vacillated between allowing states some degree of regional autonomy and a centralist predisposition, inclined to limit regional power. Responding to this vacillation, Yucatecan politicians declared Yucatán's independence from Mexico on three separate occasions during the nineteenth century.

During the last repossession of Yucatán, the Mexican government decided to split the regional forces into three different federal states. As a result, the state of Campeche was created in 1857 so that the Yucatán peninsula was split into two states. Then, the federal territory of Quintana Roo was created in 1902 to be occupied and controlled by the military in order to subdue the Maya rebels, heirs of the Caste War of Yucatán. Quintana Roo later became a state in 1974 (see Aliski 1980; Joseph 1985; *Enciclopedia de México* 1993; Ramírez Carrillo 2003). During the French occupation of Mexico and during the Mexican Revolution, Yucatán's and Mexico's paths often failed to converge. Some from among the Yucatecan elite saw the French/ Habsburg period as an opportunity to gain independence from Mexico. Yucatán also entered the Mexican Revolution late and refused to participate in the military quests of the revolutionary government. However, through federal control of taxes and revenues and through the political manipulation of development programmes, the Yucatecan administration eventually gave up its outspoken demand for autonomy (Joseph 1979, 1985; Aliski 1980).

The revolutionary state in Mexico fostered the integration and assimilation of the Yucatecan Maya into hegemonic Mexican society and economy. After the Caste War of the mid-nineteenth century, through agrarian reforms and with the support of rural socialist brigades, ethnic relations in Yucatán assumed a gentler face. No longer called 'Indians' but *mestizos*, peasants were publicly more readily accepted into urban society and culture. Until recently, Maya speakers have not been seen as radically different from other sectors of the rural and urban population. This is possibly related to the fact that Korean, Chinese and European immigrants were often assimilated either into Maya-speaking or mainstream society (Burns 1983; Gutiérrez Estévez 1992; Roggero 2001; Hervik 2003 [1999]).

Yucatán's relations with the centre of Mexico remained diffident. It was not until the first half of the twentieth century that the state was finally linked by land to the rest of Mexico (Joseph 1985). Before that, travelling to Mexico City was more complicated than travelling to New Orleans, Texas, Miami, France or the rest of the Caribbean. Rather than using Mexico as a blueprint for regional culture, Yucatecans borrowed from other Caribbean countries, France and some regions of the United States. Many Yucatecan musicians learned or developed their rhythms and musical style from forms of music and musicians in New Orleans, Cuba, Puerto Rico, Colombia, Venezuela and New York (Dueñas 1990; Heredia and De Pau 2000). Current Yucatecan gastronomy borrowed from French, Spanish, Italian, Caribbean and, since the late nineteenth century, Syrian and Lebanese cuisines (Ayora Diaz 2001).

Yucatecan intellectuals also used the pre-Hispanic past to explain the cultural values of the present. Pointing at the archaeological record, the Maya were portrayed as a peace-loving people concerned with science and culture. They were contrasted to the Aztecs, war-mongers and cannibalistic people from central Mexico. The relations between the Yucatán peninsula and Mexico were often likened to those between Classical Greece and Imperial Rome (Sullivan 1989; Castañeda 1996). It is with this background in mind that we can now turn to the locally meaningful differences between Yucatecan and Mexican cultural productions.

Being Yucatecan: Food, Alcohol and Musical Taste

In regional discourse, Yucatecans proudly proclaim a 'gentle' culture: women are respected and loved; the distaste for violence is expressed through local music and songs that praise women, love and the regional landscape; Yucatecan food is not spicy hot (though one can have as a side-dish the fiery *habanero* pepper); and there is a local preference for cold beer and iced rum or brandy cocktails rather than for straight strong alcohols such as tequila or mescal. This discourse can be better understood in the contrast often established, explicitly or implicitly, between Mexican and Yucatecan culture. Mariachi music, identified with the centre of Mexico, is often seen in Yucatán either as suitable for cantinas (places where people go to drink alcohol) or for celebrating national festivities such as Independence Day. Yucatecan food resembles neither that of Tex-Mex restaurants in the United States nor the food of other Mexican regions. There is no tradition of drinking tequila in Yucatán.

A European friend of ours, who has resided in Yucatán since 1998, told one of us that when she first arrived she was expecting to find a large range of tequila brands and quality. She was amazed at the fact that at that time only two brands were locally available, and not necessarily of the best quality. The market for tequila has been growing nationwide and now one can find in Mérida specialty stores a wide range of tequila brands. Yucatecans are gradually developing a taste for tequila, but it is not yet an integral part of the regional gastronomic field, nor is it the chosen drink for social interaction. In fact, there has been a renewal of feelings of regional identity, which is grounded in cultural preferences. Some local groups distinguish themselves from immigrants through participation in a local way of life widely identified as 'Yucatecan'. But Yucatecans also like to feel worldly. Different times of the day and annual festivities provide occasions for commensality, and are turned into spaces and times for the reaffirmation of local identity *vis-à-vis* a homogenizing national identity or, if the event demands it, the demonstration of local ties either to the nation or to cosmopolitan culture.

Food and the Construction of the Yucatecan Region

Food and cooking, through their formalization into cookbooks, have been seen to contribute to the construction of national or regional (Appadurai 1981, 1988; Camporesi 2001 [1970]; Belasco and Scranton 2002), ethnic (Cusak 2000; Innes 2001) and gendered identities (Theophano 2002). Cookbooks support the construction of imagined communities through their diffusion and use in the kitchens of a region. Food preferences and avoidances, systematized and normatively embodied in textual forms (whether oral or printed), establish and attach a moral meaning to what one eats or refuses to eat. Food also enforces the ties among those who share a taste of a dislike for certain types of ingredients or the cuisine in which they are used (de Garine 2001b). The development of a regional or national cuisine, therefore, generally informs local identities.

The development of a Mexican national cuisine, as Pilcher (1998) and Juárez López (2000) have illustrated, was based on the appropriation of recipes from different regions within the context of central Mexican cuisine. Thus, *pozole*, attributed to the state of Jalisco, in the west of Mexico, and *mole*, attributed to the central state of Puebla, have become two of the paradigmatic Mexican recipes to be adapted and marketed all over the country. However, it was only during the late 1970s that *pozole* arrived in Yucatán through 'Mexican' restaurants. Tacos, today very common, especially as *tacos al pastor* (a form of shish kebab meat tacos), are not much older in the state. Mexican cuisine has been promoted in Yucatán, and some Mexican restaurant chains can be found in strategic points of the city of Mérida. Local people explain the increasing demand for Mexican dishes as arising from the growing numbers of central Mexicans who have moved to Yucatán during the last two decades of regional economic boom. Friends of ours have lamented that, in their neighbourhoods, they are unable to find Yucatecan tamales and other dishes;

surrounded by 'Mexicans' they can only find Mexican-style tacos and tamales and must drive to other neighbourhoods to find their favourite regional food.

Because the peninsula of Yucatán is flat lowland close to sea level, cooking ingredients are different from those available in the Mexican highlands. Pork, fish, poultry and seafood are more common than beef in the local diet. Cooking often involves wrapping meat or tamales with banana leaves instead of yellow corn husk, more common in other parts of Mexico. In contrast to other Mexican regions, Yucatán, for most of the second half of the nineteenth century and the first half of the twentieth, was home to a wealthy elite profiting from the production and trade of henequen fibre, the 'green gold' (Wells 1985). Its members travelled to and received news from Europe, the United States and the Caribbean. Thus, since the nineteenth century, regional cookbooks have included dishes of putative European, US and Caribbean origin, such as Cod Biscay, Malaga Eggs, Stuffed Edam Cheese and Asturias Beef, as well as a few thought of as being of Mayan origin, such as *papadzules*, *sikilpac* and *dzotobichay* (see, among others, Aguirre 1980 [1832]; Arjona de Morales 1992 [1976]; Carrillo Lara 1994). Syrian and Lebanese immigrants have also contributed to the development of Yucatecan cuisine (Infante Vargas and Hernández Fuentes 2000). Having witnessed the everyday preparation of different dishes for some time now, we have found such variation in the preparation of recipes which are often considered to be 'classical' Yucatecan that what two families eat under the same name may be very different things. For example, Cod Biscay is a Christmas dish for many Yucatecan and Mexican families in the state and in the Mexican Republic, and yet versions are sometimes so different that one could hardly identify them as corresponding to the same dish.

In local perception, Yucatecan cooking includes very few recipes prepared with spicy hot peppers. Food, as cooked, is thus gentle to the palate, although hot peppers are made available on the table for those who prefer their food spicy hot. While Mexican food is perceived as always hot and full of milk products, in Yucatán very few specialties are cooked with cream or have cheese added on top. Yucatecan cooks profit from the wide availability of citrus fruits and often cook soups, or marinate meats, game, fish or poultry in Seville orange, lemon or a lime (*lima*) indigenous to the region (this is an Arab custom adopted in southern Spain and probably transferred to the peninsula of Yucatán by Spanish immigrants [Vargas and Casillas 1996]). Yucatán cooking is known in other regions of Mexico through adaptations of the regional *panuchos*, *cochinita pibil* and *queso relleno*. Yucatecans in general do not see wine as being a suitable accompaniment for local food. Instead, the Yucatecan combination of spices and fragrances is considered to be best matched by beer, *horchata* (a non-alcoholic drink of rice and almond) or cola drinks. Drink preferences, which may shift according to context, are also used in everyday life to mark one's group identity.

Alcohol, Culture and the Gastronomic Field

In Malcolm Lowry's *Under the Volcano*, Geoffrey Firmin, the British Consul who is the main character in the novel, is an alcoholic. With a tequila glass in his hand, Firmin confesses: 'It's mescal with me . . . Tequila, no, that is healthful . . . and delightful. Just like beer. Good for you. But if I ever start to drink mescal again, I'm afraid, yes, that would be the end' (Lowry 1984 [1947]: 225, ellipsis in the original). This passage suggests that alcoholic beverages are inscribed in moral, cultural and social structures of meaning. Our drink of preference often traces our reference to a local, regional, national, international or cosmopolitan group. After all, each environment favours the growth of different plants and allows for different speeds of fermentation (Toussaint-Samat 1992 [1987]; Unwin 2001 [1991]).

In contrast to the northern Europeans who colonized North America, and had an inclination for beer (Smith 1998), when the Spaniards landed in the New World they brought a taste for wine which led to a growing demand first for Spanish wine and later for local wines (Corcuera de Mancera 1991). Mexico's territory did not lend itself to a successful cultivation of wine grapes (except for a couple of regions in the centre and north-west) and the Spaniards had either to import wine from Spain and other regions of the Americas, or to content themselves with the local brews. When the Spaniards arrived in the centre of Mexico, local indigenous groups were already producing their own fermented drinks. Pulque, the fermented pulp of maguey, was very common among the inhabitants of the highlands of Mexico (Taboada Ramírez 1997), and *balché*, made from fermented honey, was an important part of agricultural ceremonies in Yucatán. When the Spaniards brought the *alambique*, the distilling apparatus developed by the Arabs and appropriated for the distillation of spirits in the Mediterranean, it was put to use in the production of mescal in central Mexico (Lozano Armendares 1997).

Mescal is a generic name for the distilled spirits from different types of agaves. It was the distillation of the blue agave that gave rise to a mescal produced in the tequila region. Though its production was banned, it was produced illegally from the 1500s, and later, during the 1700s, under restricted permission from the Spanish Crown (Muría 1995). In 1795 the Cuervo family was granted a licence to produce mescal in the tequila region of today's state of Jalisco (de Orellana 1995). However, the production and consumption of tequila mescal was a regional matter for a long time. Rums and brandies were imported from Europe and were favoured by the ruling Spaniards and creoles. Pulque and mescal remained favourites, the former among the lower rungs of society, and the latter among the regional elites of Jalisco. It was only during the twentieth century that tequila became highly differentiated from mescal (their distillation processes are now different and mescal, not tequila, may include a worm in the bottle). The demand for these liquors grew in Mexico and the United States, and subsequently in Europe, in the second half of the 1900s (Guzmán Pereda 2002).

With time, tequila became associated with the macho and cowboy culture of the centre of Mexico as presented by Mexican cinema (and later by Hollywood) (Quirarte 1995). With the help of the movie industry, tequila was launched as the paradigmatic drink of Mexico and Mexicans. In the peninsula of Yucatán, however, isolated from Mexican nationalist cultural constructions for more than a century, Yucatecans had developed different inclinations: the regional trade with the United States and the Caribbean had favoured the introduction of rum and brandy, and the descendants of Spaniards enjoyed sherry as an appetizer. Many Yucatecans remember their grand-parents' affection for sherry and muscat, and some Yucatecan specialty dishes included meats marinated with those wines.

The importation of cooling technology was auspicious for the establishment of a brewery in 1899, Cervecería yucateca, in an environment of year-round hot weather. The brewers launched a Vienna-style beer, León Negra, later followed by a lager-style Carta Clara, and in the 1960s by the pilsner-style Montejo. These beers were marketed as suited to the regional palate and cuisine. They rapidly became favorites of Yucatecans both in the cities and the countryside. In 1979 the Mexican mega-brewery Cervecería Modelo acquired the Yucatecan brewery and attempted to liken the quality and flavour of the local products to that of generic national beers in their category (Grupo Modelo 2000). This change was met by a decline in the local market and the demand for a return to the old quality. The beers' quality eventually im-proved, but older Yucatecans affirm that it never regained the old standards. In 2002 Cervecería Modelo decided to close the Mérida plant and take the production of Montejo and León Negra to Oaxaca (Diaz Rubio 2003). Some locals have told us that they regret the end of a regional industry, but are happy at the wider access to other beer brands, while others lament the Modelo corporation move as an attack on Yucatecan symbols.

Yucatecan food and beer are well integrated within the regional gastronomic field. Dark León Negra and pilsner Montejo are seen as the correct accompaniment for the spicy, fragrant and flavourful regional cooking. The delicate flavour of most wines is said to be overpowered by Yucatecan dishes and strong alcohols are well accepted in cocktails at night parties, but are hardly seen as the drink of choice to go with a meal. The perceived integration of beer and Yucatecan food is well illustrated by the short-lived Yucatecan restaurant *El Mural*, which opened in 2001 in one of the upscale city hotels. This restaurant lasted only about a year before its takeover by a growing chain of Yucatecan restaurants. It displayed a menu that included exclus-ively Yucatecan dishes, beer, desserts and fruit, and soft drinks (there is also a Yucatecan soft drink industry). Because of its construed authenticity, it drew local and visiting customers and its success aroused the interest of the larger restaurant chain that finally acquired it in 2002. Most of the menu has been preserved but national beers and tequila are now available, while 'rustic' dishes have been sup-pressed. For example, *El Mural* used to offer a regional dip called *sikilpac* to accom-pany the first round of drinks while the food arrived. This dish met with good acceptance from both local and foreign customers, but the new management withdrew it because of its supposed lack of sophistication.

Tequila production has grown during the last ten years responding to its increasing demand in Mexico and abroad (Cámara Nacional de la Industria Tequilera 2003). Yucatán's henequen has been long pushed off the international market of fibres. Nonetheless, the inability of Jalisco producers to satisfy the demand for tequila (due to lack of the agave itself) moved some Yucatecan producers to sell the hearts of local henequen for the liquor's production. However, given that tequila *must* be produced (1) in the town or at least in the region of Tequila and (2) from the blue agave, a group of Yucatecans has now launched commercially a new alcoholic drink distilled from the henequen plant. Their intention is twofold: they wish to fill the gap left by the faltering production of tequila and, at the same time, take advantage of the inchoate but growing demand for agave liquors in the peninsula of Yucatán (*Diario de Yucatán*, 2003a). So far, this new product has been met with reservations by Yucatecans.

Sipping a beer was, and continues to be, seen as conducive to friendly gatherings under the shade of one's house or in local cantinas, but hardly conducive to, or a justification for, macho displays. The latter are often described as a 'Mexican' propensity but hardly a Yucatecan one. Yucatecans claim to be, on the contrary, a peaceful people who enjoy life, each other's company, love and romantic songs.

Music and Moral Differences

The musical exchange between the Yucatán peninsula and the Caribbean region has fostered the development of a local genre described as *trova yucateca*. The fathers of this genre were members of the middle and upper middle classes of Mérida and other important Yucatecan towns who travelled to New Orleans, Cuba, France and Puerto Rico and exchanged their musical creations with musicians there. In recent years the City of Mérida has organized *bambuco* festivals and invited musicians from other Caribbean regions to come and perform for local audiences. During one of these performances, a singer introduced a song as a traditional song of Colombia, by an unknown composer. To her surprise, people sang along with her, since this was a song by renowned Yucatecan composer Pastor Cervera. *Trova* music in Yucatán is thus related to other *trova* music from the Caribbean. Its rhythms include *clave*, which is a local adaptation of the *Cuban Havanera* song; *bambuco*, originally from Colombia; mazurka; Peruvian waltz; schottische, imported into Yucatán at the end of the nineteenth century; bolero and *guaracha*, both originally developed in Cuba; and *Jarana* (Manuel 1990; Manuel *et al.* 1995; Vargas-Cetina 2001–3). *Jarana* is a danceable rhythm based on Spanish folk dances which seems to have originated during or after the Caste War (Stanford 2003). Songs eulogize the virtues of women, the repressed passion or love for a distant woman, platonic affection, or pride in the beauty of the local landscape and the virtues of local people and food (Bock 1992; Pérez Sabido et al. 2000).

Trova is locally contrasted to mariachi and ranchero music, where men and women sing about despair, bitterness and the violence between men and women, or between men competing for a woman's love. Besides the specific content of 'Mexican' songs (such as 'La Vida No Vale Nada' ['Life is Worth Nothing']), this perception of Mexicans' behaviour is reinforced by filmic representations of the violent life of people in the central and northern regions of the country, and by the tabloid-style reporting prevalent in national television and newspapers. Moreover, these songs seem to have a direct relationship with the violent lifestyle of peasants and drug dealers in other parts of Mexico (McDowell 2000; Valenzuela 2002). Yucatecan songs, instead, are contemplative and rarely reveal violent or 'uncouth' emotions. The lyrics are seldom, if at all, sexually explicit, although a sexual tension can be perceived by the attentive listener. For example, *'El Pájaro Azul'* ('The Blue Bird') (1928, words: Manuel Diaz Massa; music: Pepe Saldívar) is considered paradigmatic as an expression of the Yucatecan 'soul'. Trios sing this song, with its *clave* and bolero rhythms, in serenades and in restaurants and it can be found in numerous recordings available in the local market. Its lyrics (in Vargas-Cetina's translation) are as follows:

> I have a blue bird
> Inside my soul
> A bird who sings and cries
> And who in my nights of infinite quietness
> Is like a miraculous hope.
> I have a blue bird
> Inside my soul
> This blue bird is the fondness
> That I feel for you; but do not be surprised . . .
> It was my greatest dream when I was a child
> And it has turned to pain now that I am a man
> That blue bird is my fondness [for you].

In recent years the local musical scene in Mérida has become more inclusive, although Yucatecan genres still dominate. The city has maintained a number of weekly shows from the time of the competition between political parties: Monday night one finds *Jarana* dance in the city's main square; Tuesday nights are for *trova* at the Olympus Theatre; Wednesdays offer more Yucatecan *trova* in the Museum of the Yucatecan Song (founded and supported by a music lovers' club and now housed in a magnificent palace though the auspices of the past PRI governor); Thursday nights are for the Yucatecan Serenade in Sta. Lucía Plaza (a night with Yucatecan dances, songs and poetry, though it now includes 'Mexican' musical and poetic creations); Saturday is the PAN's municipality's Mexican Night, showcasing marimba and mariachi music; and on Sunday, during the day, the city's historic centre is closed to traffic, transforming the area into a flea market, with food stands and open music stages. Some of the regional and national breweries sponsor popular dance events, where people can dance to *cumbia* music and other tropical genres, highly appreciated by the popular classes of the city and the state. Once a year, City Hall sponsors the Festival of Electronic Music in the Park of the Americas, bringing together Yucatecan and other DJs from the rest of Mexico and abroad. This musical scene affirms the joy and love for life that is locally constructed as an attribute of the 'Yucatecan soul', seen as opposed to the preoccupation with violence and death that many local people describe as characteristic of 'Mexicans'.

Drinking Occasions: Sociability, Space, Regionalism and Cosmopolitanism

There are many circumstances and places where people get together and consume beverages, including alcoholic ones, while building or reaffirming their sense of community (Heath 2000). Consumption marks individuals' identities and supports the construction of communities of lifestyle, or communities of meaning (see also Ayora-Diaz 2003; Vargas-Cetina 2003). The collective production and consumption of particular foods and drinks have often been linked to the establishment of social and cultural ties that ground ethnic, class, regional, gendered and national identities (Guy 1999; Lockie 2001). Drinking is necessary on many occasions, and alcoholic beverages are among the range of drinks that participants can choose from. Stimulants, such as coffee, tea and alcohol, are a common accompaniment to social gatherings everywhere (see, for example, Kondo 1985; Schivelbusch 1992; Houston 2001), and this is no exception among Yucatecans. In what follows we describe a number of occasions and places that are locally instrumental in the construction of shifting affiliations and different senses of belonging. Alcohol consumption is not mandatory but it is legitimate in these environments, since they all imply enjoying oneself in the company of family or friends.

The Hora Cristal

Yucatán, in general, and the city of Mérida, in particular, have year-round warm weather. The average annual temperature in Mérida is in the high 30s (centigrade). During the noon work break, many people go to their favourite cantina or bar. They have one or more beers as appetizers before going home to eat, or have beers with their friends accompanied by abundant *botana* (see below) before returning to work or going home for a nap. Noon is often referred to as the *hora cristal*. According to an informant, some fifty years ago a local radio station began broadcasting a noon programme with that name. This programme was sponsored by the local brewery and a number of local cantinas. It encouraged people to drink beer with their friends, particularly in sponsoring cantinas, during the time of the radio programme; later it became a general custom that remains to this day, although the radio show has been long discontinued and most people no longer know how the *hora cristal* first originated.

Visitors from the centre of Mexico have often expressed their surprise at the fact that most Yucatecan cantinas are presented as 'family restaurants'. In fact, one often finds whole families having drinks (alcoholic or otherwise) and eating *botana*; but one also finds mixed-gender groups of friends and even groups made up of only women enjoying drinks at local cantinas, without fear of being harassed by others. In contrast to other regions of Mexico, where women were admitted in cantinas only some twenty years ago (Avila Palafox 2001), in Yucatán, since at least fifty years ago many cantinas have had a *salon familiar* (family room) where women, children and men together consume *botanas* and drinks. Friends of ours from other parts of Mexico whom we have taken to local cantinas and bars have been favourably surprised to see that even at night, in local bars, it is common to find groups of young women having drinks and chatting away.

Cantinas promote the presence of a mixed clientele through the serving of *botanas*. This is a usage probably related to the *pinchos* and tapas (Millán 2001) offered in Spanish bars, where customers get their glass of wine with a small dish on top of the glass containing food (thereby *tapa*, lid). As per the local adaptation of the tapas custom, Yucatecan cantinas offer *botanas*. With the first beer one usually receives a number of small plates with offal, pickled potatoes and/or beets, pickled mangoes and *jícama* (a watery tuber), Lebanese hummus and *ceviche* (fish and seafood marinated in lime juice). When delivering the second round of beers, the waiter serves an assortment of regional dishes such as tamales, Lebanese kibbehs and tacos of different meats prepared according to regional recipes. Thus, drinking more than one beer ensures that everybody, including children who may be sipping on cola, will be fed. While the quality and abundance in the servings of *botana* sway one's preference, the musical ambience and the beer brands available also influence the choice as to where to enjoy the *hora cristal*.

The cantinas also provide music, though only the upscale cantinas can provide live entertainment, usually in the form of a band that performs tropical rhythms and/ or romantic ballads. The hot weather encourages the consumption of cold beer rather than straight alcohol. During extremely hot days (sometimes the temperature reaches 44°C), when the beer never feels cold enough, Yucatecans may opt for regional beer cocktails: *Cheladas* and *Micheladas*. In Yucatán, *ch'el* is a blond person, beer is blond, thus *chelada* is a cold blond (*chela/helada*): a mix of beer, salt and lime juice served on ice; *Michelada* is similar, with the addition of ground red pepper or Tabasco and Worcester sauces. These cocktails are usually preferred over hard alcohols. After the noon meal many customers usually turn to an iced cocktail, such as rum with cola or sodas, as a digestive, instead of tequila or mescal, which people outside the peninsula usually drink straight.

Thus, cantinas and their *hora cristal* offer a propitious environment for the celebration of birthdays, graduations, occupational achievements, business deals or simply to meet with one's friends in the middle of the day. Although some cantinas attract a rough crowd and are avoided by families, most provide a friendly environment. This fact has encouraged a recent project by young artists who, excluded from elite art circuits, have decided to organize a poetry and painting show called the *'hora cristal art exhibit'*. In September 2003 they began to show their work in the cantina circuit, and every week they establish a roster of places to showcase their products (*Diario de Yucatán*, 2003b). The perception and rhetoric around the *hora cristal* allow for a local distinction between local customs and those of the 'Mexicans'. Cantinas in other parts of Mexico, including Mexico City, are often male spaces closed to 'decent' women because there is always the possibility of violence as a result of rowdy customers' uncontrolled behavior (Avila Palafox 2001). This is something Yucatecans know from their trips to other parts of the Mexican Republic and it is an image often confirmed by the national film industry (Quirarte 1995). Thus, Yucatecans find in the cantina environment a confirmation of the moral superiority of the local over the 'Mexican' customs and 'soul'.

The 'Happy Hour'

Often at night, after work, friends get together in restaurants or bars. At this time, in the warm weather or inside air-conditioned establishments, Yucatecans find a favourable environment to display their cosmopolitan affiliations. Many upscale bars and restaurants promote a 'happy hour' of two drinks for the price of one and, although some confine their offer to national brands, others appeal to customers by not restricting choice. This is a time when one hardly looks for Yucatecan food, usually deemed fit for lunch but not the type of meal to be consumed before going to bed (Yucatecans also find, in general, fish and seafood inappropriate for night consumption). At night one faces a choice of Argentinean meats, Chinese, Japanese or Italian food or Mexican tacos (there are also 'Arab tacos'), which are locally perceived to go well with wine, beer or mixed cocktails. However, even at this time of the night, we have seldom found Yucatecan customers ordering tequila shots. Yucatecans usually have tequila in mixed drinks such as a Tequila Sunrise and a Margarita. However, to display their sophistication, instead of ordering their drink mixed with white tequila, they usually request aged tequilas for their drinks, something that in our experience tequila lovers elsewhere find wasteful.

In restaurants, Yucatecan customers often order beer. Locally, Mexican wines tend to have a bad reputation and Chilean, Argentinean or Spanish wines are considered better. Italian restaurants often carry Italian wines, though often one finds a small and overpriced selection. Mexican food is generally accompanied with rum or brandy drinks, or with beer. United States beer brands are considered of lower quality than

Mexican and Yucatecan beers. Customers from other parts of Mexico or from abroad sometimes order tequila and use beer as a chaser (as a thirst-quenching drink to 'lower' the effect of the straight alcohol). Yucatecans are usually disinclined to do this. The drinking of straight alcohol is locally seen as leading to drunkenness and therefore not encouraged in public situations.

Music is one of the attractions to consider when choosing restaurants and bars at night. Most establishments offer recorded or cable broadcast music. However, many try to have live bands at least once a week, featuring rock, jazz or romantic music. One 'Mexican restaurant' (specializing in tacos, grilled meat and soups from the center of Mexico) presents a well-established *trova* trio in an outdoors patio. One restaurant of 'Yucatecan food' stays open all day long and presents, from morning to evening, live *trova* music. *Trova* music itself, in these occasions, becomes part of a wider context of cosmopolitan culture, since during 'happy hour' Yucatecans show their knowledge and taste for the food, drinks and music from outside the peninsula and can stress their connections to a global, cosmopolitan culture.

Ephemeral Nationalists

A TV show aired at the beginning of 2002, as part of the series *Caminos de México* ('Mexican Roads'), emphasized the unity of the nation through its culinary taste. Profiting from the celebration of 2001 Independence Day, a reporter toured different regions of Mexico to show how all Mexicans consumed *mole*, *chiles en nogada* and *pozole*, and drank tequila, joining together in the construction of the nation's spirit. In the segment on Yucatán, it was a state politician affiliated with PAN who stressed the nationalist feeling of Yucatecans, who by the thousands flooded streets, bars and restaurants to celebrate the *Grito de independencia* (proclamation of Independence), and shared a taste of the nation by eating *pozole*, *chiles en nogada* and Mexican tacos and by drinking tequila during Mexican night. The interpretation offered by this politician was in line with the explicit current federalist inclination of the state government. In contrast, many Yucatecans displayed on the streets signs of their regionalist feelings: once more, Yucatecan flags and emblems sprouted among street vendors.

While Mexican restaurants have been fashionable in Mérida since the late 1970s, we have found that Mexican foods are usually consumed as one more exotic type of cuisine, like the Chinese, Italian, Argentinean, Lebanese, Japanese and German cooking also available in the city. In fact, some Mexican, Chinese and Lebanese recipes have now been incorporated into the everyday cooking of Yucatecan families. Other than during Independence Day, in mid-September, Yucatecans seldom long for *pozole* or *chiles en nogada* during the week, although there are Yucatecan versions of *mole* and *pozole*.

During the celebration of Independence Day, even in the area where the Mérida politician was interviewed by the TV crew, informal vendors offered passers-by

Yucatecan flags, pins and licence plates with the Yucatecan flag, and small brochures with the history of Yucatán's independence movement, competing with vendors of Mexican flags. For the 2003 Independence Day, new T-shirts appeared with the legend '*Soy Yucateco*' ('I am Yucatecan', counterposed to 'I am Mexican'). Nonetheless, this is the main national celebration when Yucatecans, massively, willingly, fully and publicly celebrate as Mexican citizens, accepting with gusto Mexican food and tequila, and listening to mariachi and ranchero music. Once the celebration ends, however, Yucatecans return to their customary food and drinks and, when the occasion demands it, reaffirm the local difference from Mexican culture.

Reaffirming Yucatecan Identity

Though no organization publicly celebrates the independence of Yucatán from Mexico, there are many occasions when Yucatecans stress their difference from Mexican culture and symbols. Although in recent years the cult of the Virgin of Guadalupe has grown under the push exerted by Catholic Church ideologues and institutions, Yucatecans celebrate a number of important regional festivities. These are related to the Catholic calendar, but reflect local affiliation rather than universal ones: the festivals of the Tetiz Virgin in the village of Tetiz, the Izamal Virgin in the town of Izamal, the Virgin of Candelaria in Valladolid, the three Magi of Tizimin, together with local carnivals, are meaningful occasions on which to visit shrines and fairs and to consume local foods and drinks, often sponsored by regional and national breweries and producers of alcohols.

Dance and music are also present during these festivities. Many Yucatecans are proud to say that the local culture is a musical one. Even outsiders stereotypically expect most Yucatecans to play the guitar and to sing *trova* love songs. Groups of friends, men and women, often get together in *grupos bohemios* (bohemian groups) to play music and sing while enjoying food and non-alcoholic drinks such as coffee and soda. In their gatherings some groups sing mostly Yucatecan songs, but others are proud of their international repertoire, including love songs in French or English or in their Spanish versions. Nonetheless, an implicit requisite is that songs must be about love or, minimally, appeal to romantic sensibilities. One of us witnessed the discomfort caused by a participant when she broke the rule and performed the bitter songs written by a female composer from the centre of Mexico. The men present at that gathering complained that they were not represented by the wife-beaters and cruel machos in those lyrics, and they told the performer that she should sing about consuming love and beauty, instead of bringing to the gathering ill feelings expressed in her *despecho* (resentment) songs.

In 2001 one of the *trova* associations of the city decided to start a choir dedicated exclusively to Yucatecan music and, particularly, to the songs of composers from the end of the nineteenth and the beginning of the twentieth centuries. In 2002, after the presentation concert of this choir, the patron of the association decided to celebrate the group's success by giving a party for the choir members and their spouses. On the day of the party, a Saturday at noon, the attendees arrived with their spouses, girl-friends or boyfriends. A large table was set in one of the corridors of the association's building and in one of the rooms a group of waiters and a cook were fixing *chicharra* to be served as *botana*, and *cohinita pibil* to be served in tacos as the main meal. Sodas and a national brand of beer that comes in 190-ml bottles were served (Yuca-tecan beers are sold in 325-ml or 940-ml bottles, and the smaller bottles are preferred on hot days when one wishes a beer while it is still cool). No hard liquors were available, stressing the coherence of the regional sensibility: Yucatecan food was to be accompanied by beer and Yucatecan music.

Once guests had their fill of beer, *chicharra* and *cochinita pibil*, the choir mem-bers began taking turns at singing for the group. Everything went 'normally' until one of the members, who was born in Yucatán but grew up in the centre of Mexico, moved to the stage. First, instead of carrying his own guitar, he brought out a tape player and karaoke tapes with (of all things!) ranchero music from the centre of Mexico. His first song was met by the loud protests of the choir's patron and other guests. He was unable to complete his second song. The patron scolded him, saying that this was an occasion to be marked only with Yucatecan music. He was offended and puzzled because, as he asked us, 'Are not all types of music worthy to be sung?' Then, to appease the choir's patron, one of the guests, a local composer in his sixties, moved to the stage. Attendees moved and pushed a piano in from the corridor, and a pianist began to accompany him in the interpretation of his own songs. When the composer returned to his seat, the pianist began to play American and French jazzy romantic songs. But the patron and her friends immediately asked him to stop playing non-Yucatecan songs. That day, even love songs composed by outsiders were off-limits.

Although this particular occasion was rather extraordinary, it must be understood in the context of an existing feeling of the Yucatecan way of life being currently under threat by the cultural dominance of central Mexico (something we did not find in Chiapas, where the fear was not that of regional culture being overtaken by national culture, but, after the Zapatista uprising, rather that of 'white' culture being superseded by the ways of the indigenous people of that state). In Yucatán, some people express hostile feelings toward the 'Mexicans' moving into the peninsula because they are not adopting Yucatecan customs but rather changing local manners and tastes. All contemporary social ills and nuisances (the increasing number of robberies, domestic violence, sexual assaults, murders, unemployment and street vendors) are often explained by making reference to the growing numbers of 'Mexi-cans' in Mérida and the rest of Yucatán. We have found that in some circles 'Mexican' food, ranchero music and tequila play a negative role and are rejected in favour of Yucatecan cultural products. 'Yucatecan values' are said to need active protection (though no one ever defines with clarity what those values are). There is thus a segment of the population that actively pursues the reaffirmation of Yucatecan identity and slowly constructs a normative canon of cultural consumption, so as clearly to mark those people who are 'truly Yucatecan' and those who are not. Beer, particularly Yucatecan beer (despite the fact that it is no longer produced in Yucatán, and also is popular among non-Yucatecans), is sometimes consumed as an act of vindication against the 'tequila invasion'. Businesses specializing in tequila are to be found mainly in Mérida's main square, a space occupied by outsiders (tourists and immigrants). There, a broad range of tequila brands is readily available for the tourists while Yucatecans acquire their own drinks (including a more limited number of tequila brands) outside the city centre, in shopping malls and supermarkets.

Conclusion: Food, Alcohol, Music and the Yucatecan Identity

We have shown in this chapter how identities have a shifting character in the construction of local cultural affiliations. Identities have acquired this shifting nature through the historical experience of conflictive and, sometimes, ambivalent relations with nationalist ideologies, which are in turn perceived as tied to an outside project of nation building. At least some Yucatecans among the people we know are inclined to construct a regional sense of belonging based on a local history of economic and cultural trade with Europe and the Caribbean region. Local identities are then actively and purposely marked through the instrumental use of explicit symbols, such as carrying Yucatecan flags and shirts proclaiming 'Republic of Yucatán' or 'I am Yucatecan'. Furthermore, regional identity is based on the appropriation and sometimes implicit, sometimes explicit, negotiation of the limits of local communities of meaning and lifestyle. As happens elsewhere, with whom one eats or drinks, and what one eats or drinks in that company, will signify the inclusion in, or exclusion from, the group.

Based on a regional history that has appropriated Maya civilization's alleged inclination towards science and the arts, and a supposed regional sensitivity expressed in the rejection of violence, respect for each other, and a local affection for the arts (Terry 1989), Yucatecans mark themselves as culturally different from people in the rest of Mexico. Through this local collective self-perception, locals re-signify their established tastes for love songs (for women, men or the land), fragrant and flavourful dishes and beer as different from the preferences of other people in the rest of Mexico. Tequila and mescal, the paradigmatic Mexican national drinks, must be drunk straight and this is often underlined as one of the reasons behind the domestic and street violence supposedly rife in everyday life outside the peninsula of Yucatán (overlooking, of course the fact that violence also exists among Yucatecans). Thus, when Yucatecan friends get together for 'happy hour' after work, or to have a drink during the *hora cristal*, or when they are celebrating regional saints and events, they reaffirm their sense of belonging by endorsing local values and regional foods, beverages and music. At other times, however, Yucatecans like to feel Mexican and cosmopolitan; it all depends on the time of the day, the company, the mood and the general environment. Both regionalist and nationalist feelings are aroused during political confrontations and during the national festivities promoted by the central government (which collects taxes in the region and funds regional economic pro-grammes) or by the central bureaucracy of the Catholic Church (which promotes the cult of the Virgin of Guadalupe and the recently created 'Indian' saint, Juan Diego). At these times, food, music and social interaction are accompanied by the consump-tion of alcohol, and these habits are often held as examples of the gentle nature of the Yucatecan character. They are seen as supporting an environment of peace and respect for men and women and marking the boundaries between Yucatán and a 'Mexican' culture and cultural products that foster violence. On these occasions, the consumption of alcohol, food and music is turned into a defining marker of local identity. In fact, identity markers linked to food, music and alcohol in the state of Yucatán would seem to suggest that, even after almost two centuries of federalism, Mexico continues to be a strongly regional country.

Glossary of Frequently Mentioned Dishes

Chicharra is a local Yucatecan dish prepared with chopped pieces of fried pork skin rinds, offal, some meat and fat, mixed with parsley leaves, chopped tomatoes, onion, and the juice of Seville oranges. It is often accompanied by minced *habanero* pepper which one can sprinkle on top.

Chiles en nogada is a dish from the centre of Mexico, representative of Mexican cuisine as it displays the colours of the national flag. It consists of stuffed green peppers covered with a walnut cream and sprinkled with pomegranate seeds.

Cochinita pibil is one of the most representative dishes of Yucatecan cuisine. It is pork marinated in Seville orange and *achiote*, as well as other spices, wrapped in banana leaves and baked in a pit hole.

Dzotobichay are tamales with *chaya* leaves (a plant native to the peninsula).

Mole, a dish attributed to the state of Puebla, is usually poultry cooked in a dense sauce of an assortment of peppers, nuts, melted dark chocolate and tomatoes.

Panuchos are Yucatecan fried corn tortillas stuffed with fried black beans and topped with pickled onion and one of different meats.

Papadzules are a form of tacos in which the tortilla is soaked in a green sauce of ground squash seeds and *epazote* leaves, and covered with a fried tomato sauce.

Pozole is a dish from the state of Jalisco. It is a stew of veal or pork with aromatic herbs and abundant grains of corn.

Queso relleno is stuffed cheese: an emptied shell of Edam stuffed with ground beef and/or pork, capers, almonds, raisins, onion and herbs, served with a sauce based on corn flour. Considered also paradigmatic of Yucatecan cuisine, many variations can be found in the Caribbean.

Sikilpac is a blend of roasted tomatoes with ground roasted pumpkin seed and parsley leaves.

Note

1. Both of us moved from Yucatán to Canada to follow graduate studies at the University of Calgary and at McGill University, in Montreal. After conducting research in Sardinia for our Ph.D. dissertations and then writing up in Canada, in 1993 we moved to the southern Mexican state of Chiapas, to take up research positions. In January 2000 we moved to Mérida, Yucatán's capital city, to work in the Autonomous University of Yucatán.

References

Aguirre, M. I. (1980) [1832], *Prontuario de cocina para un diario regular: Por doña María Ignacia Aguirre bien conocida por lo primorosa en el arte*, Mérida: FONAPAS Yucatán.

Aliski, M. (1980), 'The Relations of the State of Yucatán and the Federal Government of Mexico, 1823–1978', in E. H. Moseley and E. D. Terry (eds), *Yucatán: A World Apart*, Alabama: University of Alabama Press, pp. 245–63.

Appadurai, A. (1981), 'Gastropolitics in Hindu South Asia', *American Ethnologist*, 8 (3): 494–511.

—— (1988), 'How to Make a National Cuisine: Cookbooks in Contemporary India', *Comparative Studies in Society and History*, 30 (1): 3–24.

Arjona de Morales, E. M. (1992) [1976] *Cocina Yucateca e Internacional*, Mérida: Talleres Gráficos del Sudeste.

Avila Palafox, R. (2001), 'Cantinas and Drinkers in Mexico', in I. de Garine and V. de Garine (eds), *Drinking: Anthropological Approaches*, Oxford: Berghahn, pp. 169–80.

Ayora-Diaz, S. I. (2000), 'Hospitality in Sardinia: The Moral Construction of Identities', *Europaea* VI (1–2): 229–57.

—— (2001), 'The Identity of Food in the Maya World', paper presented at the annual meetings of the Society for Applied Anthropology, Mérida, Mexico, 31 March–3 April.

—— (2003), 'Re/creaciones de la comunidad: Espacios translocales en la globalización', *Cuadernos de Bioética* 7 (10): 27–45.

Belasco, W. and P. Scranton (eds) (2002), *Food Nations: Selling Taste in Consumer Societies*, London: Routledge.

Bennett, J. M. (1996), *Ale, Beer, and Brewsters in England: Women's Work in a Changing World, 1300–1600*, Oxford: Oxford University Press.

Bock, P. K. (1992), 'Music in Mérida, Yucatán', *Latin American Music Review*, 13 (1): 33–55.

Burns, A. (1983), *An Epoch of Miracles: Oral Literature of the Yucatec Maya*, Austin: University of Texas Press.

Camporesi, P. (2001) [1970], 'Introduzione', in Pellegrino Artusi *La scienza in cucina e l'arte di mangiar bene* (1891), Rome: Einaudi Editore, pp. xv–lxxviii.

Carrillo Lara, S. L. (1994), *Cocina yucateca tradicional: Platillos rescatados de antiguos recetarios*, Mexico City: Diana.

Cámara Nacional de la Industria del Tequila (2003) *Informe de la cámara nacional de la industria tequila sobre su comportamiento en 2002*; consulted September 2003: *www.camaratequilera.com.mx/informe/informe.htm*

Cantarero Abad, L. (2001), 'Gender and Drink in Aragon, Spain', in I. de Garine and V. de Garine (eds), *Drinking: Anthropological Approaches*, Oxford: Berghahn, pp. 130–43.

Castañeda, Q. E. (1996), *In the Museum of Maya Culture: Touring Chichén Itzá*, Minneapolis: University of Minnesota Press.

Chatwin, M. E. (2001), 'Tamadoba: Drinking Social Cohesion at the Georgian Table', in I. de Garine and V. de Garine (eds), *Drinking: Anthropological Approaches*, Oxford: Berghahn, pp. 181–90.

Corcuera de Mancera, S. (1991), *El fraile, el indio y el pulque: Evangelización y embriaguez en la Nueva España (1523–1548)*, Mexico City: FCE.

Cusak, I. (2000), 'African Cuisines: Recipes for Nation Building', *Journal of African Cultural Studies* 13 (2): 207–25.

de Garine, I. (2001a), 'For a Pluridisciplinary Approach to Drinking', in I. de Garine and V. de Garine (eds), *Drinking: Anthropological Approaches*, Oxford: Berghahn, pp. 1–10.

—— (2001b), 'Views about Food Prejudice and Stereotypes', *Social Science Information* 40 (3): 487–507.

de Orellana, M. (1995), 'El agave tenaz: Microhistoria del tequila: El caso Cuervo', in *Artes de México, No. 27: El tequila. Arte tradicional de México*, Mexico City: Artes de México, pp. 28–36.

Diario de Yucatán (2003a), Sección *Local*, 28 August, p. 1.

—— (2003b), '¡A brindar por el arte joven! Promueven la muestra hora cristal', Sección *Imagen*, 7 September, p. 2.

Diaz Rubio, M. (2003), 'Renglones: Petición a la cervecería', Sección *Local*, in *Diario de Yucatán*, 7 September, p. 4.

Douglas, M. (1987), 'A Distinctive Anthropological Perspective', in M. Douglas (ed.), *Constructive Drinking: Perspectives on Drink from Anthropology*, Cambridge: Cambridge University Press, pp. 3–15.

Dueñas, P. (1990), *Historia Documental del Bolero Mexicano*, Ciudad de Mexico: Asociación Mexicana de Estudios Fonográficos AC.

Enciclopedia de México (1993), Vol. 12, Mexico City: Sebeca Internacional Corp.

Grupo Modelo (2000), 'Cervecería Yucateca', retrieved from *www.gmodelo.com/ ingles/Grupo_Modelo/Plantas/yucatan/yucatan.html* on 21 September 2003.

Gutérrez Estévez, M. (1992), 'Mayas y "mayeros": Los antepasados como otros', in M. L. Portilla, M. Gutiérrez Estévez, G. Gossen and J. Klor de Alva (eds), *De palabra y obra en el nuevo mundo. Vol. I: Imágenes interétnicas*, Mexico City: Siglo XXI, pp. 417–42.

Guzmán Pereda, M. (2002), 'Tequila, bebida nacional e internacional', in *Patrimonio Cultural y Turismo. Memorias del Congreso Sobre patrimonio Gastronómico y Turismo cultural en América Latina y el Caribe, Vol. 1*, Mexico City: CONACULTA, pp. 193–206.

Guy, K. M. (1999), '"Oiling the Wheels of Social Life": Myths and Marketing in Champagne during the Belle Époque', *French Historical Studies* 22 (2): 211–39.

—— (2001), 'Wine, Champagne and the Making of French Identity in the Belle Epoque', in P. Scholliers (ed.), *Food, Drink and Identity: Cooking, Eating and Drinking in Europe since the Middle Ages*, Oxford: Berg, pp. 163–77.

Heath, D. (1987), 'A Decade of Development in the Anthropological Study of Alcohol Use, 1970–1980', in M. Douglas (ed.), *Constructive Drinking: Perspectives on Drink from Anthropology*, Cambridge: Cambridge University Press, pp. 16–69.

—— (2000), *Drinking Occasions: Comparative Perspectives on Alcohol and Culture*, Philadelphia: Brunner/Mazzel, Taylor & Francis.

Heredia, B. and R. De Pau (2000), *Pepe Domínguez: Un Pilar de la Canción Yucateca*, Mérida: Gobierno del Estado de Yucatán/Instituto de Cultura de Yucatán/ Consejo Nacional para la Cultura y las Artes/Dirección de Culturas Populares de Yucatán.

Hervik, P. (2003) [1999], *Mayan People within and beyond Boundaries: Social Categories and Lived Identity in Yucatán*, London: Routledge.

Houston, C. (2001), 'The Brewing of Islamist Modernity: Tea Gardens and Public Space in Istanbul', *Theory, Culture and Society* 18 (6): 77–97.

Infante Vargas, L. and L. Hernández Fuentes (2000), *Las cocinas del mundo en México: Sabores del mundo árabe*, Mexico City: Clío.

Innes, S. A. (ed.) (2001), *Pilaf, Pozole, and Pad Thai: American Women and Ethnic Food*, Amherst: University of Massachusetts Press.

Joseph, G. M. (1979), 'Mexico's "Popular Revolution": Mobilization and Myth in Yucatán, 1910–1940', *Latin American Perspectives* 6 (3): 46–65.

—— (1985), 'From Caste War to Class War: The Historiography of Modern Yucatán (c. 1750–1940)', *The Hispanic American Historical Review* 65 (1): 111–34.

Juárez López, J. L. (2000), *La lenta emergencia de la comida mexicana. Ambigüedades criollas, 1750–1800*, Mexico City: Porrua.

Kondo, D. (1985), 'The Way of Tea: A Symbolic Analysis', *Man* (N. S.), 20 (2): 287–306.

Lockie, S. (2001), 'Food, Place and Identity: Consuming Australia's "Beef Capital"', *Journal of Sociology* 37 (3): 239–55.

Lowry, M. (1984) [1947], *Under the Volcano*, New York: Perennial Books.

Lozano Armendares, T. (1997), 'Mezcales, pulques y chinguiritos', in J. Long (ed.), *Conquista y comida: Consecuencias del encuentro de dos mundos*, Mexico City: UNAM, pp. 421–35.

McDowell, J. H. (2000), *Poetry and Violence: The Ballad Tradition of Mexico's Costa Chica*, Urbana: University of Illinois Press.

Mancall, P. C. (1995), *Deadly Medicine: Indians and Alcohol in Early America*, Ithaca, NY: Cornell University Press.

Manuel, P. (1990), *Popular Musics of the Non-Western World: An Introductory Survey*, Oxford: Oxford University Press.

Manuel, P., K. Bilby and M. Largey (1995) *Caribbean Currents: Caribbean Music from to Rumba to Reggae*, Philadelphia: Temple University Press.

Martin, A. L. (2001), 'Old People, Alcohol and Identity in Europe, 1300–1700', in P. Scholliers (ed.), *Food, Drink and Identity: Cooking, Eating and Drinking in Europe since the Middle Ages*, Oxford: Berg, pp. 119–37.

Menéndez, E. (1990), *Morir de alcohol: Saber y hegemonía médica*, Mexico City: CONACULTA/Alianza Editorial.

Menéndez, E. and R. B. di Pardo (1996), *De algunos alcoholismos y algunos saberes: Atención primaria y proceso de alcoholización*, Mexico City: Ciesas.

Milano Borruso, M. and S. Lerín Piñón (2001), 'Del beber y el tomar en Juchitán, Oaxaca', *Cuicuilco* (Nueva Época) 7 (22): 229–47.

Millán, A. (2001), 'Tapeo: An Identity Model of Public Drinking and Food Consumption in Spain', in I. de Garine and V. de Garine (eds), *Drinking: Anthropological Approaches*, Oxford: Berghahn, pp. 158–68.

Muría, J. M. (1995), 'El Agave histórico: Momentos del tequila', in *Artes de México, No. 27: El tequila. Arte tradicional de México*, Mexico City: Artes de México, pp. 17–27.

Patico, J. (2002), 'Chocolate and Cognac: Gifts and the Recognition of Social Worlds in Post-Soviet Russia', *Ethnos* 67 (3): 345–68.

Pérez Sabido, L., C. Medina Hadad and R. de Pau (2000), *La canción yucateca: Semblanzas y letras*, Mérida: Museo de la Canción Yucateca, AC.

Pilcher, J. (1998), *¡Que vivan los tamales! Food and the Making of Mexican Identity*, Albuquerque: University of New Mexico Press.

Quirarte, V. (1995), 'El agave imaginario: Poética del tequila', in *Artes de México, No. 27: El tequila. Arte tradicional de México*, Mexico City: Artes de México, pp. 58–67.

Ramírez Carrillo, Luis A. (2003), 'La ronda de las élites: Región y poder en Yucatán', in J. Preciado Coronado, H. Rivière d'Arc, L. A. Ramírez Carrillo and M.

Pepin-Lehalleur (eds), *Territorios, actores y poder: Regionalismos emergentes en México*, Guadalajara: Universidad de Guadalajara, Universidad Autónoma de Yucatán, pp. 191–219.

Rehfisch, F. (1987), 'Competitive Beer Drinking among the Mambila', in M. Douglas (ed.), *Constructive Drinking: Perspectives on Drink from Anthropology*, Cambridge: Cambridge University Press, pp. 135–45.

Roggero, F. S. (2001) 'El "peligro indio": La Guerra de Castas en Yucatán en el imaginario histórico regional', *Cuicuilco* 8 (21): 231–49.

Sarasúa, C. (2001), 'Upholding Status: The Diet of a Noble Family in Early Nineteenth-Century La Mancha', in P. Scholliers (ed.), *Food, Drink and Identity: Cooking, Eating and Drinking in Europe since the Middle Ages*, Oxford: Berg, pp. 37–61.

Schivelbusch, W. (1992), *Tastes of Paradise: A Social History of Spices, Stimulants, and Intoxicants*, New York: Vintage.

Smith, G. (1998), *Beer in America. The Early Years – 1587–1840. Beer's Role in the Settling of America and the Birth of a Nation*, Boulder, CO: Siris Books.

Stanford, T. (2003), 'Música maya en Yucatán y Quintana Roo', paper delivered at the workshop *Coloquio U paaxil in kaajal: La música de mi pueblo* (sponsored by CONACULTA and the Autonomous University of Yucatán), Salón del Consejo Universitario, Universidad Autónoma de Yucatán, 25 June, Mérida, Yucatán.

Sullivan, P.(1989), *Unfinished Conversations: Mayas and Foreigners between Two Wars*, New York: Alfred A. Knopf.

Taboada Ramírez, J. (1997), 'Bebidas fermentadas indígenas: Cacao, pozol, tepaches, tesgüino y tejuino', in J. Long (ed.), *Conquista y comida: Consecuencias del encuentro de dos mundos*, Mexico City: UNAM, pp. 437–48.

Taylor, W. B. (1987) [1979], *Embriaguez, homicidio y rebelión en las poblaciones coloniales mexicanas*, Mexico City: FCE.

Theophano, J. (2002), *Eat My Words: Reading Women's Lives through the Cookbooks They Wrote*, New York: Palgrave.

Terry, E. D. (1989), 'A Panorama of Literature in Yucatán', in E. H. Moseley and E. D. Terry (eds), *Yucatán: A World Apart*, Alabama: University of Alabama Press, pp. 264–305.

Toussaint-Samat, M. (1992) [1987], *History of Food*, Oxford: Blackwell.

Unwin, T. (2001) [1991], *El vino y la viña: Geografía histórica de la viticultura y el consumo del vino*, Barcelona: Tusquets.

Valenzuela, J. M. (2002), *Jefe de jefes: Corridos y narcocultura en México*, Mexico City: Raya en el Agua/Plaza Janes.

Vargas, L. A. and L. E. Casillas (1996), 'La integración de los alimentos del Viejo Mundo a la dieta mexicana', in I. González Turmo and P. Romero de Solís (eds.), *Antropología de la alimentación: Nuevos ensayos sobre la dieta mediterránea*, Seville: Universidad de Sevilla.

Vargas-Cetina, G. (2001–3), *La Trova Yucateca*, fieldnotes.

—— (2003), 'La asociación efímera: Repensando el concepto de comunidad desde la literatura cyberpunk', *Cuadernos de Bioética* 11. Retrieved 28 September 2003 from *www.cuadernos.bioetica.org/doctrina38.htm*

Viqueira Albán, J. P. (1987), *¿Relajados o reprimidos? Diversiones públicas y vida social en la ciudad de México durante el Siglo de las Luces*, Mexico City: FCE.

Wells, A. (1985), *Yucatán's Gilded Age: Haciendas, Henequen, and International Harvester, 1860–1915*, Albuquerque: University of New Mexico Press.

–9 –

Cheers and Booze
Football and *Festa* Drinking in Malta

Jon P. Mitchell and Gary Armstrong

Like the consumption of food, the imbibing of alcohol has been a relatively neglected area of study for anthropologists (as suggested in Douglas 1987 and elsewhere in this volume). However, alcohol has a meaning and a sensorial effect that ensure it is both a cultural artefact and a demarcator of time (Gusfield 1996). As Barthes (1977: 21) recognizes, it is a 'system of communication, a body of images, a protocol of usages, situation and behavior'. Social and cultural patterns determine drinking rituals (Bales 1980; Heath 1981; Conniffe and McCoy 1993), and as Douglas (1987) postulates, alcohol events offer a vision of the world *as it is*, yet may also reflect an *ideal* world loaded with symbolism and religious ideas. This ideal world is reinforced through drinking because of its effects on the senses (Seremetakis 1996: 28). Douglas (1987) also emphasizes the extent to which alcohol consumption produces social identity, as people engage in 'constructive drinking'. Moving beyond the pathologizing tendency of most approaches to alcohol, she argues that rather than destroying social relations through its associated social problems, alcohol – or, more specifically, drinking alcohol – is just as often central to the production of social relations. Drinking is a social, rather than anti-social, act.

This chapter addresses the social significance of drinking in Malta, demonstrating how acts of drinking, both in everyday contexts and in the relatively 'extraordinary' drinking events associated with saints' feasts and football celebrations, produce and demarcate social boundaries. The articulation and maintenance of boundaries have become central to an anthropological understanding of processes of identification.[1] Working within a largely semiotic or symbolic framework, a range of scholars have demonstrated how boundaries of locality are symbolized (Cohen 1985, 1986); how ethnic groups are demarcated through boundary processes (Barth 1969; Epstein 1978); how nations – and even regions such as Europe – have their identities imagined through the articulation of boundaries, be they the literal boundary of a geographical border (Wilson and Donnan 1998) or the political and social boundaries of citizenship (Stolcke 1995). More recently, scholars have emphasized the performative nature of boundary production and reproduction, drawing in particular on 'post-representational' or 'post-semiotic' work from gender studies (Butler 1990) to further confirm the processual or 'in the making' nature of identity. Our analysis of Maltese drinking highlights performance in two senses: first, the performance of sociability in everyday drinking and the extent to which it produces masculine subjectivity; second, the performances of local commitment to football team and patron saint that produce more localized identifications. In both cases, these perform- ances also contribute to the articulation of national boundaries, as they demarcate a space that is exclusive to the Maltese and apart from the ever-present foreigners.

Malta has always been full of foreigners. Its history is one of cross-currents and successive colonizations that in recent years have turned from explicit political hegemony to the more haphazard, though no less significant, invasion by hundreds of thousands of tourists each year. This has led to a situation in which the demarca- tion of inside and outside, and the establishment of a 'buffer zone' of tolerant accommodation, have become significant. The demarcation of inside and outside has become possible through local associationism that marks off certain spaces – certain bars – as the province of the local. Here, outsiders are neither expected nor particu- larly welcome. Such places can be contrasted with more cosmopolitan bars, which are aimed at accommodating outsiders in a tolerable – and tolerant – environment. This chapter concerns local bars and local drinking in Valletta, the capital of Malta. It is based on fieldwork by both authors during the 1990s and the first two years of the new millennium. Its scope is primarily ethnographic – to describe the context of drinking in contemporary Malta and explain the significance of both drinking places and the drinks that are imbibed. The main body of the chapter contrasts 'everyday' drinking patterns with 'extraordinary' drinking patterns which occur during special events such as saints' feasts and football celebrations, events which are extremely important in Maltese society, wherein football runs a close second in popular identifi- cation and support to the official national religion of Roman Catholicism. These extraordinary events are not the preserve of the local, but they nevertheless also have an important role in the articulation of local identity – both national and local within Malta. Such events enact a claiming – or reclamation – of space on the part of local associations in the name of the local and/or the national.

Alcohol is a major part of such extraordinary events, but also part of the fabric of everyday Maltese life. The Maltese routinely drink wine with meals, introducing generations of children to the joys of alcohol. Wine is notably absent, though, from most public drinking occasions, when chilled local beer is the routine, and it is replaced by whisky on special occasions such as a birthday or feast day. As in other gift-giving situations, the offer of a drink implies an obligation to receive (Mauss 1966), with refusal causing offence. If workmen are offered a beer, for example, in appreciation of their tasks, refusal is considered a great insult. The offer of whisky – particularly in a domestic context – is seen most commonly when priests, polit- icians or doctors visit the house. Whisky is made available to those considered morally superior and/or more discerning in their tastes. It is therefore loaded with ideas of power and inequality.

Drinks are also gendered in Malta. A female visitor is not normally expected to accept alcohol, and if she does it is normally a 'woman's' drink such as Pimms or Campari. The public consumption of alcohol is similarly gendered, being primarily a masculine pursuit loaded with displays of masculine competence, competition and worth. The main drink taken on public occasions is lager because its consumption permits prolonged socialization – the volume of beer slows down the process of inebriation. If drinking shorts, the Maltese male chooses 'JB and Coke' or 'Whisky Coke' whereas Maltese females drink vodka or tequila accompanied by a fruit-based mixer or the recently fashionable Red Bull 'booster' drink. While beer consumption is 'routine', occasions also present themselves which are conducive to excess, and encourage the exhibitionist, the vulgar, the insulting and the carnivalesque.

Bearing this in mind, the analysis that follows links everyday drinking patterns to the development of Maltese civil society, or what we call 'associational culture', which was established under colonial rule as a means by which Maltese could establish authority and autonomy. This is significant not only in the context of colonization but also in that of stratification, which sees a highly elaborated micro-politics of distinction and respectability governing participation in 'polite society' (Mitchell 2002: 93–119). The creation of associations allows less respectable Maltese to enhance their reputation through active participation in association activities, although certain of them – such as the footballing celebrations discussed below – are regarded in some polite circles as vulgar. The dynamics of associational civil society are rooted in ideas and practices of masculine reputation and masculine friendship that are played out in everyday interactions in Maltese bars. Inherent in this process is the need to establish a specifically local context for social life. This chapter links extraordinary drinking patterns to symbolic claims – or reclamations – over public space, in which the boundaries of the local drinking places are expanded outwards into the streets to re-establish legitimate control over them. In the patterns of everyday and extraordinary drinking, then, the relationship between the local and the supra-local, the Maltese and the foreigner, is manifest in two contrasting, but complementary, ways. The first establishes a discrete zone away from the non-local; the second reclaims space from the non-local. The local bar is precisely that – a space apart from the ever-present foreigners. Here foreigners are seldom seen, and when they are, both they and the locals experience the encounter with a certain discomfort. The extraordinary drinking events discussed here – a saint's feast and a football celebration – are orientated in different ways around claiming space. In the former celebration, the space of the parish is given over to a series of marches and proces-sions which demonstrate the patronage of the saint over this space, but also claims the streets for the feast. In Valletta, these streets are normally 'open' for tourists to stroll around, but during the feast their freedom to do so is curtailed by their redefinition as ritual space. During marches and processions, they must abide by the conventions of such events, moving as they do through space that has been appropriated by the feast. In the latter celebration, a similar claiming of space takes place, as a mock funeral celebrates footballing success and the death of the rival teams.

A Short History of Maltese Drinking

The Knights of St John of Jerusalem ruled Malta from 1530 to 1798. Although they were the controlling elite, the seventeenth and eighteenth centuries saw a consolidation in Malta of a local mercantile bourgeoisie centred on harbour areas (Cassar 1994). At the centre of the harbour was the Knights' capital, Valletta, which served as a hub of commercial and social activity. During the time of the Knights, and indeed during the British colonial rule of 1800 to 1964, Malta had an import economy, depending on imported food and wine – mainly from Italy (Blouet 1989: 105ff.). Before British rule, wine was the principal drink, with urban, elite tastes in imported wine complemented by the rural production of local wines. The period was characterized by a rural–urban distinction. Villagers would daily visit the city – which indeed came to be known as 'the city' – *Il-Belt*. Here they would rub shoulders with a variety of different types of people, both Maltese and foreign. Central to Valletta life at the time were the cafés or coffee-shops that developed in the city. Cassar (1988) refers to them as 'cosmopolitan places' where one could meet visitors and/or locals to discuss the matters of the day. As in other European countries, he implies, the coffee-shop became the space for the emergence of a sphere of public opinion (Habermas 1989; see also Ors 2002). These exclusively male domains are regarded by Cassar (1988: 109) as places of elite sociability, where commoners would 'never dream of being seen'. In his account they contrast with the rural wine-shops, which were more local and less elite in character and clientele.

However, there is also evidence of less respectable establishments in Valletta, which, like the coffee-houses of other European countries had a problematic reputation. In the 1770s British traveller Patrick Brydone (1776: 338) heard of a recent conspiracy to overthrow the Knights, which had been planned by Turkish slaves in a Valletta coffeehouse. An Arab visitor to Valletta in the 1850s saw not open, cosmopolitan coffee-houses but, rather, exclusive, even hostile, establishments: 'As for the cafés of Valletta, they are no more than dim shops without a window overlooking the sea or some garden; if you sit long in one, the waiter will come and wipe the table before you, hinting that he is expecting other customers, his whole attitude seeming to say "You weary me, when are you leaving?"' (Cachia 1962: 112). Given Malta's many years of conflict with North African and Levantine powers, there might be historical reasons for this hostility, but it does seem indicative of a prevailing localism that, alongside the above observations, suggests that a classification of coffee-houses as elite and respectable is over-simplistic. Writing of the 1960s

Maltese village wine-shop – the rural counterpart to the urban coffee-house – Boissevain (2000: 420–1) observes that while some are associated with local elites, others remain 'commoner' bars. The same might be true of Valletta coffee-houses, and indeed is true of its bars today. They are not categorically respectable or non-respectable, but depend on who drinks there. Bars become associated with particular masculine friendship groups – cliques or *klikek* (sing. *klikka*) – which spend most of their social time there, and often share a religious devotion, a political commitment and/or a hobby or pastime.

The Emergence of 'Associational Culture'

The nineteenth century saw the development of brass Band Clubs in both rural and urban Malta, which were both important features of an emergent Maltese civil society and significant new loci for drinking. The Band Clubs emerged out of the politico-religious factionalism that Boissevain (1965: 75) traces from the 1850s onwards, in which lay organizations developed to challenge the spiritual hegemony of the established Church by forming competing devotional cults. The cults organized competing saints' feasts (*festi* – sing. *festa*) at which brass bands would play. The new Band Clubs served the newly established *festa partiti* (*festa* factions). They were not merely religious organizations, though, and their members and office-holders were frequently also activists of the developing political parties. For example, the two Valletta Band Clubs – La Valette and the King's Own Band Club – list as their early committee members figures from the early years of Maltese party politics. The Band Clubs were part and parcel of an emerging civil society that was to develop into party politics in this colonial setting.

In the early twentieth century the political parties themselves started to form clubs, and most Maltese settlements now have clubs dedicated to one of the two main political parties: the Labour Party and the Nationalist Party. Naturally formed to promote the interests of the political parties, these clubs – like the Band Clubs – are also important drinking places. Indeed, the roles of bar and that of promoter of political association are mutually sustaining. Both types of club continue to be places of conviviality and of sociopolitical organization where alliances and plans are made.

The twentieth century also saw the emergence of football clubs and football supporters' clubs. Club bars are more than just businesses; they are orientated towards groups of men with particular *hobbies*,[2] especially those of bands and football. Particular groups are associated with particular bars. These are *klikka* of men who will spend time together in the bar. They are sites of political canvassing by political candidates, and are the primary location for organizing clientelistic practices, or what Pardo (1996: 30) has called 'the mass diffusion of favours'.

As well as indigenous Maltese politics, the British period also saw the development of indigenous Maltese wine and beer production. With the stationing of British garrisons on the island, the importation of beer became an important industry, and when in 1929 the major importation company H. & G. Simonds amalgamated with the recently established Farsons brewery they established what was to become one of the largest companies in Malta.[3] Simonds Farsons Cisk – Cisk was added after the 1948 merger with another brewery – is currently the highest-performing non-financial company in the Malta Stock Market (<http://www.borzamalta.com.mt/>). It not only produces Malta's most popular beers, but also now owns the franchise for and imports other beers, including Tetleys, Carlsberg, Budweiser, Becks, Kilkenny – as well as the spirits Ballantine's, Famous Grouse, Bacardi, Campari and others. At the same time as local beer production was developing, so too local wine was being produced more systematically than hitherto. In the early years of the twentieth century a number of wine makers established themselves as companies, initially producing cheap, basic wine for local mass consumption but more recently experimenting in fine wine production by refining the local grape varieties and importing vines from Italy.

These new products had a local market – or market of local Maltese – and also had a significant market among visitors. The presence of the British garrisons led to the emergence of 'sailor bars' in Valletta and the other towns around Malta's Grand Harbour, most famously on Valletta's Strait Street, known as 'The Gut'. This is a narrow alley-street that runs parallel to the city's main thoroughfares, and until the 1970s – when the British troops withdrew from Malta – it was lined with bars and dance-halls to service the troops.

With the withdrawal of the troops, the beer and wine market continued to expand alongside the expansion of tourism. Tourism was seen as a potential saviour for the Maltese economy after independence (1964). From the 1960s onwards, the numbers of tourists visiting Malta expanded, from 334,500 in 1975 (National Tourism Organization of Malta 1994) to 1,180,145 in 2001.[5] (<http://www.maltatourismauthority.com/research/statistics/geograph01.xls>). As a consequence, the older sailor bars of Valletta were replaced by newer tourist bars in the coastal resorts along Malta's north shore, particularly in Paceville, which has become not only the centre of tourist activity but also a major attraction for Maltese youth during weekends and the summer. This night city of excess has become the post-independence site of the *rite de passage* for young Maltese – of growing up and throwing up due to excessive alcohol consumption. Indeed, consumption in general has expanded exponentially since independence, but particularly after the election of 1987, which saw the end of sixteen years' protectionist economic policy by the Malta Labour Party and its replacement with a more free-market-orientated Nationalist Party, which liberalized the economy and encouraged consumption. Per capita expenditure at constant prices rose by 33 per cent between 1984 and 1992 whilst private consumption at current prices rose from 317.3 million Maltese lira to 417.1 million over the same period (Tonna 1994).[4] This overall expansion in consumption has also manifested itself in the expansion of drinking – and particularly drinking to excess in centres such as

Paceville, which has become an important icon for Maltese popular culture and has consequently suffered a degree of demonization in the press (Sammut 1991; Mitchell 2002).

The cosmopolitanism of the eighteenth-century Valletta coffee-house has therefore been replaced by the cosmopolitanism of the twenty-first-century Paceville tourist bar. This development has had important consequences for Valletta as a whole, which since the 1960s has become increasingly depopulated and run-down (Mitchell 2002: 35–61). However, it still maintains a lively bar culture that is sustained partly by the large numbers of non-Vallettans who enter the city each day to work and/or shop. It is estimated that although the resident population of Valletta is only around 9,000, over 40,000 people – tourists, office workers, shoppers – enter the city every day. The bars are also sustained by locals and ex-locals who maintain a close attachment to Valletta and are dedicated to their bars.

Bar *San Paolo Naufrago*

Bar *San Paolo Naufrago* – St Paul's Shipwreck – sits on one of the steep, stepped streets that slide down from Valletta's central ridge towards the Grand Harbour. A cave-like opening is flanked by green wooden shutters that close on those rare occasions when the bar is not open. The bar is more commonly known as *Ghand Lawrenz* – Lawrence's place – after its current owner, but sometimes also as *Ghand Censu*, after his father Censu.[5] Although not formally classified as a male domain, in practice it is predominantly masculine and women say that they are *tisthi* – ashamed – to enter on their own; when they do enter, their presence is usually mediated by the men there. Women would only normally enter on Sunday mornings and during the days of *festa* – the celebration of the local patron Saint Paul, after whom the bar is named. At these times the women sit in the small side-room used during the week for draughts matches, and have drinks brought to them by men. At other times, women who work in the nearby shops might quickly go into the bar to buy a drink or a sandwich, but seldom stay there to eat or drink. While in the bar, they strictly avoid eye-contact with anybody but those serving, and are usually teased by Lawrence for entering. Some women prefer not to enter at all, choosing instead to stand outside the open bar-front and catch the attention of somebody who might help them buy what they need.

The bar acts as a kind of club-house for the *Pawlini* – 'Paulites' – who participate in the organization, design and management of street decorations and fireworks during the feast. The term *Pawlini* broadly denotes supporters of the *festa*, be they locals to the parish or outsiders, but since the early 1970s it has also marked members of the organization that was set up to oversee its administration – the Ghaqda tal-Pawlini (Association of Paulites). This Association sits alongside Valletta's two Band Clubs as the most significant institutions of Valletta civil society. Office-holders in the Ghaqda are considered important local figures, but also command a position which enables them to pursue links with other associations and with political institutions.

The bar serves as a *de facto* club for the men at the centre of the Ghaqda. Many of these are Valletta locals, but just as many are former residents of Valletta who have either been moved out of the city after the controversial slum-clearances of the 1970s (Mitchell 1998a) or have left the city to find more comfortable housing. It is the place where these men establish and consolidate their reputations as 'good men' – *ragel sew* – who are trustworthy, reliable and sociable. Conversation in the bar revolves around notions of masculinity. In particular, the phrase *tkun ragel* – 'be a man' – is often used, and in a variety of contexts, as a form of sanction against behaviour or attitudes considered un-masculine. It is most often used in arguments, when it is felt that someone has lost and should concede the fact. The implication is that to admit defeat is to be sufficiently resilient and sufficiently sure in one's masculinity. The dominant – or hegemonic (Cornwall and Lindisfarne 1994; Connell 1995) – male ideology emphasizes both heterosexuality and fatherhood, together with trustworthiness and reciprocal sociability. The latter require considerable effort and expenditure, whilst the former are questioned when men fail to deliver that effort and expenditure. Friendship in Malta is a precarious business in need of reproduction and reaffirmation. Offence is quickly taken at those who fail to fulfil the obligation to participate in the daily rounds of visiting and socializing. Those who do not live up to the expectations of sociability are referred to as *pufta* – 'poofter', a derogatory slang for homosexual – or *haxxej* – 'fucker'.

Maintaining a reputation as a good, upstanding man means a sustained and intensive commitment to bar sociability. The core *klikek* of the *Pawlini* visit the bar twice daily, and often several times a day, for coffee in the morning and alcoholic drinks in the evening. Ghaqda office-holders, who are often also political or other important local figures, are expected to come to the bar frequently, particularly on Sunday, which is the most important day for drinking. Members of the *klikka* employ a mental system of checks and balances whereby they monitor who has been buying which drinks, and what favours have been reciprocated with a drink bought. The method of drink buying, however, makes the resulting reciprocity implicit rather than explicit. The focus, rather, is on generosity. Drinks are bought in rounds and in a style that serves to emphasize the largesse of the drink buyer. People do not wait for others – or indeed themselves – to buy a new round, nor do they ask whether a round is needed. Rather, they will approach the barman – Lawrence – to make a round, who will discreetly ask who is to be included in the round. The drinks are then 'sent' to the recipients. On Sundays and feast days, the exuberance of the occasion leads to a quick-fire provision of rounds, such that in no time each table is full of undrunk and half-drunk rounds. Buying rounds like this is also the way local dignitaries – be they important office-holders in the Ghaqda tal-Pawlini or local politicians – demonstrate their largesse. They will walk into the bar and order a round to be sent to everybody there. As Lawrence places the drinks in front of each recipient, a querying eye will draw the discreet response as to who 'sent' the drink.

Different bars in Valletta – and indeed in Malta – are associated with different *klikek*, which are considered by their members to be the smallest and most intimate level of social grouping outside the household. *Klikek* are often referred to metaphorically as *qaqocca*, or artichoke heart. Men will demonstrate the closeness of their *klikka* by taking the fingers of one hand and squeezing them together. The other hand is wrapped around this cluster of fingers, to resemble an artichoke heart, and the shoulders are arched slightly in a gesture that involves the whole upper half of the body, to demonstrate togetherness. In a quiet and serious tone of voice they then affirm: 'We're a small clique, like an artichoke heart.'

The notion of *klikka* refers both to actual social groups and to the influential groups thought to sit at the centre of political, religious and other important institutions. It is also used rhetorically to emphasize a unity that transcends apparent social divisions. To this extent, the boundary of the category *klikka* is a flexible one. In the early 1990s, the locals of *Ghand Lawrenz* divided into three *klikek*. The divisions between the different *klikek* manifested themselves in different ways of using the bar, in the occupation of different space within it, and in drinking different drinks. The first *klikka* comprised older, more established *Pawlini* – *festa* enthusiasts *par excellence*. The second was a younger group who were also involved in *festa*, but in a rather less committed way. They were seen by the older *klikka* as lacking commitment to the cause of *festa*, and rather flighty – less responsible than they. The third *klikka* were also *Pawlini*, but less interested in direct involvement in *festa*. Rather, their *hobby* was football, which they followed avidly and played regularly for minor local teams.[6] Despite these divisions, however, the *Ghand Lawrenz Pawlini* would frequently refer to themselves as *klikka wahda* – one clique.

Space, Authority and Masculinity

Of the various criteria demarcating a good man – *ragel sew* – the most important relates to marital status. Here, being a man confers responsibility and authority. Married men are responsible for the household, and to this extent are recognized as responsible for the single most important institution in Malta: the family. Authority and marital status were represented in the use of social space *Ghand Lawrenz*.

In most bars, both in Malta and elsewhere, the boundary between that part of the bar private to the proprietors – the area behind the bar itself – and that open to the public is rigidly adhered to. Although bars are 'public', this public is always tempered by the presence of an off-limits, private zone that lies behind the counter and through the door marked 'private' (Strathern 1992: 128–9). *Ghand Lawrenz*, this boundary is often transgressed, most often by younger, unmarried men and by a local woman called Lela.

Lela was something of an anomaly, as a beer-drinking woman who came into the bar on a daily basis. In the early 1990s she was in her mid-thirties and worked as a housemaid for a local bourgeois family. However, her use of the bar space both explains how she managed this anomalous status and invites its classification in terms similar to the gendered classification of space in other Mediterranean contexts – the distinction between public and private as gendered masculine and feminine (Friedl 1962; Reiter 1975). When she came into the bar, Lela would walk straight through the main room and into the apparently 'private' space behind the counter. Here, she would help herself to a bottle of beer from the large fridges underneath, and leave the money on top. The implication is that, as a woman, she is better placed to transcend the apparent boundary between public and private areas of the bar, and effectively help herself to hospitality.

However, it was not only Lela who felt able to enter this private space. As mentioned, the boundary was also routinely transcended by the younger, unmarried men who spent their time *Ghand Lawrenz* – both those who were involved in *festa* and those more interested in football. Of these, there were perhaps twenty who regularly spent time in the bar. This meant that on Sunday mornings, the most significant social occasion of the week, the space behind the bar was very cramped.

The fact that younger, unmarried men occupied this space is significant. These were men who were actively or potentially in the process of looking for a partner, rather than those who had resolved their sexuality, and hence their adult personhood, through marriage. It was rare to see married men, older, unmarried men, or men who expressed a lack of interest in courtship behind the bar. This suggests that the bar, in replicating, via Lela, a gendered division of space between the public and private domains, also replicated the sexual careers of the men who spent their time there. Indeed, more broadly, it replicated their passage to adult masculinity through fatherhood.

As well as occupying this ambiguous position behind the bar, the young men involved in courtship were also generally more mobile than the older men. They would pull up in cars outside *Ghand Lawrenz* and run into the bar, straight to the back, and quickly order a drink. They would often only stay for one, before moving off to other places, where they might meet young women. Particularly popular were the bars of Paceville. Their participation in the system of round buying was therefore sporadic. On Sunday mornings, when they would stay in the bar for a full 'session' – from around 10.30 a.m. to 1 p.m. – they would buy rounds, but at other times they would not. This mobility of the younger men led to a certain scorn from the older regulars. They often questioned the commitment of these younger, more mobile, men, to the local social groups – the *klikek* and the Ghaqda tal-Pawlini. The behaviour of the younger men also contrasted with the solidity and stasis of men who occupied the main 'public' part of the bar, sitting and sharing drinks together in a stable, round-buying *klikka*.

Foreign and Local Drinks

There was also a distinction between the drinks drunk by the two younger *klikek* and the older one. While the older men drank local beer – produced locally by Simonds Farsons Cisk – either lager or pale ale, the younger men would drink imported beers, particularly Heineken. On Sundays and on other special occasions, drinking would move on from beer to spirits, and again there was a distinction. Whilst the older men would drink whisky, the younger would drink other things – vodka, Campari and particularly the artichoke-based Italian aperitif Cynar.

The significance of these choices – as with other areas of consumption – goes beyond the particularities of personal taste. As a number of scholars have testified, consumption choices are socially determined, and relate to consumers' self-identity. Through consumption, people constitute themselves as persons – they construct their identity (Friedman 1994; Miller 1995). The younger men's choice of imported beer and particularly of the Italian spirits signals a certain pursuit of European sophistication. The Italian drinks are significant in that they link the young men to Malta's historically influential Italianate bourgeois elite. The mercantile bourgeoisie that developed in Valletta and the other harbour areas during the Knights' era was both Italian-focused and Italian-speaking. As the families consolidated economically, they also established themselves as leaders in the clergy and judiciary, and in the late nineteenth century it was this group that provided Malta's party politicians (Frendo 1979). Consuming Italian drinks therefore signifies influence and connectedness as well as sophistication.

Consuming foreign drinks also has party political significance. In an intensely polarized political environment, Valletta, and particularly St Paul's parish, is renowned as a hot-bed of support for the Nationalist Party. The Nationalists have historically been an Italianate party, emphasizing Malta's historical and cultural links with Italy, rather than the more exclusivist Labour Party (Hull 1993). This in itself encourages the younger *Pawlini* to consume Italian drinks. However, there is a more specific politics of consumption that links back to the 1970s and 1980s, when the Labour Party was in government. Like many socialist governments of the era, it was strongly protectionist in its policies, and restricted imports on all goods, to protect local production. The commodities that particularly captured the national imagination were imported chocolate and toothpaste, which adopted the status of luxury contraband. Meanwhile, the status of locally produced goods fell *vis-à-vis* the imported ones, and this distinction has remained. Imported goods are still regarded as of higher quality than locally produced ones, and are thus associated with higher status.

The older *Pawlini*'s preference for local beer did not express any lack of commitment to the Nationalist cause, but rather the fact that they remembered a time when local production was not associated with Labour protectionism, and so was something to be proud of rather than denigrated. Whisky, introduced by the British, was the 'traditional' spirit for special occasions. Most households had a bottle of whisky, which, as noted above, was produced for important visitors such as politicians and priests. Their commitment to local beer and whisky represented a less self-conscious attitude towards the semiotics of consumption than that of the younger *Pawlini* – a factor that can also be linked to their differential masculinity. The self-conscious young men are differentiated from the older, more comfortable, *klikka* not only by their use of space within the bar, but also by what they drink.

Everyday Drinking and *Festa* Drinking

If sociability in bars such as *Ghand Lawrenz* requires a daily attendance – a daily commitment – by the *Pawlini*, this regular, quotidian drinking is punctuated by a cycle of 'extraordinary' drinking. Sunday, as noted, is a significant day in the weekly calendar, when the rhythm of everyday drinking is intensified. This is a time when *Pawlini* from outside Valletta who are unable to come into the city on a daily basis will certainly make a point of coming to the bar. It is also a time when women – and sometimes children – are seen in the bar.

As well as this weekly intensification, drinking *Ghand Lawrenz* also takes on these extraordinary qualities during the various annual public holidays. It is during the time of the *festa*, the feast of St Paul, that drinking takes on a very different character. To begin with, *Ghand Lawrenz* becomes permanently open to *Pawlini* and non-*Pawlini* alike. The normal spatial dynamics break down and the bar serves the wider *festa* constituencies – *Pawlini,* other locals and non-local Maltese, visitors, tourists.

Meanwhile, the normal denizens of *Ghand Lawrenz,* the dedicated *Pawlini klikek* who normally spend long hours in the bar, loosen their allegiance and become locals of all the neighbourhood bars. The logic of this follows the logic of *festa* itself. During the five days of *festa* leading up to 10 February – the feast day *proper* – a series of solemn liturgical functions in the parish church are accompanied by a series of more ludic events outside, particularly brass band marches. These events effectively mark out the territory over which St Paul is patron, creating a new, temporary geography for *festa*-time.

During band marches, crowds line the streets but also, significantly, large groups of *festa* enthusiasts – those normally seen *Ghand Lawrenz* – follow the band through the streets, shouting praise to the saint, singing along to the tunes, and drinking. The followers divide into round-buying *klikek,* who stay together during the march. Throughout the march they move from bar to bar along its route, always ahead of the march, to anticipate it. Early on in the march, the aim is to arrive at the next bar on the route with enough time to buy and drink a single round so that as the drinks are finished, the band arrives and can be escorted for a few metres before the group moves on to the next bar. As the march progresses, though, the timing becomes increasingly difficult, because the round-buying system breaks down, and in their enthusiasm several members of the *klikek* will order rounds simultaneously, leaving not one but several drinks to be drunk in each bar. Drinks are also 'sent' to these itinerant drinkers by locals in each bar who are friends or relatives of the group. Again, this leaves a surplus of drinking to be done. Eventually, the pattern of entering a bar to drink and then leave breaks down. Rather than staying in the bar, the revellers take their drinks with them, entering the next bar to restock their supply of drinks to carry along the way. Most of the revellers drink beer, and have developed a technique in which spare bottles of beer are held between the fingers of one hand while the one that is being drunk is held in the other. Doing this, they can carry five bottles at a time, and it is not unusual to see *Pawlini* doing just that. Those who drink spirits – usually whisky – will adopt a glass to carry along into which all new measures are poured. Inevitably, as the band marches progress, their followers get more and more raucous as they get more and more drunk. By the end, the singing, dancing throng is more like something one would expect at a rock concert or football match than a brass band march during a religious feast.

These *festi ta'barra* – outdoor, street festivities – climax on *festa* day with the much-loved *marc tas-siegha* – one o'clock march – and the final procession, during which the massive statue of St Paul is taken out of the church and processed around the parish. These are both important drinking events and festive occasions for the commemoration of the saint, and they follow a different logic from everyday drink-ing – a logic that opens out the intimacies of the bar space to the public space of the street, thereby expanding the domain of the local into the whole parish.

Although outsiders are tolerated at these events – and in some senses actively encouraged to attend – they are never full participants in the festivities. Rather, they are expected to act as a passive audience; they should watch, perhaps take photo-graphs but certainly not sing, dance or drink to excess. The boundary between insiders and outsiders is therefore maintained through the sensorial and experiential distinction between observers and participants in the *festi ta'barra*, a distinction that is not only marked but constituted through the use – some might say abuse – of alcohol. Because of the disinhibiting effect of alcohol, the boundary between the sober observer and the drunken participant enables the latter to dominate the relation-ship between the two, and ensures that *festa* goes further than merely opening out the local to the supra-local. It enables local people to effectively *claim* the public space of the streets for the local *festa* and its participants. The same is true of other events in Valletta, which in various ways enact a claiming – or reclamation – of public space by local groups. Prominent among these are the periodic celebrations associated with football.

Everyday Drinking and Football Drinking

There are no shortages of public rituals on the streets of Valletta. As well as *festa*, since being awarded the status of a World Heritage Site in 1980, the city is now host to a proliferation of antiquated and militaristic parades, which have little connection to the population of the city and in their enactment seem to be of passing interest to the variety of mainly European tourists. Whilst some occasions are promoted in the tourist industry, the biggest parades in the city are primarily 'private' occasions for the Valletta population and its diaspora. The surface level of celebrations often belies deeper and long running antagonisms. The annual pre-lenten carnival enacted every March sees a parade of floats with effigies. The majority of the participants hail from Valletta and can often trace a long dynasty in their costume and float designs. In classic carnival style this event for decades ended with a lavish ball where the elite of Maltese society would rub shoulders with their social inferiors, both parties resplendent in masks and lavish costumes. Today, the significance of the carnival has been occluded by the emergence of many other, equally spectacular events throughout the year. The number of carnival floats and troupes has fallen, as has participation in the ball; the affair has become more of a children's event, and spontaneity, wit and satire have disappeared. What was once an occasion loaded with alcohol is now a sober affair verging on the kitsch for the benefit of tourists. In fact today, no matter how celebrated is a saint or a carnival, nothing can attract the numbers and alcoholic excess that is manifest when Valletta city celebrates winning a football trophy.

Football is routinely an occasion for drinking, and the main sites for everyday drinking are the supporters' clubs – dedicated either to local or to prominent international teams – which operate for football *klikek* in the same way as *Ghand Lawrenz.* Adjacent to the law courts in Valletta, and a few metres from Strait Street, is a door which leads to a marble staircase with peeling plaster walls which after thirty-five steps leads to the bar of the Valletta City supporters' club. Established in 1991, the bar is the contemporary meeting place for committee members and active supporters – those in the club's central organizing *klikka.* Although linked to the club's functionary elite, there is an egalitarian ethos in the bar, and politics is actively discouraged in favour of football-related debate and general gossip. Round buying is here an established practice, and again the most common drinks consumed are local beer and whisky. The bar is significant to those who support the team but no longer live in Valletta, particularly when trophies are won and brought 'home' to the bar, to riotous and drunken celebrations. At such moments it unites a series of 'satellite' bars where groups of less directly active – though no less fanatical – fans regularly gather to drink.

The Defilé

In April 2001, the first round of what was to be a month of football-related celebration took place in Valletta, not far from a bar made famous by an intoxicated British actor – Oliver Reed – who during an eight-hour drinking session in the company of British sailors and Maltese locals slumped drunk in a corner and died in his slumbers. Never people to miss a business opportunity, the Maltese owners of the small establishment – which for forty years had been known simply as 'The Pub' – was renamed 'Ollie's Last Drink'. Gathered a few hundred yards away were hundreds of Valletta fans, colonizing the staircase at the top of which stood the Siege Bell monument that had been erected to commemorate fifty years since Malta was awarded the George Cross for its gallantry during the 1942 Axis Siege. This memory was subsumed by the enthusiasm of football supporters in search of a party, although events later in the month suggest it was a fitting site for celebration. For over four hours they listened to speeches celebrating Valletta's victory in the Maltese Premier League, sang along to popular anthems that blasted out from the massive public address (PA) system, and cheered as children and adults took their turn at the microphone to perform their own songs. It was a joyous and relatively spontaneous family occasion.

Two weeks later, at the end of the season – Valletta had won the league with a fortnight to go – a grand defilé was organized through the streets of Valletta. The days between the celebration and the defilé were ones of frantic preparation by the fans. Superstition prevented them from preparing in advance any of the paraphernalia, the Maltese proverb *Ahseb fil-hazin biex it-tajjeb ma jonqosx* – 'Expect the bad so you don't lose the good' – dictating this relative inactivity prior to the moment of victory. That said, the people of Valletta had years of experience in organizing such events. Originating in 1943 to commemorate Valletta winning the Malta Cup, the original defilé was a joyous celebration not only of victory but also of the birth of a new club – Valletta FC. The club had been established the same year when five of the fourteen clubs that existed in the city joined together to conform to a new Malta Football Association (MFA) regulation that permitted only one club per town, village or city. The MFA were concerned about intra-town rivalries, but the move to 'one town, one team' merely shifted antagonisms from *within* different towns to *between* them (Armstrong and Mitchell 2001). The 1943 victory was over Valletta's traditional rivals Floriana, and occurred at the same time the island was recovering from the Axis bombing of the Valletta harbour area, and the Siege for which the Siege Bell was a commemorative monument. The elderly of Valletta recall the defilé as an event where people manifested hitherto unseen elation, which went beyond celebration of a football victory and was more a reaffirmation of the vitality of a war-devastated city and population.

The cup final had permitted the population of Valletta, who had been dispersed due to the bombing, to gather at the Empire Stadium, Gzira, to witness the victory.

Following the match, thousands of fans then followed their victorious team back to Valletta, on foot or on the backs of trucks, many of which also carried brass bands. They shouted, cheered and sang their way back the four miles to their bomb-devastated city. This was the first defilé, and it is now repeated whenever Valletta FC wins the championship. In the early 1980s, the Empire Stadium was replaced as the national stadium by Ta'Qali, some eight miles from Valletta, but the parade still attracts thousands of Vallettans as it winds its way back to the capital.

Euphoric, uproarious and drunken, the 2001 defilé expanded on this model. Because the victory was already secured, it took supporters from Valletta to Ta'Qali to watch the final game of the season, who then returned to Valletta to celebrate. The event was beyond formal structure and control. The team's triumphal return reached its climax with the entrance of the truck holding the players, the football club committee and the trophy through the City Gate. A retinue of trucks and trailers followed, ranging from four- to sixteen-wheelers bedecked in carnival paraphernalia – with papier mâché figures ridiculing characters seen as antagonists. The trucks were bedecked with slogans, insults, cartoons and graffiti directed at football opponents. There were at least 100 vehicles in the procession, some officially part of the proceedings, others not. The celebration had begun mid-morning even though the final match did not kick off until 8 o'clock in the evening. Thus, by the time the parade arrived at the stadium, most people had had a drink or two, and the majority could be said to have been under the influence of alcohol. At this stage, though, there was a sense of moderation and only a few participants were seriously drunk. The same could not be said of the same people by 10 o'clock. On the return to Valletta, crates of beer adorned every truck and bottles of beer were a vital accessory of the football paraphernalia worn by every participant. Beer, both local and Belgian – in honour of the Stella Artois brewery who sponsored the Valletta team shirt – were the essential items of consumption. The raised bottles manifest on every float were reciprocated by those following and a shower of beer was not received with anger but in the spirit of this occasion. Behind the defilé a trail of broken and discarded beer bottles marked the path of celebration.

While the central focus of the parade was obviously the all-male football team, pride of place on the largest truck was also taken by club committee members and the boys of the Valletta nursery team. On the other floats the participants were predominantly male whilst the expectant crowd that thronged the main thoroughfare of Valletta was mixed – at least 50 per cent female. This matches the pattern of *festa*, in which a predominantly male procession 'performs' to a mixed 'audience' (Mitchell 1998b). Both participants and spectators drank to excess, and normal taboos against female and childhood drinking were suspended. On this liminal occasion public drunkenness was not merely committed, it was expected.

It took over two hours for every vehicle to pass through the City Gate, which meant that the defilé proper ended around midnight. The party continued, however, and by 3 a.m. was firmly centred on the Valletta City club bar, in which some three hundred drunken revellers sang along to songs that blared out from the PA system. The floor was awash with beer, and four players, finding it difficult to stand, heroically continued drinking beer bought by loyal fans. Outside, a self-appointed squad of responsible fans gathered debris from the streets to leave them clean for the morning arrival of office workers, shoppers and tourists. The newspapers reported the collection of three tons of discarded beer bottles.

Il-Funeral

A few days after the defilé, Valletta fans organized a public 'funeral' of their opponents. It began in a Valletta bar, and proceeded through the streets from bar to bar, ending again at the Valletta City club bar. Like the defilé, *Il-Funeral* was a liminal occasion of substantial drinking, but also manifested a certain contempt for Malta's dominant Roman Catholicism, in its inversion of the accepted and expected conventions of a religious funeral. In this funeral, loud music, irreverent comments, speaking ill of the dead, drinking *en route* and defiling the dead were all par for the course. The proceedings presented a 'reversible world' (Babcock 1978) in which the structures of normal society were not merely suspended, but inverted.

Il-Funeral has also become an integral part of Valletta's invented traditions, although it dates back only to the early 1990s, when a coffin bearing Floriana colours was processed through Valletta after the city's arch rivals were beaten to the championship. Since then it has become more elaborate, and is now a regular and much lauded ritualistic finale to the football season by the die-hard fans. It effectively enacts a public execution and burial of football enemies.

At first sight the funeral procession looks authentic. A 'cadaver' wearing full ceremonial robes is carried in an open cask by pall-bearers in funeral attire. The cortège winds its way up Valletta's main street from its origins in the dark and narrow streets in the lower areas of town. Accompanying these are men in the costumes of bishops, monsignors, nuns and standard- and candle-bearers. Behind and alongside these 'officials' walk the Valletta FC committee members and other die-hard fans. Immediately behind the coffin as it approaches the higher part of the city is a brass band playing New Orleans Funeral blues. Suddenly the dead body comes alive and conveniently a glass of scotch whisky is placed in his hand. In true biblical tradition a miracle is performed and alcohol has played its part. The reborn raises his glass, to the cheers and ridicule of the crowd. The makeshift coffin (a real one would be blasphemous) teeters precariously as the bearers feign drunkenness. The procession also includes the traditional mourners (*bikkejja*), who wail in sadness at the death. Characteristically for the event, though, the women who would normally wail are replaced by men in drag. Indeed, all the participants in the funeral are male, as are 90 per cent of the audience.

While 'lifeless', the body is carried in and out of various bars along the route. Each time, as it is offered a drink, the body comes to life. As it leaves the King's Own Band Club, the body comes to life once more, raising its arms in synchronized movements, causing much mirth among the three hundred or so spectators. As the ridicule and irreverence reach their peak, the body is carried to Valletta's main square, where another three coffins appear, painted in the colours of the club's main opponents. In a ceremony of mock seriousness, the three painted coffins, together with the fourth minus its body, are slung on ropes and hung on poles some ten metres high. The ropes are pulled and the coffins hoisted. As they rise to a brass band's lament, a drum roll begins to mimic an execution. At the final drum beat, huge cheers and raised glasses salute the four coffins as they dangle in symbolic death. Later, when the coffins are lowered, a group of young boys kick the coffins to pieces, to complete the act.

Conclusion: The Future of Maltese Drinking

Like the *festa* before them, the defilé and funeral enact the claiming of public space for local interests. While everyday drinking such as that performed *Ghand Lawrenz* establishes a zone of local activity at a remove from the public spaces in which Maltese encounter foreigners, such extraordinary drinking events expand this local zone out to appropriate public space. In all three types of event, an egalitarian principle prevails that subordinates everyday hierarchies to the camaraderie of collective drinking and celebration. In *festa* this is achieved through the levelling effect of a ritual that subordinates the individual to the collective religious power and authority of the Church, the saint and, ultimately, God. In the funeral, it is achieved through the deliberate undermining of religious authority but also the similarly levelling invocation of mortality. Here, participants speculate on death – not only that of their rival teams, but also perhaps the potential of their own team to 'die', or indeed the inevitability of their own, physical death. In the defilé, participants re-enact the reclamation of Valletta in 1943, but also lay claim to the routes between city and stadium. Fortified by alcohol, and safe in their sheer weight of numbers, participants know that they will not be challenged by either rival fans or the police. Claiming space is also therefore claiming a time to rule. Such demarcation of space establishes a boundary between Maltese and the ever-present foreigners, and therefore contributes to the process of national identification. It does so through the performance both of everyday sociability – itself contributing to the constitution of masculinity – and of the more extraordinary sociability and camaraderie required during *festa* and football celebrations – which is orientated to localism. Through these acts of 'constructive drinking' (Douglas 1987), therefore, numerous intersecting processes of identification are produced and reproduced.

It is clear that, despite the ability of Valletta people to stage these elaborate festive occasions, there is residual concern about an apparent decline in local life, and the replacement of Valletta as the main social centre for Malta's young people. The concern is manifest *Ghand Lawrenz* in the tensions between the older *klikka* and the younger men in the bar. The replacement of the British forces with (also mainly British) tourists has led to the development of tourist bars in Malta's coastal resorts and a gradual replacement of Valletta as the site of fashionable sociability. This development has coincided with – and indeed is related to – the emergence of a more generalized concern within Malta about the erosion of 'traditional' values of family, community, religion (see Mitchell 2002). Such concern has twofold implications for Maltese drinking: first, that local bars such as *Ghand Lawrenz* will become increasingly untenable, as their main constituency is drawn towards the new Paceville bars; second, that the locally produced drinks – beers and wines – will be taken over by imported drinks.

Paradoxically, the rise of the tourist economy has led to a valorization of the traditional and the local, encouraging tourists to seek out local bars and drink local drinks. Of particular importance has been the diversification in local wine production, which has led to the development of fine wines and the emergence of a number of wine bars that are popular with the Maltese middle classes. It seems possible, then, that the masculine practices of everyday beer drinking will be replaced among Maltese by a more sophisticated, wine-drinking mode that is a marker of distinction, whilst the local bars will become the objects of the tourist gaze. Although this may be the fate of everyday drinking, the celebratory excesses of *festa* and football seem here to stay. The decades since the 1960s have seen a marked escalation of *festi ta'barra* throughout Malta (Boissevain 1992), and with each new football season, fans organise celebrations with bigger and more elaborate ritualizations. As long as this is the case, the cheers will continue while the booze goes down.

Acknowledgements

Thanks are due to Jean-Paul Baldacchino, Tanya Cassidy, Paul Clough, Victoria Galea, Matthew Vella and *The Setting Sun*.

Notes

1. We use the language of identification rather than identity to avoid reifying identity itself. See Brubaker and Cooper (2000).

2. The word *hobby* – pl. *hobbies* – is the Maltese word for the English 'hobby'. As a loan word it is nevertheless vernacularized and so presented here in italicized form, as is the common practice for 'indigenous categories' in ethnographic writing.
3. *www.farsons.com/home.htm*
4. The Maltese lira is worth around £2 sterling.
5. The Maltese *Ghand* means 'at the house of', and operates in the same way as the French *chez*. It is therefore used in this chapter without prepositions 'in' or 'at'.
6. The length of this chapter does not allow us to explore the full implications of football in Maltese society, which is discussed in Armstrong and Mitchell (1999) and (2001). We are also currently working on a book-length treatment of this theme.

References

Armstrong, G. and J.P. Mitchell. (2001), 'Players, Patrons and Politicians: Oppositional Cultures in Maltese Football', in G. Armstrong and R. Giulianotti (eds), *Fear and Loathing in World Football*, Oxford: Berg.

—— (1999), 'Making the Maltese Cross: Football in a Small Island', in G. Armstrong and R. Giulianotti (eds), *Football Cultures and Identities*, London: MacMillan.

Babcock, B.A. (ed.) (1978), *The Reversible World: Symbolic Inversion in Culture and Art and Society*, Ithaca: Cornell University Press.

Bales, R. (1980), *The 'Fixation Factors' in Alcohol Addiction: An Hypothesis Derived from a Comparative Study in Irish and Jewish Social Norms*, New York: Arno Press.

Barth, F. (1969), *Ethnic Groups and Boundaries: The Social Organisation of Cultural Difference*, London: Allen and Unwin.

Barthes, R. (1977), *Elements of Semiology*, New York: Hill and Wang.

Blouet, B. (1989), *The Story of Malta – fourth edition*, Malta: Progress Press.

Boissevain, J. (1965), *Saints and Fireworks*, London: Athlone.

—— (1992), 'Play and Identity: Ritual Change in a Maltese Village' in J. Boissevain (ed.), *Revitalising European Rituals*, London: Routledge.

—— (2000), 'Looking Back: An Anthropologist's Perspective', in P. Catania and L.J. Scerri (eds), *Naxxar: A Village and its People*, Malta: The Editors.

Brubaker, R. and F. Cooper. (2000), 'Beyond Identity', *Theory and Society* 29 (1): 1–47.

Brydone, P. (1776), *A Tour Through Sicily and Malta in a Series of Letters to William Beckford*, London: Strahan.

Butler, J. (1990), *Gender Trouble*, London: Routledge.

Cachia, P. (1962), 'An Arab's View of XIX C. Malta', *Maltese Folklore Review* 1(2): 110–116.

Cassar, C. (1988), 'Everyday Life in Malta in the Nineteenth and Twentieth Centuries', in V. Mallia-Milanes (ed.), *The British Colonial Experience 1800–1964: The Impact on Maltese Society,* Malta: Mireva.

—— (1994), *Economy, Society and Identity in Early Modern Malta*, PhD thesis, University of Cambridge.

Cohen, A.P. (1985), *The Symbolic Construction of Community*, London: Tavistock.

—— (ed.) (1986), *Symbolising Boundaries: Identity and Diversity in British Culture*, Manchester: Manchester University Press.

Conniffe, D. and D. McCoy. (1993), 'Alcohol in Ireland: Some Economic and Social Implications', Research Paper no. 106. Economic and Social Research Institute: Dublin.

Connell, R.W. (1995), *Masculinities*, Cambridge: Polity Press.

Cornwall, A. and N. Lindisfarne (eds) (1994), *Dislocating Masculinity: Comparative ethnographies*, London: Routledge.

Douglas, M. (ed.) (1987), *Constructive Drinking: Perspectives on Drinking from Anthropology*, Cambridge: Cambridge University Press.

Epstein, A.L. (1978), *Ethnos and Identity: Three Studies in Ethnicity*, London: Tavistock.

Frendo, H. (1979), *Party Politics in a Fortress Colony: The Maltese Experience,* Malta: Midsea Books.

Friedl, E. (1962), *Vasilika: A Village in Modern Greece,* New York: Holt, Rinehart and Winston.

Friedman, J. (ed.) (1994), *Consumption and Identity,* London: Harwood Academic Press.

Gusfield, J. (1996), 'Passage to Play: Rituals of Drinking Time in American Society', in J. Gusfield (ed.), *Contested Meanings: The Construction of Alcohol Problems,* Madison: University of Wisconsin Press.

Habermas, J. (1989), *The Structural Transformation of the Public Sphere,* Cambridge, Mass: MIT Press.

Heath, D. (1981), 'Determining the Socio-Cultural Context of Alcohol Use', *Journal of Studies on Alcohol* 9: 9–27.

Hull, G. (1993), *The Malta Language Question: A Case Study in Cultural Imperialism*, Malta: Said.

Mauss, M. (1966), *The Gift: Forms and Functions of Exchange in Archaic Societies*, London: Routledge and Kegan Paul.

Miller, D. (1995), *Acknowledging Consumption*, London: Routledge.

Mitchell, J.P. (1998a), 'The Nostalgic Construction of Community: Memory and Social Identity in Urban Malta', *Ethnos* 63(1): 81–101.

—— (1998b), 'Performances of Masculinity in a Maltese *Festa*', in F. Hughes-Freeland and M. Crain (eds), *Recasting Ritual: Performance, Media, Identity*, London: Routledge.

—— (2002), *Ambivalent Europeans: Ritual, Memory and the Public Sphere in Malta*, London: Routledge.

National Tourism Organisation of Malta. (1994), *Summary Statistics*, Malta: National Tourism Organisation of Malta.

Ors, I. (2002), 'Coffeehouses, Cosmopolitanism, and Pluralizing Modernities in Istanbul', *Journal of Mediterranean Studies* 12(1): 119–45.

Pardo, I. (1996), *Managing Existence in Naples: Morality, Action and Structure*, Cambridge: Cambridge University Press.

Reiter, R.R. (1975), 'Men and Women in the South of France: Public and Private Domains', in R.R. Reiter (ed.), *Toward an Anthropology of Women*, London: Monthly Review Press.

Sammut, F. (1991), *Paceville*, Malta: Merlin Library.

Seremetakis, C.N. (1996), 'The Memory of the Senses, Part I: Marks of the Transitory', in C.N. Seremetakis (ed.), *The Senses Still: Perception and Memory in Material Culture and Modernity*, Boulder, Colorado: Westview Press.

Stolcke, V. (1995), 'Talking Culture: New Boundaries, New Rhetorics of Exclusion in Europe', *Current Anthropology* 36 (1): 1–24.

Strathern, M. (1992), *After Nature: English Kinship in the Late Twentieth Century*, Cambridge: Cambridge University Press.

Tonna, B. (1994), *Malta Trends 1994*, Malta: Centre for Research into Signs of the Times.

Wilson, T.M. and H. Donnan (eds), (1998), *Border Identities: Nation and State at International Frontiers*, Cambridge: Cambridge University Press.

–10–

Drinking Rituals, Identity and Politics in a Basque Town

Sharryn Kasmir

The medieval centre of the Basque town of Arrasate (Mondragón in Spanish) houses the fourteenth-century, Gothic-style Church of San Juan. The church is one of Arrasate's few distinctive monuments, and it stands out in an architectural environment dominated by factories, apartment houses and parking lots. In another town, the church might well be an object of local pride, but in Arrasate it is a victim of disregard. When I first arrived in Arrasate in 1987, the church was in a state of disrepair. Like the façades of many public buildings, its stone walls were painted with political slogans in support of Basque causes: *Gora ETA*! (Long live ETA!) was the most striking graffiti. ETA (Euskadi Ta Askatasuna, Basque Homeland and Freedom) is the armed organization that fights for an independent and socialist Basque state; even to paint the initials ETA is an illegal act. In 1989, the parish priest organized a lecture to garner community support for a restoration project for the church. Only ten people attended the event, a poor showing in Arrasate, where political lectures by representatives from other nations-without-a-state, international volunteers home from a trip to Chiapas, or union leaders from other regions in Spain regularly draw crowds of one hundred or more. When the renovation finally got underway some years later, the labour was performed by out-of-town youth volunteers who were recruited for the project through church organizations. Residents of Arrasate were largely uninvolved in the work.

In noticeable contrast to the lack of interest in the church, a single feature of the building attracts adoration. In a niche above a church archway sits a small statue of the Virgin Mary holding the baby Jesus. The statue is neither large nor beautiful; indeed, it is not remarkable in any way. Yet this Mary is the focus of the annual festival called '*Maritxu Kajoi*' (little Mary in a box), so named because she is encased in a wooden cabinet. *Maritxu Kajoi* was invented in 1977 by young men from Arrasate who resurrected the largely forgotten icon and designated her patron saint of the partakers of the *txikiteo* (bar round).[1]

Maritxu Kajoi is celebrated on the first Friday of October when participants dress in evening wear and spend the night making rounds of town bars. *Maritxu* shares aspects of burlesque and inversion that characterize popular festivals cross-culturally. Arrasate is located in the Basque province of Gipuzkoa in the north-east corner of Spain. It is a densely populated town of 23,000 with an economy that has been based in industry since the late nineteenth century. In the 1970s, when the Maritxu festival was invented, most residents lived in households in which the primary wage earner was a factory worker. Working-class identity was, and still is, central to many townspeople's self-consciousness and to Arrasate's regional reputation. For this reason, the preferred *Maritxu* costume – cocktail dresses or gowns for women and top hats and tails for men – enacts a class inversion that turns jeans-and-T-shirts-wearing workers into pretend bourgeoisie. The clothing is uncomfortable, not warm enough for the cool October air, and not easily cleaned, making it wholly inappro-priate for the long night of drinking and therein exaggerating the burlesque. Further-more, celebrants magnify the parody of the 'high life' by drinking champagne (actually cava) instead of the wine or beer ordinarily consumed at the bars, thus revelling in extravagance and spending. The demand for champagne grew so great over the years that bartenders contracted with a supplier to provide a specially bottled vintage that carries a *Maritxu Kajoi* label.

The festival mocks religion, as well as the distinctions of class. Rather than revering the Church of San Juan, which honours the town's official patron saint, revellers turn their devotion to the dubbed patron of the *golfuenak* (riffraff or layabouts) and they pay tribute to her by drinking to excess. More than this, partici-pants parody the Virgin's supernatural powers. Each year, the fiesta commission – a committee of volunteers, charged by town hall to organize public festivals – arranges a miracle for Mary to perform. One year, the fountain in the central plaza ran dark with red wine piped in from barrels; the Virgin had turned water into wine. In 1988, during the growth of international AIDs organizing, the statue was rigged to throw condoms to the crowd (Maritxu Kajoi Komisiñue 2001: 29). Mary is induced to perform her miracle after a crowd gathers below and sings to her; this act caricatur-izes the drama of Holy Week as it is celebrated in southern Spanish cities, where penitents sing devotionally to religious statues. Participants further mock Holy Week by choreographing a procession that begins at the gate to the medieval city and stops at eight bars. At each station, worshippers sing songs of pretend prayer, and the procession concludes with a devotional sung underneath *Maritxu*.

Ridiculing the practices of Catholicism is a major theme of *Maritxu Kajoi*. During the Franco dictatorship (1939–75), the Spanish Church allied with the regime to shore up fascism, and town parishes often operated as local arms of the state, repressing Basque language and culture along with most institutions of liberal, civil society. As a result, in the 1970s, as the protest movement against Franco grew, many youth turned away from the Church. The *Maritxu Kajoi* celebration recorded the local history of this anticlericalism. Anti-church sentiment is still prevalent among politically radical Basques and is reproduced and enacted during *Maritxu Kajoi*.

The holiday assumes an oppositional posture beyond its critique of religion. When devotees present themselves to the Virgin, they sing '*Maritxu Nora Zoaz?*' ('Mary Where Are You?'). A popular Basque rock group recorded this song to the tune of the communist 'International', contributing a socialist register to the event. Moreover, festival posters, which are designed by town residents, often carry political messages. In 1978, the poster featured a drawing of two Civil Guardsmen (members of the Spanish state paramilitary force) armed with automatic rifles. *Maritxu* was pictured above a crowd of drunken celebrants who were singing '*Que se vayan, se vayan, se vayan*' ('That they go, they go, they go') (Maritxu Kajoi Komisiñue 2001: 15). This refrain is chanted at police during demonstrations; it demands that Spanish law enforcement officials leave Euskal Herria (the Basque Country) and thereby suggests that the Basque Country is policed by an occupying force and that Basques are a colonized people. The words '*Ez gaude denok*' ('We are not all here') regularly appear on festival posters. This slogan refers to those who are absent from the festivities because they are in jail for their association with ETA, and the phrase infuses the fiesta with support for the most radical expression of Basque nationalism.

The festival also contributes to Euskera (Basque language) revival. Since the re-emergence and radicalization of Basque nationalism in the 1960s, the revival of Euskera – banned during the Franco regime – has been a primary goal of the Basque movement (see Urla 1987; Tejerina 1992). Festival posters were printed in Euskera from the first year of its celebration, a time when the majority of the population did not know the language, and the prayers of mock devotion sung to the Mary statue and to the bars are in Euskera. In these ways, *Maritxu Kajoi* is associated with the Basque project of language activism.

Maritxu Kajoi has grown considerably since it was first celebrated over twenty-five years ago. Visitors come from far away to spend a night of excess in Arrasate, and restaurants and bars are crowded beyond their capacity. While the festival attracts a broad spectrum of townspeople and tourists, *Maritxu Kajoi* remains infused with local meanings of class, anticlericalism, Basqueness and leftist politics. *Maritxu Kajoi* is one of many drinking rituals that constitute and express working-class, Basque and radical identity in Arrasate. This reflective chapter draws on my long research acquaintance with Arrasate, where bars are a centre of social life. Bars are not primarily places of drunkenness or sexual pairing, though these do occur; instead, they are above all locations for association. Like bars in other Basque towns and cities, many of Arrasate's pubs are identified with different political parties and ideologies: Basque nationalist versus pro-Spanish, and left-wing versus right-wing. Here I show how bars contribute to the *izquierda abertzale* (Basque left) social world, and I explore the complex and rich interplay between drinking, identity and politics.

This ethnographic case contributes broader insights regarding drinking customs, identity and power. In circumstances where class and ethnic inequality characterize the social terrain, informal gathering places such as bars can become important venues for creating identity, challenging the power of dominant groups or the state, and building alternative sources of symbolic, social and political power. Scholars and activists who care about issues of inequality and power cannot afford to see bars as marginal places or drinking rituals as insignificant cultural practices.[3] Rather, these spaces and forms of culture can be central to the formation of identity, affiliation and consciousness that is acted upon in larger, more formal political arenas. The goings-on in bars, as the Basque example shows, may even have the potential to upset the existing cultural and political order and reshape local and national politics.

'Constructive Drinking'

This chapter develops a theoretical approach to drinking that illuminates the many and important connections between the places and practices of drink and the processes of identity, political opposition and power. A related approach to drinking is outlined by anthropologist Mary Douglas (1987). From Douglas's perspective, the consumption of alcohol is not seen as pathological or addictive behaviour (though of course it has these potentials), but, like other collective practices, drinking is envisioned as a field of action in which social groups and identity are constructed, important social information is transmitted, and boundaries of inclusion and exclusion are marked. Hence she coins the term 'constructive drinking' to indicate the role of alcohol in creating and maintaining social relations.

Extending this perspective to a concern for nationalist and working-class struggles, it becomes apparent that in many places and historical contexts, 'constructive drinking' is associated with political consciousness, organizing and power. For example, Lele men in the Democratic Republic of Congo participate in drinking clubs in clearings in the forest. These clubs are forums for discussing political topics, but they are different from formal political meetings, which are coded as 'work' and where participants do not drink (Ngokwey 1987). Bars have been nuclei for nationalist political culture in Ireland and in other anti-colonial contexts. One observer wrote of the way in which bar culture figured into the struggle for Congolese independence:

> [T]he bar is freedom. A white informer will not go to a bar because a white person stands out. So you can talk about everything. The bar is always full of words. The bar deliberates, argues and pontificates. The bar will take up any subject, argue about it, dwell on it, try to get at the truth. Everybody will come around and put in their two cents' worth. The subject doesn't matter. The important thing is to participate. To speak up . . . You have to take account of the bars and Lumumba understood this perfectly. (Kapuscinski 1992: 52–3)

This passage paints urban bars in the Congo as dynamic, talkative places, and it portrays independence leader Patrice Lumumba as utilizing bars to build support for the nationalist movement. Drinking culture in that colonial setting defined social groups, included and excluded, and was a context for sharing information, arguing and developing opinions.

Bars are also hubs of working-class culture, places where class experiences are shared and grievances aired. Kathy Peiss portrays taverns in New York City in the early twentieth century as spaces for workers to mould identities, engage in rituals, and build independent class-based organizations:

> Workers who sold their time and labor and submitted to the bosses' control could daily assert a sense of independence in the public spaces of the saloon or lodge. This was linked to the notion of reciprocity among one's working-class peers, both institutionally, in such organizations as mutual aid societies, and interpersonally, in such common practices as treating to rounds of beer. (Peiss 1986: 4)

Bars are after-work spaces, where workers can invent communal practices that subvert the alienation and discipline of the factory. In his study of nineteenth-century Oldham, England, John Foster (1974: 218) demonstrates that pubs were important venues for working-class politics and that the politics of pub owners were gauges of working-class views, and vice versa. Similarly, Wolfgang Schivelbusch (1993: 15–85) discusses the intersection of class politics and drinking culture in nineteenth-century British and German working-men's taverns. He notes a persistent conflict in socialist movements: on the one hand, anti-alcohol puritanism saw drinking as a plague on workers, but, on the other hand, bars hosted political discussion, friendships and networks that bolstered working-class activism. These ethnographic and historical reports show drinking places to be social arenas in which alternative cultural forms are invented and nourished, and in which ethnic and national minorities and working people articulate political opposition and will.

Using the framework of 'constructive drinking', I take an ethnographic look at the bars associated with the radical Basque-nationalist milieu. Radical Basque nationalism is a loosely affiliated sector that aspires to an independent Basque state and promotes a leftist social agenda. The movement includes a political party, a labour union, a youth wing, an organization for the families of ETA prisoners, a feminist collective and Basque language schools.[4] The radical-nationalist world has politicized much of social life in Euskal Herria, including language, music, fiestas and bar going (for a critique of the politicization of Basque culture, see Legasa n.d.). Arrasate has a somewhat more radical profile than other Basque locales, though it is not exceptional; from 1987 until the most recent elections in 2003, the radical-nationalist electoral coalition (originally Herri Batasuna, People United, and more recently Batasuna, United) held the town mayorship and the greatest number of council seats.[5]

In the Basque Autonomous Community – consisting of the three provinces of Gipuzkoa, Araba and Bizkaia and governed by its own regional parliament (with a population of 1.8 million) – radical nationalists averaged 15 to 20 per cent of the popular vote for much of the post-Franco period (higher in Arrasate). The political field consists of five to six competitors, including the moderate Basque nationalist parties Partido Nacionalista Vasco (Basque Nationalist Party, PNV) and Eusko Alkartasuna (Basque Alliance, EA), the right-wing Partido Popular (Popular Party, PP), Partido Socialista Obrero Español (Spanish Socialist Party, PSOE), the left-wing Izquierda Unida (United Left, IU) and the anti-ETA but Basque leftist Aralar (which ran its first candidates in 2003). In the 2001 regional elections, however, radical nationalists made a poor showing, capturing only 10 per cent of the vote, while the moderate Basque nationalists won 43 per cent of the vote and the presidency of the Basque parliament, and Partido Popular and the Spanish Socialist party won 23 and 24 per cent, respectively. In the 2003 municipal elections, radical nationalists suffered a devastating blow when their party Batasuna was banned from participating in elections for its alleged support of ETA. Radical nationalists reconfigured themselves and distributed their own (illicit) ballots; while these protest ballots were a symbolic demonstration of popular support, radical nationalists were dispossessed of formal political power.

In good measure, radical nationalism's decline reflects growing disillusionment with ETA, particularly ETA's new tactic of assassinating politicians and other non-military and non-police personnel. Radical Basque nationalism also suffered the effects of increased state repression. From 1996 to 2004, the ruling right-wing Partido Popular enacted strong measures to crack down on ETA and to suppress civic groups and individuals, including politicians, journalists and writers who were associated with Basque causes. The cycle of political violence and state repression intensified in 1998 after the failure of a unilateral cease-fire that was declared by ETA. The cease-fire was announced one week after twenty-four political parties. labour unions and grassroots groups signed the Lizarra-Garazi Peace Accord; modelled on the Northern Ireland peace agreement, the Basque initiative called for all-party negotiations regarding territoriality and sovereignty. When the Spanish government refused to negotiate with ETA and continued to repress Basque groups, ETA ended the cease-fire. Subsequently, the broad alliance that produced the accord fell apart, and the state strengthened its crackdown on ETA and on the Basque left, manifested most recently when radical nationalists were banned from participation in fundraising, campaigning and other electoral activities. The surprise victory of the Spanish Socialist Party in the 2004 state-wide elections – which took place in the aftermath of Partido Popular's false attribution of the al-Qaeda-authored bombings of a Madrid train station to ETA and the government's unpopular support for the US-led Iraq war – has done little to reverse this repression of Basque radicals. Basque newspapers remain closed, and Batasuna remains outlawed.[6]

Even though its electoral strength has declined, radical nationalism's presence in demonstrations, festivals and public messages in the form of posters, murals and graffiti remains strong and is greater than that of other parties.[7] Radical nationalism dominates *kalea* (the street), an important dimension of public life. Bars are chief among the locations belonging to the street, and drinking culture is a vehicle for reproducing radical-nationalist identity and politics. As the cross-cultural and historical material on drinking shows, joining together after work, buying rounds, singing and discussing political philosophies are common habits of workers in many places. Similarly, in the midst of nationalist struggles, bars are often places of political talk, off-limits to colonists and police. Further, long nights of bar going are a notable feature of public life in much of Spain. Yet in Euskal Herria, these drinking rituals are marked as distinctly Basque. Indeed, the very fact of having a dense associational life, largely rooted in local bars, is considered by Basques to be a defining cultural trait. In this way, drinking culture is used to construct Basque identity in the context of the long-standing struggle against the Spanish State for Basque self-determination. *Maritxu Kajoi* is perhaps the most distinctive of the rituals that tie drinking to class, national and political identity. Other drinking customs (rough-housing, talking politics, treating to rounds) are more ordinary and can be found in many locales, but the political and cultural field of radical life in Arrasate brands them as Basque.

The *Cuadrilla*, *Caja* and Political Identity

The bar round is variously called *txikiteo*, named in Euskera for the small glasses of wine (*txikito*) that are most typically ordered, *vuelta* (circuit, walk) and *poteo*, from the Spanish word for the jug used to hold wine (*pote*). The linguistic connection of bar going to wine – and small amounts of it at that – is relevant for understanding the character of Basque drinking customs. Bar goers commonly drink *txikitos* or *zurritos* (half glasses of beer) so that even though they spend many hours in bars, they consume less alcohol (and spend less money) than one might imagine, and drunken, belligerent behaviour is not prevalent. In the many years I have been a patron of Arrasate's pubs, I have never witnessed a fight; bars are not aggressive or violent places, including along sexual lines.

The *tixkiteo* (*poteo* or *vuelta*) involves going from bar to bar. Most Basque towns and cities are crowded with bars (Arrasate has upwards of 100) and there is ample variation according to style, location and political affiliation, such that one's choice of bars can be a statement of social identity. Most of the time, radical Basques stay away from conservative and Spanish-affiliated bars and conservatives tend to avoid radical establishments (see Vazquez [1998] for a discussion of more conservative Basque pubs).

The fundamental elements of bar going are the *cuadrilla* (friendship group) and the *caja* (common pool of money). *Cuadrillas* are relatively stable, mixed-sex friendship groups that are first formed in childhood among neighbourhood or school mates. *Cuadrillas* typically amass ten to thirty people, and they have a name, perhaps taking the name of one of the most active or notable members of the group. *Cuadrillas* are durable social institutions but they are flexible. As personal style and political opinion develop in the teen and young adult years and individuals take different paths, the formal *cuadrilla* may recede into the background, gathering for fiestas or other special events, while a more informal group becomes the social mainstay.

For young people in their teens and twenties, the friendship group (whether the childhood or more recent group) is the primary social unit, rather than the family, sports team or couple. Indeed, the *cuadrilla* and the couple exist in a certain degree of tension; when a couple forms, the pair has to balance their time between their two cuadrillas, and the time they spend alone together detracts from their participation in their respective groups. *Cuadrillas* prize the group as a whole; they are not personal spaces and for the most part personal problems are not discussed there (Pérez-Agote 1987: 97–8). In the many hours I spent with my own and other *cuadrillas*, we rarely engaged in the mutual disclosure that characterizes my dyadic friendships in New York City. Friends do offer each other support, but this happens in smaller groupings, in more private settings. Just as they did not discuss their own problems, in my experience, *cuadrilla* members did not often indulge in disclosing private information about others. *Cuadrillas* are not vehicles for social one-upmanship or gossip.

Bar going begins in adolescence, before the legal age for consuming alcohol, when young people spend after-school hours in pubs talking with friends and playing backgammon, cards (especially *mus*) and video games. They may drink soda, juice or glasses of water, spending an allowance given to them by their parents. Their choice of bars is important. If they select bars in the radical sphere, usually because they are already attracted to politics, they will begin to see and hear political messages, become part of the radical social world, and potentially make up the next cohort of radicals.

A typical night of drinking for older teenagers and adults begins when *cuadrilla* members meet in their favourite bar. Usually, explicit plans are not made. Rather there is an assumption that those who want to spend the evening together will arrive after dinner.[8] (Older people with more money to spend may dine together in a restaurant and then gather in the bar.) The first one to arrive waits for another friend or two, and after some time, the group heads out to a second bar. Latecomers will catch up along the way and will find their *cuadrilla* by looking in likely bars or asking bartenders or patrons if they have seen their group. Since a *cuadrilla*'s route is fairly predictable, the town centre is small and radical-identified *cuadrillas* limit themselves to visiting about nine bars, friends find each other quickly. If the group gets sizeable, and if members spend many hours together, they will likely form a *caja* or common bank. Each of the participants puts in an equal sum from which everyone's drinks are paid. One person is selected or volunteers to be the *cajero* (cashier), and he or she holds the money and pays the tabs. There is no tally of individual bills, nor is there a calculation of who may have paid too much or too little, rather there is a presumption of generalized reciprocity – that is, it is taken for granted that acquaintance will be long and there will be equivalence over time. Therefore, little tension is provoked when one *cuadrilla* member orders an expensive gin and tonic while another has the more inexpensive *txikito* of wine or *zurrito* of beer, or when one person stops drinking early in the rounds while the others continue to spend the *caja*. Should the money run out, everyone may add an additional sum. If at the end of the night there is money left over, it may be deposited into the collection jars for Basque causes that can be found in many pubs. In cases when a considerable sum remains, the *cajero* is likely to go home with the money, saving it for collective use on some other occasion. Again, there is both durability and flexibility of the collective. On a future date, if some but not all group members are together, this may constitute enough of the original personnel to use the *caja*. Future plans, such as a group dinner, may also be made for the money, thereby requiring further expenditure and extending the time frame of the transaction.

The *cuadrilla* and *caja* shape bar rounds as collective activities. Typically people do not drink alone, and payment is a mechanism for generalized reciprocity and future sociability. More than this, in the worldview of my informants, the *cuadrilla* and *caja* structure bar going as a Basque custom. During my years of participant observation in bars, people often commented that Catalans pay separately for their own drinks, unlike Basques, who pay collectively. This crude but friendly stereotype of another national group (for they recognize the autonomous region of Catalonia in north-east Spain as having a claim to sovereignty like their own) reflects an emic connection of the *caja* to Basqueness. In this equation, Basque society is more collectivist than other national or ethnic cultures in Europe, and this finds expression in modes of paying. The tradition of the *caja* is also inflected with class sensibility. Friends often told me that Basques (and people from Arrasate more than most) spend freely on eating and drinking; they are not 'middle-class' savers, they claim, but have what they defined as a working-class or 'popular' ethos of spending in the moment. The veracity of these claims aside, my informants' manner of constructing Basqueness is noteworthy: collectivity and working classness are called upon as characteristics that differentiate them from other groups and as features of Basqueness. These qualities are elaborated in drinking rituals.

Basque social scientists likewise argue that the *cuadrilla* and *poteo* are signifiers of Basqueness (Gurruchaga 1985: 365–74; Pérez-Agote 1984: 105–10; 1987: 286–97). During the Franco regime, police monitored the public domain, and Basque activists were forced to operate in secrecy. In the 1960s and 1970s, politicized *cuadrillas* began to rupture this code of silence and began to discuss politics and plan actions during bar rounds. Gurruchaga (1985: 365–74) argues that by commanding the space of the bar in this way, political *cuadrillas* brought Basque nationalism into the public sphere. The bar round was thus a form of resistance to the dictatorship and a vehicle for reproducing Basque nationalism.

Notably, however, these authors also suggest that the *cuadrilla* and the *poteo* were masculine forms. Women have frequented bars since the 1970s, when the Franco regime passed laws allowing married women to work, and women sought factory jobs. In their experiences as industrial workers, many young women did as men were already doing: they repaired to the bars after work. Today, women have full access to pubs, and the absence of sexual prowling in bars means that women feel comfortable and respected there. Teenage girls and women (myself included) enjoy the rough-housing, playing, drinking, music and political discussion of the bars; however, the integration of bars did not automatically make them fully responsive to women nor did it remake bars as gender-neutral environments, a fact that becomes salient as women mature and have children.[9]

As bar goers grow older and become parents, their habits change. The prevalence of smoking and drinking in bars limits pregnant women's (and children's) participation in bar culture, and parents of young children are less able to partake of bar life. When I returned to Arrasate in 2001 with my eighteen-month-old son, we joined friends with their babies and toddlers and sat outside of bars which gave onto plazas or open areas where our children could play. Still, our patterns were curtailed: we went home earlier than we used to, and we watched our children more than we talked politics. For parents, participation in the radical milieu is centred on other pursuits, such as raising their children as Euskera speakers and belonging to political and civic organizations. When their children enter the teenage years, parents become freer to take up bar going anew.

Drinking Culture and *Ekintza*

Radical bar culture further signifies Basque identity because it values and advances the cultural codes of participation and *ekintza* (action). Basque anthropologists (Zulaika 1988; Valle 1994) describe a symbolic world in which *ekintza* itself conveys Basqueness. In this worldview, the Basque self, especially the radical Basque, is made in action: 'a Basque person is defined by and communicates by *doing*' (Valle 1994: 43, emphasis added). Basque drinking culture involves men and women in activities of many sorts, primarily talking. This talk takes several forms, including telling stories, recounting plots of movies or books, sharing information, and heated and intelligent debate. Often, in the midst of this talk, plans (both social and political) are made – a trip, a *cena popular* (popular dinner, which can include hundreds) or a new celebration, such as *Maritxu*. A dimension of being Basque is taking part in the self-conscious creation of *more* cultural activities, particularly those that support nationalism.

In her study of Korrika, a biannual relay race organized by the Basque left to support Euskera education, Teresa del Valle (1994) teases out the relationship between talking, planning and action, which she deems to have deep roots in Basque culture. The idea for Korrika came about during a dinner among friends. Valle (1994: 42) describes this process:

In the context of a cuadrilla, a conversation initiated during dinner easily goes on for one or more hours. Topics move quickly from banal commentary and jokes to profound philosophical conversation. Thus it is not difficult to imagine how a serious project could arise in this friendly, relaxed context where exposition, confrontation, and group participation convert an individual idea into a group product.

Valle explains that often no one remembers who came up with the idea; rather, the decision is attributed to the group and is thereby turned into a collective project. This process also characterizes conversations that take place during a night out with a *cuadrilla*, when talk can turn into plans and plans to action. Consequently, the *cuadrilla* is not only a unit of friendship but also of action, and the *poteo* is a space not only for leisure but also for producing a social, cultural and political world.

The most prized participants in the *poteo* are those who create fun for others. One night during the 1992 Olympics in Barcelona, I was out with friends, and we initiated our own 'Olympics'. The Barcelona games were criticized among Basques for the way the Spanish state used them to promote itself and for the commercial nature of the event. Our game began when one friend, known for being energetic and provoking others, found a large tree branch with which we invented several sports contests. We spent hours prolonging the fun. On other evenings, *cuadrillas* might serenade fellow bar goers or develop a night-long prank. This kind of *jola* (play, game) is considered a valuable contribution to the ambiance of the evening; it is understood to transform the night from one of consumption (after all, we are purchasing and imbibing mass-produced drinks) to one of social production. Activism negates the passivity associated with being consumers because bar goers *make* culture.

Since bar going is a sphere of participation and *ekintza*, it is marked as Basque. Furthermore, the prank or play might have an explicitly political referent thereby strengthening the connection of the *poteo* to Basque identity. In 1989–90, a boycott of French goods was called by radical nationalists because the then-ruling French Socialist Party cooperated with the then-ruling Spanish Socialist Party to extradite ETA refugees from the French Basque provinces. For several weeks, smashing French goods, such as Bic pens and cigarette lighters, was a running *jola* during the *poteo* (see MacClancy 1993).

The Radical *Vuelta*

Several bars in Arrasate's town centre constitute the milieu in which these rituals take place. When one enters a radical pub, as opposed to a conservative or apolitical establishment, one immediately sees the telltale sign of radicalness: photos of Arrasate's ETA prisoners are prominently displayed. Like the slogan 'We are not all here', these pictures recall the prisoners' absence from daily life, and they evoke the prisoners' symbolic presence in the social world of the radical *vuelta* and offer examples of national heroism. Prison addresses are printed below the pictures, in a gesture that encourages patrons to write to them in jail and keep them part of the community. In most Basque towns and cities, radical bars display photos of their own local prisoners, and adherence to this code makes radical bars recognizable even if one is in a new place where one does not know the establishments. Nonetheless, radical pubs are heterogeneous and reflect the plurality of leftist expression within the radical-nationalist movement.

A radical *cuadrilla* might begin its night out in Arrasate in Bar Jai. Jai attracts teenage *cuadrillas* and older regulars in their thirties and forties who have frequented the bar since they were adolescents. On weekend nights, the pub is overcrowded and the *cuadrilla* will have a hard time finding a place to stand. Images of Arrasate's political prisoners hang above the bar, and posters advertising upcoming demonstrations are taped to the walls. During the quiet hours of the afternoon, patrons go to Jai to reserve bus seats for radical-nationalist demonstrations, read a newspaper or strike up a conversation with the bartenders. Bar Jai is run by four women and one man, most of whom are in their early forties. They have rented this property for over two decades, and long-term, stable leases have enabled the barkeepers to invest in and design the space according to their own tastes and political beliefs. Because the bar is run by activist women, Jai has a feminist feel. It is decorated with positive imagery of women, such as a witch doll that hangs in the centre of the bar. The witch symbolizes Euskal Herria's pre-Christian and mythologically matriarchal past, both of which imagine a pre-modern epoch when Basque culture flourished 'untainted' by Spanish and European influence (see Ortiz-Osés and Mayr 1988).

The town centre is off-limits to cars (except for deliveries), so when the *cuadrilla* leaves Jai, it steps carelessly into the cobblestone lane and heads around the corner to Txalaparta Taberna. Txalaparta's bartenders are young men in their twenties who attend radical-nationalist demonstrations. Txalaparta is a small place, with four tables and a dozen or so stools pulled up to the bar. On weekend nights, Txalaparta cannot accommodate the crowd, and the street outside is often filled with customers, extending the ambiance beyond the doors of the pub. Like in Jai, photos of ETA prisoners are hung behind the bar, political T-shirts and pins are displayed for sale, and political posters fill the walls. Txalaparta opens earlier than other radical establishments, and in the morning hours customers come to read the newspaper, meet a friend, or learn about a recent political development. While Txalaparta's clientele overlaps considerably with that of Bar Jai, the bar appeals especially to those who prefer its more stylistically (though not politically) conservative character. Txlaparta is brighter than Jai and its decor is neater. The tables and stools are free of graffiti, and 'tradition' is invoked by a ceramic wall plaque of a peasant grandfather in his *boina* (Basque beret).

The *cuadrilla* might then make its way down a narrow alley to the recently opened Bar Jola. As they approach, they see young customers smoking, drinking and talking on the steps adjacent to the bar. Radical Basque rock, a homegrown music movement that takes up political themes, is often playing in this small pub.[10] Jola's interior is painted black. Stickers left over from many political campaigns decorate the bar, and the area behind the bar is filled with magazines, T-shirts and the pictures of political prisoners. Older people do not favour this tavern, and it has the reputation for being a place for young *cuadrillas*. After leaving Jola, the *cuadrilla* will make its way to one of four or five other radical bars and then begin the circuit again. The *cuadrilla* picks its route from among nine or so places in a way that reflects its stylistic, personal and political preferences. Some *cuadrillas* have enduring friendships with particular bartenders, others may prefer a quiet environment, and various dimensions of leftist politics (e.g. feminism, youth politics, ultra-leftism) shape routines.

Though they are heterogeneous, Arrasate's radical bars have a collective identity. During the days-long fiesta for the town's patron saint of San Juan, bartenders work extended hours. After the festival is over, radical bartenders close their businesses and take a day off for a group dinner. One year, a local artist designed a T-shirt for the San Juan holiday that depicted Arrasate's town centre with the radical bars marked. Each bar bore the symbol or slogan of one radical Basque organization. As is common for political T-shirts issued for fiestas, the back read '*Ez gaude denok*', recalling the absence of ETA prisoners. Like the post-fiesta group dinner, this T-shirt gave material representation to the informal collective of radical establishments by mapping the various businesses as one social unit. Radical bartenders form a solidaric group, whose relations are not unduly strained by competition. While particular pubs may make more profits because their overhead is lower or one business may be experiencing a phase of heightened popularity, good business for one bar typically means good business for others, since the customs of drinking dictate that *cuadrillas* move along in their *vuelta* from one establishment to the next.

Each year, the town council sets the prices for all drinks, from the small servings of beer and wine that cost about US50 cents to soda and bottled water at US$1.50 to more expensive mixed drinks at US$4.00. Balancing economic rationality and social purpose, radical bartenders fight to keep the prices of drinks low, especially for the cheaper beverages favoured by young people. Although they share the class interests of other bar owners, and therefore should share a desire to raise prices, radical barkeeps often pursue a different strategy. In part, their position is economically motivated since a larger portion of their business comes from teenagers who are spending small allowances, and lower prices can help to regularize that customer base. But their stance is politically and socially motivated, as well: lower prices keep the establishments hospitable to young people. Given that going to radical bars is often young people's earliest experience of participation in the radical world, it is important from a political standpoint to facilitate access. For this reason, bars even welcome non-consuming customers. Many young people with no money still pass after-school hours in bars. They may share a drink or ask for a glass of water and then borrow a backgammon set from the bar and spend the afternoon with their friends. Consequently, bars are public spaces that transcend pure business logic.

In addition to fostering a radical milieu, bars are more explicitly stages for political education and mobilization. People talk about politics in bars, and news about recent arrests, demonstrations and current political events is shared there. Bars are among the most timely venues for spreading information: when there is a political development of note, such as the arrest or police killing of an ETA militant, activists go to radical establishments to find out if there will be a protest. Demonstrations can be organized quickly and effectively in this way. Customers come to pubs during the day to read newspapers, and they periodically look up from their reading to discuss an article with the bartender or fellow patron. At times these conversations become analytical, comparative and theoretical, and bar talk can be sophisticated and intelligent. This rich environment of thought and debate is highly valued, especially given that most residents of Arrasate have not been educated beyond secondary school. One of my friends affectionately dubbed one of our favourite bars 'The University'.

Defending Bars/Defending Basqueness

In my decade-and-a-half acquaintance with Arrasate, I have seen the rise and fall in popularity of particular bars, recession and unemployment take their toll on business, and radical bars face collective challenges and undergo change. Sky-rocketing real estate prices and what is referred to as the 'Europeanization' of Basque society pose threats to bar culture. Today, a bar can cost several hundreds of thousands of dollars (US) to purchase and thousands a month to rent. Where running a bar was once a modest pursuit, requiring relatively little capital, over the last decade it has become prohibitively expensive.

In the early 1990s, real estate pressures jeopardized three of Arrasate's radical bars. Their leases were about to expire and in each case the property owner indicated a desire to sell rather than renew the lease, but the barkeepers were in no financial position to buy the expensive properties. More than this, their lease problems were compounded by recent regulations that were enacted by town hall to modernize Arrasate's eating and drinking establishments. Sound-proofing, two exits, ventilation systems and separate bathrooms for men and women were required for all new constructions and at the time of a lease renewal or property transfer, thereby adding US$50,000 to the cost of starting or buying a bar. Moreover, drink prices were raised and pub hours were limited to 1.00 a.m. on weeknights and 3.00 a.m. on weekends; this constrained social patterns and profitability since bars customarily stayed open later on busy nights.

Regulations regarding safety, hours of operation and alcohol prices are decided upon by the town commission on urbanism, which was headed by a council member from Partido Nacionalista Vasco (PNV), the moderate Basque nationalist party. PNV condemns ETA and largely accepts the terms of regional autonomy granted by the Spanish Constitution; it stands in measured contrast to (and electoral competition with) the leftist and independentist Basque Liberation Movement. At the time, Spain was readying itself for full membership in the European Community and the legal changes were justified by the need to bring Basque businesses in line with European standards. In the several-week period between the proposal and the passing of the codes, the new regulations were the subject of considerable discussion. The bartenders' guild fought against the ordinances (and they won small modifications) and bartenders and customers opined on the intent and impact of the laws. Mocking what they supposed was the rationale for the changes, radical nationalists I talked with invented what they imagined was PNV's argument:

Basques drink too much. We smoke too much. We spend too much time in bars.

In Europe, people are not out in the street, making noise all night.

We could do a lot of other things. We could take up kayaking or go away for the weekend. We are too provincial.

Like the above comment regarding the Basque proclivity to spend freely and not to be 'middle-class' savers, when radicals mimicked the remark: 'Basques drink too much. We smoke too much. We spend too much time in bars,' they voiced a class image they have of themselves: they implied that they do not engage in the self-conscious guarding of the body that they associate with bourgeois norms of selfhood, and they claimed the working-class self as the Basque self. The sarcastic tone of the declaration: 'In Europe, people are not out in the street, making noise all night,' suggests that the street is a public and popular arena that should be filled with noise and people. Europe is too quiet because social life takes place in the private realm. Similarly, 'We could take up kayaking or go away for the weekend' satirizes a lifestyle of expensive leisure activities that supposedly make people 'modern' and sophisticated. The imagined PNV speaker is projecting a kind of cosmopolitan, middle-class person who stands opposed to the provincial, working-class subject. The radical inventor of this pronouncement instead embraces the provincial and popular subject who stays in town with nothing to do but go to the bars.

Radical Basques whom I knew interpreted the bar regulations as an effort to reform social practices and impose cultural values. Interestingly, though the codes were written by the local government which was headed at the time by the radical-nationalist coalition Herri Batasuna, radicals talked about them as if they had originated elsewhere and were the work of a foreign, colonizing culture. PNV was conceptualized as the local agent of this colonization. (Perhaps unfairly, the radical-nationalist mayor was not held responsible, as he was seen as acting even-handedly by letting the commission do its work autonomously.) The codes were considered to be a manifestation of Europeanization, or the spread of a bourgeois ethos that prized the modern and standard and encouraged home-centred and individualized leisure pursuits. In this emic calculation, Basque is equated with public sociability and popular, active participation in social life, while Europe is paired with the bourgeois, passive consumption and private leisure. This worldview constructs a distinctive and politicized Basque identity.

The potential closing of these three bars was seen as a threat to the radical-nationalist social world. On the street, there were quiet warnings that if someone else bought the spaces, they would find their establishments boycotted. Eventually, rental or purchase agreements were negotiated for all of the bars, permitting them to stay open. At the same time, another bar in the radical orbit was inaugurated, adding variety to the daily circuit. When the fate of the bars was uncertain, the discussion and analysis made it clear that according to radical Basques, to damage bar culture was to threaten the collective self. Radical Basques used the term 'Europeanization' to refer to the dismantling of public culture. They understood the communality of street life and bar culture as an alternative mode of life and a defence against these pressures. Laws that regulated conditions for consuming alcohol, age of consumption and beverage prices proved to them that Europe is about controlling regional and working-class customs and spaces. Following this logic, allegiance to bar going was a form of resistance to globalization.[11] The rituals of bar going, the equivalents of which could be found in a working-class district of Manchester or Detroit, were thereby turned into constructive practices, for they constituted and demonstrated Basque distinctiveness, identity and political will.

Conclusion

The anniversary of Fidel Castro's 26 July insurrection that led to the Cuban Revolution is celebrated in Arrasate in the town's radical bars. *Mojitos* (a Cuban drink made of rum, soda water, lime, mint and sugar) are served for the occasion, and this special drink, not normally available, becomes the focus of the bar round. Bars fly Cuban flags and play Cuban music. The 2001 celebration did not go off as planned. Early in the day, a young ETA militant was killed when a bomb exploded in her apartment. Typically, radical nationalists in towns and cities throughout Euskal Herria would respond to this news by holding acts of homage or demonstrations for the fallen militant; however, the Basque regional government announced that any such gatherings would be prohibited. (Earlier that year, the Spanish legal code had been changed, and the radical ritual of paying tribute to a dead ETA member, as well as the tradition of the public homecoming for a freed prisoner, were now considered to be acts of 'apology for terrorism', a crime punishable by several years in prison.) As a result, planned demonstrations were cancelled. The radical-nationalist party instead issued a call for bars to shut for the day, as a statement of solemnity and nationalist action.

In Arrasate, activists found a way to protest despite the ban. Small groups of people met in various spots in the town centre; they stood in silence and held *ikurrinas* (Basque flags) with a black ribbon pinned to the middle as a symbol of mourning. Since there were fewer than ten individuals in each location, none of the groups could be charged with holding a public gathering. While participants showed determination in subverting the ban, their numbers were few. The more significant message was created by the radical taverns. Even though they had already prepared tens of gallons of *mojitos*, barkeepers locked their doors and suspended the Cuba festivities, leaving the streets oddly quiet and creating a tone of mourning rather than of mass protest and collective anger. The next day when the pubs re-opened, the *mojitos* were no longer fresh, and bartenders recorded considerable monetary losses.

Fear of arrest and violent confrontation with the police kept many from participating in the vigils, but more than this, the poor showing also reflected recent changes in the radical social world. Supporters of Basque independence, who might have joined the protest in past years, have become increasingly sceptical of ETA's tactics. Others are weary of political terrorism and critical of *kale borroka* (street fighting), the radical-nationalist campaign in which young people battle police during demonstrations (see Aretxaga 2000). Many people suspected that the vigils would develop into *kale borroka* (though in this instance, they ended peacefully), and for this reason they stayed away. Moreover, the Spanish state's strategy of criminalizing certain political rituals and of targeting civic organizations created a generalized climate of fear.[12]

In past years, the death of the ETA militant would have been marked by demonstrations, and the banning of political acts would have sparked yet more protest. Groceries and other kinds of shops would have closed with the bars, as people took to the street. But in the present climate, the bars were counted on to make the political moment on their own. In a sense, closing the bars was the easiest and most visible way to create a public response without mobilizing the masses. Though this episode evidences the intensification of state repression and the waning of support for radical causes, and though bars suffered economic losses, it also demonstrates the continued intimate connection between bars and politics. On this day, the activism of bartenders stood in for broader political action and bartenders publicly represented the radical stance. Bars stood as a symbol of Basqueness, radicalness and activism.

This connection between bars, politics and identity that was so plain on 26 July has many manifestations. The festival of *Maritxu Kajoi* is perhaps the most unusual of the rituals, but it is not singular in its embellishment of the relationship between drinking, political identity and action. People from Arrasate are proud of *Maritxu Kajoi*. The festival is considered 'genuine' or 'authentic' culture because town residents actively participate in the celebration: it was invented by local men, in the years just after the end of the Franco regime when public traditions were being created anew. *Cuadrillas* plan and organize the event, and the fact that this labour is performed by community volunteers strengthens the festival's popular or authentic image. Furthermore, *Maritxu Kajoi* is not commercialized by the rides, stalls and food stands that are ubiquitous in patron saint feasts in many places and lend a kind of pre-packaged or generic feel to those events. *Maritxu*'s particularity marks it as a Basque celebration. Basques have a history of distinguishing between popular festivals and those that are state-controlled or ersatz. In Arrasate, during the dictatorship, the San Juan feast was associated with the government and therefore it was poorly attended. In 1964, at the time of the emergence of ETA and the underground Basque movement, town residents reclaimed San Juan as a popular and 'Basque' festival rather than a state-controlled one (Kasmir 1996: 103). *Maritxu Kajoi* is appreciated for its ironic critique of religion and of class inequality but also for its valorization of the mundane and obvious: that is, the connection of Basqueness, working classness and radicalness to drinking.

The *cuadrilla*, *caja*, *ekintza* and the presence of political messages and debate transform the daily habits of bar going into performances of Basque identity and radical political affinity. Drinking is a collective behaviour which creates fields of social identity, includes some people and excludes others, and transmits information among group members. As the recent commemoration of the Cuban Revolution demonstrated, even as radical nationalism suffers the effects of state repression and negative public opinion, bars are a mainstay of Basque opposition. Yet these changes raise important questions about the future of bar culture. What will happen if bars are continued to be asked to bear the brunt of radical public expression? Will radical bars become socially isolated and vulnerable to state repression? These are important questions for the upcoming years as the battle between radical nationalism and the Spanish state continues.

Acknowledgements

I would like to thank Tom Wilson for inviting me to contribute this chapter and Edward Hansen for alerting me to the importance of bar culture for nationalist movements. I also wish to extend my sincere gratitude to my dear friends in Arrasate who showed me the intimate and daily connections between friendship, social life and political commitment.

Notes

1. A local newspaper noted in 1981, 'The little, quiet Virgin, which until four years ago had been forgotten and which many people from here in Mondragón did not even know existed, became the centerpiece of the day on Friday' (Maritxu Kajoi Komisiñue 2001: 15).
2. Elsewhere I analyse the gender dynamics of radical Basque youth culture, and I show how bars and youth culture are arenas for forging a non-ethnic Basque identity. Industrialized towns and cities of Euskal Herria, including Arrasate, are home to many immigrants (and their children and grandchildren) from other regions of Spain who are not ethnically Basque. The codes of radical political culture described in the present chapter allow working-class immigrants and their offspring to identify as Basque (Kasmir 1999, 2002).
3. Edward Hansen (1983) took a mindful approach to drinking customs in Catalonia in north-east Spain. He showed how during the Franco regime, Catalan bars were locations for patron–client relationships that bolstered Catalan business success, which itself was a component of the Catalan claim to national rights.
4. The structure of the Basque left is pluralistic and its history is complex: the Basque National Liberation Movement (MLNV) is a social movement that includes a feminist organization, a labour union, neighbourhood associations, cultural groups, an international solidarity brigade, an environmental organiza- tion, an amnesty organization for ETA prisoners, a peace group, a Marxist- Leninist political party and an electoral coalition. Herri Batasuna was formed in 1978 to present radical-nationalist candidates in state, regional and local elec- tions. Its members vary in their support for socialism and for ETA's armed tactics. The Socialist Coordinating Committee (KAS, now illegal) oversaw the activities of these groups and authored the KAS Alternative, a programme for Basque self- determination. This programme was intended as an alternative to the Autonomy Statute enacted in 1978 by the post-Franco Spanish state. The Autonomy Statute created the Basque Autonomous Community from the Spanish-Basque provinces of Gipuzkoa, Bizkaia and Araba. The fourth Spanish-Basque province of Nafarroa is governed by its own statute, and both autonomous communities have their own parliaments and police forces. The Basque left considers the Autonomy Statute inadequate for genuine self-determination, and it calls for the unification of all of the Basque provinces, including (eventually) the three Basque provinces across the border in France.

   From the transition period after Franco's death in 1975 until 1996 when the conservative Partido Popular won state-wide elections, most of the constituent groups of the Basque left were legal and operated openly in Basque civil society. They distanced themselves from political violence, even if they refused to publicly condemn ETA, and they were careful to call for 'self-determination' but not 'independence', as the latter is illegal according to the Spanish Constitution.

In this way, they engaged in legal political dissent without risking charges that they were collaborating with or supporting a terrorist group. Over the past several years, there has been an escalation of violence by ETA and an intensification of repression by the Spanish state. In this context, several Basque civic and cultural organizations have been declared illegal, accused of supporting or apologizing for terrorism. This has instigated a restructuring or dissolution of several left organizations, most notably Herri Batasuna. Herri Batasuna reconstituted itself first as Euskal Herritarrok, and then as Batasuna to accommodate the changing political climate and to stay one step ahead of the increasingly harsh Spanish judicial system. Most recently, Batasuna was barred from participating in elections. This was the first banning of a political party since the end of the dictatorship, and it was the first time since 1978 that radical nationalists were prohibited from holding office. For reports of these and other recent political events see *Euskal Herria Journal*'s useful website: www.ehj-navarre.org/html/ecnomy.html/ld980912.html

5. For an analysis of how class formation in Arrasate contributed to its history of radicalism, see Kasmir (1996).

6. The Spanish Socialist Party (PSOE) held state power from 1982 to 1996, during which time it embarked on its own strategy of controlling Basque separatism. In the 1980s, it negotiated a partnership with the Socialist-led French state to seek out and deport Basque refugees in the French Basque provinces, areas that had provided safe haven during the Franco years and beyond. The Socialist government in Madrid also engineered a 'dirty war' to kidnap and assassinate suspected ETA members; the Minister of the Interior, PSOE leaders and members of the national police, among others, were determined to be members of the right-wing death squad Grupos de Antiterroristas de Liberación (GAL). The exposure of GAL and its link to the state was a decisive factor in PSOE's electoral loss to Partido Popular in 1996 (see Woodworth 2003).

7. See Chaffe (1988) on the Basque left's use of 'the street' as a forum for public communication.

8. Bar rounds can take place several times during the day: before and after lunch, for the unemployed or for those whose jobs still grant the traditional long lunch break, and before and after dinner. Budgets permitting, bar goers may eat *pintxos* (small snacks, appetizers) which are served in some of Arrasate's bars. During the deindustrializing and recessionary period from the 1980s to the late 1990s, there was a very high rate of youth unemployment, and jobless youth spent several hours every day in bars (see Kasmir 2002).

9. Basque feminist anthropologists have analysed the relationship between space and gender. Valle et al. (1985: 226–56) found that their informants conceptualized ETA, prison and other sociocultural spheres associated with politics as being masculine, while they saw domestic space as feminine (see also Aretxaga 1988).

10. See Lahusen (1993), Kasmir (1999, 2002), Urla (2001, n.d.) for discussions of how these musical forms express Basque identity and radical politics.
11. For a related academic critique of globalization from a radical Basque perspective, see Mendizabal (1998).
12. In 1997, all twenty-three leaders of Herri Batasuna were sentenced to seven years in jail. They were found guilty of collaboration with ETA because the party distributed an election video in which three masked ETA members presented a proposal for Basque self-rule. The arrests were a primary motivation for the reorganization of Herri Batasuna into Euskal Herritarrok. These were the first of many arrests that resulted from Partido Popular's policy of pursuing civic groups. On suspicion that it was channelling funds to ETA, the offices of the radical-nationalist newspaper *Egin* were raided by police in 1998, and its property was seized.

References

Aretxaga, B. (1988), *Los funerales en el nacionalismo radical vasco: Ensayo antropológico*, Barcelona: Anthropos Editorial del Hombre.

—— (2000), 'A Hall of Mirrors: On the Spectral Character of Basque Violence', in W. Douglass, C. Unza, L. White and J. Zulaika (eds), *Basque Politics on the Eve of the New Millennium*, Reno: University of Nevada Press, pp. 115–26.

Chaffe, L. (1988), 'Social Conflict and Alternative Mass Communications: Public Art and Politics in the Service of Spanish-Basque Nationalism', *European Journal of Political Research* 16 (5): 545–72.

Douglas, M. (ed.) (1987), *Constructive Drinking: Perspectives on Drink from Anthropology*, Cambridge: Cambridge University Press.

Foster, J. (1974), *Class Struggle and the Industrial Revolution: Early Industrial Capitalism in Three English Towns*, London: Methuen.

Gurruchaga, A. (1985), *El código nacionalista vasco durante el franquismo*, Barcelona: Anthropos Editorial del Hombre.

Hansen, E. C. (1983), 'Drinking to Prosperity: The Role of Bar Culture and Coalition Formation in the Modernization of the Alto Panádes', in J. C. Aceves (ed.), *Economic Transformation and Steady State Values: Essays in the Ethnography of Spain*, Publications in Anthropology 2, Flushing, NY: Queens College, pp. 42–51.

Kapuscinski, R. (1992), *The Soccer War*, New York: Alfred A. Knopf.

Kasmir, S. (1996), *The 'Myth' of Mondragón: Cooperatives, Politics, and Working-Class Life in a Basque Town*, Albany: State University of New York Press.

—— (1999), 'From the Margins: Punk Rock and the Repositioning of Ethnicity and Gender in Basque Identity,' in William Douglass, Carmelo Unza, Linda White and Joseba Zulaika (eds), *Basque Cultural Studies*, Reno: University of Nevada Press, pp. 178–205.

—— (2002), '"More Basque than You!": Class, Youth, and Identity in an Industrial Basque Town', *Identities: Global Studies in Culture and Power* 9 (1): 39–68.

Lahusen, C. (1993), 'The Aesthetic of Radicalism: The Relationship between Punk and the Patriotic Nationalist Movement of the Basque Country', *Popular Music* 12 (3): 263–80.

Legasa, F. J. (n.d), 'Re-defining Basqueness: Politics, Popular Music and Cultural Identity in *Bilboa 00:00h*, unpublished manuscript.

MacClancy, J. (1993), 'At Play with Identity in the Basque Arena', in Sharon MacDonald (ed.), *Inside European Identities: Ethnography in Western Europe*, Oxford: Berg, pp. 84–98.

Maritxu Kajoi Komisiñue (2001), *Maritxu Kajoi 25 Urte*. (booklet).

Mendizabal, A. (1998), *La Globalización: Perspectivas desde Euskal Herria*, Hondarribia: Argitaletxe Hiru.

Ngokwey, N. (1987), 'Varieties of Palm Wine Among the Lele of the Kasai', in Mary Douglas (ed.), *Constructive Drinking: Perspectives on Drink from Anthropology*, Cambridge: Cambridge University Press, pp. 102–12.

Ortiz-Osés, A. and F.-K. Mayr (1988), *El Matriarcalismo Vasco: Reinterpretación de la cultura vasca*, Bilboa, Spain: Publicaciones de la Universidad de Deusto.

Peiss, K. (1986), *Cheap Amusements: Working Women and Leisure in New York City, 1880–1920*, Philadelphia: Temple University Press.

Pérez-Agote, A. (1984), *La reproducción del nacionalismo: El caso vasco*, Madrid: Centro de Investigaciones Sociologicas, Siglo Veintiuno.

—— (1987), *El nacionalismo vasco a la salida del franquismo*, Madrid: Centro de Investigaciones Sociologicas, Siglo Veintiuno.

Schivelbusch, W. (1993), *Tastes of Paradise: A Social History of Spices, Stimulants, and Intoxicants*, New York: Vintage.

Tejerina, B. (1992), *Nacionalismo y lengua. Los procesos de cambio linguistico en el Pais vasco*, Madrid: Centro de Investigaciones Sociologicas, Siglo Veintiuno.

Urla, J. (1987), 'Being Basque, Speaking Basque: The Politics of Language and Identity in the Basque Country', doctoral dissertation, University of California, Berkeley.

—— (2001), 'We are all Malcolm X! Negu Gorriak, Hip Hop, and the Basque Political Imaginary', in T. Mitchell (ed.), *Rapping the Globe: Rap and Hip Hop Outside the USA*, Middletown: Wesleyan University Press, pp. 171–93.

—— (n.d.), 'Basque Hip Hop? Language, Cultural Identity and Popular Music', unpublished manuscript.

Valle, T. del (1994), *Korrika: Basque Ritual for Ethnic Identity*, Reno: University of Nevada Press.

Valle, T. del, J. M. Apalategi and B. Aretxaga (1985), *La mujer vasca: Imagen y realidad*, Barcelona: Anthropos Editorial del Hombre.

Vazquez, R. (1998), 'A Critique of "Ideology": The Social Bases of Basque National-ist Politics', conference paper, Basques in the Contemporary World: Migration, Identity and Globalization, 6–9 July, Reno, NV.

Woodworth, P. (2003), *Dirty War, Clean Hands: ETA, the GAL, and Spanish Demo-cracy*, New Haven, CT: Yale University Press.

Zulaika, J. (1988), *Basque Violence: Sacrament and Metaphor*, Reno: University of Nevada Press.

–11–

Alcohol and Masculinity
The Case of Ethnic Youth Gangs

Geoffrey P. Hunt, Kathleen MacKenzie and
Karen Joe-Laidler

Masculinities have become the subject of much scholarly discussion and debate in many fields of study, with calls to 'take men seriously' particularly as the 'crisis of masculinity' heightens in postmodern society (Jefferson 1996; Connell 2000). The movement to seriously consider the experience and construction of men and masculinity in a variety of settings and cultures has been prompted by the recognition that there is no one single or universal male role. Instead, researchers have learned that there are what Connell (1995, 2000) calls a multiplicity of masculinities, such that what is distinctly 'male' may vary across time and place. Moreover these multiple masculinities must be understood in the context of the social structure within which the social interaction takes place. That is, acts of manliness must be located within the broader economic and social class context but, at the same time, understood in relation to social interaction and human agency. Masculinity, then, is produced through interaction with others and with resources from a particular time and place.

One particularly important area within this masculinities debate is the study of crime (Messerschmidt 1986, 1993, 1997; Connell 1987; Newburn and Stanko 1994; Bourgois 1996; Collison 1996; Jefferson 1996). Essentially, masculinities and crime studies examine 'varieties of real men' in relation to their differential access to power and resources, and how different groups of men construct and negotiate the meaning of manliness with similarly situated others (Messerschmidt 1993; Newburn and Stanko 1994). Messerschmidt (1993, 1997), in particular, suggests that the social structure situates young men in relation to similar others so that collectively they experience the world from a specific position and construct cultural ideas of hegemonic masculinity, namely dominance, control and independence (Joe and Chesney-Lind 1995).

Much of the discussion on masculinities and crime has focused on aggression and violence as strategies for individually and collectively expressing hegemonic masculinity. At the individual level, intimate partner violence can be understood as a strategy for affirming one's masculinity to oneself and to one's partner, particularly for lower- and working-class males, who lack the conventional resources open to their middle class counterparts to produce a sense of manliness (Messerschmidt 1993). In the United States, a number of researchers have focused particularly on the nature and levels of violence associated with the collective behaviour of youth gangs. According to these studies, young ethnic and minority male gang members living in marginalized communities have little access to masculine status in the economy and in education (Joe and Chesney-Lind 1995; Messerschmidt 1997). This collectively experienced denial of access to 'legitimate' masculine status creates an arena for exaggerated public and private forms of aggressive masculinity, where participation in street violence demonstrates to one's fellow gang members that one is a 'man' (Messerschmidt 1993). 'Street elite posturing' (Katz 1988) among male gang members with dramatized displays of toughness accounts for one cultural form of public aggressiveness. Male gang members' constant and aggressive pursuit of 'respect' represents another way to construct and affirm manliness in an alienated environment. Gang intimidation and violence are more than simply an expression of the competitive struggle in communities with little to offer, but also vehicles for a meaningful identity and status. At the immediate level of interaction, the street is a battleground and theatre for young marginalized minority males to define, shape and do gender (Connell 1987, 1995). Unlike middle-class boys, who can gain status and respect through academic success and participation in sports, working-class minority youth gain respect through their ability to perform well on the street.

Although efforts to understand the collective experience of marginalized youth in relation to violence and masculinities in the United States have shed new light on the multiplicities of masculinity, one factor has remained largely absent from the discussion, namely alcohol. This is particularly surprising in light of a large body of international evidence which shows that the chances for violence are greater when alcohol use is involved (Graham and Wells 2003). A small but growing number of UK and Australian studies have emerged on the culture of drinking and the construction of hegemonic masculinity. For example, Gough and Edwards' (1998) discursive analysis of 'four lads' suggests that the 'male talk' often involved in drinking at the pub frequently centres on the discursive subordination of 'others', particularly women and gay men. This form of male bonding, through drinking, acts as an important resource in the production of masculinity. Graham and Wells (2003: 548) found that while the 'lads'' use of alcohol made them 'more willing to take risks, more stimulated, more emotional and more aggressive', their aggressive behaviour in pubs was motivated in the proximal sense by 'male honour, face saving, group loyalty, and fun'. In a somewhat similar vein, Tomsen (1997) describes how masculine social identity is affirmed during heavy group drinking in Sydney bars, and in the interactional process, questions of male honour are resolved through violence. In light of these recent attempts in the United Kingdom and Australia to understand the role of alcohol in collective violence and its relationship to masculinity, the purpose of this chapter is to explore this theme in relation to US youth gangs.

Drinking, Gender and Masculinity

Gender is a strong predictor of drinking behaviour (Wilsnack et al. 1994). As Lemle and Mishkind (1989: 213) note, gender differences 'in drinking behavior are so ubiquitous that men's drinking predominates for virtually all ages, ethnic groups, religions, education levels, incomes and categories of marital status'. In general, men are more likely to drink, are more likely to drink heavily, and are more likely to experience problems with their drinking. These overall gender characteristics are also true cross-culturally. In almost every culture men drink more than women (Heath 2000). For example, Fillmore et al.'s (1991) analysis of thirty-nine longitudinal studies from fifteen countries highlights the extent to which men 'in every country and every age group . . . drank larger quantities, drink more frequently and report more drinking problems than women' (cited in Wilsnack et al. 1994: 173). Although these differences existed across all age groups, age does influence the extent to which male and female drinking differ. Alcohol consumption tends to increase rapidly among youth until the age of 18 and then begins to decline after the age of 20 depending on the extent to which young people take on additional responsibilities of work or marriage. As Foxcroft and Lowe (1997: 215) have noted, 'in a period of approximately ten years young people go from individuals who have never had an alcoholic drink to individuals who as an age group comprise the heaviest drinking section of the population'. During this period male adolescents in general drink more heavily than their female counterparts, although the extent of the differences varies by age.

Not only is drinking primarily a male activity, but initiation into drinking for boys is also viewed as a *rite de passage* into manhood. 'Along with his first sexual experience, [drinking] . . . is one of the fundamental activities by which a boy is initiated as a man' (Lemle and Mishkind 1989: 214). To drink is to be masculine, and to drink heavily is to be even more masculine. According to McClelland and his colleagues (1972: 284), such heavy drinking occurs in men who are 'obsessed with manly virtues'. Men use alcohol to gain a sense of power. For example, as Park (1995) has shown, the 'New Zealand "kiwi bloke" sees drinking as a badge of masculinity' (cited in Heath 2000: 74). Male drinking, especially in young male groups, is often prescribed male behaviour (Gutmann 1996) and is associated with risk-taking activities, excitement and aggression. Consequently, drinkers are viewed as manly not solely because they drink, but also because their drinking is linked with other behaviours which are also connected with the image of being masculine (Lemle and Mishkind 1989). For example, notions of honour are frequently intertwined with drinking, and when the drinker's honour is impugned then violence may be the result (Burns 1980; Parker 1995). Some writers (Riches 1986; Block and Block 1995) have distinguished between instrumental violence, which operates to achieve practical purposes, for example to acquire money or property, and expressive violence, which operates in a much more symbolic way, for example as a way of demonstrating to one's peers that one is a dependable member of the group (Vigil 1988; Padilla 1992; Messerschmidt 1993), or as a way of gaining recognition, status and affirming masculinity.

As boys grow up, they also become accepted into male-dominated groupings, which are often associated with drinking. For example, Bales (1962), in his work on drinking in Ireland, demonstrates how young boys become accepted into male drinking groups and subsequently increase their separation from the women in the society. The groups produce and confirm male solidarity and male dominance, and the division between male and female social life becomes consolidated. Hence alcohol is used both as a way of asserting male togetherness and as a convenient symbolic tool for separating men from women. The male drinking group creates a social distance from other groups and specifically from women. The distancing process can be further enhanced through male discourse which constructs the 'other' (Fisher 1998). For example, in the case of male gangs, women are referred to as hos, bitches, broads, breezies, tricks, honeys, jigs, hootchies, females or ladies, and are classified as status symbols, sources of sexual pleasure or monetary suppliers. This terminology allows men to effectively 'dehumanize' women, which in turn may justify violent behaviour in certain circumstances.

These gender divisions can be substantiated in two additional ways: first, occupations and related occupational drinking groups; and, second, the drinking arena. Sociologists and anthropologists in studies on fishermen (Peace 1992; Tunstall 1962), miners (Dennis et al. 1969), factory workers (Ames and Janes 1987) and longshoremen (Mars 1987) have noted the extent to which group solidarity at work is further established by drinking together on and off the job. The second way in which men consolidate their separation from women by drinking is through the drinking arena. A drinking arena can be defined as a space with a surrounding boundary which has symbolic or material connotations. The boundaries serve as both physical barriers and symbolic barriers. The arena can be, for example, a space such as a park bench or railway arch (Archard 1979) or demarcated 'pitches' (Sansom 1980). Within the arena, the drinkers are controlled by a series of group-defined obligations and reciprocities. The arena can also be a more elaborate material structure, which physically separates activities within the building from those outside. Such physical structures include taverns, bars, pubs, wine shops and pulquerias (a bar for drinking pulque). A sense of belonging within a particular drinking arena is the result of an individual becoming an accepted member of a particular group. Members can expect a certain type of treatment which differs from non-members, who by their non-membership can be excluded. Given the dominance of men in public drinking places (Hunt and Satterlee 1987; Sulkunen et al. 1997), it is not surprising that the drinking arena further consolidates gender divisions.

Ethnicity is an additional factor which influences gender differences in youth drinking. For while female drinking among African-Americans, Latinos and Asian-Americans is lower in frequency and quantity than for males (Gilbert and Collins

1997), the extent of the difference varies by ethnicity (Edwards et al. 1995: 373–5). Male drinking patterns also vary by ethnicity. In general, data from the 2002 Monitoring the Future survey reveal widespread alcohol consumption among school children in general. 'Approximately three-quarters of white, Mexican American, Cuban American, Puerto Rican, and other Latin American . . . seniors reported using alcohol during the preceding year' (Wallace 2002: 71). However, when analysed by ethnicity and gender, clear differences emerge in the consumption rates of high school seniors. Although heavy drinking rates were highest among Caucasian seniors, they were 'lower among Mexican American and Cuban American seniors, even lower among other Latin American and Puerto Rican seniors and lowest among Asian American and African American seniors' (Wallace 2002: 72).

We have, then, two distinct sets of literature. One area of study has examined the extent to which notions of masculinity are inter-related with violent behaviour. The precise type and style of violence is mediated by the interplay of social structure and social interaction. The second area, the alcohol literature, has emphasized the extent to which drinking is a male-dominated activity that both enforces and enhances gender divisions within the society. The following analysis, using data from our ongoing research on ethnic youth gangs in the San Francisco Bay area,[1] attempts to unify these two sets of literature by suggesting that alcohol affirms expressions of masculinity in an environment where drinking and violence are endemic. Our discussion focuses on this process. First, we demonstrate how alcohol is integrated into the everyday lives of male gang members, including both the extent and context of drinking. Second, we consider the way that alcohol and group drinking work to maintain group solidarity and camaraderie, while, at the same time, operating as a distancing mechanism to exclude 'others', including both women and rival gang members. Third, we examine the role of ethnicity in mediating both the style of drinking found in the gangs and the different forms of cultural identity associated with it. We also contend that notions of masculinity within the gang, when coupled with drinking, create environments in which disrespect can easily be perceived and honour equally quickly called into question. On these occasions, violent behaviour swiftly follows.

Research Design and Sample

Methods

San Francisco, the source for the data in this chapter, is an important location for conducting research on youth gangs due to its compact geographical area and its concentrated ethnic and cultural diversity. Currently, the 2000 census estimates the total population of the city to be 776,733 (US Census Bureau 2002). While the area continues to attract newcomers, and the ethnic composition of the city continues to grow, the overall population in San Francisco has increased by little more than seven per cent since 1990 compared to a statewide increase of more than thirteen and a half per cent. Given the relatively small topographic area of the city, a 46.7 square mile fist of land confined by the Pacific Ocean and the San Francisco Bay, the city is comprised of a diverse mix of racial and ethnic groups. According to 2000 census figures, 43.6 per cent of the inhabitants of the city were white (not of Hispanic origin), with Asians the next largest ethnic group, representing 30.7 per cent of the population. Slightly more that 14 per cent of residents were of Hispanic origin, 7.6 per cent were African-American, 3 per cent were two or more races, and approximately one per cent were of all other races (US Census Bureau 2002).

Between 1997 and 1999, we conducted face-to-face interviews with 383 male gang members (see Table 11.1). These respondents were members of 92 different gangs, of which 32 were African-American, 28 were Latino, 28 Asian and Pacific Islander, and 4 Caucasian. Gang members, located using a snowball or chain referral sampling approach, were interviewed in two stages. In the first stage, the respondent answered questions from a quantitative interview schedule covering topics such as basic demographic data, work and criminal histories, patterns of alcohol and drug use, activities of gang members and violence experienced by gang members. The second stage was an in-depth focused interview that explored topics such as the respondent's background and early life; their experiences of alcohol use within their families; history of involvement in the gang; relationships with gang members; and experiences of drinking and violence within the gang. The interviews were conducted in a variety of settings ranging from the respondent's or peer's residence, parks, youth centres and coffee shops. Interviews lasted, on average, two hours, and respondents received an honorarium for their participation and time. The interviews with the African-Americans were conducted in English. The Latinos and Asian men were interviewed in English or their native language (or a combination), depending on their preference. The fieldworkers assisted in translating the Spanish interviews. All of the fieldworkers were familiar with the gang scene in their communities, having either been directly involved in the street scene or as community workers (e.g. youth workers, public housing liaison). Given their role within the community, they had no difficulties in establishing rapport and trust with the young men.

We took several steps to address validity and reliability issues. Given the field-workers' familiarity with the scene and with some of the respondents, the respondents were less likely to exaggerate or minimize their experiences. During the course of the interview, the fieldworkers rephrased questions at different times to detect inconsistencies and to ensure truthfulness. The interviewers also were required to assess the respondent's veracity at the end of the interview, and found them to be truthful. There were no instances in which the respondent gave inconsistent responses. Fieldworkers also conducted periodic field observations to cross-check respondents' veracity.

Table 11.1 Social demographic characteristics of homeboys

By ethnicity	African-American (N = 177)		Latino (N = 103)		Asian (N = 64)		Pacific Islander (N = 15)		Other (N = 24)		Total (N = 383)	
	n	*%*	*n*	*%*	*n*	*%*	*n*	*%*	*n*	*%*	*n*	*%*
Median age	19		18		18		20		19		18	
Place of birth												
San Francisco	149	84.2	53	51.4	19	29.7	10	66.7	15	62.5	246	64.2
Other US city	15	8.5	7	6.8	3	4.7	1	6.7	2	8.3	28	7.3
Latin America	0	0.0	39	37.9	0	0.0	0	0.0	0	0.0	39	10.2
Hong Kong/ China	0	0.0	0	0.0	16	25.0	0	0.0	0	0.0	16	4.2
Asian countries	0	0.0	0	0.0	14	21.9	4	26.7	1	4.2	19	5.0
Other	0	0.0	0	0.0	10	15.6	0	0.0	4	16.7	14	3.6
Unknown	13	7.3	4	3.9	2	3.1	0	0.0	2	8.3	21	5.5
Last grade completed												
8th or less	12	6.8	15	14.6	15	23.4	1	6.7	1	4.2	44	11.5
9th	21	11.9	17	16.5	13	20.3	2	13.3	7	29.2	60	15.7
10th	35	19.8	25	24.3	10	15.6	1	6.7	3	12.5	74	19.3
11th	65	36.7	23	22.3	14	21.9	1	6.7	3	12.5	106	27.7
12th	42	23.7	21	20.4	10	15.6	10	66.7	7	29.2	90	23.4
Some college	2	1.1	0	0.0	1	1.6	0	0.0	2	8.3	5	1.3
Unknown	0	0.0	2	1.9	1	1.6	0	0.0	1	4.2	4	1.0
Current school attending												
None	102	57.6	48	46.6	30	46.9	8	53.3	11	45.8	199	52.0
Regular	22	12.4	9	8.7	15	23.4	0	0.0	2	8.3	48	12.5
Alternative	18	10.2	32	31.0	5	7.8	2	13.3	2	8.3	59	15.4
Vocational	6	3.4	1	1.0	0	0.0	0	0.0	0	0.0	7	1.8
General Education Development	16	9.0	7	6.8	4	6.3	0	0.0	2	8.3	29	7.6
College	13	7.3	0	0.0	6	9.4	5	33.3	4	16.7	28	7.3
Other	0	0.0	2	1.9	3	4.7	0	0.0	3	12.5	8	2.1
Resided with most up to age 16												
Mother and father	28	15.8	33	32.0	41	64.1	5	33.3	9	37.5	116	30.3
Mother only	96	54.2	42	40.8	12	18.8	7	46.7	9	37.5	166	43.3
Father only	10	5.6	7	6.8	2	3.1	1	6.7	0	0.0	20	5.2
Mother and stepfather	1	0.6	1	1.0	0	0.0	1	6.7	0	0.0	3	0.8
Grandparents	28	15.8	9	8.7	0	0.0	0	0.0	1	4.2	38	9.9
Other relative	9	5.1	2	1.9	7	10.9	0	0.0	3	12.5	21	5.5
Foster care	3	1.7	1	1.0	0	0.0	0	0.0	1	4.2	5	1.3
Other	2	1.1	8	7.8	2	3.1	1	6.7	1	4.2	14	3.7
Living in housing project	124	70.1	20	19.4	18	28.1	2	13.3	3	12.5	167	43.6

Table 11.1 Social demographic characteristics of homeboys (continued)

By ethnicity	African-American (N = 177)		Latino (N = 103)		Asian (N = 64)		Pacific Islander (N = 15)		Other (N = 24)		Total (N = 383)	
	n	%	*n*	%	*n*	%	*n*	%	*n*	%	*n*	%
Marital status												
Single	141	79.7	80	77.7	51	79.7	15	100.0	19	79.2	306	79.9
Married, living with spouse	4	2.2	5	4.8	1	1.6	0	0.0	1	4.2	11	2.9
Married, not living with spouse	4	2.2	3	2.9	0	0.0	0	0.0	0	0.0	7	1.8
Living with girlfriend	27	15.3	14	13.6	11	17.2	0	0.0	4	16.7	56	14.6
Unknown	1	0.6	1	1.0	1	1.6	0	0.0	0	0.0	3	0.8
Number of children												
0	126	71.2	70	68.0	60	93.7	15	100.0	18	75.0	288	75.2
1	31	17.5	23	22.3	1	1.6	0	0.0	2	8.3	58	15.1
2	14	7.9	4	3.9	1	1.6	0	0.0	3	12.5	22	5.7
3 or more	6	3.4	6	5.8	1	1.6	0	0.0	1	4.2	14	3.7
Unknown	0	0.0	0	0.0	1	1.6	0	0.0	0	0.0	1	0.3
Fathers' occupation												
Professionals	5	2.8	3	2.9	5	7.8	1	6.7	1	4.2	15	3.9
Clerical/retail/sales	15	8.5	8	7.8	4	6.2	1	6.7	6	25.0	34	8.9
Skilled manual	11	6.2	22	21.3	7	10.9	0	0.0	2	8.3	42	11.0
Semi-skilled	35	19.8	13	12.6	16	25.0	4	26.7	2	8.3	70	18.3
Unskilled	36	20.3	27	26.2	11	17.2	3	20.0	5	20.8	82	21.4
Unemployed/welfare	15	8.5	1	1.0	8	12.5	0	0.0	1	4.2	25	6.5
Criminal activity	9	5.1	0	0.0	1	1.6	2	13.3	0	0.0	12	3.1
Other	5	2.8	2	2.0	0	0.0	2	13.3	2	8.3	10	2.6
Unknown	46	26.0	27	26.2	12	18.8	2	13.3	5	20.8	93	24.3
Mothers' occupation												
Professionals	26	14.7	9	8.7	2	3.1	3	20.0	2	8.3	42	11.0
Clerical/retail/service	56	31.6	18	17.5	12	18.8	7	46.7	9	37.5	102	26.6
Skilled manual	1	0.6	0	0.0	1	1.6	1	6.7	0	0.0	3	0.8
Semi-skilled	13	7.3	4	3.9	7	10.9	1	6.7	0	0.0	25	6.5
Unskilled	16	9.0	25	24.3	6	9.4	3	20.0	3	12.5	53	13.8
Housewife	17	9.6	19	18.4	13	20.3	0	0.0	5	20.8	54	14.1
Childcare	5	2.8	3	2.9	0	0.0	0	0.0	0	0.0	8	2.1
Unemployed/welfare	22	12.4	9	8.7	15	23.4	0	0.0	1	4.2	47	12.3
Criminal activity	1	0.6	0	0.0	0	0.0	0	0.0	1	4.2	2	0.5
Other	3	1.7	0	0.0	3	4.7	0	0.0	0	0.0	6	1.6

Table 11.1 Social demographic characteristics of homeboys (continued)

By ethnicity	African-American (N = 177)		Latino (N = 103)		Asian (N = 64)		Pacific Islander (N = 15)		Other (N = 24)		Total (N = 383)	
	n	*%*	*n*	*%*	*n*	*%*	*n*	*%*	*n*	*%*	*n*	*%*
Unknown	17	9.6	16	15.5	5	7.8	0	0.0	3	12.5	41	10.7
Source of income last month												
Welfare	2	1.1	2	1.9	2	3.1	0	0.0	2	8.3	8	2.1
Job	12	6.8	30	29.1	15	23.4	6	40.0	7	29.2	70	18.3
Family	4	2.2	16	15.5	16	25.0	1	6.7	2	8.3	39	10.2
Hustle	151	85.3	35	34.0	18	28.1	5	33.3	9	37.5	218	56.9
Friends	0	0.0	2	1.9	2	3.1	2	13.3	0	0.0	6	1.6
Combination	7	4.0	13	12.6	9	14.1	1	6.7	4	16.7	34	8.9
Unknown	1	0.6	5	4.9	2	3.1	0	0.0	0	0.0	8	2.1
Median monthly personal income($)												
	1,300		600		600		1,200		750		950	

Characteristics of the Sample

Almost three-quarters (274) of the respondents were born in the United States. Forty-six per cent (177) of the respondents were African-American, while just over a quarter (103) were Latino, 17 per cent (64) were Asian and 4 per cent (15) were Pacific Islanders. Of the remaining twenty-four respondents, seven were Caucasian, one Native-American and sixteen were of mixed ethnic background. The overall age range was 13 to 50 with a median age of 18 years. Almost two-thirds of the respondents (243) were 18 or younger. The African-Americans had the widest age range with a median age of 19. The Asians and Latinos had a median age of 18, Pacific Islanders 20 and the others 18. The majority (55 per cent) had been involved in gangs from one to five years, a quarter from six to ten years, and only 5 per cent for less than a year (data not shown). Despite their age, only one-quarter of them had completed high school. Forty-five per cent of them, however, were still attending some form of educational programme, including General Education Development classes and alternative school. The majority of the young men were single (80 per cent), and had no children (75 per cent). Slightly more than one-quarter of the African-American and Latino men reported that they had at least one child.

The majority of the respondents were unemployed at the time of the interview, and overall only 18 per cent of them reported that their job was their main source of income during the last month. Hustling, usually defined in terms of drug sales and other illegal activities, represented the major source of income for 57 per cent of the young men. There were differences, however, among the different ethnic groups. Hustling represented the primary income source in the last month for over 85 per cent of the African-Americans. The median monthly personal income among

African-Americans was $1,300. By comparison, slightly more than one-third of the Latinos, one-third of Pacific Islanders and slightly more than one-quarter of the Asians relied on hustling for money. The latter group were equally likely to rely on hustling as on family members for income. Forty per cent of Pacific Islanders, nearly 30 per cent of the Latinos and one-quarter the Asians relied on their job for income in the last month. These groups reported lower levels of a monthly median income of $600 among Latinos and Asians and $1,200 for Pacific Islanders.

Among the 18 per cent of respondents who were working either full- or part-time jobs, almost half of them were in unskilled occupations. This latter characteristic reflected the occupations of the respondents' fathers, who tended to be employed in either unskilled or semi-skilled occupations, such as janitors, labourers, delivery drivers, roofers, cooks and landscaping workers. Approximately 27 per cent of the mothers were employed, and worked in clerical, retail and service orientated occupations, and 21 per cent of them in either unskilled or semi-skilled occupations. Overall, our respondents were the sons of working- and lower-working-class minority families. There were significant differences among the young men, however, in relation to their family connections and residence. Importantly, over one-half of the African-American respondents reported that they lived only with their mother until at least their sixteenth birthday. Sixteen per cent of them were equally as likely to live with both parents or with their grandparents. Latinos were slightly more likely to live with their mother only (40 per cent) than with both parents (32 per cent). Almost two-thirds of Asian respondents lived with both parents and less than one-fifth lived with only their mothers. Almost half of the Pacific Islanders were raised by their mothers only and one-third lived with both parents.

Almost half of all the respondents lived in three districts in San Francisco. The largest number of respondents (85 or 22 per cent) lived in the Bayview/Hunter's Point District, an area populated predominantly by African-American families. The second most concentrated number of respondents (53) lived in the Mission district, a busy and crowded area in the city with a high Latino population (including 41 per cent of the Latino respondents), followed by Visitacion Valley (47), a district which contains one of the city's larger housing projects. The highest concentration of Asians in San Francisco resided or hung out in Chinatown and North Beach, two neighbouring districts. Seventy per cent of the African Americans lived in public housing, compared to 28 per cent of Asians and 19 per cent of Latinos.

Alcohol, Masculinity and Gang Life

To understand the role of alcohol in the lives of gang members, we must begin our analysis by considering the characteristics and dynamics of street life. As many researchers have noted, being on the streets is a natural and legitimized social arena for working-class and minority male adolescents. For many of these young men, life is 'neither the workplace nor the school; it is the street' (Messerschmidt 1993: 102). Their entrée to life on the street is through the street gang. Gang members are primarily male and it is therefore not surprising that life on the streets is governed by rules of masculinity, where notions of honour, respect and status afford outlets for expressing and defending one's masculinity. The gang epitomizes masculinity and ensures male bonding. Given this masculine culture of the street, how extensive is drinking in gang life and what role does it play?

Gang members spend the majority of their day 'hanging around' (Corrigan and Firth 1976) and typically describe this activity in the very mundane terms of 'doing nothing'. Seventy per cent of the respondents indicated that they hung out with their homeboys every day. Even for those gang members who worked or went to school, when their workdays or schooldays were over they headed for the streets. Of the 178 gang members who were still in school, almost two-thirds hung out with their homeboys on a daily basis, and of the 115 who worked, more than half hung out with the gang on a daily basis.

Although adults perceive these activities as a waste of time, the everyday practice of 'doing nothing' is often an intense and busy period of time and the activities that occur include talking, recounting details from previous events, joking, discussing business, defending one's honour, maintaining one's respect, 'handling their business', fending off insults, keeping the police at bay, 'cruising' around in a car, doing a few deals, defending turf, and getting high. During most of these activities gang members drink. 'Hanging out' is also immensely important for newcomers to the gang to learn the codes of behaviour that exist on the street and in the gang. By 'hanging out' they learn to distinguish between acceptable and unacceptable behaviour. The novitiate also learns the hierarchy of the gang and how to behave differentially with young gang members, leaders and OGs.[2] The following quote by a Latino gang member illustrates the ways in which drinking accompanies the activities of a 'normal day':

I: Describe the activities of a usual day of a homeboy. What time did you get up?

R: 6.30 or 7.00, because I take the people who are going to go to work, they want to stop off and get their morning fix [buying/obtaining drugs].

I: You take care of the morning crowd?

R: Right that involves getting my morning beer you know. I drink down the beer which calms my stomach you know. I fix [taking drugs] and then I go out and hit the Mission [a district in San Francisco] between 16th and 18th. I can make up to like $800. You know what I mean, selling quarters [a measured quantity of drugs] at $30 to $45 a thing depending on how square they [the customers] are or if they are regulars. Then after that I go take me a nap. The other one [fellow drug dealer] comes on and I rest for a couple of hours. I get up at 10:00. I take a shower and get dressed, change clothes, so that the narcs [the police] don't start to recognize me because I am wearing the same thing constantly. . . . I will come out and maybe work an hour or two for the afternoon. A group of us, we work the afternoon and drink a bunch of beers. Just get kind of buzzing. Then you kill time until the evening crowd. . . . What is good about the homeboys, man, is that one will go out and spend $25 on food . . . bring a bunch of tacos and burritos back and say it is time to eat. Because you got to make sure you put some nutriment in that body. And after that, after lunch time some of us kick back smoke a little herb [marijuana] and drink some more beer. . . . Now this is getting to be about 6.00 or 6.30. Throughout this . . . there is drinking you know you are always having your cerveza [beer], man. And okay so like about 6.30 it slows down a little bit. (G101)

This vivid account demonstrates the intensity and order in 'hanging out': meeting up with others; earning a day's pay; getting energy to last through the day; and avoiding police attention. Importantly, it also underscores the extent to which drinking is an integral part of those activities. The homeboy begins drinking with an early morning beer, in the afternoon he consumes a 'bunch of beers', supplemented with a 'little herb', and at this point the 'buzzing' begins. Once the evening commences, drinking becomes continuous. Given the fact that drinking permeates all of these activities, how extensive is their drinking?

Drinking Patterns and Characteristics

As table 11.2 indicates, the majority of young men had their first drink in their very early teen years, typically at the age of 12 for beer, the age of 13 for wine and the age of 14 for hard liquor. Drinking units were measured by the number of beer bottles/cans, wine glasses/wine coolers and shots of hard liquor. Within a year, respondents began drinking more than once a month, with beer being consumed more regularly at the age of 14, and wine and liquor at the age of 15. Few respondents reported that they did not drink regularly (8 per cent). African-Americans preferred liquor (60 per cent) and, to a lesser extent, beer (35 per cent). The reverse pattern was found for Latinos, Pacific Islanders and Asians, whose beverage of choice was beer.

Initiation into drinking differed between ethnic groups. While African-American gang members and Pacific Islanders tended to learn to drink on the streets in peer groups, Asians were more likely to commence drinking for the first time at off-street parties they attended with their friends. Latinos were introduced to drinking in two ways: either through street activities with their peers, or within the family context, most often by older male family members but occasionally with family members of the same age. [3] In the family context, the offering of alcohol was usually casual, for instance at a family gathering:

I was around 10. They brought some liquor from my home country. And then my uncle gave me some. He said, 'You want some?' Yeah, all right. That's how it goes or whatever. And then I went like to make a phone call and then I was like getting drunk. I was getting

Table 11.2 Drinking characteristics of homeboys by ethnicity

By ethnicity	African-American (N = 177)		Latino (N = 103)		Asian (N = 64)		Pacific Islander (N = 15)		Other (N = 24)		Total (N = 383)	
	n	*%*	*n*	*%*	*n*	*%*	*n*	*%*	*n*	*%*	*n*	*%*
Median age of first use												
Beer	12.0		12.0		13.0		13.0		13.0		12.0	
Wine	13.0		13.0		13.5		12.5		13.0		13.0	
Liquor	14.0		14.0		14.0		14.5		14.0		14.0	
Median age of regular use												
(more than once a month)												
Beer	14.0		14.0		15.0		15.0		14.0		14.0	
Wine	15.0		14.5		15.0		13.0		13.0		15.0	
Liquor	15.0		14.0		15.0		16.0		14.0		15.0	
Alcohol type used most often												
None	4	2.3	14	13.6	12	18.8	0	0.0	1	4.2	31	8.1
Beer	62	35.0	60	58.3	28	43.8	9	60.0	13	54.2	172	44.9
Wine	3	1.7	0	0.0	2	3.1	0	0.0	0	0.0	5	1.3
Liquor	106	59.9	23	22.3	22	34.4	6	40.0	9	37.5	166	43.3
Unknown	2	1.1	6	5.8	0.0	0.0	0	0.0	1	4.2	9	2.3
Current drinking pattern												
Abstinence	9	5.1	26	25.2	15	23.4	0	0.0	4	16.7	54	14.1
Current (not binge or heavy)	118	66.7	29	28.1	24	37.5	7	46.7	12	50.0	190	49.6
Binge*	15	8.5	10	9.7	9	14.1	3	20.0	0	0.0	37	9.7
Heavy†	34	19.2	36	35.0	15	23.4	5	33.3	7	29.2	97	25.3
Unknown	1	0.6	2	1.9	1	1.6	0	0.0	1	4.2	5	1.3

*Five or more drinks at one sitting fewer than five times per month.

†Five or more drinks at one sitting more than five times per month.

drunk and I fell. I was trippin' out. And then I really got into it when I was around 15. (H059)

One-quarter of the respondents were heavy drinkers, having drank five or more drinks in a short period of time on five or more days in the last month. The largest percentage of heavy drinkers were among the Latinos (35 per cent), followed by Pacific Islanders (33 per cent), then Asians (23 per cent). African-Americans had the lowest numbers of heavy drinkers with only 19 per cent. Binge drinkers, having five or more drinks at one sitting fewer than five times in the last month, accounted for only 10 per cent of drinkers. Half of all drinkers were current drinkers who did not binge or drink heavily. The largest proportion of African-Americans (67 per cent) and Asians (38 per cent) fell into this category. Sixty-five (almost 20 per cent) indicated that they drank daily in the last month (data not shown), and at least half of these were either binge or heavy drinkers. Of the daily drinkers, more than two-thirds were African-Americans and two-thirds were aged 19 or older. Forty-five drank beer everyday and twenty-eight drank hard liquor daily (of these, eight respondents drank both beer and hard liquor daily). Latinos accounted for 15 per cent of the daily drinkers, while only five Asians drank on a daily basis. All in all, Asians drank less than the other groups, while Latinos, when they drank, tended to drink more.

Drinking Contexts and Ethnicity

Drinking patterns of gang members tell us much about the extent to which drinking is a part of their daily experiences. However, the contexts of their drinking and the activities that they are involved in while drinking can provide a more complete picture of the role that alcohol plays in their everyday lives on the streets and with other gang members. In a typical day gang members meet up with each other at some point to 'hang out' or 'chill', and group drinking and drug use begins. Some significant differences exist between ethnic groups in their day-to-day activities. For instance, African-American gang members were the most entrepreneurial in their daily activities. On a typical day they tended to rise early, head for the corners where they 'posted up' to sell their drugs while drinking and hanging out with their homeboys. More than 85 per cent of the African-American respondents had sold drugs in the last month, most of them on a daily basis. They often gambled together while they hung out, shooting dice being the most popular diversion, as well as the cause of some contention from time to time. On occasions they would go to the courts and play basketball. The majority of their time was spent out on the streets, followed by hanging out in individuals' homes.

The Latino respondents[4] were similar to the African-American respondents in that they typically headed out onto the streets and met up with their homeboys at their park or street corner early in the day. Like the African-American gangs, they tended to spend most of their days and evenings out on the streets, or hanging out in the homes of other gang members. Latinos' daily activities differed from the African-American respondents in that they were more leisurely because there were fewer drug sellers (approximately 43 per cent sold in the last month) among this group. Their activities primarily involved hanging out, drinking and getting high. On occasions, they would get together and have picnics and BBQs in the parks, and from time to time would rent a hotel room in order to have parties. Pacific Islanders similarly hung out primarily on the streets with their fellow gang members. They also frequented beach areas, parks and private homes. Few were drug sellers, but many liked to gamble.

Asian respondents were the most diverse of all groups in their activities. They usually slept longer hours during the day and headed out to meet up with their groups in the mid-afternoon to early evenings. They tended to 'hook up' at someone's residence or at a public place as opposed to having a specific meeting place out on the streets. Their daily and nightly activities also differed from African-American and Latino gang members. Like the Latinos, most of their activities were leisure, but they were more inclined toward entertainment, such as shooting pool, bowling, hanging out in coffee shops or going to Karaoke clubs.

It is important to keep in mind that many gang members also had jobs or were still in school. For those individuals, their drinking activities took place after they had finished for the day and on the weekends.

Table 11.3 provides information about the most common contexts in which gang members are likely to drink most of the time, and the details of their most extreme binging event in the last year. Among all ethnic groups, drinking is most typically associated with socializing events such as group parties, hanging out with their gang members, and after fights. Although the overall median number of drinks consumed among all respondents during their most extreme binge was ten drinks, there were significant differences among the groups. African-Americans reported a median number of seven drinks, and over two-thirds drank liquor. By comparison, Latinos reported a median of twenty drinks, and had different drinking preferences. While 20 per cent drank only beer, another 32 per cent drank only liquor, and another 26 per cent mixed their drinks. Asians reported a median number of ten drinks, and, like Latinos, were more diverse in their drinks. While almost 30 per cent drank only beer, another 17 per cent kept to liquor, and almost one-third mixed their drinks. Pacific Islanders were the heaviest bingers, with a median of twenty-two drinks, most of which were liquor, or a combination of different types of alcohol.

Very few gang members binged alone. Binging events were essentially social events, which, in three out of four instances, involved either gang members or friends. Only 1 per cent of respondents had binged with a girlfriend or spouse, and only twenty-five respondents binged in a family context. The setting for binge drinking was typically in the private domain of someone's house or outdoors such as at the beach, in parks or at neighbourhood corners. Bars and clubs were not the scene for binging for Latinos, Pacific Islanders and African-Americans. By comparison, bars and clubs were the most common site of binging by Asian respondents (more than one-quarter), followed by private residences.

Alcohol, Masculinity and Group Solidarity

Drinking works in several symbolic ways in the gang. Because drinking is an integral and regular part of socializing within gang life, drinking operates as a social 'lubricant' or social 'glue' working to maintain the social solidarity of the gang. In this

Table 11.3 Drinking contexts and single event characteristics

By ethnicity	African-American (N = 177)		Latino (N = 103)		Asian (N = 64)		Pacific Islander (N = 15)		Other (N = 24)		Total (N = 383)	
	n	%	n	%	n	%	n	%	n	%	n	%
Most common use contexts												
Cruising in cars	48	27.1	17	16.5	4	6.3	4	26.7	4	16.7	77	20.1
Group parties	114	64.4	72	69.9	39	60.9	10	66.7	19	79.2	254	66.3
Hanging out with group/ night	100	56.5	48	46.6	27	42.2	10	66.7	14	58.3	199	51.9
Hanging out with group/ day	63	35.6	23	22.3	9	14.1	7	46.7	4	16.7	106	27.7
School	4	2.3	1	1.0	3	4.7	0	0.0	0	0.0	8	2.1
Before fight	33	18.7	14	13.6	5	7.8	2	13.3	3	12.5	57	14.9
After fight	82	46.3	37	35.9	14	21.9	7	46.7	11	45.8	151	39.4
At home with family	24	13.6	4	3.9	4	6.3	1	6.7	0	0.0	33	8.6
Alone	35	19.8	13	12.6	6	9.4	0	0.0	1	4.2	55	14.3
Median no. most drinks in one event	7		20		10		22		13		10	
Type of alcohol												
Beer	26	14.7	21	20.4	19	29.7	2	13.3	5	20.8	73	19.1
Wine	5	2.8	1	1.0	1	1.6	0	0.0	0	0.0	7	1.8
Liquor	118	66.7	33	32.0	11	17.2	7	46.7	8	33.3	177	46.2
Combination	22	12.4	27	26.2	20	31.3	6	40.0	9	37.5	84	21.9
Unknown	2	1.1	3	2.9	3	4.7	0	0.0	0	0.0	8	21
Setting												
Residence	54	30.5	33	32.0	17	26.6	6	40.0	9	37.5	119	31.0
Bar/club	16	9.0	5	4.9	18	28.1	1	6.7	3	12.5	43	11.2
Outdoors	61	34.5	23	22.3	5	7.8	4	26.7	6	25.0	99	25.9
Party	31	17.5	18	17.5	8	12.5	4	26.7	3	12.5	64	16.7
Car	9	5.1	1	1.0	1	1.6	0	0.0	0	0.0	11	2.9
School	1	0.6	1	1.0	3	4.7	0	0.0	0	0.0	5	1.3
Other	5	2.8	21	20.4	11	17.2	0	0.0	3	12.5	40	10.4
Unknown	0	0.0	1	1.0	0	0.0	0	0.0	0	0.0	2	0.5
With whom												
Alone	10	5.6	2	1.9	2	3.1	0	0.0	2	8.3	16	4.2
With friends	39	22.0	27	26.2	18	28.1	9	60.0	8	33.3	101	26.3
With gang members	107	60.5	44	42.7	27	42.2	4	26.7	10	41.7	192	50.1
With spouse or girlfriend	3	1.7	1	1.0	0	0.0	0	0.0	0	0.0	4	1.0
With family	13	7.3	8	7.8	2	3.1	2	13.3	0	0.0	25	6.5
With other	1	0.6	2	1.9	5	7.8	0	0.0	2	8.3	10	2.6
Unknown	4	2.3	19	18.5	10	15.6	0	0.0	2	8.3	35	9.1

way, as a number of researchers have noted (Bales 1962; Szwed 1966; Waddell 1975), alcohol can be fundamentally important in producing and maintaining cohesion within a community or part of a community. Among Chinese gangs, male members frequented night clubs to drink together. In fact, night clubs were the most common setting in which Asian gang members got together to drink other than at private residences. In some of these public gatherings, drinks were paid for by the Dai Lo, or Big Brother of the group, who, through his connections and money-making abilities, had emerged as a respected leader of the group. Among Latinos, inclusion in a drinking group confirmed one's status as an insider. When gang members were short of money to buy alcohol, they pooled their funds. Even when a gang member had no money to contribute, he would still be allowed to drink with the rest of the group. The only requirement to inclusion was that 'they got to have heart . . . as long as they back you when something goes down [if trouble occurs]' (H099).

New members of a gang have to prove themselves before they can begin to attain any honour, status or respect. Their initial test is the initiation ceremony often referred to as 'jumping in' (Vigil 1988). To date, there has been an extensive literature on the initiation process or *rite de passage* of potential gang members (see, e.g., Padilla 1992; Vigil 1988). The process of 'jumping in' has often been associated with some form of physical tests. According to Vigil and Long (1990: 64), this process can serve 'to test member's toughness and desire for membership . . . and to enhance loyalty to the group'. From our data, two types of gang entry exist: the first is a formal process and similar to that outlined for the Latino gangs, the second is more informal.

In those cases where some form of formalized initiation took place, the actual content of what was required varied from having cigarette burns inflicted; doing a particular deed to prove oneself, such as stealing a car; or the more 'traditional' method of accepting a physical 'pummelling' from gang members. The informal process of joining the gang involved prospective members 'hanging around' or 'kicking back' with the gang for varying periods of time which could last anywhere from a couple of months to a whole year. If, during this period, the potential recruit could show that he 'was down' or reliable as a member of the group and was prepared to support his fellow gang members, then he became accepted as a member. In a couple of cases, the initiation involved more than one method. For example, one respondent described a fairly lengthy process which involved both 'hanging around' and being 'jumped in'. This induction process is important because it is designed to symbolically test the newcomer's toughness, his ability to defend himself and withstand physical violence. As one African-American gang member noted: 'You gotta get jumped in, that's the only way you can get in . . . they ain't gonna get in there easy, you gotta get your stripes' (H150). Once the initiation has been accomplished and the newcomer accepted, their new status is confirmed by a bout of drinking and getting drunk, as the same gang member explained:

We don't really drink before we jump in somebody, but then after it's over then everybody get drunk. The person that got jumped in, he be the most ripped [drunk]. You want him ripped like so that he can be just cool with you, he be happy that he got in.

The act of drinking and getting drunk after being 'jumped in' acts as a form of celebration and the alcohol can also help to deaden the pain.

I drank right after I got jumped in. They'll be like . . . give you hugs . . . ask what do you want, do you want a 40 [a 40 oz of malt liquor], you get a 40 and you'll drink it . . . just to ease the pain of getting jumped in. (H013)

The initiation process coupled with drinking confirms the novitiate's claim of being a gang member - he has demonstrated his toughness and is an accepted member of the gang.

Having gained acceptance to the gang, a new member must assert his masculinity to maintain respect from the other members. In this masculine context, 'respect' demands deference to, and, at the same time, commands, status, power and authority in an environment with few legitimate avenues (e.g. employment, education) through which to attain a sense of esteem and importance for oneself and among one's peers. The 'pursuit of respect' (Bourgois 1996) for young minority males is expressed through exaggerated demonstrations of bravado, fearlessness and aggressiveness with others on the street. However, the precise ways in which drinking operates to affirm masculinity are culturally determined by the respective ethnicities of the gangs. Existing research on Latino gangs suggests that drinking plays a key role in the creation of a 'macho' identity.

I: Why do you think you always wanted to drink beer?

R: Because ah, I wanted to like ah, feel that machismo. I wanted to feel like my dad. I would go to the fucking store now and get a beer or sit at a bar. I always wanted to, well what is in that places man? I used to walk by there. And I had my gear and I looked and see . . . and that is pretty cool. And it is pool there but I couldn't go in there. They would tell me you got to leave, you got to get out of here you are too young. So then I just started setting myself up. When I reach a certain age I am going to check out a bar. (H006)

'Machismo' in the gangs includes demonstrations of strength and 'toughness' as well as *locura* (wildness) (Feldman et al. 1985; Vigil and Long 1990; Moore 1991; Padilla 1992).[5] As Vigil and Long (1990) have noted, alcohol can work to encourage the observance of ritually wild or crazy behaviour, especially in violent conflicts with outsiders, but also in other types of risky activities, such as joyriding and breaking into cars.

Oh yeah. I was out drinkin and stuff, and then James, and you know, he's just tryin to get off the street himself, and then, so we go in here. He goes to the store to buy some stuff for his little late night [party], and left the keys cause we were by North [in rival gang turf], and he said just take the car, you know, or lock the doors, or somethin, or honk, or whatever, you know attract attention . . . I just took the car. 'You're drunk.' 'So what?' And I took it, and I crashed it. (H287)

Studies of African-American gang life suggest the construction of a different cultural identity, one where 'the overall street style and the desired approach to projecting an individual's personal image can be summed up in the word "cool" (Feldman et al. 1985: 124; see also Hagedorn 1988; Taylor 1990). In this subculture, occasional drinking is the norm (MacLeod 1987) in public and private settings, as long as gang members are also 'handling their business'.

We stay in the hood [neighborhood] And we just kick back. And, like I said, when we drink, we socialize at the same time. And we also even handle our business. So, when I'm up there drinkin, I also handlin my business. Cuz I got, customers that know me. So, it ain't like I gotta really . . . really gotta put myself to work. People know me. So, when I'm out there drinkin, somebody might come up to me and say, 'Hey.' You know what I'm sayin? 'Are you workin?' I'd say, 'Yeah.' And I'm makin quick money at the same time while I'm just kickin it with my homies. (H225)

The African-American gang members in our sample reported relatively higher current alcohol use than the other ethnic groups. They are not binge or heavy drinkers, since the style of drinking and the behaviour associated with intoxication can undermine the 'cool' image, and are likely to be interpreted as a sign of 'being out of control'. 'They be cool. Everybody get purved [intoxicated]. They act the same. They know how to control their purve' (H212).

In the case of Asian-Americans, the available research suggests different attitudes to drinking. On the one hand, Chin (1990) suggests that intoxication is frowned upon by Chinese gangs. On the other hand, our own work on both Asian-American and Southeast Asian gangs (Toy 1992; Waldorf et al. 1994; Hunt et al. 1996) suggests that although drinking is not heavy among these groups, it is nevertheless widespread and intoxication in public and private places appears acceptable. A Southeast Asian gang member noted that he feels less vulnerable when he is drinking:

Every time I go to the club I have a drink . . . I am less vulnerable to attack. If somebody is looking for trouble I will be the first one to boom on them because I am drunk and I don't care . . . I think it makes me more violent because you just don't care . . . you know you just get out there and start doing your thing. (H174)

However, many Asians commented on how intoxication caused them to embarrass themselves, which was one of the reasons why a number of them were concerned about controlling their drinking.

> It was at a party. I was drinking because there were a lot of girls. Drink and show off. So we was just felt really weird like dizzy and we would be walking along. . . . And then sometimes you don't even know what you did. You embarrass yourself. One time I fell in the puddles I was so drunk. I didn't even know I fell in the puddle. First it was kind of raining and then there were a lot of girls. (H313)

Alcohol, Violence and Masculinity

Alcohol and group drinking work effectively as a social lubricant to bind the group together (Hunt and Satterlee 1986). Drinking also operates to separate the individual and the group from non-members. This process of distancing and exclusion allows the group to maintain its boundaries and its commonality while opposing others. This exclusionary quality of group drinking may then create the circumstances by which violence can occur. Drinking takes place within a social arena in which macho ideals are prominent. Maintaining respect within the gang is a constant process in which status is gained or lost on the basis of individuals' ability to defend themselves, their honour and their group's honour through violent physical confrontation (Messerschmidt 1993). The process of maintaining respect continues while alcohol is being consumed. At such times, drinking, as a central feature of gang life, coupled with key notions of masculinity, may increase the likelihood that violent behaviour will erupt and embolden gang members to react to possible statements or incidences of disrespect. Violence, like drinking, is the 'currency of life' in gangs (Sanchez-Jankowski 1991). When disrespect is believed to have occurred, then a gang member must react aggressively in order to nullify the consequences of being 'dissed'. The likelihood that gang members will react aggressively is increased in situations of drinking. As our respondents regularly noted, either they themselves become emboldened while drinking or their fellow gang members' drinking results in confrontations with others where violence was necessary in order that honour be maintained. To refuse to be violent when called upon to 'be down' for the gang is to lose respect, regardless of the rights and wrongs of the situation.

Alcohol as Tension-Reduction

Given the norm of aggressive behaviour and posturing that operates in the day-to-day lives of gang members, it is not surprising that tensions in the gang, from current or previous slights, frequently erupt and conflict may then ensue. Internal conflicts frequently occur when a gang member feels that he has been disrespected for a supposed slight, an accident or an unfortunate remark, especially one perceived as an insult to a family member. In these circumstances, the gang member, while maintaining his honour, must operate within the established hierarchy of the gang and abide by its norms. In many of these cases the event occurred while gang members were drinking. As one African-American respondent remarked:

> Shooting dice up in Westpoint, it was one of my folks' friends and he didn't like the way I was playing him in dice, I didn't want to bet him or nothing so he got mad. I threw the dice away from him and then he had to scuffle, I was kind of drunk. (H230)

Many cases of internal disrespect stemmed from disagreements about women and girlfriends.

> Like we were having a birthday party for my cousin. And everybody was drunk, heavily drunk, stupid. And a thing happened where one of my friends slapped one of my other friend's girlfriend. It was accidental, but then my two friends started fighting. And then I got into it, everybody got into it, it was like a riot. We were just all drunk and stupid. (H319)

Overall, gang members while drinking, were more likely to fight with non-gang members or members of other gangs than with themselves (see table 11.4). Thirty per cent of the sample who admitted to being violent with fellow gang members in the last year implicated alcohol, whereas 53 per cent admitted to alcohol-related violence with other gang members. The figures for alcohol-related violence in the last month were 11 per cent and 25 per cent, respectively. Fortunately, conflicts within the gang appeared not to lead to any long-lasting rifts, and once the fighting was over the group reconvened, and the friendships continued.

> R: Me and my partner got into it. I was dancing with one of his ladies. He wanted to get at her. But I didn't know. I was kind of drunk and he was drunk. So kind of asking for it.
> I: What happened? Did you guys make up?
> R: Yeah it was all good . . . like nothing happened. (H240)

In such cases, as other researchers have noted, alcohol works as a 'tension-reducing' mechanism, or, as Szwed (1966: 439) called it, a 'safeguard against divisive and disruptive behavior'. In such cases, drinking provides an 'institutionalized excuse to explain away public outbursts of hostilities and at the same time a means of resolving them' (Szwed 1966: 439). In these circumstances gang members also learn when it is acceptable to back down from a perceived slight without losing respect. Once the dispute is resolved through alcohol-related violence, the group can regain its cohesion and unity. In fact, on some occasions, once the conflict has ceased, the antagonists seal their unity by sharing a beer. As one Latino respondent remarked: 'Yeah, we

Table 11.4 Violence and alcohol related violence

By ethnicity	African-American (N = 177)		Latino (N = 103)		Asian (N = 64)		Pacific Islander (N = 15)		Other (N = 24)		Total (N = 383)	
	n	*%*	*n*	*%*	*n*	*%*	*n*	*%*	*n*	*%*	*n*	*%*
Non-gang-related violence												
Last year	130	73.4	75	72.8	47	73.4	8	53.3	19	79.2	279	72.8
Alcohol implicated	93	52.5	53	51.5	14	21.9	6	40.0	12	50.0	178	46.5
Last month	45	25.4	33	32.0	13	20.3	2	13.3	8	33.3	101	26.4
Alcohol implicated	35	19.8	21	20.3	5	7.8	2	13.3	6	25.0	69	18.0
Inter-gang violence												
Last year	119	67.2	88	85.4	41	64.0	12	80.0	21	87.5	281	73.4
Alcohol implicated	90	50.8	68	66.0	19	29.7	9	60.0	16	66.7	202	52.7
Last month	48	27.1	49	47.6	15	23.4	6	40.0	9	37.5	127	33.1
Alcohol implicated	42	23.7	32	31.1	9	14.1	6	40.0	7	29.2	96	25.1
Intra-gang violence												
Last year	74	41.8	38	36.9	11	17.2	5	33.3	12	50.0	140	36.6
Alcohol implicated	64	36.2	29	28.2	6	9.4	4	26.6	11	45.8	114	29.8
Last month	28	15.8	19	18.4	4	6.2	1	6.6	4	16.6	56	14.6
Alcohol implicated	24	13.6	12	11.6	1	1.5	1	6.6	4	16.6	42	11.0

fight amongst each other, over a little argument but it never goes no further than a fist fight. And then we just shake hands and go have a beer and that is it' (G101). Unfortunately, although alcohol may operate to safeguard the unity of the gang, it may also have been the catalyst, in the first place, for gang members inadvertently to make inappropriate remarks or behave in an unacceptable way to others in the group.

Alcohol as Violence Facilitator

More respondents reported incidences of violence with people outside the gang than with their fellow gang members. The reasons for external violent activities were varied and include such issues as: gang members testing others; gang members' perceptions that they or their territories had been 'disrespected'; gang members' fears that their turfs were under threat; gang members' attempts to expand their turf; and fighting over the affections of another. On those occasions when drinking occurs, alcohol provided the circumstances for gang members to be violent and effectively enhance their status as gang members.

The most violent aggressive acts with 'outsiders' occur in inter-gang violence, or disputes between one gang and another. Notably, when gangs fight with one another, it is most often due to conflicts within their own ethnic group. Latino gangs are divided into two ideological groups, Surenos and Nortenos. The Sureno gang members are primarily of Mexican origin, while the Nortenos are of mixed Central American backgrounds; however, there is some crossover in both of these groups. The deadly rivalry between these two groups has been alive for more than the 13 years that our research has been in progress. As one homeboy illustrates, one of the easiest ways for his Norteno brothers to gain status is by fighting with their rivals:

I: How does a person get that extra respect?

R: By doin something. Like if you, you know, if you get stabbed by a Scrap [Sureno] . . . or something; you earn you a little bit a respect, you know, cuz you got stabbed. If you go to 19th Street and shoot somebody, you get respect right there straight up. (H337)

Asian gangs hang out in two districts in San Francisco, Chinatown and the Tenderloin, both areas where there is a strong entrepreneurial component. Asians generally fight with other Asian groups over turf or other territorial issues. Fights might be with others of the same ethnic background, or, particularly in the Tenderloin, where drug sales are prominent, with other ethnic groups who are involved in sales there. This Vietnamese respondent discusses a complaint that he had with a Chinese gang when he was hanging out in their area:

When I was kicking it down in Chinatown though it is like they would only let the fireworks people stay and all the other Jackson dudes 'and like gangster they would pretty much not come around. It would be just like us dudes. Yeah one time I got a beef with Chinatown Boys, dude. We was down there selling fireworks and then they, yeah one of my friends was selling with us but he was kicking it with the other Chinese group and that other Chinese group didn't like his group so we had to back up our boys too. So it was like that dude. And it was fucked up. (H174)

African-American gangs tend to gather around various housing projects in San Francisco. Rivalries between same ethnic group gangs can be among the most deadly, as one African-American gang member illustrates:

A fight, I can remember a party, people . . . were drunk, high, you know what I'm saying, and man, this one dude over there . . . tripping . . . It wasn't what he said, it was one dude dancing, and one dude tying his shoe, and it got started from then on cause the dude was kicking his foot and his face while he was bent over tying his shoe, and from then on it's been problems. Yeah, it's gangbanging[7] gonna be going on for the rest of our lives from Oakdale and Harbor, between Oakdale and Harbor, it ain't gonna never be no peace, they gonna kill, they done kill people already, it's not gonna stop. (H115)

Given the occurrence of intra-ethnic conflict, how do gang members themselves characterize the role of alcohol? Although the respondents expressed no overall agreement on the issue of whether alcohol improved their ability to fight, nevertheless two features were clear. First, confrontations between rival gang members frequently took place while gang members were drinking. In fact, 72 per cent of the respondents who admitted to being involved in violent behaviour with other gang members also admitted that they had been drinking. Second, in spite of disagreements as to the precise effects of alcohol, many of our respondents admitted that drinking assisted them to develop a sense of *locura*, or 'pumped them up', making them ready to fight. As one African-American respondent noted:

> Like before a nigger fight . . . a nigger might get drunk or something to get him pumped. Cuz drink will have you pumped, ready to fight like. It just bring out the madness in you or something. It's just something about the drink . . . I drink before I fight cuz it'll have you pumped. (H160)

In these cases, alcohol works, not as the literature would suggest, as an excuse mechanism (MacAndrew and Edgerton 1969; Heath 1978), but instead as a facilitating mechanism.

The gang members readily admitted that on some occasions the violent confrontation with another group may be senseless, and provoked by a drunken fellow homeboy. Nevertheless, because of their masculine notions of respect and honour, they must still defend their homeboy.

> We were just sitting there . . . one of my partners was drinking heavily . . . [and] . . . was talking shit to everybody . . . This guy came by, who was not drunk and my partner hit on him cuz he was drunk and saying shit . . . then we all jumped on him. . . . Even though it wasn't his [the passer-by's] fault that caused the violence . . . the dude wasn't drunk. But one of my partners was heavily drunk and started some shit. We had to get his back [protect him] . . . cuz he's one of our homies. (H169)

This case also illustrates the extent to which a gang member's respect and honour depend on his willingness to back up his fellow gang members regardless of the rights and wrongs of the incident. Failure to do so would mean a loss of face with his gang members. 'If . . . we get into some funk with another group, then you gotta show your heart. If you down, you down. If you a wimp, you better start running' (H157). These violent activities, encouraged by the young men drinking, worked to bind the group together (Sanders 1994). The identity of the group was continually reinforced by these conflicts with other gangs or with other individuals, while enforcing the gangs' separateness.

Clearly the relationship between drinking and violence is a complex one. Although gang violence is typically portrayed as an event involving planning and is inevitably associated with drug dealing (or drug using), our respondents' experiences suggest that drinking is frequently a precursor to internal and external forms of aggressive and often violent behaviour. In addition, the context of fighting, whether it is internally among members or externally with rivals or 'outsiders', is normally episodic. Members reported aggressiveness with other fellow members while drinking, and this served as a release mechanism. In cases of external violence against other gangs, although these incidences were also often unplanned, alcohol worked more as a catalyst for aggressive behaviour and a mechanism to embolden gang members to exhibit their masculinity.

Conclusion

Our analysis has examined notions of masculinity within the lives of these gang members and the ways in which these are played out in the day-to-day activities of the gang. Gang life can be described as the quintessential masculine arena in which power, aggression, violence and heavy drinking interact. Although the social life of the gang encourages a particular culture of masculinity associated with heavy drinking, male posturing, risk taking, bravado and aggressive behaviour, our data suggest that the precise ways in which masculinity is performed are complicated and mitigated by ethnicity. Ethnicity is the attribute which most clearly binds and differentiates gangs in San Francisco. With few exceptions, African-Americans hang out with African-Americans, Latinos hang out with Latinos, Filipinos with Filipinos, Asians with Asians, and gang membership reflects this. On the other hand, ethnicity does not imply that all the members of the same ethnic group will be bound to one another if they are members of different gangs. Divisions between members of different gangs within the same ethnic groups can be based on territorial, ideological and entrepreneurial conflicts. Clearly the marginalized status of ethnic minority males leaves few avenues through which to successfully express their masculine identity in the larger social structure. With limited access to status, honour and respect, the streets provide one arena in which young working-class minority males can effectively enact masculinity, jockeying for position and power in a very competitive arena.

As Connell (2000: 10) has noted, 'there is no one pattern of masculinity'. Consequently, although all gang members share some common social characteristics, they nevertheless 'do gender' in their own culturally determined way, including the way they drink. Among African-American gang members, being obviously drunk is not being cool. Their Latino counterparts, however, exhibit their machismo by being wild and reckless. Asian gang members struggle with acceptability and vulnerability in their drinking practices. In all cases gang members exhibit their masculinity to themselves, to their own homeboys and to others outside the gang.

Drinking is an essential part of 'doing gender' in the gang, and, consequently, the role of alcohol is integral to any analysis of gang life. In fact it can be argued that not only does alcohol bond gang members together and encourage social cohesion, it also provides the environment in which aggressive and violent behaviour is the likely outcome. The very process of encouraging cohesion through drinking and separating gang members from 'others' allows gang members to distance themselves more effectively from not only all non-gang members, but also members of other gangs, including others of their own ethnic backgrounds. It also encourages them, through their discourse, to dehumanize them. In so doing it provides the justification for violence to occur.

What we find is that these marginalized young men negotiate their masculine identities within the bounded and limited environment of the streets, where they earn their money, spend their leisure time, form relationships with women and other men (including some, while excluding others), and gain or lose status and respect. The ways in which they drink, the symbolic meanings of their drinking and the outcomes of their drinking are an intrinsic part of the world they live in and of their identities as men in the gang.

Acknowledgement

Collection of data for this chapter was made possible by funding from the National Institute on Alcohol Abuse and Alcoholism (RO1-AA10819).

Notes

1. The study for this discussion is based on a research endeavour, originating in 1989 and which is still ongoing. The initial study was in response to the growing public concern about youth gangs and their connection to the drug trade and to violence in the United States, particularly on the West and East Coast. In that study, we found that most gang members who did use drugs tended to confine and control their drug use, in keeping with the entrepreneurial spirit of 'not being your own best customer'. Instead, we found that gang members tended to drink more than use drugs, and found alcohol to be a better way of relaxing and socializing. Thus, in the current study, our focus has centred on the role of alcohol in gang

members' lives and its connection to violence, a behaviour often linked to gang activity. San Francisco represents an interesting locale for the study of youth gangs as they have been present in many ethnic communities since at least the 1960s in the Chinese, Latino and African-American communities.

2. The term OG stands for Old Gangster or Original Gangster - a gang member who was a founding member or has been in the gang for a long time and is now semi-retired.

3. This initiation into drinking by male family members is not unusual in Latino cultures. See Brandes (2002) and Gutmann (1996).

4. In the case of the Latino respondents we have yet to examine possible differences in drinking patterns and behaviours between Mexican, Chicanos, American-born or recent immigrants. Likewise with our Asian respondents we have not distinguished as yet between either different Asian nationalities or between American-born Asian and first-generation immigrants. Consequently, for the purposes of this chapter we have adopted more generic terms such as Latinos and Asians to discuss their overall drinking patterns or drinking behaviours.

5. For a detailed discussion of the possible different meanings of 'macho' and 'machismo', see Gutmann (1996).

6. Gang names in San Francisco are frequently named after street names, as in the cases of Jackson, Oakdale and Harbor.

7. Although the term gangbanging originally referred to gang rape, today the term more normally means inter-gang fighting.

References

Ames, G. M. and C. R. Janes (1987), 'Heavy and Problem Drinking in an American Blue-collar Population: Implications for Prevention', *Social Science and Medicine*, 25: 949–960.

Archard, P. (1979), *Vagrancy, Alcoholism and Social Control: Critical Criminology,* London: Macmillan.

Bales, R. F. (1962), 'Attitudes Toward drinking in the Irish Culture', in D. J. Pittman and C. R. Snyder (eds), *Society, Culture, and Drinking Patterns,* Carbondale, IL: Southern Illinois University Press, pp. 157–87.

Block, C.R. and R. Block (1995), 'Street Gang Crime in Chicago', in M. W. Klein, C. L. Maxson and J. Miller (eds), *The Modern Gang Reader,* Los Angeles: Roxbury Publishing Company, pp. 202–10.

Bourgois, P. (1996), *In Search of Respect: Selling Crack in El Barrio,* Cambridge: Cambridge University Press.

Brandes, S. (2002), *Staying Sober in Mexico City,* Austin: University of Texas Press.

Burns, T. F. (1980), 'Getting Rowdy with the Boys', *Journal of Drug Issues* 10 (2): 273–86.

Chin, K.-L. (1990), 'Chinese Gangs and Extortion', in C. R. Huff (ed.), *Gangs in America*, 1st edn, Newbury Park, CA: Sage, pp. 129–45.

Collison, M. (1996), 'In Search of the High Life: Drugs, Crime, Masculinities and Consumption', *British Journal of Criminology* 36 (3): 428–44.

Connell, R. W. (1987), *Gender and Power*, Stanford: Stanford University Press.

—— (1995). *Masculinities*, Berkeley: University of California Press.

—— (2000), *The Men and the Boys*, Berkeley: University of California Press.

Corrigan, P. and S. Firth (1976), 'The Politics of Youth Culture', in S. Hall and T. Jefferson (eds), *Resistance through Rituals: Youth Subcultures in Post-war Britain*, London: Hutchinson University Library, pp. 231–42.

Dennis, N., F. Henriques and C. Slaughter (1969), *Coal is Our Life*, London: Tavistock.

Edwards, R. W., P. J. Thurman and F. Beauvais (1995), 'Patterns of Alcohol Use among Ethnic Minority Adolescent Women', in M. Galanter (ed.), *Recent Developments in Alcoholism, Vol. 12*: *Alcoholism and Women*, New York: Plenum Press, pp. 369–86.

Feldman, H. W., J. Mandel and A. Fields (1985), 'In the Neighborhood: A Strategy for Delivering Early Intervention Services to Young Drug Users in Their Natural Environments', in A. S. Friedman and G. M. Beschner (eds), *Treatment Services for Adolescent Substance Abusers*, NIDA Treatment Research Monograph Series, Washington, DC: U.S. Government Publishing Office, pp. 112–28.

Fillmore, K. M., E. Hartka, B. M. Hohnstone, E. V. Leino, M. Motoyoshi and M. T. Temple (1991) 'A Meta-analysis of Life Course Variation in Drinking: The Collaborative Alcohol-related Longitudinal Project', *British Journal of Addiction* 86 (10): 1221–68.

Fisher, L. (1998), 'The Shadow of the Other', in D. Zahavi (ed.), *Self-awareness, Temporality and Alterity: Central Topics in Phenomenology, Vol. 34: Contributions to Phenomenology*, Boston: Kluwer Academic Publishers, pp. 169–92.

Foxcroft, D. R. and G. Lowe (1997), 'Adolescents' Alcohol Use and Misuse: The Socializing Influence of Perceived Family Life', *Drugs: Education, Prevention and Policy* 4 (3): 215–29.

Gilbert, M. J. and R. L. Collins (1997), 'Ethnic Variation in Women's and Men's Drinking', in R. Wilsnack and S. Wilsnack (eds), *Gender and Alcohol: Individual and Social Perspectives*, New Brunswick, NJ: Rutgers Center of Alcohol Studies, pp. 357–78.

Gough, B. and G. Edwards (1998), 'The beer talking: Four Lads, a Carry Out and the Reproduction of Masculinities', *Sociological Review* 46 (3): 409–35.

Graham, K. and S. Wells (2003), 'Somebody's Gonna Get Their Head Kicked in Tonight: Aggression among Young Males in Bars – A Question of Values?', *British Journal of Criminology* 43: 546–66.

Gutmann, M. C. (1996), *The Meanings of Macho: Being a Man in Mexico City*, Berkeley: University of California Press.

Hagedorn, J. M. (1988), *People and Folks: Gangs, Crime and the Underclass in a Rustbelt City*, Chicago: Lakeview Press.

Heath, D. B. (1978), 'The Sociocultural Model of Alcohol Use: Problems and Prospects', *Journal of Operational Psychiatry* 9: 55–66.

—— (2000), *Drinking Occasions: Comparative Perspectives on Alcohol and Culture*, Ann Arbor, MI: Sheridan Books.

Hunt, G. and Satterlee S. (1986), 'Cohesion and Division: Drinking in an English Village', *Man* (N. S.) 21 (3): 521–37.

—— (1987), 'Darts, Drinks and the Pub: The Culture of Female Drinking', *Sociological Review* 35 (3): 575–601.

Hunt, G., K. Joe and D. Waldorf (1996), '"Drinking, Kicking back and Gang Banging": Alcohol, Violence and Street Gangs', *Free Inquiry – Special Issue: Gangs, Drugs & Violence* 24 (2): 123–32.

Jefferson, T. (1996), 'Introduction to Special Issue on Masculinities and Crime', *British Journal of Criminology* 36 (3): 337–47.

Joe, K. and M. Chesney-Lind (1995), 'Just Every Mother's Angel: An Analysis of Gender and Ethnic Variations in Youth Gang Membership', *Gender and Society* 9 (4): 408–31.

Katz, J. (1988), *Seductions of Crime: Moral and Sensual Attractions in Doing Evil*, New York: Basic Books.

Lemle, R. and M. E. Mishkind (1989), 'Alcohol and Masculinity', *Journal of Substance Abuse Treatment* 6 (4): 213–22.

MacAndrew, C. and R. B. Edgerton (1969), *Drunken Comportment: A Social Explanation*, Chicago: Aldine.

MacLeod, J. (1987), *Ain't No Makin It: Leveled Aspirations in a Low-Income Neighborhood*, Boulder, CO: Westview Press.

Mars, G. (1987), 'Longshore Drinking, Economic Security and Union Politics in Newfoundland', in M. Douglas (ed.), *Constructive Drinking: Perspectives on Drink from Anthropology*, Cambridge: Cambridge University Press, pp. 73–90.

McClelland, D. C., W. C. Davis, R. Kalin and E. Wanner (1972), *The Drinking Man*, New York: Free Press.

Messerschmidt, J. W. (1986), *Capitalism, Patriarchy and Crime: Towards a Socialist Feminist Criminology*, Totowa, NJ: Rowman & Littlefield.

—— (1993), *Masculinities and Crime: Critique and Reconceptualization of Theory*, Lanham, MD: Rowman & Littlefield.

—— (1997), *Crime as Structured Action: Gender, Race, Class, and Crime in the Making*, Thousand Oaks, CA: Sage.

Moore, J. W. (1991), *Going Down to the Barrio: Homeboys and Homegirls in Change*, Philadelphia: Temple University Press.

Newburn, T. and E. Stanko (eds) (1994), *Just Boys Doing Business.* London: Routledge.

Padilla, F. (1992), *The Gang as an American Enterprise*, New Brunswick, NJ: Rutgers University Press.

Park, J. (1995), 'New Zealand', in D. B. Heath (ed.), *International Handbook on Alcohol and Culture*, Westport, CT: Greenwood, pp. 201–12.

Parker, R. N. (1995), *Alcohol and Homicide: A Deadly Combination of Two American Traditions*, Albany: State University of New York Press.

Peace, A. (1992), 'No Fishing without Drinking: The Construction of Social Identity in Rural Ireland', in D. Gefou-Madianou (ed.), *Alcohol, Gender and Culture*, New York: Routledge, pp. 167–80.

Riches, D. (ed.) (1986), *The Anthropology of Violence*, Oxford: Basil Blackwell.

Sanchez-Jankowski, M. (1991), *Islands in the Street*, Berkeley: University of California Press.

Sanders, W. B. (1994), *Gangbangs and Drive-Bys: Grounded Culture and Juvenile Gang Violence*, New York: Aldine de Gruyter.

Sansom, B. (1980), *The Camp at Wallaby Cross*, Canberra: Australian Institute for Aboriginal Studies.

Sulkunen, P., P. Alasuutari, R. Nätkin and M. Kinnunen (1997), *The Urban Pub*, Lähiöravintola, Finland: Stakes.

Szwed, J. F. (1966), 'Gossip, Drinking, and Social Control: Consensus and Communication in a Newfoundland Parish', *Ethnology* 5 (4): 434–41.

Taylor, C. S. (1990), *Dangerous Society*, East Lansing: Michigan State University Press.

Tomsen, S. (1997), 'A Top Night: Social Protest, Masculinity and the Culture of Drinking Violence', *British Journal of Criminology* 37 (1): 90–102.

Toy, C. (1992), 'A Short History of Asian Gangs in San Francisco', *Justice Quarterly* 9 (4): 601–19.

Tunstall, J. (1962), *The Fisherman*, London: Macgibbon & Kee.

US Census Bureau (2002), 'The Asian Population: 2000', accessed at: *www.census.gov/prod/cen2000/index.html*, Census 2000 Brief Series.

Vigil, J. D. (1988), *Barrio Gangs: Street Life and Identity in Southern California*, Austin: University of Texas Press.

Vigil, J. D. and J. M. Long (1990), 'Emic and Etic Perspectives on Gang Culture: The Chicano Case', in C. R. Huff (ed.), *Gangs in America*, Newbury Park: Sage, pp. 55–68.

Waddell, J. O. (1975), 'For Individual Power and Social Credit: The Use of Alcohol among Tucson Papagos', *Human Organization* 34: 9–15.

Waldorf, D., G. Hunt and K. Joe (1994), *Report of the Southeast Asian Gangs and Drugs Study*, San Francisco: Institute for Scientific Analysis.

Wallace, J. M., J. G. Bachman, P. M. O'Malley, L. D. Johnston, J. E. Schulenberg and S. M. Cooper (2002), 'Tobacco, Alcohol, and Illicit Drug Use: Racial and Ethnic Differences among US High School Seniors, 1976–2000', *Public Health Reports* 117 (Supplement 1): 67–75.

Wilsnack, S. C., R. W. Wilsnack and S. Hiller-Sturmhofel (1994), 'How Women Drink: Epidemiology of Women's Drinking and Problem Drinking', *Alcohol Health & Research World* 18 (3): 173–81.

–12–

Drinking Politics

Alcohol, Drugs and the Problem of US Civil Society

Anthony Marcus

A Place Where Everybody Knows Your Name?

In 1995, Robert Putnam, director of the Center for International Affairs at Harvard University, published a brief article in the *Journal of Democracy* entitled 'Bowling Alone: America's Declining Social Capital'. In it he made the observation that bowling continues to be one of the most important leisure pursuits in the United States, but the bowling league, which has long been a symbol of working-class community life everywhere from rural small towns to sprawling modern suburbs and even inner cities, is disappearing. Posing bowling alone as emblematic of a growing trend away from community engagement and voluntary association, Putnam (1995: 77) advanced the thesis that America is faced with a crisis of democratic participation that 'may be linked to a broad and continuing erosion of civic engagement that began a quarter century ago'. He attributes this primarily to the technological transformation of leisure and changes in the structure of work. Using the concept of social capital, which he borrowed from James Coleman (1988, 1990), as a means to operationalize and quantify civic engagement, Putnam (1995: 67) argues that

> life is easier in a community blessed with a substantial stock of social capital. . . networks of civic engagement foster sturdy norms of generalized reciprocity and encourage the emergence of social trust. Such networks facilitate coordination and communication, amplify reputations, and thus allow dilemmas of collective action to be resolved. . . . networks of civic engagement embody past success at collaboration, which can serve as a cultural template for future collaboration.

'Bowling Alone' put Putnam at the centre of a public discussion about contemporary democracy in America. Appearing on television, radio and in the national press, Putnam (1995: 77) warned of a 'democratic disarray' confronting the United States and argued that 'high on America's agenda should be the question of how to reverse these adverse trends in social connectedness, thus restoring civic engagement and civic trust'. Tying his concern for the erosion of civil society in the United States to broader discourses on 'democratization', governance and civil society in the developing world, Putnam's work became the pole of debate for a generation of post-cold war scholars and policy makers who struggled to make sense of the collapse, reorientation and reconstruction of states across the globe. In the following year, US 'first lady' Hillary Rodham Clinton joined Putnam in the neo-Toquevillian renaissance, publishing her manifesto on children and community *It Takes a Village* (1996). Finally, in 2000, Putnam published the best-selling *Bowling Alone: The Collapse and Revival of American Community* (2000), capping a decade of discussions of voluntarism in the United States, NGO-led civil society projects in 'democratizing' nations and research into social capital formation in first, second and third world contexts.

However, some critics of Putnam have questioned the value of social capital (Portes 1998; Durlauf 2001). Writers in the Durkheimian tradition have pointed to changes in the division of labour in society, and concomitant new social solidarities, such as professional networks and work-related contacts (Reeves 2001). Others have looked at the problems and possibilities of democratic, civic engagement and community tied to new information and communications technology (Castells 1996; Burbach et al. 1997; Norris 2001). Finally, Marxian critics have argued that Putnam presents democracy and civic engagement as existing completely outside the realm of politics. They have compared him to past communitarians such as de Toqueville and Tönnies and levelled the criticism that he presents social ties as socio-technical matters, rather than issues of political ideology, economic control, social power and political repression (Pollitt 1996; Robin 2001). Corey Robin (2001: 111) argues that Putnam, 'longs for a vibrant public square where men and women meet to discuss the great questions of the day and then continue the conversation over beers. But he won't touch the political conflicts – particularly about capitalism and economic inequality – that drive people in and out of that square.' In particular, Robin (2001: 110) identifies the crushing of the US labour movement as part of 'how elites have consciously restricted participation over the last thirty years'.

In this chapter, I explore some of the Marxian critiques of Putnam's 'bowling alone' thesis. I look at the way in which, in the absence of a strong 'counter-hegemonic' political project, social categories of difference and division such as race, ethnicity and gender underwrite civic engagement and support a status quo that is neither democratic nor participatory. By comparing the uses and spaces of social drinking and those of marijuana and heroin, it will be argued that in a uni-polar political environment organized and administered by the capitalist state, the social engagement, civil society and social capital that Putnam, Clinton and other communitarians seek to strengthen have a class nature that intimately links them to a project of hegemonic social control, and conservation of the status quo. The strengthening of this hegemonic project through the publicly visible community activity advocated by 'social capitalists' may actually yield greater social divisions, less social trust and weaker democratic institutions.

Though Putnam's article reviews many areas of American community life, and actually mentions beer and pizza as intrinsic to league bowling (1995: 70), he ignores what is possibly the oldest, most ubiquitous and most paradigmatic site of community participation and social capital building – the neighbourhood bar.[1] Despite the fact that social drinking does not neatly correspond to the moral tone that drives much of the social capital literature, the neighbourhood bar remains one of the primary locations to which people go to exchange ideas, make connections for business or employment, and create a place for themselves in public life and community. Furthermore, the well-documented and long-standing connection between drinking and politics makes the study of drinking alone versus drinking together potentially far more important for discussions of community life, civic engagement and social capital than bowling leagues, which only meet once a week, and have little documented evidence of being politically charged.

This chapter, based on eighteen months of participant-observation fieldwork in New York City bars from 1997 to 1999, conducted for a National Institute on Drug Abuse-funded study of illicit drug marketing and use, examines the role of social drinking, alcohol intoxication and civic engagement in the creation of political power. Through a comparative examination of the rituals of social drinking and those of illicit drug use among the same adult male peer groups, it will be argued that there is a special relationship between drinking, social capital and social violence that reflects and is determined by the close connection between alcohol production, distribution and use, on one hand, and state power, civil society and the formal economy, on the other. By comparing the different political and social uses of alcohol and illicit drugs in different civic contexts and spaces, I suggest ways that social drinking in bars is tied to political-economic and ideological processes of group identification and social boundary creation and maintenance that drive people apart, reduce 'social trust', silence alternative voices, and ultimately support a hegemonic process of the administration of state power.

Anthropology and Political Drinking

Despite nearly forty years of discussion and debate within the anthropology of substance use, there has been little explicit theorizing of the relationship between alcohol and politics. Instead, most anthropological treatments of social drinking have been primarily concerned with Durkheimian questions about social order, community creation, standards of behaviour, violence, deviance, 'drunken comportment' and social solidarity (Mandelbaum 1965; Cavan 1966; MacAndrew and Edgerton 1969; Everett et al. 1976; Greenberg 1982; Douglas 1987; Collins 1989; Fagan 1990). Such basic problems as the role of social drinking in organized political violence, voluntary association, political mobilization and ideologies of left and right have generally been ceded to historians, studying everything from the relationship between wine and medieval conflicts in the Vatican over papal succession, to comparative readings of the Boston Massacre, eighteenth-century American slave conspiracies, the origins of the workers' movement and decolonization (Maier 1970; Davis 1971; Thompson 1980; Amber 1990; Salinger 2002).

The closest the anthropology of substance use has come to the study of such instances of political drinking has been the work of feminist and gender studies scholars who have developed a problem-orientated view of social drinking as a part of masculine identity formation. Focusing on rituals of homosociality, trust and community building, male bonding and in-group/out-group exclusion, they have argued that drinking is part of the negotiation and instantiation of masculinity. Though political in their view of masculinities, they have made little attempt to tie identity-formation processes to political coalition mobilization, civil society or the state. This has left much of the anthropology of drinking at the positivist interface between anthropology, public health and social welfare (McGregor 1990; Tomsen 1997; Bernat et al. 1998; Hunt and Barker 2001; Room 2001; West 2001; Bachman and Peralta 2002), and symbolic and often functionalist readings of masculinity, group behaviour and national selfhood (Kapferer 1993; Kimmel 1996; Millan 2000).

The type of close contemporary ethnographic readings of the politics of the Bavarian beer uprisings of 1844 or the inebriated reactionary mob violence of the unemployed in nineteenth-century Europe with which Karl Marx and Frederick Engels concerned themselves is largely absent from contemporary anthropological investigations of alcohol. Such concerns occasionally appear in literature on political entrepreneurship and ethnic conflict in the third world (Wolcott 1974; Marshall 1979; Graves et al. 1982; Colson and Scudder 1988; Bourgois 1989), and Mediterranean patronage networks (Hansen 1988). However, the relationship between alcohol and politics remains largely untheorized in the anthropological literature that specifically addresses substance use, and largely outside the purview of the growing field of the anthropology of the United States.

Similarly, the obviously political relationship between the rejection of social drinking and voluntary associations, political mobilizations and the ideologies that underwrite them has also been generally regarded as the domain of historians of social reform (Crowe 1968; Foner 1970; Kerr 1980), or part of the anthropology of indigeneity (Leland 1976; Saggers and Gray 1998; Eber 2000, 2001; Spicer 2001). Even studies of powerful voluntary associations built explicitly around alcohol rejection such as Alcoholics Anonymous (mentioned by Putnam) have usually had little concern for issues of politics, governance and ideology, though there are some recent exceptions (Makela 1996; Morrell 1996; Zajdow 1998)

As an example of this lacuna in the literature on the anthropology of alcohol and social drinking, neither D. B. Heath's *Annual Review of Anthropology* essay (1987) nor the comprehensive review essay by Hunt and Barker (2001) in the *Social Science and Medicine* special issue on the anthropology of alcohol and drugs has a section on politics and drinking. The closest that either of these major review essays comes to providing a discussion of such an approach is in Hunt and Barker's section entitled 'Relations of Substance: Power, Elites, and Sumptuary Regulation' (Hunt and Barker 2001: 181), where they call for the incorporation of power into anthropological studies of alcohol and drugs. However, their view of how this would best be accomplished focuses exclusively on taste, status and elite behaviour, citing only an essay on yuppie coffee by William Roseberry (1996) as their guide. Finally, Merrill Singer's 1986 essay 'Toward a Political Economy of Alcoholism' also fails to address civil society, voluntary association, political clientelism, governance, hegemony or the exercise of state power.

Anthropology, Substance Use, Civil Society and the State

There is a cliché that holds that 'all politics are local'. Such a view has, historically, been particularly appealing to anthropologists, whose concern with culture and 'community' has often missed or even obscured the operation of larger-level political processes (Wolf 2001). Although this anthropological view of political processes as existing within the largely unconscious bounded systems of culture remains common, since the 1960s anthropology has became far more cognizant of the role of the state in determining the human environment in which sociocultural innovation occurs (Roseberry 1989). It is not uncommon in contemporary anthropology to identify political mobilization, voluntary association, ideological participation and the twisted root systems where civil society meets state power as crucial to, if not determinative of, anthropological explanations. This has been particularly true for the anthropological literature on social movements, which has explicitly taken up the issue of civil society and theories of the state (Ginsburg 1998; Doane 2001; Edelman 2001).

However, political anthropology often fails to identify the successful operation of state power. Instead the state is typically identified only in the places where it is weak, in doubt or raises irresolvable contradictions that make its operations and attempts to 'naturalize' power in everyday life readily visible. This empirical problem-oriented view of the state tends to focus on the social margins of strong state nations of the advanced industrial world, and on places in the former colonial world where the ideological functions of the state are weak and where power centres on tax collectors and the military rather than on structures of 'governmentality'.

It is perhaps for this reason that anthropologists have generally been far more cognizant of issues of civil society, politics and the state in the production, marketing, and use of illicit drugs, which test the limits of state control, than they have of alcohol and drinking, which exist within a 'naturalized' structure of social regulation. Some of the more prominent examples of this are the well-documented relationship between illicit drugs (production, marketing and use) and guerrilla war, agrarian political economy, neo-imperialism, law enforcement, urban patronage, banking and commerce, border maintenance, political office, voluntary association and ideology. These topics have been studied quite extensively, particularly in Latin America, Southeast Asia and East Africa.

Even in the advanced industrial world, where strong states usually naturalize the operations of power, there have been a few significant discussions of the contradictions, fissures and disturbances in the operations of state power and the social spaces created by illicit drug economies (Williams and Kornblum 1994; Maher 1995; Bourgois 1996, 1997). However, the successful regulation of alcohol production, distribution and consumption in the United States since Prohibition has yielded few visible contradictions. This has tended to obscure the political aspects of alcohol and has left the anthropology of the United States with little literature that addresses political drinking.

The data contained in the following pages derive from research undertaken between September 1997 and September 1998 in a National Institute on Drug Abuse-funded study of heroin marketing and use in New York City. The study, entitled 'Heroin in the 21st Century', looked at the role of heroin in the lives of 'functional' 'ordinary' people, rather than using the 'deviance model' that has typically governed research among 'junkies' and 'addicts', recruited from methadone clinics, jails, 'flophouses', mental health facilities and other places where heroin users in crisis appear in public. This study focused on heroin users who hold full-time jobs and maintain some respectability and control over their lives, typically hiding their use.

As with research on homosexuals in the 1950s and 1960s, there were difficulties in recruiting informants, in this case heroin users, whose survival depends on secrecy about their private lives. The technique that was typically used for recruitment was 'snowball' networking. New informants were taken out to dinner and an interview, on the theory that, as relatively successful people, a $10–$25 informant gift is of little use to them, but the chance to develop a peer relationship with a confidant somewhat outside their lives might be appealing.

I began my research in a bar in Manhattan's ever-gentrifying East Village. I knew the area well, having lived there and done fieldwork for a year in 1989. I chose a bar, which I will refer to as Bianca's, that had a long-standing reputation for attracting heroin users and was one of the few 'neighbourhood bars' that was racially and ethnically diverse. Like many of the bars in this neighbourhood, it was owned by an older Eastern European immigrant. However, there was little of the well-ordered small town neighbourhood bar feel that many nearby bars had. Bianca's did not open until after 6 p.m., had few of the Eastern European regulars that so many of the neighbourhood bars had, and depended almost entirely on a young hip crowd that had been brought in during several waves of gentrification. As an earlier informant had once put it, inverting the slogan of the popular TV show *Cheers*, 'it's the bar where nobody knows your name'. This meant that I could cast my net quite widely and not have to worry too much about either my reputation or that of my informants. I joined Monday- and Tuesday-night pool teams that used Bianca's as their 'home', giving me an excuse to be in the bar, talking to people until midnight two days a week. In addition to my two league nights each week, I passed many non-league nights playing pool, drinking beer and talking with people.

Social Drinking, Sniffing and Smoking

In the following pages I discuss incidents occurring over three nights which are particularly emblematic of the different relationships that alcohol, marijuana and heroin have to civil society, sociability and the creation of social capital. Though all three intoxicants lowered social inhibitions and created some form of 'relaxation', the different ways in which these three different intoxicants, generally thought to be depressants, were used in different social spaces suggest the degree to which politics and social custom, rather than chemistry, determine the contours of use, abuse and function.

On a warm evening in early April I hurried off to Monday-evening pool. We were playing an 'away game' about three blocks from our home bar, but I went to meet Andre,[2] a key informant, before the match. Andre, who had started using heroin about five months earlier at the instigation of a new girlfriend, was a slight, red-bearded Euro-American from the Midwest who had recently come to New York with the hopes of becoming a writer and was now working as a low-level employee at a dotcom. I had recruited him to both the Monday- and Tuesday-night teams that were based at Bianca's. The Tuesday-night team was a mix of post-college Euro-Americans and neighbourhood characters, some of whom I knew to be heroin users, and the Monday night team had a Latino identity, with a Spanish name, a Latino captain, whom I had known from my previous fieldwork in the neighbourhood, and four Latinos from around New York City.

When I arrived at Bianca's, Andre was practising for the match with Oswaldo and Gonzalo, the team captain, both Central Americans in their early forties, who worked in the social services and had spent many years organizing New York City support committees for political movements in their native countries. The bar was empty save for the barkeep and my three teammates. Gonzalo and Oswaldo were complaining to Andre about the other team. 'You'll see, it's a bunch of ugly racists,' Gonzalo the team captain told Andre, 'Have you ever seen a single Latino or black go into that bar? Some of those people are probably in the KKK.' He looked to his friend Oswaldo for confirmation. 'Yeah, they're cold. I don't like them,' his friend intoned. Gonzalo looked over to me for further confirmation. 'Come on Gonzalo, this is New York City, you make it sound like they're from rural Georgia,' I said. 'Some of those guys work in the entertainment business, Chris is an accountant. None of them have the time for pool, much less night riding.' 'You know what I'm saying,' Gonzalo asserted in Spanish, smiling and wagging his finger. 'Yeah, ok, its not the friendliest bar,' I agreed, not wanting to let Gonzalo take me into Spanish, where he would be able to silence me and exclude Andre. 'I'm just saying, don't go overboard. Let's just crush 'em at pool tonight and not worry about what they do under their sheets.' We practised for another twenty minutes before it was time to go to the other bar.

We entered the bar and were immediately confronted with the dramatic differences from the anarchic open feel of Bianca's. This was a neighbourhood bar, with a protected, tucked-away feel. A row of neighbourhood regulars, all male and Eastern European, were sitting along the bar drinking, under a glass case behind the bar where pool trophies from past years and team pool cues were stored. There were booths along the sides and each team claimed a booth for their evening drinking and team conferencing. By about 9.30 p.m., everybody was drunk and our team was behind two matches to one in a best of five. Oswaldo was playing against the sister of the captain of the other team and he made a shot that looked as if it might have been a foul. An argument arose and the other team's captain quickly joined in, bearing down on Oswaldo and trying to convince him to give in. Gonzalo sprung to his friend's defence and reassured him in Spanish that his shot was clean and fair and that he should not allow the white guys to bully him. The other team's captain said, 'If you're going to discuss this, do it in English so everybody can understand.'

Gonzalo turned to me in shock. 'This bastard (*pendejo*) told me to speak English,' he said in Spanish. The other team captain exploded. 'I fucking know what *pendejo* means. You think I'm fucking stupid? I've lived in New York long enough to know what a *pendejo* is,' he said, only inches from Gonzalo's face. Gonzalo responded by backing him across the room, shouting in English, 'This is my fucking country, you motherfuckers should know how to speak my fucking language. I should get an AK 47 and kill you, you racist shit.'

Everybody involved in the pool game was shouting at each other, with some trying to break up the fight and others trying to start it. The bartender, a burly Eastern European immigrant in her fifties, stepped out into the combat zone and read the riot act, making the original disputants flip a coin. This was enough to diffuse the situation and the match continued in relative silence, with only Gonzalo going on in Spanish to a Puerto Rican used car dealer on our team about the history of Anglo chauvinism in the Americas. Andre asked if I wanted to go outside and smoke marijuana. We went out to a stoop near the bar with a Dominican short-order cook from our team and the guy Andre had played against from the other team.

A few minutes later two members of the other team came out and joined us, bringing their own marijuana. They passed around the joints and watched for the police. Andre started a conversation about what he called my 'anthropologist's get out of jail free card' that I was supposed to give to police if I was caught in a bust. I told them that I doubted that even in the best of circumstances it could be counted on to trump 'Rudi's law' (the mayor of New York at the time, Rudolph Guiliani). Oswaldo joined us for a greeting and a quick puff on his way to get a sandwich at a deli. When we went back inside the bar, things were a bit more relaxed for the rest of the evening, but some tension remained between the two teams, which had, indeed, been constituted and recruited in very different bars, based on somewhat incompatible identities.

When the game ended, everybody went home, except Gonzalo, who decided he wanted to shoot more pool at a Puerto Rican nationalist bar in *El Barrio* (Spanish Harlem), where, as he put it, 'these gringos would be afraid to go'. Gonzalo invited the team to join him, but Andre headed home and the other Latinos, including the one Puerto Rican on the team, all made disparaging comments about Puerto Rican nationalist bars 'filled with old men obsessed with ancient history'. I decided to accompany Gonzalo and we caught a taxi up to Spanish Harlem. We drank, played pool and argued about nationalist politics until about 3 a.m., with a crowd of aging Puerto Ricans who were indeed very concerned with history. This was a striking contrast to the bar I had just come from with its smattering of Eastern European immigrants and crowd of twenty- and thirty-something Euro-Americans discussing work, television and life in the East Village.

On Tuesday night, the Euro-American team played a home game at Bianca's and Andre was the first to play. He quickly lost to his opponent from an all-girl team and we drank beers and talked about work. A little later, his girlfriend, Patricia, a Euro-American in her early twenties, who was doing a Masters degree in politics, came bursting into the bar with an old friend from her undergraduate days. 'Ok, everybody out of the pool, I want some smack,' she said to Andre. He invited me to come along with them. The four of us went off to her apartment, which was about a ten-minute walk from the bar. I was scheduled to play last and had at least two hours to kill until I was due to play.

At Patricia's apartment, she made us some tea and Andre unfurled a little foil cylinder with heroin in it and distributed a little to each of them to inhale. Their friend started to nod off in his chair and Patricia unbuttoned her shirt and invited Andre to suck on her breasts. He seemed a bit embarrassed in front of me, but assented. 'You don't mind?' she asked, answering her own question with, 'It's data, right?' 'Everything's data,' I said, but was a bit uncomfortable, nonetheless. 'I'll have to get back to playing pool soon anyhow,' I told her. 'I took a course in anthropology,' she said, dividing her attention between Andre's sexual attentions and trying to impress me with her knowledge of social science. Their friend was nodding stupidly on his chair and I decided to take my leave. Andre looked up, embarrassed. 'I'll catch up with you later in the week,' I told him. He told me to take it easy and I headed back to the bar.

In less than twenty-four hours I had participated in public drinking that had nearly turned into a race riot, gone to a bar that seemed like a permanent study group on Puerto Rican history, and finally watched a private heroin party that felt like a prelude to group sex. If alcohol had magnified and defined the distance between people, causing them to erect barriers and boundaries between them and a social 'other', heroin had encouraged what seemed to be nearly the opposite form of transgression. At the time, I was still thinking in terms of social drinking and social drugging and looking for where and how these various substances were connected to identities, rather than social spaces and the larger political forces that define them. The mariju-ana smoking session on the stoop in the East Village had seemed so normal, ordinary and lacking in issues of identity and social definition that I had barely mentioned it in my field notes or even seen it as data. Poised between the highly regulated, socially acceptable and completely public use of alcohol and the stigmatized, criminal and completely private use of heroin, marijuana had provided an interstitial respite from both the pressures of public performance and their opposite, the highly fraught negotiations of private transgression.

Later that year, in the winter, I made a trip to a small town in rural Western New York to visit family and was confronted with some of the same issues of social drinking, social drugging and marginal marijuana use. A friend of the family there learned that I worked as a heroin researcher and wanted to ask me about the long-term health prospects for heroin users. He nervously explained that he and his two housemates were using. They were a woman and two men in their early twenties, living together in an old rented house in the town. Both men were gay, claiming to be the only two male hustlers in town, and the woman was bisexual, making them all social outlaws due to their sexual orientation. Nonetheless, they were very secretive about their heroin use, making regular trips to the nearest city to buy heroin.

One night I accompanied them to their favourite local bar. Like Bianca's it was not a neighbourhood bar but a big crowded place where townies and the crowd from the local college both went and sometimes even mixed. Also, like Bianca's, accord-ing to my informants, it had been shut down by authorities several times, for permit-ting underage drinking and allowing drug transactions to occur on the premises. Clinging close to the bar and taking up the barstools was an older crowd of regulars from the town. In the cavernous dark room to the side of the bar, groups of local college students and 'townies' stood separately drinking beer with their friends. At the very front of the room, separated by an old barroom pool table, was a group of about a half dozen Mexican farmworkers and children of farmworkers in their late teens and early twenties standing dramatically apart from the main mix of young people.

I 'put quarters up', waited for my turn to play, and tried, unsuccessfully, to strike up a conversation with some of the Mexicans who were also waiting to play pool. When I returned to the crowd with whom I had arrived, they told me that they had decided to buy marijuana from the Mexicans and return home. I asked if I could come along. One of them went over to negotiate with the dealer and returned almost immediately. About five minutes later we tramped through the snow to a doorway in the parking lot behind the bar where two Mexicans were waiting. I was introduced to the two Mexicans. Money was exchanged for a few pre-rolled joints, one of which was lit and passed around. They stood out in the cold snow-covered back parking lot behind the tavern smoking together.

When my companions explained that I worked for a university in New York City and got paid to hang out with people who do drugs, one of the Mexicans became very animated and peppered me with questions about my research and what you had to do to get such a job. He apologized to me for his friends being so unfriendly in the bar, telling me that, 'People don't mix much up here. You will never see Mexicans hanging out with gringos. It just doesn't happen.' 'What about the *pachecos*?' I said, using the Mexican term for marijuana user and pointing to us. 'You know how it is,' he answered, '*pachecos* are more open, marijuana makes people more friendly.'

The cases presented above involving the public use of alcohol, the private use of heroin and the interstitial use of marijuana are, of course, not representative of all the different contexts within which people use these and other intoxicants. Similarly, the distinctions that I have drawn between public and private, and the interstitial spaces that fall between those two categories, are heuristic and therefore contingent, somewhat difficult to operationalize and subject to challenge. However, I believe that the cases cited provide a useful point of departure for discussing some of the ways that state regulation of space, social intoxicants and individuals do much to determine the sociocultural environment within which substance use can be converted into a political tool in civil society, by a variety of social actors, yielding outcomes as diverse as ethnic violence, ethnic conciliation or merely avoidance.

Regulation, Social Space and Substance Use

It is arguable that social drinking stands as the primary form of state-sanctioned intoxication in most societies in the world today. In the United States, alcohol is highly taxed, closely monitored and thoroughly regulated by the government at every stage from production to consumption, and even after consumption in the form of strict drinking and driving laws. The public use of alcohol is generally restricted to licensed restaurants and bars, or 'public houses', and the vast majority of those who purchase alcohol do so from state-sanctioned merchants, in a legally regulated way. Individual alcohol purchase is socially acceptable and does not bear any resemblance to the purchase of marijuana, heroin or other narcotics, where the simple act of purchase puts one outside the law.

Within the public house, where buildings cost money to purchase, leases may last for twenty years, state licensing can involve large amounts of time, money and even bribery, inspection is frequent and often unannounced and the owner's livelihood depends on outcomes, there is very little room for making enemies or subversion of the dominant social ethos. Although the very purpose of drinking is bound up with civil society and social transgression, as a general rule, public houses represent one of the least subversive environments in US society. It is one of the great clichés of television police drama that bar owners will tell police anything if threatened with more attention from law enforcement. In fact, public social drinking is one of the most carefully monitored and regulated areas of civic engagement and everything from the serving of alcohol to the opening and closing hours may be subject to alteration or termination by a multitude of actors, such as 'the community', hostile police officers or local, regional or national government. Whether a bar is one 'where nobody knows your name' that is watched, regulated and frequently closed by the state, or a self-regulated neighbourhood bar with a 'respectable' regular crowd who share high amounts of legitimate social capital, the public drinking house is a stage on which there is little room for social experimentation and collective social performance cannot deviate far from the dominant script.

In contrast to alcohol, heroin is illegal and criminal at every stage from production to consumption. Any contact with heroin at any point in the journey from production to consumption is illegal and so strongly socially proscribed that it may cause isolation from friends, family and associates. Heroin's criminality, along with its status as the most dangerous and tabooed drug, tends to individualize those who use it, effecting an overall reduction in social capital. Millions of people put themselves outside the law as lone individuals or small collections of individuals, but there is no public or civic role for heroin and its use typically involves rituals with little political value in civil society. It is the ultimate private drug. Individuals generally use it within relatively circumscribed social networks that typically isolate them from anybody who is not using. The fact that it is not only used in private but also typically sold in private through 'house connections' tends to make the transgressions that are facilitated by its use socially invisible. Regardless of whether boundaries of race, ethnicity, class and social identity are being crossed or maintained, like furtive interracial sexual activity, the social combinations created by heroin have little overall effect on civil society. With no public performance, the rituals involved remain personal and social, but largely apolitical. It is only where heroin meets the state, such as in drug rehabilitation centres, police stations, jails and prisons, that brief opportunities are afforded for heroin users to identify each other, make fleeting connections, and appear in civil society.

Andre, for instance, did not meet heroin users outside his circle of friends until he was arrested while attempting to buy heroin. During his time in custody he met several African-American and Latino users and dealers who provided him new networks for heroin purchase and use. This was all at the cost of becoming part of a vast network of known heroin users, each with a computer file containing fingerprints, a photograph and a suspended sentence that required 'good behavior' for at least a year. Though Andre probably raised his stock of 'drug capital,' he came out of the experience with less social capital, and abandoned his one conscious political commitment, marijuana law reform, which he feared might create difficulties with the authorities.

If alcohol is one of the primary lubricants of public life, civic engagement and community, and heroin is a highly proscribed criminal substance that socially taints all who touch it, marijuana exists in a peculiar interstitial limbo that often brings together surprising combinations of individuals. The most widely used illegal drug in the United States and one of the largest domestic cash crops, marijuana, is in many instances illegal but not criminal. Like social drinking during the Depression, marijuana cannot be used openly as a public act, but is generally tolerated in private and easily obtained and used in semi-public spaces, where anonymity is greater and law enforcement is difficult. In short, marijuana is easy: almost anybody can use it (even a future president), the degree of danger and social proscription is limited, and one need not even inhale to participate in a social ritual that brings people together to talk furtively in doorways, on stoops and in parks, while putting their lips to the same rolled-up paper cylinder.

It is, of course, impossible to generalize about every case of marijuana use. The contexts within which it is used are countless. However, the examples presented above, where marijuana is sold and used in social spaces that typically defy the distinction between public and private, will be recognized as representative by most who have had some experience with the drug. A drug that is neither fully legal nor fully illegal, marijuana can be grown in a suburban basement and lacks either the federal regulatory apparatus attached to alcohol, tobacco and firearms or the vast law enforcement efforts directed towards 'harder' drugs such as cocaine, heroin and ecstasy. Like Prohibition-era 'hootch', marijuana brings people together in surreptitious social combinations that do not challenge or threaten the hegemonic social categories of civil society, but do sometimes have the potential to defy them.

Civil Society and Political Drinking

St. Patrick's Day – that's white people's day. They get scary when they drink – all in a big crowd pretendin' they're Irish and looking for trouble.

William, unemployed African American in his mid-twenties

They used to call St. Patrick's Day servant's day, because it stood for the New York working class. In the nineteenth century they'd get drunk and march up Fifth Avenue hurling Irish confetti – that's cobble stones – into rich people's houses. Now they drink green beer and pat each other on the back for living in the suburbs and supporting the system.

A gay activist discussing the exclusion of the Irish Lesbian and Gay Organization from the St. Patrick's Day parade

Alcohol is bad. . . . It can bring out the cracker in anyone. Remember that police brawl down at city hall? Even the black mayor wasn't safe that day.

Henry, retired African-American in his early fifties, discussing a September 1992 rally by New York City police against a civilian review board

The relationship between politics and the use of intoxicants is well known and well documented. In the United States alcohol has been recognized as a powerful political tool by both state and extra-state forces since the Whisky Rebellion of 1794, which stands as the first major test of the post-confederationist United States state. Local bars remain one of the key sites of civil society and political organizing in many towns and cities across the country, with a wide variety of organizations and political committees making use of public drinking spaces that are often closely linked to political, economic or social identities. During my fieldwork in Upper Manhattan between 1990 and 1994, frequent conflicts broke out between Dominican, Irish and Puerto Rican factions of the local Democratic Party organizing committee over which neighbourhood bars would be used for fundraisers and political gatherings.

Despite the often seamless quality of modern governmentality and democratic process, the explicit relationship between alcohol and political mobilization sometimes becomes readily apparent, as suggested by the incidents of political drinking referred to in the epigraphs to this section. The first two involve political contestation over the meaning of New York City's large and highly political St Patrick's Day parade, which has always been associated with public drinking and in recent years has seen tremendous conflict over the exclusion of the Irish Lesbian and Gay Organization from the parade. The final quotation refers to an almost classic example of political drinking that could have come out of nineteenth-century New York City. In 1992, David N. Dinkins, New York City's first African-American mayor, supported a civilian review board to act as a check on police brutality. In response mayoral aspirant Rudolph Guiliani led 10,000 mostly white off-duty police in a march on city hall to oppose the review board. Encircling City Hall, many of the protesters were publicly drinking beer, visibly intoxicated and threatening, particularly to non-white passersby (Chevigny 1995). Though the mayor technically had the mantle of governmental power, the large mobilization of off-duty police who were breaking public drinking laws shifted the terms of civil power, paralysing on-duty police, who did not know how to regulate the disturbances. While it is not clear what was actually planned or even condoned by Guiliani, the use of intoxication and white caste privilege in a political event that included physical and verbal attacks on civilians, racial epithets and posters representing Dinkins' African descent as simian suggests the real power of alcohol as a political tool that must be regulated and managed.

Though bars and pubs are generally under closer control than political demonstrations and parades, the social performances that are enacted in them may also become violent. However, the relationship between the state and the production, distribution, and consumption of alcohol tends to ensure that such performances closely follow the standard, acceptable and hegemonic scripts of civil society[3] and they are unlikely to challenge existing categories and concerns of contemporary public life. Neighbourhood bars, where regulars create strong networks of civil society, and more anonymous bars like Bianca's, where individuals and groups of friends 'drink alone', are equally political civic spaces, and as such are closely shaped by the forces of the state.

It is not the greater civic engagement and social capital of drinking with 'regulars' that produce tolerance and collective practice, as suggested by Robert Putnam and other communitarians. To the contrary, it is the anonymity of drinking alone or with small groups of friends that allows the space for people to pursue new networks, replenish old ones, and coordinate and cooperate for mutual benefit in a plural society. Putnam (1995: 76) actually suggests in passing that the erosion of civic engagement may have also yielded a 'decline in intolerance and probably also in overt discrimination'. However, he never explores the possibility that intolerance and discrimination may not be incidental to the organs of civic engagement that he believes are the core of successful and effective American governance.

If there is any validity to structural-conflict models of society, governance based on divide and rule, and the class nature to the state, the argument may be made that, in the absence of viable political alternatives, 'bowling alone' (informally with friends and family) may be safer, healthier and present more potential for the development of a true American democracy than bowling in leagues that are the most public face of the largest and most visible small businesses in most towns. Similarly drinking alone may be better for overall 'social trust', ethnic peace and a plural community than drinking in civic spaces whose political use is generally defined and recognized from the first drink.

This is why I chose Bianca's as a research site; it is why undocumented Mexicans in Western New York drink in dark cavernous bars filled with many different types of youth; and it is why Gonzalo, a Central American revolutionary, who spends most of his time talking politics, recruiting to local anti-intervention networks, and looking for young white women with whom to have affairs, would not have been welcome on pool teams in many of the bars in the East Village, where the level of social capital was high enough that they knew him as 'that Spanish communist'.

When Gonzalo was tired, frustrated and feeling intolerant of gringos, he retreated to the Puerto Rican nationalist bar, where there was no danger of a real fight and little chance to encounter anyone new in a plural society. Though this bar was filled with *independentistas*, some of whom had fallen afoul of the law, they were in a historically Puerto Rican neighbourhood, in an era when only old men and dreamers are actively supporting an independent Puerto Rico. Perhaps most significantly, Puerto Ricans had already fought their way into the state apparatus in New York City during the 1970s when there were licensing problems, police raids and battles by groups like the Young Lords.[4] The level of social trust and social capital was high in such a public drinking site, but the social script and caste of characters were also safe, predetermined and fairly exclusionary.

Puerto Rican nationalist bars in Spanish Harlem and American nationalist bars in Western New York are political spaces, but not democratic ones. It is in more plural and anonymous public drinking sites, where the level of social capital is lower, and encounters between people who know each other and people who do not are more dependent on chance, that the script of public life sometimes strays from the hegemonic socially prescribed one. Such bars may be the public drinking equivalent of bowling alone, but they are also generally positioned just a tiny bit further from the places where civil society meets state power. As such, they are typically the ones that have the most trouble with the law, for a variety of reasons from underage drinking, to community concerns about race mixing and drugs, to issues as vague as the influence on the community. However, even the most plural and anonymous of bars must stay very close to the hegemonic standards set by the state and by the sectors of civil society closest to the state.

Conclusion

Craig MacAndrew and Robert B. Edgerton (1969: 173) end their classic monograph *Drunken Comportment: A Social Explanation* with the following story:

> Not long after James I acceded to the throne, a certain English nobleman gave a dinner party to which he invited a large number of luminaries. After the goblets had been filled and refilled several times and the liquor had taken hold, an English general named Somerset rose from his chair and proclaimed: "Gentlemen, when I am in my cups, and the generous wine begins to warm my blood, I have an absurd custom of railing against the Scottish people. Knowing my weakness, I hope no gentlemen in the company will take it amiss". Having thus delivered himself, he sat down, and a Highland chief, one Sir Robert Blackie of Blair-Atholl, rose and with singular dispassion addressed his fellow celebrants as follow: 'Gentlemen, when I am in *my* cups, and the generous wine begins to warm my blood, if I hear a man rail against the Scottish people, I have an absurd custom of kicking him at once out of the company, often breaking a few of his bones in the process. Knowing my weakness, I hope no gentlemen will take it amiss.' The story concludes, we need scarcely add, that General Somerset did not that night follow his usual custom of denigrating the Scottish people. The moral, then, is this. Since societies, like individuals, get the sorts of drunken comportment that they allow, they deserve what they get.

The preceding story represents what I suggest is the predominant view of social drinking in advanced industrial societies. In such a view, the codes of conduct around alcohol use are different for different categories of people in different contexts, with individuals engaging in transgressions of varying degrees depending on their ability to 'get away with it'.[5] Like those who believe that the effects of alcohol are biochemically determined, those who accept the view of MacAndrew and Edgerton that alcohol is a socially determined tool of social release assume that society can set higher or lower standards of behaviour for social drinking and therefore regulate the degree to which people act out. Whether these are 'hate crimes laws' connected to drinking, stricter drunk driving laws or more intense forms of regulating the sale of alcohol, the social regulation approach misses the political dimensions of alcohol use or conscious 'non-use'.

Just as the politics of anti-drinking in America have a long history of being intimately tied to a variety of political projects, such as evangelism, segregation and the politics of gender, from nineteenth-century presidents publicly displaying their lemonade parties in the White House to direct actionists like Carrie Nation, so too do the politics of drinking. The social norms model represented by MacAndrew and Edgerton is unable to illuminate or explain either the ethnic divisions that emerged among public drinkers during my fieldwork nor the long-standing use of public drinking and certain neighbourhood bars for a variety of political projects in New York City.

These examples of political drinking go far beyond social rituals of identity building, to the connections between collective social life and state power. Social drinking could be viewed as a public political tool whose power is jealously guarded and tightly regulated by the state. Such drinking is used consciously and unconsciously by a variety of actors to fight for space in civil society, and it is difficult to imagine that even a powerful counter-hegemonic force would derive benefit from political mobilizations connected to the rituals of a substance that is so closely tied to state power. As suggested by Guiliani's police rally, political drinking involves a substance which is legally and effectively regulated at every stage and in every place and is therefore more likely to produce rearguard, conservative or even reactionary political outcomes than vanguard, progressive or even resistant ones.

It is probably no accident that drinking rituals and public drinking spaces are so deeply segmented, segregated and imbued with the predominant social hierarchies of gender, race and class. Even health clubs, where people are vulnerable and often naked together, are rarely as segregated and segmented as a neighbourhood bar, which may not welcome African-Americans, Jews, women or people who do not believe in Puerto Rican independence. If a political view is taken of alcohol use, rather than a social, psychological or pharmacological one, phenomena such as 'hate crimes' and 'bias attacks', which nearly always involve alcohol use, are no longer the product of psycho-social hatreds, 'drunken comportment' and explosive deviant behaviour, or even national tropes of masculinity and race, but rather the waste products of the project of state control and political hegemony that typically determines the contours of civil society in the absence of counter-hegemonic 'strong forces'.

Acknowledgements

I would like to acknowledge the help of Andy Dawson, Mary Patterson, Vicky Schubert and Salim Lakha, who have provided a world of intellectual stimulation, as well as practical suggestions, bibliographic heads-ups and collegial nurturing. I would also like to thank my sister Abigail Marcus for her assistance in fieldwork and Jo Sanson for countless hours of discussion and brainstorming about the problem of civil society, along with crucial editorial help.

Notes

1. In the book *Bowling Alone*, Putnam mentions, in passing, a Roper poll finding that bars have seen a decline in customers over the last decades. As social drinking is entirely incidental to Putnam's view of social capital creation, there is no discussion of whether these lost bar customers are casual ones or the regular customers who make bars sociopolitical spaces.
2. All names have been changed for the purpose of confidentiality.
3. The July 2003 defence by New York City Mayor Michael Bloomberg of the New York Police Department policy of allowing predominantly white and affluent outdoor classical music concert-goers to freely drink alcoholic beverages in city parks during the summer months, while fining poorer, often non-whites who drink at social events in public parks suggests the degree to which state policy involves close attention to sociocultural details in regulating alcohol use.
4. It is consonant with this argument that the defining moment of the gay liberation movement, 'Stonewall' in 1969, was a fight for the right to have a gay bar in Manhattan.
5. In a different way, this is the same for illegal drugs, where the inequalities of the criminal justice system affect the types of behaviour that different categories of people believe they can risk.

References

Ambler, C. (1990), 'Alcohol, Racial Segregation and Popular Politics in Northern Rhodesia', *Journal of African History* 31 (2): 295–313.

Bachman, R. and R. Peralta (2002), 'The Relationship between Drinking and Violence in an Adolescent Population: Does Gender Matter?', *Deviant Behavior* 23 (1): 1–21.

Bernat, J., K. S. Calhoun and S. Stolp (1998), 'Sexually Aggressive Men's Responses to a Date Rape Analogue: Alcohol as Disinhibitive Cue', *Journal of Sex Research* 35 (4): 341–8.

Bourgois, P. (1989), *Ethnicity At Work: Divided Labor on a Central American Banana Plantation*, Baltimore: Johns Hopkins University Press.

—— (1996), *In Search of Respect*, Cambridge: Cambridge University Press.

—— (1997), 'In Search of Horatio Alger: Culture and Ideology in the Crack Economy', in C. Reinarman and H. G. Levine (eds), *Crack in America: Demon Drugs and Social Justice*, Berkeley: University of California Press.

Burbach, R., O. Nuñez and B. Kagarlitsky (1997), *Globalization and Its Discontents: The Rise of Postmodern Socialisms*, London: Pluto Press.

Castells, M. (1996), *The Rise of the Network Society*, Cambridge, MA: Blackwell.

Cavan, S. (1966), *Liquor License: An Ethnography of Bar Behavior*, Chicago: Aldine.

Chevigny, P. (1995), *Edge of the Knife: Police Violence in the Americas*, New York: New Press.

Clinton, H. R. (1996), *It Takes a Village: And Other Lessons Children Teach Us*, New York: Simon & Schuster.

Coleman, J. S.(1988), 'Social Capital in the Creation of Human Capital', *American Journal of Sociology*, supplement 94: 95–120.

—— (1990), *The Foundations of Social Theory*, Cambridge, MA: Harvard University Press.

Collins, J. (1989), 'Alcohol and Interpersonal Violence: Less Than Meets the Eye', in N. Weiner and M. Wolfgang (eds), *Pathways to Criminal Violence*, Newbury Park, CA: Sage.

Colson, E. and T. Scudder (1988), *For Prayer and Profit: The Ritual Economic, and Social Importance of Beer in Gwembe District, Zambia, 1950–1982*, Stanford, CA: Stanford University Press.

Crowe, C. (1968), 'Racial Violence and Social Reform – Origins of the Atlanta Riot of 1906', *Journal of Negro History*, 53 (3): 234–56.

Davis, T. (1971), 'The New York Slave Conspiracy of 1741 as Black Protest', *Journal of Negro History* 56 (1): 17–30.

Doane, M. A.(2001), 'A Distant Jaguar: The Civil Society Project in Chimalapas', *Critique of Anthropology*, 21 (4): 361–81.

Douglas, M. (ed.) (1987), *Constructive Drinking: Perspectives on Drink from Anthropology*, Cambridge: Cambridge University Press.

Durlauf, S. N. (2001), 'Bowling Alone: A Review Essay', *Journal of Economic Behavior and Organization*, 47 (1): 259–73.

Eber, C. (2000), *Women and Alcohol in a Highland Maya Town: Water of Hope, Water of Sorrow*, Austin: University of Texas Press.

—— (2001), 'Take My Water: Liberation through Prohibition in San Pedro Chenalho, Chiapas, Mexico', *Social Science and Medicine* 53 (2): 251–62.

Edelman, M. (2001), 'Social Movements: Changing Paradigms and Forms of Politics', *Annual Review of Anthropology* 30 (1): 285–317.

Everett, M., J. O. Waddell and D. B. Heath (eds) (1976), *Cross-cultural Approaches to the Study of Alcohol: An Interdisciplinary Perspective*, The Hague: Mouton.

Fagan, J. (1990), 'Intoxication and Aggression', in M. Tonry and J.Q. Wilson (eds), *Crime and Justice: A Review of Research, Drugs and Crime*, Vol. 13, Chicago: University of Chicago Press.

Foner, P. (1970), 'The IWW and the Black Worker', *Journal of Negro History*, 55 (1): 45–64.

Ginsburg, F. D. (1998), *Contested Lives: The Abortion Debate in An American Community*, Berkeley: University of California Press.

Graves, T., N. Graves, V. Semu, and I. A. Sam (1982), 'Patterns of Public Drinking in a Multi-ethnic Society: A Systematic Observational Study', *Journal of Studies on Alcohol*, 43: 990–1009.

Greenberg, S. (1982), 'Alcohol and Crime: A Methodological Critique of the Literature', in J. Collins (ed.), *Drinking and Crime*, London: Tavistock.

Hansen, E. C. (1988), 'Drinking to Prosperity: Hedonism and Modernization in Vilafranca', in J. B. Cole (ed.), *Anthropology for the Nineties*, New York: Free Press.

Heath, D. B. (1987), 'Anthropology and Alcohol Studies: Current Issues', *Annual Review of Anthropology* 16: 99–120.

Hunt, G. and J. Barker (2001), 'Socio-cultural Anthropology and Alcohol and Drug Research: Towards a Unified Theory', *Social Science and Medicine* 53 (2): 165–188.

Kapferer, B. (1993), *Nationalist Ideology and a Comparative Anthropology*, Colombo: Studies in Society and Culture.

Kerr, K. A. (1980), 'Organizing for Reform: The Anti-Saloon League and Innovation in Politics', *American Quarterly* 32 (1): 37–53.

Kimmel, M. (1996), *Manhood in America: A Cultural History*, New York: Free Press.

Leland, J. (1976), *Firewater Myths: North American Indian Drinking and Alcohol Addiction*, New Brunswick, NJ: Rutgers Center for Alcohol Studies.

MacAndrew, C. and R. B. Edgerton (1969), *Drunken Comportment: A Social Explanation*, Chicago: Aldine.

Maher, L. (1995), *Sexed Work: Gender, Race, and Resistance in a Brooklyn Drug Market*, New York: Clarendon Press.

Maier, P. (1970), 'Popular Uprisings and Civil Authority in Eighteenth-Century America', *William and Mary Quarterly* 27 (1): 3–35.

Makela, K. (ed.) (1996), *Alcoholics Anonymous as a Mutual-help Movement: A Study in Eight Societies*, Madison: University of Wisconsin Press.

Mandelbaum, D. G. (1965), 'Alcohol and Culture', *Current Anthropology* 6 (2): 281–93.

Marshall, M. (1979), *Weekend Warriors: Alcohol in a Micronesian Culture*, Palo Alto, CA: Mayfield.

McGregor, H. (1990), 'Domestic Violence, Alcohol and Other Distractions', in J. Vernon (ed.), *Alcohol and Crime*, Canberra: Australian Institute of Criminology.

Millan, A. (2000), 'Tapeo: An Identity Model of Public Drink and Food Consumption in Spain', in I. and V. de Garine (eds), *Drinking: Anthropological Approaches*, New York: Berghahn Books.

Morrell, C. (1996), 'Radicalizing Recovery: Addiction, Spirituality, and Politics', *Social Work* 41: 306–12.

Norris, P. (2001), *Digital Divide: Civic Engagement, Information Poverty and the Internet in Democratic Societies*, New York: Cambridge University Press.

Pollitt, K. (1996), 'For Whom the Ball Rolls', *Nation*, 262 (15): 9.

Portes, A. (1998), 'Social Capital: Its Origins and Application in Modern Sociology', *Annual Review of Sociology* 24: 1–24.

Putnam, R. D. (1995), 'Bowling Alone: America's Declining Social Capital', *Journal of Democracy*, 6 (1): 65–78.

—— (2000), *Bowling Alone: The Collapse and Revival of American Community*, New York: Simon & Schuster.

Reeves, R. (2001), 'We Bowl Alone, But Work Together', *New Statesman*, 130 (4531): 23–4.

Robin, C. (2001), 'Missing the Point', *Dissent*, Spring: 108–11.

Room, R. (2001), 'Intoxication and Bad Behavior: Understanding Cultural Differences in the Link', *Social Science and Medicine* 53 (1): 189–98.

Roseberry, W. (1989), *Anthropologies and Histories: Essays in Culture, History, and Political Economy*, New Brunswick, NJ: Rutgers University Press.

—— (1996), 'The Rise of Yuppie Coffees, and the Reimagination of Class in the United States', *American Anthropologist* 98 (4): 762–75.

Saggers, S. and D. Gray (1998), *Dealing with Alcohol: Indigenous Usage in Australia, New Zealand, and Canada*, Cambridge: Cambridge University Press.

Salinger, S. V. (2002), *Taverns and Drinking in Early America*, Baltimore: Johns Hopkins University Press.

Singer, M. (1986), 'Toward a Political Economy of Alcoholism: The Missing Link in the Anthropology of Drinking Behavior', *Social Science and Medicine*, 23 (1): 113–30.

Spicer, P. (2001), 'Culture and Restoration of Self among Former American Indian Drinkers', *Social Science and Medicine*, 53 (2): 227–40.

Thompson, E. P. (1980), *The Making of the English Working Class*, London: Gollancz.

Tomsen, S. (1997), 'A Top Night: Social Protest, Masculinity and the Culture of Drinking Violence', *British Journal of Criminology* 37 (1): 90–102.

West, L. (2001), 'Negotiating Masculinities in American Drinking Subcultures', *Journal of Men's Studies* 9 (3): 371–92.

Williams, T. and W. Kornblum (1994), 'Saving Kids in the Projects', *Nation* 258 (14): 484–8.

Wolcott, H. F. (1974), *African Beer Gardens in Bulawayo: Integrated Drinking in a Segregated Society*, New Brunswick, NJ: Rutgers Center for Alcohol Studies.

Wolf, E. (2001), *Pathways of Power: Building an Anthropology of the Modern World*, Berkeley: University of California Press.

Zajdow, G. (1998), 'Civil Society, Social Capital and the Twelve Step Group', *Community, Work & Family* 1 (1): 79–91.

Index